HOW INDUSTRY ANALYSTS SHAPE
THE DIGITAL FUTURE

How Industry Analysts Shape the Digital Future

NEIL POLLOCK

ROBIN WILLIAMS

OXFORD

UNIVERSITY PRESS

OXFORD
UNIVERSITY PRESS

Great Clarendon Street, Oxford, OX2 6DP,
United Kingdom

Oxford University Press is a department of the University of Oxford.
It furthers the University's objective of excellence in research, scholarship,
and education by publishing worldwide. Oxford is a registered trade mark of
Oxford University Press in the UK and in certain other countries

First Edition published in 2016

Impression: 1

Published in the United States of America by Oxford University Press
198 Madison Avenue, New York, NY 10016, United States of America

British Library Cataloguing in Publication Data
Data available

Library of Congress Control Number: 2015948866

ISBN 978-0-19-870492-8

Printed in Great Britain by
Clays Ltd, St Ives plc

Acknowledgements

This book draws on several years of fieldwork. During this time we have benefitted greatly from the help and support of many individuals and organisations. Neil Pollock would like to acknowledge the support of the Economic and Social Research Council (ESRC) in funding his fellowship 'The Social Study of the Information Technology Marketplace(s)' (RES-063-27-0221) which allowed him the time to carry out the bulk of the research that is reported here. The book also makes use of material from an older study conducted under the ESRC grant (RES-000-23-0466) on 'The Biography and Evolution of Standardised Software Packages'.

In terms of accessing the field of study, we would like to recognise and thank the following for giving us a glimpse of the exciting world they inhabit and providing information or data that we have used in writing this book: Jonny Bentwood, Duncan Chapple, Jon Collins, Khalda De Sousa, Jane Doorly, Nancy Erskine, Richard Garrett, Gideon Gartner, James Governor, Paul Hopkins, Jennie Lehman, Ludovic Leforestier, Simon Levin, Efrem Mallach, David Mitchell (now sadly deceased), Rick Nash, and Neil Ward Dutton. We owe a special note of gratitude to the members of the Institute for Industry Analyst Relations (IIAR), especially its current and past directors Ludovic Leforestier, Simon Levin and Duncan Chapple, who have been particularly generous with their time and hospitality. In writing this book, we have also interviewed a number of Gartner analysts who, for reasons of sensitivity, we have decided not to name explicitly here. Nonetheless, it goes without saying that we are also very grateful to these people for their input.

This work has also benefitted directly and indirectly from many discussions, at various times and places, with the following academics and doctoral students: Luis Arujo, Barry Barnes, Barbara Czarniawska, Gian Marco Campagnolo, Chris Carter, David Cooper, Luciana D'Adderio, Simon Down, Wendy Espeland, Michael Faust, Gary Alan Fine, Jamie Fleck, Royston Greenwood, Gordon Haywood, C. F. Helgesson, Sampsa Hyysalo, Ingrid Jeacle, Jannis Kallinikos, Antonios Kaniadakis, Karin Knorr Cetina, Kornelia Konrad, Benjamin Koeck, Irvine Lapsley, Eric Laurier, Mike Lynch, Kalle Lyytinen, Donald MacKenzie, Arthur Mason, Katy Mason, Peter Miller, Nathalie Mitev, Eric Monteiro, Fabian Muniesa, Carrie Paris, Alex Preda, Paolo Quattrone, Bill Rees, Arie Rip, Dan Robey, Steve Sawyer, Susan Scott, Peter Skaerbaek, James Stewart, Lucy Suchman, Burt Swanson, Barbara Townley, Harro van Lente, and Ping Wang.

Acknowledgement is also necessary for the input of Gian Marco Campagnolo, who accompanied us during the final period of fieldwork and co-authored Chapter 7, and Luciana D'Adderio who was a co-author on Chapter 9.

C. F. Helgesson, Paolo Quattrone, Brent Gallupe and Barbara Townley provided comments on the key arguments of the manuscript. We are grateful for the critical insight they have provided.

Sue Hancock and Matthew Hollow completed a marvelous job of proof-reading and copy editing our manuscript. Thanks to Moyra Forrest for excellent indexing. We are very grateful for their many suggestions in improving the flow of our argument. We would also like to acknowledge the support of David Musson and Clare Kennedy from Oxford University Press.

We thank the following individuals for allowing us to reproduce material here: Portia Isaacson Bass for use of the early Gartner advert which appears in Chapter 3; Thom Erbé from KeaCompany for the photos that appear in Chapter 10; the Knowledge Capital Group for the diagram included in Chapter 10; and Dave Noble of Intelligen Analyst Relations for the chart that appears in Chapter 2.

An early version of Chapter 5 appeared previously in *Social Studies of Science*. Elements of Chapters 6 and 7 were originally published in *Information and Organisation*. Chapter 9 previously appeared in *Accounting, Organisations and Society*. We are grateful to the copyright holders for permission to reproduce this material.

Contents

List of Figures

List of Tables

Abbreviations and Acronyms

AMR	Advanced Market Research
ANT	Actor Network Theory
ATA	All The Analysts
BCG	Boston Consulting Group
BoB	Best of Breed
BPO	Business Process Outsourcing
BPR	Business Process Reengineering
BW	Business Warehouse
CEO	Chief Executive Officer
CIO	Chief Information Officer
CQA	Catalyst, Query, Answer
CRM	Customer Relationship Management
CTI	Computer Telephony Integration
EDS	Electronic Data Systems
EFM	Enterprise Feedback Management
EFSS	Externally Facing Social Software
ERP	Enterprise Resource Planning
ETL	Extract, Transform, Load
FM	Feedback Management
FMV	Fair Market Value
FT	*Financial Times*
HE	Higher Education
HR	Human Resources
HQ	Headquarters
IBM	International Business Machines Corporation
IIAR	Institute for Industry Analysts Relations
ICT	Information and Communication Technology
IDC	International Data Corporation
IP	Intellectual Property
IPO	Initial Public Offering
IS	Information Systems
IT	Information Technology

KCG	Knowledge Capital Group
KPI	Knowledge Performance Indicators
M&A	Mergers and Acquisitions
MBA	Master of Business Administration
MIS	Management Information Systems
MOM	Marketing Operations Management
MQ	Magic Quadrant
MRM	Marketing Resource Management
MRP	Manufacturing Resource Planning
NCVI	Net Contract Value Increase
NP	Neil Pollock
PLC	Public Listed Company
SaaS	Software as a Service
SAP	Systems, Applications, Products in Data Processing (SAP AG)
SME	Small and Medium-sized Enterprises
SOA	Software Oriented Architecture
SPA	Strategic Planning Advice
SSK	Sociology of Scientific Knowledge
SST	Social Shaping of Technology
STS	Science and Technology Studies
TCE	Transaction Cost Economics
TERM	Technology Enabled Relationship Management
VP	Vice President
WEF	World Economic Forum

Prologue: King of the Hill?

Gartner Inc. HQ, Stamford, Connecticut (approx. 1995). Mike Brodie was sitting looking across the sea of new faces in the classroom. The 'recruits' attending the Gartner boot camp had just survived a long and difficult recruitment process. They seemed thrilled to be working at the firm that was overwhelmingly seen as the leader in the field. They were not put off because some from outside thought Gartner an '800lb gorilla' that threw its weight around. On the contrary, certain of the group were becoming 'heady and giddy with the power' their new career promised to bestow on them. They were working for the firm that was at the head of a multi-billion pound industry offering research and advisory services that appeared to exercise considerable influence over the information technology (IT) market. Gartner produces predictions about new digital solutions and the future markets for these technologies, it assesses and classifies the vendors producing these products, including creating potent rankings that pitch one vendor against another. And because its research reports are read (and often acted on) by those buying expensive IT systems, this grants Gartner substantial access to the places where these products are made. Vendors have no choice but to open their doors to these people. 'Woa! I get to meet all the senior execs', 'I get to see everything that is going on', 'all the information is flowing in my direction', 'God, I am all powerful', was just some of the excited chatter flying around the room. One of the recruits, Elias Thomas, was arriving at the same electrifying conclusion, that he too would soon be 'king of the hill'. Another echoed these sentiments aloud to Mike Brodie: 'surely, we are telling the market where to go?'

Mike Brodie was a respected figure at Gartner, having risen to the position of Head of Research. He was remembered as 'very, very sharp, very intellec-tual' but also at times as 'vicious': 'You're an arrogant little shit!' was how Mike Brodie responded to the question, and the recruit just shrank in his chair. 'You really seriously think that what you are doing is actually setting the pace of the market, setting the direction. No you are not! You are not writing software. You are not making a technology. You are not commission-ing something to be built. You know nothing. You are just sitting there observing'. Mike carried on. 'Our role is to either pour petrol or put a fire retardant on things. We press the accelerator button or the brake. You are not pointing the direction of the car; you are not on the steering wheel. But you are pushing the accelerator or brake. But if you say that is 'fantastic', you have just hit the accelerator, and if it is heading over a cliff, you have just accelerated it over the cliff. That is all you have done. You have not made it a better, fantastic product. Likewise, on the brake thing as well, if you slam the brake on, if it is a brilliant product, it is still going to go down that road and make millions. It is just that you have made it take an extra year to get there. You have slowed it all up'.

With Mike's Brodie's intervention, Elias Thomas remembers 'being brought down a few pegs as well'. 'Yeah, Mike is right', he thought, 'we're not actually writing software, we are not actually doing it, we are just observing. We might be right on their shoulders, looking over their shoulders as it is done, and we might be closer to it than everybody else, but that does not mean we are setting the direction of the market. And those vendors who listen to us, if they are idiots and we give brilliant advice, they *might* ignore it; and if we give lousy advice and they are clever, then they *will* ignore it. So it is not like our feedback loop is perfect; we are not influencing it as much as we think we are'. He thanked his lucky stars that it was not him who had 'opened his mouth'.

But the Gartner recruits are not completely alone in their view. We are no longer in Stamford, but Edinburgh and the year is 2010. One of the authors (NP) is sitting in his university office interviewing another industry analyst, David Mitchell, Head of Research at the UK firm Ovum. The conversation is flowing such that NP plucks up the courage to ask him the question which everyone from outside this domain wants to put to these experts: how on earth do they come up with their predictions? How can they possibly know what is coming next? Which technology trend will catch on? The next big thing? The response is insightful. 'A Gartner analyst or one of my team', David Mitchell says, 'might write down that the next trend in Enterprise Resource Planning is Software Oriented Architecture componentisation and Business Process Management orchestration across that. And someone says how do you know that? What the average Gartner analyst will say, is "well I have had 15 enquiries about these topics in the last quarter, so I have a really good sense that people are asking about it, so it is very likely to be true"'. And it is here that the discussion begins to echo that of the recruits, for David Mitchell too thinks that industry analysts often direct the market. In his view, industry analysts are like 'ethnographers' that look over the shoulders of technology vendors. And, because they are 'deep in the heart of all these software companies, they know what they are working on next'. But 'like any good ethnography', he says, 'you recognise that you change a system by being *part* of it. You are never outside it. The deeper you are inside some of these vendors the more you are actually influencing what is coming next. So that is how you know what is coming next: because you are *making* it come next'.[1]

NOTE

1. The following discussion is based on interviews conducted with Gartner analyst Elias Thomas and Ovum analyst David Mitchell.

1

The Social Study of Information Technology Markets

1.1. HOW TO UNDERSTAND THE NEW ACTORS WHO SEEM ABLE TO SHAPE THE IT MARKET?

How should we understand the recent emergence of actors who appear to set the direction of information technology (IT) markets? How is it that these experts apparently hold the success of new technologies in their hands? What do we make of their claimed capacity to 'predict' the future of the digital world? What gives them the power to 'name' entire generations of technology, and then decide which products fit into their classifications? How is it that they are able to say whether one technology vendor performs better than a rival? Why is their advice able to push a £5m procurement decision in a certain direction? Where have they come from? How have they been able to develop what appears to be considerable influence over market processes in such a short period of time? How are we to understand and theorize their influence on technology markets?

Remarkably little attention has been given to these questions amongst those from within Information Systems and related areas. This includes scholars across Information Systems, Organization Studies, Science and Technology Studies and the more socially oriented Computer Sciences, such as Social Informatics and Computer Supported Cooperative Work, with a potential interest in the markets for digital technologies. Informed by diverse perspectives, a considerable body of work has been amassed on digital technologies, which encompass technology design, development and their organizational implementation and use, but only a handful of studies address how the same 'markets' for these technologies are constructed and function. This stands in contrast to innovation economists who have paid attention to the building and operation of IT markets (Fransman 2010). It was economists who predicted the emergence and growth of 'intermediaries' in various markets to 'lubricate economic exchange' (Sharma 1997: 762).[1] However we still know very little about the role of such intermediaries (Hennion 1989,

Carruthers & Stinchcombe 1999, Bessy & Chauvin 2013) in the marketization of new digital innovations. Even though Information Systems scholars acknowledge that digital innovation is distributed along a chain of players—what Avgerou et al., (2004: 2) call the 'ICT innovation scene'—they have yet to directly take on the challenge of understanding the role of mediators in shaping innovation and technology markets. Whilst there is occasional mention of 'third party information providers' in the field of Information Systems (Keil & Carmel 1995, Sawyer 2001), their influence over market processes and technology development and adoption remains for the most part 'black boxed' (Latour 1987).

When market practices have been discussed, Information Systems and Organization Studies scholars have focused predominantly on large-scale industry-forming processes that surround new generations of technologies (Chiasson & Davidson 2005). Often drawing on institutional perspectives, the focus has been on 'managerial fads and fashions' (Abrahamson 1996, Newell et al. 2001, Baskerville & Myers 2009, Hirschheim et al. 2012), prevalent supplier 'rhetorics' (Pettigrew 1973, Swan & Clark 1992, Knights & Murray 1994), and broader 'organizing visions' (Swanson & Ramiller 1997, Ramiller & Swanson 2003, Currie 2004, De Vaujany et al. 2013, Meyer & Kearnes 2013) that herald in new technological and market opportunities, etc. Though the Information Systems literature provides occasional glimpses of the numerous intermediaries supporting the market-based supply of digital technologies, we know little about the complex interplay between these actors and how their work influences and alters the shape of technologies.

This book is the outcome of an interdisciplinary research project on the *Social Study of the Information Technology Marketplace(s)* that had substantive and conceptual aims. Firstly, we sought to carry out empirical work on the processes by which IT markets were constructed and maintained by various intermediaries. Our investigation focussed in particular on the role of a specific form of market intermediary, the 'industry analyst', in shaping how the markets surrounding new digital technologies were created and organized. From fieldwork, we saw how the development and operation of IT markets could not be properly understood without taking into account the research outputs of these experts. Some have suggested that today there could hardly be IT markets without the intervention and tools of these kinds of actors.

Here we take our cue from the economic sociologist Karpik (2010: 14) who, in a provocative phrase writes, the 'market is "equipped" or it does not exist'. What he means by this is that without the mechanisms to sort and compare goods, particularly complex products, where qualities cannot be assessed prior to consumption, buyers could not easily make purchase decisions. We also make use of Hennion's (1989: 414) suggestion that when the adopter has to take on a complex purchase choice there is not the 'chasm' normally thought between producer and consumer; there is instead the work of the intermediary that attempts to bridge these worlds (to link production with consumption). If we lose sight of the intermediary, Hennion (1989) warns, then it will not be clear as to how these two poles hold together. Indeed, it will be a surprise they combine at all (Carruthers & Stinchcombe 1999).

Our earlier research into the market for enterprise systems demonstrated how potential technology adopters experienced difficulties in assessing the qualities and performance of these hugely complex IT applications (Pollock & Williams 2007, 2009). These are 'non-fungible' goods, whose properties cannot readily be established (e.g. by inspection). For such multifaceted and expensive products, markets are a very inefficient mode of discovery. User organizations buy these products rarely—perhaps once a decade—and thus have little knowledge of the market and limited experience in assessing the performance and promises of vendor organizations. Procurement decisions, in other words, are made in contexts characterized by incomplete and uneven access to information. Would-be adopters are therefore forced to resort to indirect indicators. Indeed the starting point for our enquiry was the observation that where user-organization members might have traditionally sought advice from trusted peers about vendor offerings (Fincham et al. 1994), this form of information sourcing was no longer seen to provide an efficient means of discovery (Glückler & Armbrüster 2003). It is in this context that industry analysts have emerged, providing such advice on a commercial basis. Just how and in what way these new experts might 'equip' (Karpik 2010) technology consumers, or 'lubricate' market processes (Sharma 1997), will be the focus of subsequent pages.

Secondly, the project wished to explore whether the exciting new dialogue recently opened up between the disciplines of Science and Technology Studies (Callon 1998, Callon et al. 2007), Accounting (Milller & O'Leary 1987, Miller 2008, Vollmer et al. 2009), Economic Sociology (Pinch & Swedberg 2008, Stark 2009, Beckert & Aspers 2011), the Sociology of Finance (MacKenzie 2006, Preda 2009), Organization Studies (Cabantous & Gond 2011, Muniesa 2014, D'Adderio & Pollock 2014) and Marketing (Cochoy 1998, Kjellberg & Helgesson 2007, 2010, Araujo 2007, Mason et al. 2015) might be extended to include the field of Information Systems. At the heart of this dialogue was the suggestion that certain forms of knowledge output were not simply descriptive of markets but could be seen to be actually 'doing things' in the economy. To use the example discussed by Callon (1998), economic theories and models were able to bring into being that which they initially attempted to describe. This idea holds out the promise of needed impetus to the study of the construction and workings of IT markets.

Our focus in the book is the role of industry analysts in shaping innovation and markets and the extent to which their advice is 'performative'. By this we refer to the ways in which their research actively pushes or 'nudges' innovation pathways or technology procurement choices in certain directions. Indeed, industry analysts firms would be an ideal site to build on what has since been dubbed the 'performativity programme' (Callon 2007). Here we are arguably dealing with more complicated forms of influence than economic or financial theories. Whilst Hardie and MacKenzie (2007), for instance, show how financial research can modify a 'price', the assessments of industry analysts can change the trajectory of a complex product such as enterprise resource planning (ERP) systems (see Pollock & Williams 2009).

This opening chapter attempts to carry forward the two aims identified in our initial project. We set out why the market intermediaries described here are important, how their research has begun to govern and direct the activities of technology vendors and adopters alike, and why we think the process of marketization they are involved in should become a central topic of interest for Information Systems researchers and others. One reason there has been limited interest in the study of actual IT market situations thus far is because markets—presented as entirely 'abstract spaces' (Callon & Muniesa 2005), as economists have done—are difficult to study. There is a paucity of frameworks to guide the researcher in this kind of endeavour. We think the performativity programme offers help here. Its advantage is that it puts 'knowledge', as well as 'practices' and 'artefacts' (MacKenzie 2009) at the centre of the analytical lens. But we also want to show that just as there are similarities between IT procurement markets and the economic or financial trading markets on which much of this new literature has been constructed, there are also pertinent differences. If the performativity programme is to be useful for our purposes therefore, it will also need to be extended. This is a further goal of the book.

1.2. NEW FORMS OF KNOWLEDGE PRODUCER

The last three decades have seen the emergence in IT markets of new types of knowledge producer together with novel forms of knowledge production and distribution. We note the rise of a number of related groups coming under a variety of headings—'commercial research firms', 'advisory firms', 'research analysts', 'market analysts', 'technology analysts', 'IT research firms' and 'industry analysts' etc.,—all of whom perform related roles in providing research for enterprise technology buyers and producers. Though there is often much crossover between these groups it is the latter, industry analyst firms, that we will focus on here. Industry analyst firms have expanded from a small group of specialist players in the 1980s based mainly in North America to today where there are several hundred such firms around the world. We highlight the work of a number of core and leading analyst firms but foreground the work of Gartner Inc. in particular, and how it has emerged ahead of competitors such as Computer Intelligence, Dataquest, Forrester, Input,

International Data Corporation, Ovum and Yankee Group. Gartner is the largest of the industry analyst firms, having grown dramatically in size and influence over a short period of time. Partially this is through subsuming its larger rivals, but it is also because of its innovative practices that will be described here. Like the other industry analyst firms, it appears to have created and captured a lucrative and prosperous market, reporting large growths in revenues and client numbers, and selling its research and services to more than 10,000 of the world's most important companies.[2]

Industry analyst research is read and acted on by a number of key constituencies. These include Chief Information Officers (CIOs) planning organizational IT strategies, IT procurement teams choosing between multi-million pound workplace IT solutions, and company managers and employees wanting to learn more about the potential benefits of digital technologies for their business (Firth & Swanson 2005, Burks 2006). Industry analyst output is also extensively read by technology vendors and investor analysts (Snapp 2013). Ikeler (2007: 234) writes that industry analysts are the 'single most influential validators of the technical products and complex services that dominate the business-to-business world'. In a 2003 industry survey, for instance, it was found that technology buyers were already beginning to source advice not just from peers but also from industry analysts (Chapple 2007). Other surveys confirm this change in how technology purchases are being influenced (Hill & Knowlton 2013). By 2013, it was estimated that between 40–60 per cent of all IT decisions were shaped to some extent by industry analysts (Dennington & Leforestier 2013). The knowledge products that Gartner and the other firms produce appear to be appreciated by those who consume them. The *Edelman Trust Barometer* regularly finds industry analysts highly placed amongst those professionals seen to provide not just 'useful' but 'impartial' business advice. In 2008, they were ranked as the 'most trusted' source of advice, narrowly coming ahead of 'academics' (Edelman 2008).

Not a day passes, it seems, without a major announcement or high-profile report from these firms or discussion of their research in the industry and mainstream press. The annual Gartner Symposium in Orlando is now routinely covered on prime-time television for instance. Yet despite their increasingly prominent role, the academic study of these experts has not kept pace. Information Systems researchers, the group of scholars most centrally placed to address these actors, note their influence, but have not systematically sought to study them. When we first came across these firms during fieldwork, in the early 2000s, by chance and as part of a wider study into the biography of the enterprise resource planning (ERP) system (Pollock & Williams 2007, 2009), we struggled to place their work in a literature. In a review of the research conducted on industry analysts thus far Bernard & Gallupe (2013) counted only half a dozen mentions of these actors in the Information System field (Mallach 1997). Moreover, most of the studies discussing these actors appear to be rather speculative with a weak empirical base. Existing scholarship does offer insights into how into how analysts coin new technological terminologies (Wang & Ramiller 2009, Swanson 2010) and how they have had a hand in shaping technological paradigms like ERP or Customer Relationship Management (CRM) (Wang & Swanson 2007). However, whilst valuable, these studies have not focused in any detail on these issues.

There are further scattered insights to be found into these experts from across the social sciences (and we hope the programme of study outlined here might help link these up to provide a more coherent discussion of the general category of 'the analyst'). Firstly there is an established body of work on 'financial analysts' (including 'investment analysts' and 'security analysts') that we will draw on (Hong & Kubik 2003, Beunza & Garud 2007, Wansleben 2012). We will show that whilst there are parallels and linkages between industry analysts and this more established group, there are also significant differences, particularly in terms of the characteristics of their knowledge production process (Knorr Cetina 2010, 2012).

Secondly, there is a large body of work on 'management consultants' that has helped us reflect on how this relatively new form of expertise has been able to establish itself. Interestingly, many industry analysts insist they are *not* management consultants, even if to outsiders they appear similar. Their reasons for this distinction forms part of *Chapter 4: The Professionalization of Business Knowledge,* where we discuss industry analysts in relation to other groups such as the above mentioned consultants, financial analysts and also journalists. Thirdly, there is a relevant body of work from Economic Sociology on the role 'critics' play in mediating markets (as in 'restaurant', 'film', 'theatre', 'art' critic etc.). Critics have attracted the attention of scholars because they are seen as influential not only in composing actual evaluations but also through grouping and comparing offerings within consequential 'product categories' (Zuckerman 1999, Rosa et al. 1999, 2003). Because this has potential direct analogies with the study of industry analysts we thus concentrate and build on this literature in *Chapter 6: Who Decides the Shape of Product Markets?*

Finally, whilst our own field of Science and Technology Studies (STS) has made specific reference to industry analysts, it has been somewhat dismissive of these experts—presenting their knowledge as 'simplistic', 'flawed', or, in some cases, 'wrong' (see Borup et al. 2006, Rip 2006). We find this odd when one considers the founding concerns of STS were to avoid adopting a judicatory position on the accuracy, effectiveness, appropriateness etc., of knowledge. STS instead seeks to explore what comes to count as knowledge in specific locations (e.g., how particular knowledge artefacts become 'successful', 'diffused', 'believed' etc. [Shapin 2001]). Yet this stance does not appear to have been granted to industry analysts. Why is this? Moreover, despite becoming interested in the performativity of knowledge, particularly, as already mentioned, the performativity of economic theories (Callon 1998) and financial knowledge (MacKenzie 2006), STS has (paradoxically) ignored or 'deflated' certain forms of business knowledge, in some cases portraying it as 'arbitrary', whose methods and content do not deserve enquiry (Rip 2006).

1.3. WHO ARE THESE EXPERTS?

Our aim in writing this book is to open a window onto this distinctive 'epistemic culture' (Knorr Cetina 1999). These are experts not always appreciated or understood by those outside this domain. Who are these specialists who command the attention of vendor and user communities? What is the nature of their technical knowledge, the outputs they produce, the organizational configurations in which they work and from which their knowledge and products emerge? How do they explain their skills and practices to themselves and others? How is their knowledge warranted or validated? We want to learn about this new specialism. We want to understand how this research is entwined with what Knorr Cetina (ibid) terms 'machineries of knowing'. Knorr Cetina (ibid: 363) developed this conceptualization to capture not just knowledge construction but the 'construction of the machineries of knowledge construction'. The so-called Knowledge Society is not simply about the proliferation of evermore varieties of expertise, she argues, but also about the various machineries that serve and shape this expertise. In this introductory chapter, we begin to unpack the work of these industry analysts and their machinery through considering the narrative presented in the Prologue above. We use this to set out the rationale for the book and then to identify some initial questions that will form the basis of subsequent chapters.

1.3.1. What is an analyst?

Analyst: "*A specialist or expert in the analysis of events and situations or the prediction of future developments in a particular field*". "*A person who approaches a situation, event, etc., analytically or who tries to consider all the factors involved before forming an opinion*".

(Oxford English Dictionary, 1989)[3]

The Prologue provides a sense of the rise of a new powerful body of technical and market expertise. These are people who claim and who are increasingly able to demonstrate specialized knowledge (and being able to 'demonstrate' their expertise turns out to be important for the story we will tell) about vendors and products in the IT marketplace. This is not an insignificant group. One practitioner repository (the 'ARchitect' database) contains the details of over 700 industry analyst firms from around the globe (see Appendix 1 for a list). Despite these large numbers, however, there is little public knowledge about the nature of the industry analyst role, who they are, or what they actually do. Some definitions may be helpful here. The Oxford English Dictionary (1989) describes 'an analyst' as someone who 'stands back from the situation' they are observing, who 'considers all the factors involved' before forming 'an opinion' or 'to producing a prediction or statement of future developments'. A more specific definition, this time from those working for/within IT vendors, describes them as experts 'whose business model incorporates creating and publishing research about, and advising on how, why and where ICT-related products and services can be procured, deployed and used' (Dennington & Leforestier 2013: 4). Going back in time, an analogy from 1988 describes Gartner analysts, in making business predictions, as similar to meteorologists who plot the weather. 'If managers were pilots, then Gartner Group would provide flight planning maps and the weather forecast. The pilot charts his or her course, but the maps provide the context' (*Future Thinker*, 1988: 31).

One broad aim then will be to map this expertise empirically to show the boundaries beginning to emerge around this role. We will investigate whether they are 'standing back observing the situation' as they gather insights or if they go about their work in some other way? We will ask the question whether industry analysts in making predictions are similar to other groups, such as meteorologists or financial analysts, who produce forecasts on a regular basis. Also, to make sense of this expertise, it is necessary to say something about how it started out, which includes providing a discussion of past and current business model(s), and how these specialists were able to establish a market for their knowledge. To throw light on this we will also investigate the leadership role of Gideon Gartner in starting the firm that would bear his name, and subsequently how Gartner Inc. has gone on to shape the technology analysis world more generally.

1.3.2. Starting out

The usual way of introducing Gideon Gartner is to stress how he invented an entire industry. 'It's too easy to categorize Gartner Group as something we already know. It's not. At the very least, Gartner Group has reinvented market information publishing' (Future Thinker 1988: 31). But Gideon Gartner's firm was not the first analyst organization. As far as we can establish, the origins of this industry can be traced back to the 1964 International Data Corporation (IDC) offices in Framingham, Massachusetts. Gideon Gartner did however set out on his own innovative pathway that other firms have since attempted to emulate. At the origins of this specialism, there were self-evidently no established models for what an industry analysis firm should look like. Having broken from his Wall Street investment analyst job, Gideon Gartner reports that he knew little about running a technology analyst firm (Fredman & Gartner 2014). There were no ready-made plans for establishing and running an analyst business. These things had to be worked out. As Gideon recalled: 'Like Rome, I could not build our system in a day; in fact it took a period of over two years!' (Gartner 2011).

Accounts of Gideon Gartner's life, including those he has written himself, insist on the unconventionality of his choices. Gideon Gartner describes how in 1979 the early firm was a 'hodgepodge of ideas', deploying 'unusual research methods' (Gartner 2011d). He drew on ideas from a range of domains: 'I knew the layout of the computer industry because I was working in the competitive analysis department of IBM, which was studying the competition' (interview, Gideon Gartner). He also drew on his Wall Street experiences where he had worked for the investment analyst firms E. F. Hutton and later Oppenheimer (Gartner 2011d). Gideon Gartner joined two IBM user groups,[4] and noted that Wall Street technology analysts lacked understanding of user perspectives on technology (Gartner 2010b). In seeking to create 'visible and meaningful differentiation' from the existing players in the field (like IDC, Computer Intelligence, Dataquest, Yankee and Input), Gartner also drew upon academic writing on 'decision theory' (Gartner 2010). The radical feature of his firm was that it apparently shifted the industry from providing 'market research' to 'decision support'. The growth of Gideon Gartner's firm since has been nothing short of spectacular. Much of what he set out back then, particularly his vision of how the industry should develop and the distinctive business model he would adopt—whereby Gartner were 'paid by everyone they talked to' (interview, Governor)—has gone on to be seen as the template for the contemporary technology analyst firm.

1.3.3. Learning the tricks of the trade

The Prologue also provides evidence of an ongoing process of *socialization* within these firms whereby neophytes learn the theory and practice of this new role. This includes attending 'boot camps' initially run by Gideon Gartner himself but later by other research leaders such as Mike Brodie. It was in these spaces that novice industry analysts were first encouraged to master the methodologies and techniques surrounding this specialism. Gideon Gartner depicts himself as a 'kindergarten teacher', standing at the front of the room writing 'research directives' onto a flip chart to instil into neophytes 'a discipline' about how they should approach their work ('be enthusiastic', 'self-critical', 'proponents of change' etc.) (Gartner 2011). Technical and market knowledge was crucial but in itself not enough. Analysts had to go about the collection, production and communication of their research in a programmed way. Gideon Gartner described himself as determined to instil 'strong discipline' into those present regarding, for instance, the quality ('correct errors of fact immediately') and clarity of the research ('advocate positions explicitly', 'improve abilities to sell a specific point of view'). In just a few short years this hodgepodge of ideas would become formalized and structured into something grander and more distinct—what became known internally as 'Theory G'. Later these early schemes would be detailed and distributed to all staff as the 'Gartner Group Research Notebook'. It was the 'very existence' of Theory G, now spelt out and embodied in a physical manual that, according to Gideon Gartner, would 'lend credibility' to his new enterprise and even perhaps the entire industry (Gartner 2011).

Very quickly, the recruits would learn that this was no ordinary firm. Gartner's early research meetings were described as a cross between an 'academic seminar' and a 'think tank' culture, but with an emphasis on 'confrontation' (interview, Thomas). The recruits thus found themselves entering an organization where those around them were 'strong willed', and above all else loved 'challenging each other' (Gartner 2011). Gideon Gartner wanted to promote an 'aversion to groupthink' and expected the analysts to 'think outside the box' (Fredman & Gartner 2014). Passionate debate was thus a routine part of the weekly Friday research meetings: 'When I joined', describes an ex-Gartner analyst, 'you'd have certain analysts who would present their research to that audience to have much wider peer review. That was physically brutal as in people would throw things at you - the sweets off the table - they'd actually throw them' (interview, Levin). The peer critique was apparently straight to the point: '"That's a piece of crap", "I don't know where you came up with that", "I don't know what you're thinking but you just need to go away and start that from scratch"' (interview, Levin).

A further aim of the book will be to map the practices and techniques of this firm. This includes building an understanding of the research directives and contemporary templates and methodologies that have superseded Theory G. We will also enquire into how the knowledge contained in industry analyst outputs is collected and compiled. Developing insights in this domain appears heavily dependent on the creation and maintenance of formal and informal channels with technology buyers, vendors and others. We shall analyse these networks (and associated network-building processes) as part of Gartner's distinctive knowledge building practices.

1.3.4. A developing occupation

The Prologue also points to an emerging *occupation*. In just a few short decades, these specialists have matured from an informal rudimentary and inchoate group to a developed and formalized occupation that has come to exert considerable authority over large parts of the IT market. Comparing the early accounts described in Gartner's recent biography (Fredman & Gartner 2014) with our own fieldwork, for instance, we find that analyst roles and careers are becoming more structured. In some cases, we find them beginning to emulate more established expertise. A further question will be to understand the unique characteristics of this body as compared to other apparently similar groups. To what extent can we say that a new type of professional community is emerging? Indeed one central question will be to understand whether and in what ways these groups are attempting to professionalize. We were told the story of a 'failed' attempt to set up a professional association—the European Analysts Group in the 1990s. It never took off because, as one of our informants put it, Gartner would not 'allow it' (interview, Collins). This begs the question, if industry analysts are not following a traditional professionalization path, what other means have these groups used to establish the value of their knowledge?

1.4. HOW IS THEIR WORK ORGANIZED? HOW DO THEY KNOW WHAT THEY KNOW?

Talking to and observing industry analysts we learn that this is a highly demanding occupation. Many things seem expected of them. What are the requirements and qualities of an analyst? We have already seen that some of these can be taught at a boot camp. Others come only after years of experience in the field. We identify two issues: 'productivity' and 'sensibility'.

1.4.1. Organization of work: Productivity is key

The Prologue gives an indication of the unique organizational culture established within these firms. These are highly prolific groups of people. In 1985, for instance, with only 160 analysts, Gartner Inc. were already 'pumping out over 10,000 pages a year of analysis' (Fredman & Gartner 2014). With nearly a thousand analysts today, Gartner's output is significantly higher. It releases dozens of reports about a vast range of innovations on what seems an almost daily basis. Indeed all the analyst firms appear to have extremely high levels of productivity. An industry commentator writes: 'Every year industry analysts publish over 17,000 research reports, influencing over $250bn in tech buying decisions'.[5] How are we to understand these kinds of highly prolific organizations? What drives this constantly moving research front?

Clearly, the 'external' context plays a role. The computing industry is extremely fast moving: technology vendors are rarely still, there is constant innovation, and the products they produce are always evolving (Fransman 2010). But the 'internal' dynamics of analysts firms play their part too. The promissory machinery created by Gartner, and emulated by later firms, has served to accelerate this pacing. Much of what was taught in those early boot camps revolved around conversations about 'productivity'. Gartner set out the 'publish or perish' system (interview, Thomas). He described himself as 'neurotic' about output. Employees were taught from day one that a key reason for being fired was if they 'stopped writing' (interview, Thomas). Individual analysts were continuously 'measured on productivity—how many research notes they wrote and how many inquiries they answered from clients' (Fredman & Gartner 2014). A further aim of the book therefore will be to understand how such large-scale and intensive forms of envisioning can be maintained. Chapter 5: *The Business of Technology Expectations*, investigates the kinds of knowledge and market infrastructure needed to make this kind of research production possible. Another important question is how analysts are able to keep on top of contemporary developments. What kind of research practices and methods are necessary to uphold these levels of output?

1.4.2. How do they know what they know: A sensibility?

But how do analysts know what they know? Their object of study, as we will show throughout the book, is far from simple. They are attempting to get a handle on situated technology practices dispersed over a vast array of organizational sites but which must be relayed in something close to real time (for whatever else happens, technology predictions cannot be late). The analysts we spoke to were aware of their privileged perspective ('looking over [technology developers] shoulders', 'closer to it than everybody else' [interview, Thomas]). They articulated very particular conceptions of their own research process ('like any good ethnographer' [interview, Mitchell]). Of course, the methods and practices of these people can be criticized, most obviously, as alluded to above, for their role in the production of this constant flow of seemingly transitory ideas. Notwithstanding this we think that how they describe themselves—as 'ethnographers'—is not just to provide an empty gloss to their activities.

To be an industry analyst one has to do more than simply churn out research reports. The people who excel in this occupation have something of an 'ethnographer's sensibility' towards their object of study. Industry analysts do not actually 'test' the software solutions they write about (Snapp 2013).[6] Many will have technical knowledge and experience of the technologies they review (garnered in a previous career for instance: see *Chapter 3: The Organization of Analyst Work*); but this is not always the case. They are able to produce their research because they are in constant conversation with an extraordinary number and range of people (from vendors, current and potential adopters, colleagues, investors, executives and even sometimes academics). They acquire what Collins & Evans (2002) would call 'interactional' expertise rather than 'contributory' expertise. Whilst they may not be able to build the software systems they write about, they do seem quite capable of sustaining detailed and probing conversations with those that can. Through cultivating extended networks of 'informants' who operate in strategic positions in the technological decision making process they are amassing a huge amount of data and insight related to how vendors organize themselves and orient their markets. But this is not only what we mean by 'sensibility'.

We came to see some within these groups as having much in common with what Holmes and Marcus (2006, 2008) describe as 'para-ethnographers'. The term captures how business experts working within organizations performing research-like roles not only mimic or draw on the intellectual tools favoured by anthropologists but then go on to exhibit some of the same sensitivities. This includes an appreciation of more 'situated' forms of knowing that can work alongside or instead of conventional quantitative methods for aggregating data (Suchman 1987). We describe the research processes through which these experts attempt to collect and make sense of several hundred hours of qualitative discussions, described by Gartner as 'subjective enquiries'. Subjective enquiries are Gartner's learnt response to the inherent problem of tracking 'illusive' issues. It is the sensibility that provides them with their unique purchase on contemporary developments. Some of those we met seemed to have acquired a 'subtlety' towards the settings they studied that would not be out of place in a traditional organizational ethnography ('I have a really good sense that people are asking about it'; 'you recognize that you change a system by being part of it' [interview, Mitchell]).

However, there are also important differences that we should not underestimate. One is that the objects of industry analyst research are unlike those typically encountered by the social scientist. Though analysts may appear to have borrowed from traditional ethnographers 'the role of disinterested outsiders and observers' (Knorr Cetina 2010: 19), the people they meet are not disinterested subjects. They are usually the objects of assessment (e.g., they are being 'ranked' by the analysts). This makes them highly 'interested' and in some cases 'calculating' towards the shaping of such assessments. This is another feature of the sensibility mentioned above. As one industry analyst told us, in their interactions with vendors there is a 'game' being played out where the technology vendor and others will attempt to represent things in a certain way (to improve their position on a ranking). In turn, the industry analyst will be mobilizing his or her own 'strategies' to get behind 'the façade' as they put it. This includes modes of questioning where they will seemingly 'provoke' a vendor, or 'push things too far', with the aim of trying to get them 'to react' (interview, Thomas). How they do this—these multilateral games—is an important theme of the book (and especially *Chapter 7: Marketing of Quantifications*).

1.5. DO INDUSTRY ANALYSTS DIRECT THE MARKET?

It is clear from the excited chatter of the recruits described in the Prologue that there is more to the boot camp than just acquiring narrow technical skills or learning about research productivity. The socialization process also included the adoption of wider beliefs about the efficacy of these knowledge practices when applied to market situations. There was the realization that to be a Gartner analyst was unlike work at other industry analyst firms. The sense that they could potentially direct the market excited the recruits, such that they wanted to talk about it, to make sense of it, to ask if it was true. Not only would they get to meet all the 'senior execs' from the world's most important IT vendors but apparently there was little need for them to leave their offices to do so. 'They come to *us*. We *don't* go to them' (interview, Winter) crowed one Gartner analyst as he spelt out how the late modern technological hierarchy has been refashioned. This begs the question as to how Gartner has been able to manufacture this situation in a relatively small amount of time. Is it really able to direct the market?

1.5.1. Four different positions on their influence

We have arrived at the key aim of the book. This is to describe the contribution of industry analysts to the marketization of the IT realm and to develop an appropriate conceptualization and theorization of this contribution. The Prologue tries to capture how industry analysts have varying conceptions of their influence over markets, how they move between different positions when talking about what they do. Let us spell out these differences:

i) *Industry analyst research simply 'describes' a technology trajectory*: One part of the discussion of what an industry analyst does echoes the general dictionary understanding above, that is to get as close as possible to an innovation so that ultimately the analyst can *predict* its course. It does not matter whether the analyst is describing something that currently exists (an already established technology) or does not yet exist (a technology still in a vendor lab); the research is meant to be external to the thing described.

However, many analysts acknowledge that the separation between the writing and the state of affairs described in the research was rarely clear-cut.

ii) *Industry analyst outputs 'accelerate' a technology trajectory along the direction it was already travelling*: This is the recognition that, in writing about an innovation, an industry analyst may also end up pushing or nudging it in a certain direction. Mike Brodie and Elias Thomas acknowledge how they may 'accelerate' the success of a new product or, in the case of a negative review, 'slow' or retard it along its route. But they are clear that they do not change its course: a 'brilliant product' will still get to where it should be going and a less than fantastic one will still go 'over the cliff'.

If this were all industry analysts were to do then this already would be highly significant (and still give plenty of reason to write this book). But Mike Brodie's view is not shared by all those we interviewed. Nor does it fully reflect our own observations captured during several years of fieldwork. There are further positions:

iii) *Industry analyst reports 'modify' a technology trajectory so that the direction of travel is changed*. There is the acknowledgement that industry analysts are not external to the state of affairs but 'part of the system' that they are attempting to describe. Rather than observe technology from afar, the industry analyst David Mitchell describes how they are 'deep inside' the technology vendor organizations described. And they realize they 'change a system by being part of it'. In producing research, they are not just writing about technological innovation but they begin to take control of the 'steering wheel'—to direct it in one-way or another.

iv) *Industry analysts direct a technology trajectory according to 'presumptions' about what constitutes effective technological development*. This brings us to a variation of the last position where these experts are as much 'innovators' as the innovative actors they are describing. In the process of their writing and analysis, the industry analysts move from a position where they are describing how the market or technology could develop to prescribing how it *should* develop. That is, they *purposefully* begin to shape the thing they initially set out to describe: they 'tell the market where to go'.

The central goal of this book is to begin to flesh out these different kinds of influence that industry analysts might have on markets. The book speculates that, for at least some of the time, these specialists seek to reformat IT markets according to their presuppositions about the nature of the technological developments and market processes related to these developments.

1.6. HOW WILL WE STUDY AND MAKE SENSE OF INDUSTRY ANALYSTS?

"An influential analyst can't analyze without changing what is analyzed".
Future Think Live[7]

To help with the above aim we have found useful the recent suggestion from sociologists of science and technology, particularly Michel Callon and our Edinburgh colleague Donald MacKenzie, that theories about markets can be 'performative'. Their performativity programme puts forward the idea that theory is not simply descriptive of the world but it can enact the phenomenon it is attempting to describe. The radical departure introduced by Callon (1998) and MacKenzie (2006) was to make these arguments within the context of economic and financial markets. They sought to show the formative relationship between economic or financial theory and actual market processes. In attempting to theorize the market, economists could end up modifying actors in those markets. That is, the theory enacts the 'framing' processes that allow the operation of the same market activities described in the research (Table 1.1 presents a detailed discussion of these arguments).

There has been a recent upsurge in interest in the so-called economic performation of the economy. But the market actors we investigate are not economists. Nor are they writing theory (narrowly defined). Yet their research is important and, if the Prologue above is anything to go by, highly influential in the shaping of markets. Below we make a couple of brief points in relations to this.

1.7. A DIFFERENT MODEL OF PERFORMATIVITY: MECHANISMS OF INTERACTION; HOW TO CAPTURE THESE INTERACTIONS

In addressing this debate, Peter Miller (2008) argues against the assumption that all processes of market shaping derive simply from Economics and points to the work of other market professionals, such as accountants, in the constitution of markets. Callon (2007) makes a similar argument in later work where he begins to distinguish between 'confined Economics' and 'Economists in the wild'. The former are seen as 'academic economists' or 'text book views of the economy' and the latter 'market professionals' who operate closer to front line economic processes. Importantly, in keeping with the symmetry of Actor Network Theory, Callon does not differentiate between these types of actor. An economist may be both an 'academic researcher whose job is to produce theories on the market . . . [o]r he or she may be a market professional

Table 1.1. Performativity: Key notions

The notion of 'performativity' stems from the work of the linguistic philosopher J. L. Austin (1962) who wrote that a statement was performative when it did more than just describe a reality but was instead actively engaged in the constitution of that reality (c.f. Barnes 1983). This begs the question as to whether all statements may be performative? Do forecasts operate as self-fulfilling prophecies (MacKenzie 2006)? Could industry analysts make whatever judgement they choose? In Austin's original discussion, he was careful to avoid discussing the 'veracity' of performatives. What was important was not whether statements were true or false but how, in actually making them, the speaker was 'setting something in motion' (Callon 2007: 320). Callon has built on this argument in two ways: through replacing the concept of truth and falsity with 'success' and 'failure' and setting out a partial framework to study whether performatives have 'successfully' brought about that which they previously set in motion.

This first point is relatively straightforward, especially for those familiar with the pragmatism of Actor Network Theory, the approach that sits behind the performativity programme, but the second less so. What Callon means is that performatives do not exist in isolation; they have meaning and effect in the 'world' they create for themselves. This notion of a 'world' is important for Callon's argument. Drawing on semiotics, he points to how statements are 'indexical', meaning they are always 'located' (referring to particular circumstances, time and space). In other words, a 'statement contains its own context'; statements cannot exist outside their context but require this context or (to use Callon's terminology) 'world'. Callon describes theories and their world as a socio-technical agencement. The term (derived from the work of Deleuze and Guattari 1988) is used to denote a heterogeneous collection of material and textual elements that act on and modify each other. As Callon notes, there is nothing 'outside' a socio-technical agencement—theories or descriptions of the agencement, for instance, are not 'external' but part of the configuration, acting and bringing it into being. Callon argues that a theory is successful (performative) when it can create its corresponding socio-technical agencement. He writes that a theory or formula imposes a world or 'socio-technical agencements outside of which it cannot survive' (2007: 324). A formula 'progressively discovers its world' and there is a world 'put into motion by the formula describing it' (ibid: 320).

One other important aspect is the assertion that no one element (human or nonhuman) is assumed a priori to be more important than any other; they all, methodologically at least, have equal status, and in this sense they all can act. It is because of the implied symmetry here that Callon can argue that theories also set worlds in motion.

Employing these ideas Callon (1998, 1999) can therefore suggest that the 'market' and 'homo economicus' are no longer ideas that exist simply in economic textbooks but are continuously enacted within the economy. If people trade and purchase goods in a 'market' (as opposed to any of the other ways the exchange of goods might occur) then this is because economic notions of the market have successfully constructed a 'socio-technical agencement'. Callon emphasizes that the mechanisms enabling this are not part of human nature (actors in Callon's view have a variable ontology) but are actively constructed and that academic economics has played a role in this performation. Moreover, actors and objects are so thoroughly entangled in other (competing) socio-technical agencements that there have to be processes of 'framing' and 'disentanglement' if economic actors are to exist. If this framing is successful then a socio-technical agencement can give an actor the ability to 'act'. In this last respect, the notion of socio-technical agencement has two meanings: it depicts the various equipment, tools and prostheses that allow people to calculate and decide within markets; and it captures the fact that actors are constituted by the various surrounding agencements (Hardie & MacKenzie 2007).

---

who designs market devices, algorithms for comparing supply and demand' (Callon 2007: 336). We think this distinction deserves more attention than it has been given to date. The counter-intuitivity in Callon's argument clearly revolves around the influence of academic research rather than practicing professionals. The assumption has been that 'confined' economists are cut off from their subject matter (i.e. they are removed from the places where their work is consumed). The suggestion that their theory has transformatory rather than merely descriptive capacities is therefore something of a surprise!

For the market professional, however, there is not thought to be the same divide between the production of research and its implementation. The consumption of the research of an industry analyst can directly affect the markets it relates to. Industry analysts are dealing with the consumers of their outputs on a daily basis. There are, as we will show, substantial links and interactions between these groups. They move back and forth between the world described in their research and the world itself. At one moment they are distanced observers and at the next included in the situation. Their research aims to describe a technology in the marketplace that, at other times, it is actively concerned with transforming. The job of the industry analyst, so clearly seen from the Prologue above, can be as much concerned with the *actioning* of research as with the writing of it. It is thus less revelatory perhaps to suggest that market professionals actually transform that which they set out to describe (see Nilsson & Helgesson [2015] who make a similar point with regard to another market professional—the market researcher).

1.7.1. Interactions are important: Nowhere near the same divide

A key question to using this approach is whether it tells us something we did not already know (e.g., the counter-intuitivity sought by Callon). Whilst the performativity programme may deviate substantially from how most academic, policy or broader industry experts conceive of the influence of market theories, it carries less novelty when applied to market or business groups such as industry analysts. To argue that industry analysts directly shape technologies through writing about them will not be a great surprise to these people. The industry analysts we interviewed frequently addressed the interaction their research has with its object of study. Their work, it seemed, was not just about forming an opinion but it also involved a reflexive element that demanded that they pay close attention to what happens to that opinion once sent out into the world. Indeed, industry analysts regularly discuss their research using a vernacular version of 'self-fulfilling prophecy' (Hind 2004), the well-known theory offered by Merton (1982), and a precursor to much of the performativity debate (see MacKenzie [2006] for a discussion of how the latter builds on the former).

The fact that the performativity argument can so plausibly be applied to this area is both interesting and a concern. It is interesting because it provides (some of the) tools needed to depict the influence of the kinds of business knowledge otherwise ignored or critiqued by other related (STS and Management) approaches. But it is also a worry because it means potentially our analytical insight is weakened (Pollner 2002, Nilsson & Helgesson 2015). In discussing this line of enquiry with industry analysts, for instance, we often failed to raise eyebrows. In sharing early versions of these pages with informants, we found ourselves telling them something they already knew and in a language less nuanced than their own (Pollner 2002). What does this mean for how we study industry analysts?

We are happy to accept Callon's argument that the work of 'confined economics' and 'economics in the wild' refer broadly to similar things (insofar as they are both the work of market building). Yet to dissolve completely the distinction between these two spaces is not helpful as it masks the very different character of social and material relations potentially at play. In particular we argue that there is a close interplay between the industry analyst intervention and the setting in which they are operating, whether this is the interplay between an industry analyst talking about an imagined digital future and the technology vendors trying to create that same future, the interplay between the industry analyst creating a ranking and those attempting to provide evidence for a particular vendor rating, or the interplay between an industry analyst making a speech at a conference and the audience nodding agreement with the futuristic claims made. In short, a study of these *interactions* is necessary if we are to understand the double-sided character of theory as both shaping and shaped by wider relationships.

All this raises the further question about the kinds of templates and methods needed to study these different kinds of market building processes. A number of exciting studies embracing the performativity arguments have attempted to take seriously the influence of theory (MacKenzie et al. 2007, Kjellberg & Helgesson 2006, Araujo 2007, Muniesa 2014). Many of the studies we came across offer interesting accounts of the significance of theories (e.g. Cabantous & Gond 2011), but can only postulate about their effects on the world. Others have resorted to reading Management textbooks (Thrift 2005), market research manuals (Nilsson & Helgesson 2015), trade journals (Cochoy 2014) or attending business school courses (Muniesa 2014) and speculating how the directives inscribed in these pages or forums might be read or applied in actual settings. This is despite Callon and MacKenzie's concern from the outset to counter the argument that they were proposing a linear view of the impact of theory.[8] Yet some of this literature tends to advance a particularly 'strong' version of the performativity argument (of theory doing things to people) (Holm & Nielsen 2007). In other cases, the discussion of the impact of theory has become uncoupled from studies of organizational reality (e.g. Aspers 2007, Perkmann & Spicer 2010, Cabantous & Gond 2011). There seems to be a gap between what might be thought of as 'espoused' performativity and the studies of performativity in practice.

For our purposes, we find it more helpful to view performativity as a *set of interactions between the generators of theory and their audiences* (Alexander 2011). Yet there are few studies that come close to capturing the processes of mutual shaping that we are suggesting (D'Adderio & Pollock 2014). We have come across few discussions of how these theories are adopted in practice or where scholars look at the complex interplay between theories and actors in or across organization(s) over time or across space. Many scholars have focused on single episodes such as the creation of new markets. Even MacKenzie's (2006) investigation of the Black Scholes Merton theory looks historically at long-term processes whereby markets are made rather than how they operate or continue. Also, there has been little focus on the production and consumption of theory *in tandem*. This is a weakness, we argue, because it means we are blind to certain crucial aspects of the subsequent shaping of theory. We particularly think this kind of approach to analysing the effects of theory on markets has limitations when applied to market intermediaries (a group poised at the intersection between different worlds [Hennion 1989]).

We argue that if the notion of performativity is to be fruitful we should give attention to the issue of analytical template and research design, a feature not much discussed in studies of performativity (but see Mason et al. 2015). The current view of performativity derives from rather simplistic methodologies, often employing the 'flat ontologies' of Actor Network Theory and typically tracking *from theory out*, without giving adequate attention to the complex forms of interplay that can exist between the diverse players in the business ecology that is structured institutionally and temporally. Studies thus leave rather under-described and under-explained the ways in which theory or theory-driven tools are distributed, implemented, and used by actors from the arena or ecology in question (Holm & Nielsen 2007).

This leads us on to consider how we have gone about addressing industry analysts in a way that considers both its production and its consumption. This is linked to the performativity programme's concern to understand the mechanisms for the mutual shaping of theory and markets. In the version of performativity set out in this book, we want to move away from the view that these theories and tools could be analysed separately from the organizational reality in which they were shaped and used. Thus, where possible, we have studied the development and use of these artefacts together. Here we take the opportunity to say something about what exactly we have studied.

We have studied industry analyst research outputs from multiple viewpoints. We have been able to assemble what we would argue is a comprehensive in-depth picture of these artefacts during key stages in their biography from their design, through to application in practice, and take-up and adoption in user contexts.[9] We deliberately placed ourselves at the interfaces between industry analysts and a range of other players and audiences that we describe more fully in subsequent pages. This allowed us to understand the intricacy of the knowledge creation and reception process, as we will show below.

1.8. PLAN OF THE BOOK

The bulk of the fieldwork reported here has been carried out on the market-leading firm Gartner Inc. It would be unusual (not to say difficult) to write a book about industry analysts without giving significant attention to Gartner, such has been its influence and dominance over the IT industry in recent years. Added to this, the very limited literature on this industry is centred on Gartner (often written by current or ex-Gartner employees). The next chapter, *The Emergence of a New Expert*, provides the recent history and growth of this occupational group, through investigating some of the 'innovations' introduced by Gartner. We will discuss how Gideon Gartner founded Gartner Inc. and in so doing helped bring into being this new body of expertise known as the industry analyst.

We will also discuss how Gartner's outputs are not unproblematic forms of knowledge. Far from it! Certain of its products are viewed as highly controversial. Merely to mention the word 'Gartner' or its signature product the 'Magic Quadrant' will often provoke sharp disagreements in certain circles (and every so often 'laughter'). Given how its knowledge products are widely problematized, therefore, it would have been relatively straightforward to 'debunk' this form of expertise, as one academic colleague assumed we were doing when he heard of our research project. We could also have written a more critical account of this particular firm along the lines of McDonald's (2014) or O'Shea and Madigan's (1998) expose of management consultants. Finally, since industry analysts form part of the rapidly emerging 'privatized research industry', we could also have drawn lessons from Mirowski's (2011) trenchant critique of the 'commercialized research model'.

It will be clear to the reader who gets beyond the first few pages of this book that this is *not* what we have decided to do. Whilst this peculiar form of business knowledge is often judged, rarely is it described with much care or detail. In the main, social scientists, for whatever reason, have not sought to get close to these actors, to open this particular 'black box', to describe their skills, outputs and processes, as we have done here. In researching and writing about this group, we have learned (in part) to see the world as they do. Some have argued that getting to know and understand the detailed work of experts, including the demanding constraints they work under, inevitably blunts one's critical edge (MacKenzie 2005). Such compromises are necessary MacKenzie (ibid) argues if markets are to be understood, this includes getting close to such individuals to observe who the powerful actors able to shape market processes are and what are the consequences of that shaping. However, we do not agree that a detailed focus *inevitably* means that one has to be uncritical. We have conducted a very detailed enquiry, but, at the same time, looked to track a diversity of voices and perspectives, avoiding the risk of just finding or presenting the complacent accounts of industry analysts or the partisan views of disgruntled vendors or consumers.

Our aim then is to describe the work of these experts in as much detail as we were able to uncover and the reader can bear. The third chapter, *The Organization of Analyst Work*, begins to throw light on how these experts go about their work. 'What do you cover?' is what people in this domain typically ask when they meet an industry analyst for the first time. Industry analysts have their own 'territory': 'This is my turf and I cover it' (interview, Thomas) is a common refrain. We show that while Gartner analysts need to adhere to standardized methodologies, they can also exercise a high level of discretion in covering their turf. We also map the 'careers' of these specialists, describing the unique recruitment process they undergo as well as their training and internal management.

If the second and third chapters provide the recent history and growth of this occupational group, in the fourth chapter, *The Professionalization of Business Knowledge*, we attempt to theorize and make sense of this knowledge work. Effective study of these experts has required bringing together the tools and frameworks of a number of different disciplinary schools. This includes literature from the Sociology of Professions, Sociology of Science and Sociology of Markets. It is also here that we compare industry analysts to apparently similar bodies of expertise (e.g., management consultants, equity analysts, journalists etc).

It should be clear that 'theory' in these kinds of business settings is not the formal or confined theory described by Callon (2007) and others. It is rather a set of apparently mundane concepts, practices and artefacts. But we want to show in the book that there is a significance to the various tools Gartner deploys that extends beyond immediate appearance. In this respect, we find insightful how Gideon Gartner borrowed and adapted techniques and objects from a wide range of domain to construct 'Theory G'. Theory G has evolved considerably over the years since he left the firm. Today, it is not so much a coherent narrative but a 'hodgepodge of ideas' (Gartner 2010b). Nonetheless, these ideas continue to influence in important ways how IT markets are put together, organized and acted upon.

The five empirical chapters that follow look at various aspects of how these ideas have been rolled out or become embedded in contemporary knowledge products. The weakness when we ignore important forms of expertise is that we tend to view their outputs as monolithic and undifferentiated. The fifth chapter, *The Business of Technology Expectations*, develops this discussion through showing how Gartner have not one single mode or set of tools for acting on and in markets but a range of equipment and practices at their disposal. To show the plurality of these knowledge practices, we set out an initial typology that characterizes Gartner's research outputs according to differences in how they are produced, legitimated, distributed, consumed and achieve influence. Each of the subsequent chapters will develop one or more aspects of this typology.

One focus in this typology will be towards describing how Gartner create much of the 'knowledge infrastructures' (Edwards 2010) on which IT markets operate. 'Technology classifications' are an important part of this infrastructure. The sixth chapter, *Who Decides the Shape of Product Markets?*, looks at how Gartner makes regular 'naming interventions' within the IT domain. Existing Information Systems scholarship has tended to present terminologies as shaped by wide communities of players but this does not capture how particular kinds of intermediaries like Gartner have emerged in recent year to police the confines of technological fields. The chapter follows Gartner's current and past role in the evolution of Customer Relationship Management (CRM) software. We show how Gartner attempted to regulate the boundaries around this technology category through various episodes of 'classification' and 'categorization' work. Gartner not only attempt to exercise control over a terminology but also the interpretation of that name.

Another aspect of the typology we want to foreground is how Gartner make use of highly abridged figurations to depict and communicate their research. However, it would be a mistake to dismiss these as straightforward simplifications as critics have done. This is because much of what Gartner produce is simplified *on purpose*. Gideon Gartner is alleged to have said, 'If I can't finish the page while I'm taking a piss, then it's way too long' (Fredman & Gartner 2014). Gideon Gartner's aim was not just to streamline reporting but to shift the *raison d'être* behind this form of research. What he wanted to provide to the technology buyer was information or a picture of the market that they could immediately make sense of and act upon (Pollock & Campagnolo 2015).

There is no better example of this simplicity than the Magic Quadrant. In the seventh chapter, the *Marketing of Quantifications*, we show how this figuration has become hugely important—with some describing it as the *most influential* piece of research in the IT domain (a few have even gone as far to describe it the most significant research output *across* business domains). However, interestingly, it is also a 'dividing object'. Just as it has many followers, there are also large numbers of detractors who describe the Magic Quadrant as a mere simplification or piece of 'marketing'. Our purpose in this chapter is to investigate just why the Magic Quadrant has become so influential. We explore the intricate processes through which Magic Quadrants are constructed and consumed.

The eight chapter, the *Venues of High Tech Prediction*, attempts to understand the apparent paradox whereby, though industry analyst IT predictions often turn out to be 'wrong', there appears no obvious decline in the number of predictions made, the appetite for this kind of knowledge, or the standing of the specialist producing them. This begs the question of what *value* predictions have for those who consume them. We have been able to examine this issue empirically through ethnographic study of one of the key contemporary interfaces between the production and consumption of predictions: the industry analyst conference. Departing from studies that foreground the 'accuracy' of predictions, we describe how this knowledge is subject to more plural methods of evaluation and accountability. We discuss in particular its 'utility' amongst Gartner clients, and how Gartner analysts gauge the effectiveness of their knowledge through interacting with and provoking reactions from conference audiences.

The ninth chapter, *Give Me a 2x2 Matrix and I Will Create the Market*, builds on the initial discussion of the Magic Quadrant found in Chapter 7. It focuses on how scholars have conceptualized the influence of these kinds of rankings as encouraging 'mechanisms of reactivity' (Espeland & Sauder 2007) amongst market actors. We to whether there are additional agential aspects found within rankings that extend these 'social' accounts. We suggest that 'sociomateriality' is also a significant aspect of the Magic Quadrant's influence. Through developing the notion of a 'ranking device', we provide evidence to show that IT markets are shaped by the affordances and constraints of the Magic Quadrant.

Let us be clear; though we have focused on the leading industry analyst firm, this is not a book solely about Gartner. We conducted fieldwork on a number of other industry analysts firms and players. Amongst the developments that the tenth chapter, *The Expertise Ecosystem*, will reflect on is the broader ecosystem of industry analyst expertise that appears to be emerging. This domain appears polarized, notably between larger and smaller analyst firms, which seem to play different kinds of role. It is also changing as the barriers to entry have been lowered (through the Internet and other social media technologies), leading to a dramatic increase in 'new entrants'. This includes the introduction of so-called 'open source' or '2.0 research firms' that employ different business models or research practices and who have, in some respects, begun to compete with the incumbents. We also discuss the growth of new technical and market specialists—known as 'analyst relations' experts—that have become important in helping IT vendors make a more systematic response to the challenge of industry analyst firms.

The final chapter, *From IT Markets to the Sociology of Business Knowledge* asks whether the performativity template as it is currently construed—i.e. on understandings of markets as either partially or fully built around financial/economic theories—is useful for analysing the kinds of contexts encountered in this book. The chapter points to some of the limitations of the performativity argument when applied to business knowledge production practices more broadly and makes some tentative suggestions towards a modified analytical template on the *Sociology of Business Knowledge*.

The material presented in the book is drawn from a mix of interviews and ethnographic observations on Gartner and other related actors. In the course of our preceding investigation into enterprise systems (Pollock & Williams 2009), we spoke to many Gartner analysts as well as Gartner clients and technology vendors. We built upon and extended these contacts in the course of this project. We did not have a formal agreement with Gartner to conduct this research *ab initio* (and did not know whether Gartner would welcome such an approach). Despite these initial assumptions, we have found it relatively easy to find and interview analysts. In some cases, Gartner analysts have approached us and asked to be included in the study! We also attended Gartner conferences and listened into Webinars which are open to the public (for a fee of course!). A full list of those interviewed and observations carried out can be found at Appendix 2.

NOTES

1. As Sharma (1997: 762) observes, from an agency-theoretic perspective: 'When principals themselves cannot afford the cost of information gathering (i.e., monitoring) devices, agency theory predicts that third-party institutions will arise to fill the gap and to lubricate economic exchange . . . The existence of rating agencies, such as Standard & Poor's and Moody's, is explained by agency theory in these terms, as is the role played by investment bankers when they help firms raise money in the capital markets'.
2. http://tekrati.wikispaces.com/Analyst+Family+Tree. Accessed 25 June 2013.
3. "analyst, n." OED Online. Oxford University Press, June 2015. Web. 28 July 2015.
4. These were SHARE and GUIDE (Gartner 2010) that were both formed in the 1950s by users of IBM mainframes, making them perhaps the oldest computer user groups (Akera 2001).
5. Analyst Strategy Group, http://www.go2asg.com/menu_pages/home.html, posted by Kea Company on Twitter 17th January 2015. Accessed 11 February 2015.
6. One informant told us that it was standard practice during the early days of the industry (1990s) to write research pieces based on a rudimentary form of 'testing'. Analysts would apparently read user manuals to understand what the software could and could not do. Armed with this information they would then quiz technology vendors about choice of functionality and features etc. This is no longer common practice because the technologies have become too complex (Chapple, personal communication).
7. Future Think Live, http://pcmine.com/P/FT/Future%20Think%20Live%20III.pdf. Accessed 20 December 2014.

8. Callon offered the notion of 'overflow' to show not only how theory can 'frame' a situation, but also how aspects not included or ignored by the original theory fight back (and the introduction of a theory is thus invariably followed by processes of 'reframing' where overflows are taken into account). MacKenzie (2009), drawing on Fleck's (1988) notion of 'innofusion' (which is a concatenation of the words 'innovation' and 'diffusion'), similarly described how theories were necessarily changed and adapted as they moved across contexts.

9. To give just one example, we conducted a number of separate periods of fieldwork on Gartner's 'Magic Quadrant' over a 10-year period, each time capturing a different facet of this tool, from its production to consumption. Our rationale for studying the Magic Quadrant in this way was initially a mixture of serendipity, good fortune and then later design. For instance, during an investigation into ERP systems (Pollock & Williams 2009), we saw, by chance, how large technology vendors interacted with Gartner to attempt to shape and influence the Magic Quadrant. Curious about these kinds of interactions, and as part of a further study, we were able to find Gartner analysts willing to talk us through how they go about compiling Magic Quadrants, as well as with how they respond to the contributions of technology vendors. Shortly after, we became aware of 'analyst relations' experts—a new category of expertise that had emerged over the last few decades as a response to industry analysts. We have been able to observe these latter groups as they collect information on and attempt to wield influence on industry analyst tools. Finally, in our most recent study, we have carried out interviews and observations of how Magic Quadrants are used and consumed by technology adopters during procurement contests.

2

The Emergence of a New Expert

This chapter examines how Gideon Gartner founded Gartner Inc. and in the process helped constitute the new and distinctive category of expert we know as the industry analyst. The role of the IT industry analyst is now well established but it did not exist before the late 1970s. This was a novel category of knowledge service that developed as the market for computer hardware and software took off. Table 2.1 shows some of the main industry analysis firms, indicating when and by whom they were established. Many of these firms were formed by players who had previously worked at other analysts (notably Yankee Group and Gartner). The field has grown rapidly ever since. The *Directory of Industry Analyst Firms*, published by ATA Research (All The Analysts), lists 98 firms (ATA Research, 2008). Techra, which claims to publish 'the Web's most complete analyst firm directory', includes 500 entries from a list of 'well over 700 IT, Telecommunications and high technology analyst firms' (Techra, no date). The ARchitect database contains a list of over 700 industry analyst and related market research firms (shown in Appendix 1).

Gartner Inc. (formerly Gartner Group) is one of a number of IT Advisory firms formed in the late 1970s and 1980s, including: Computer Intelligence, Dataquest, Forrester, Input, International Data Corporation (IDC), Ovum, and Yankee Group (Bernard & Gallupe 2013). Gartner Inc., established in 1979, was by no means the first industry analyst organization but pursued an innovative pathway to become the largest player (Gartner 2010b) and in the process exercised a decisive impact on the field of industry analysts and the IT market more broadly. Table 2.1 also indicates some of the subsequent changes in ownership as the industry has restructured around Gartner and a handful of very large global players.

The category of industry analyst emerged at the interface between various kinds of commercial organizations that provided knowledge of the IT sector. This nexus included market research, investment analysis, technical publishing, and (if we include Saatchi and Saatchi's short-lived ownership of Gartner) even advertising. Though these different players all revolve around knowledge of the IT applications sector, the information needs of investors, vendors and actual/potential adopters differ markedly. As we explore in more detail later,

Table 2.1. The main industry analyst firms

Company name	Year founded	Founders	Subsequently acquired by (date of last acquisition)	Number of clients[iv]	Number of analysts[iv] [iii]
IDC (International Data Corporation)	1964	Patrick McGovern, who also founded several Industry Insights spin-offs		720+	1000+
Yankee Group Research, Inc.[ii]	1970	Howard Anderson	Primark, Reuters PLC, Monitor Clipper Partners (DMG), Alta Communications Inc. 451 Group, (2013)		100
Gartner Inc. (Gartner Group)	1979	Gideon Gartner, Dave L.R. Stein. Gartner later founded GIGA Information Group	IPO; Saatchi & Saatchi; Information Partners	10,500+	1200+
Forrester Research	1983	George Colony, who previously worked at Yankee Group	IPO	1540+	140+
META Group	1989	Marc Butlein & Dale Kutnick who previously worked at Gartner Group & Yankee Group	IPO; Gartner, Inc. (2005)	1400+	100+
Giga Information Group	1995	Gideon Gartner who co-founded Gartner	Forrester Research (2003)	1300	90+
AMR Research[i]	1986	Tony Friscia	Gartner Research (2009)	900+	100+

Adapted from http://tekrati.wikispaces.com/Analyst±Family+Tree (accessed 25 June 2013)
(i) http://en.wikipedia.org/wiki/AMR_Research (accessed 20 January 2015)
(ii) http://en.wikipedia.org/wiki/Yankee_Group (accessed 20 January 2015)
(iii) http://en.wikipedia.org/wiki/International_Data_Corporation
(iv) Ikeler 2007 (data attributed to Brodeur Partners (www.brodeur.com))

this has consequences for the research processes these different kinds of firm pursue and for the ways this data is presented and consumed. For example, classic IT market research addresses the prospects and procurement plans of potential organizational adopters to generate predictions of the rate of market growth for particular types of IT application—which can be sold to vendors (Berghoff et al. 2012). Investment analysis is based on research into particular product markets and the performance of different suppliers therein to advise investors on which vendors to invest in. Technology buyers have markedly different information needs—on the one hand, to establish the potential contribution of generic types of new technology to their needs and, on the other, as they approach procurement, to establish the specific capacities of particular suppliers and their offerings and how well they may fit with their own organizations strategy and practices.

The earliest research and analyst organizations started off conducting market research and other quantitative research for technology vendors. Most of these were also publishers. For example, IDC (formerly International Data Corporation) began in 1964 running a database of computer installations in the US. It also published *The Computer Industry Report* and launched *Computerworld* in 1967. Its claims to be the oldest player (Bernard & Gallupe 2013) might be contested by *Computer Review*, which originated in another publication, *Computer Characteristics Quarterly*, published since 1959 by Adams Associates.[1] This, as we explore in the next section, provided one established model for this kind of knowledge service. In addition, the Yankee Group, founded in 1970, claims to be the first independent technology research and consulting firm: 'We invented technology research' is the strap line on their outputs.[2]

Table 2.1 summarizes the formation and evolution of the main industry analyst firms. As it shows, many industry analyst firms can trace their roots back to IDC, Yankee Group (recently acquired by 451 Research)[3] and Gartner.[4] The close relationships demonstrated here between analyst firms in relation to firm formation and acquisitions also pertain to the development of the careers of individual analysts, as we will see in Chapter 3. The field of industry analysts has grown enormously. The big three analyst firms (Gartner, Forrester and IDC) between them account for 56 per cent of the total $4.47bn estimated industry analyst market (in 2013). With total revenue for 2013 of $1.8bn (Gartner Inc. 2014), Gartner is today by far the largest of the analyst and research organizations (about 6 times the size of its nearest rival Forrester Research). The rapid growth of Gartner Inc. to becoming worldwide leader in the field has been through a combination of organic growth and a sustained programme of acquisition of competitors and firms with complementary capabilities and market base. Through its well-established procedures for selecting and for assimilating new acquisitions it has handled over 32 acquisitions since the company went public in 1993, including most recently IDEAS International (2012), Burton Group, Inc. (2009), AMR Research, Inc. (2009) and META Group (2005).

2.1. THE DISTINCTIVE GARTNER BUSINESS MODEL

The history of Gartner Inc. is better documented than that of its rivals—not least through the efforts of the individuals and organizations involved (Gartner 2010, 2010a,b,c, 2011a,b,c,d,e). Gideon Gartner had a background in the computer industry. He had been working as a Manager of Market Information in IBM's Data Processing Division, where he undertook 'competitor analysis'. After he was recruited to Wall Street by investment analysts E. F. Hutton he gained a reputation by publishing an analysis that successfully predicted Xerox Corporation's sluggish growth and was recruited by Oppenheimer & Co—'one of the big three in Wall Street research' (Gartner 2010). As his work focused less on financial analysis than on reviewing various technical developments, he saw an opportunity to shift away from investor analysis and create a new kind of service i.e., providing advice and information to buyers and sellers of computers, building on his detailed knowledge of products offered by IBM, then the major supplier of both hardware and IT applications, and of its competitors. Gideon Gartner 'convinced Oppenheimer to establish a little business on the side' (interview, Gideon Gartner) involving regular meetings with CIOs of large corporations, discussing how the field was developing. After Oppenheimer turned down his suggestion of setting up a partnership, Gideon Gartner, together with colleague David Stein, set up the firm that dominates the field today.

To understand how Gartner has been able to achieve its position and the radical nature of its offering we first need to understand how it moved beyond what at the time was the established model of industry analysis. To do this, we first examine the UK publisher of technology market reports—Ovum. Ovum exemplifies one distinctive model of industry research and analysis in terms of the way it generates and trades its knowledge. This was the earliest model, characterized by Dennington and Leforestier (2013) as 'number crunchers'. As we shall see, it differed in significant respects to that developed by Gartner.

2.1.1. Industry publishers of market reports—one pre-existing model

Ovum, established in 1985 as a publishing house, offers a relatively traditional model of large-scale market research into technology sectors. An exhaustive research process, involving interviews with large numbers of vendors and adopters, produces an extensive database, which is then used to generate specialist reports. The upfront costs of collecting and processing this information are very high. The reports therefore need to be heavily marketed (and they can be very profitable if sufficient sales can be achieved). David Mitchell Research Director, Ovum Research, told us 'In my firm, IP [Intellectual

Property] is the main product' (interview, Mitchell). Ovum's business model involves economies of scope and scale and generating 'reproducible IP'. Mitchell contrasts this to the consultancy services offered by smaller firms, noting that 'you can never set generic questions in a consultancy project; you are always doing specific ones. So how much can you synergize across lots of different consultant projects when all the questions are very different' (interview, Mitchell). He concludes that 'the biggest firms that have grown most successfully are the ones who recognize that once you have an IP or asset drive[n] model you can then apply sales leverage to it and then grow quite successfully' (interview, Mitchell).

One of the issues confronting research organizations concerns how to scale up. As the organization extends into other countries and technical areas, it is necessary to keep existing knowledge products up-to-date and to enter new fields. The 'up front' costs of labour-intensive knowledge collection threaten to escalate and overwhelm sales income. In Ovum, this has driven important changes over the years to speed up and reduce the costs of the research process, with a more elaborate division of labour between data collection (allocated to lower paid staff) and analysis and with data collection being offshored.

This kind of quantitative research, like conventional market analysis, generates what may be described as 'synoptic research' (Tsoukas 2010). Synoptic research methods, for example based on large-scale quantitative surveys, are good at consistently and reliably summarizing existing patterns and established trends, for example growth in markets and market share. David Mitchell, Research Director, Ovum Research describes how they draw on various information sources to produce the robust and original knowledge that underpins their IP—the product they can sell:

> We'll do some interview work to get figures that are not quoted in the accounting literature . . . You aggregate that. That gives you a relatively strong model but then you need to estimate the statistical area under the curve that you don't know. So you can get the financial information from the big people but there is likely to be a tail of maybe 25, 30, or 40 of the normal distribution of the little companies that you can't figure out. So you estimate the shape of the curve that you don't know and project forward. Then when looking at future demand you do that based on a series of interviews on future technology patterns. So we do approximately 400,000 primary interviews a year on the business, on the business and technology decisions makers, what future spending patterns are. Based on that future signal of demand you put that into current state and statistically forecast the growth. So we do robust models like that (interview, Mitchell).

Though generating 'robust models', these kinds of methods are arguably less effective in identifying the possibility of shifts in existing paradigms and trajectories. Gideon Gartner, in establishing the Gartner Group developed the idea of a different kind of knowledge service—produced by a rather different research process. Speaking publicly about its origins he notes: 'Our idea was to go way beyond market research; to really help people in their decision making, to be much more strategic...to be a decision-support company' (Gartner 2007).

2.1.2. From market research to decision support

The research process that Gideon Gartner proposed was in part inspired by contemporary efforts to apply ideas from decision theory to business practice in investment analysis, marketing and company strategic planning, which suggested the need to go beyond such quantitative methods that, in his view, could simply encourage 'herd behaviour'.[5] He drew on the work of decision theory scholars Montgomery and Weinberg who note: 'The problem is not to generate data, but to determine what information is relevant and actionable' (Montgomery & Weinberg 1979: 44). Gideon Gartner concluded from this work that 'evidence to support research conclusions was often abundantly available, and should be tapped' (Gartner 2011). Drawing explicitly upon Montgomery and Weinberg's concept of Strategic Intelligence Systems, which applies decision theory to the domain of Marketing, Gartner's approach seems designed to foster sensitivity to shifts in sentiment across the analyst's network that could signal possible changes in the technology landscape. In this context, Gartner developed the idea of 'Stalking Horses', as the basis for what a former colleague, Richard Stiennon, described as 'thought experiments that would spark innovative thinking' (Stiennon 2012). Initially this was conceived in terms of discussions with peers; latterly, as we will show, they came to involve interactions with a wide range of clients and contacts.

The goal here was to generate 'original and provocative conclusions' (Gartner 2011a) rather than, for example, to reinforce existing consensus. Thus, Gartner (2011c) exhorted his analysts to 'advocate positions explicitly, improve abilities to sell a specific point of view'. As Elias Thomas, Gartner's VP Research, told us: 'We are deliberately taught to provoke, to push things too far to get people to react. I can think of lots of examples where...provoking vendors and clients is part of the game as far as an analyst is concerned, in order to get to the truth' (interview, Thomas). The key objective seems to be to tap into particular kinds of knowledge shift—emergent understandings and insights, which may be driven by client concerns or by particular successful initiatives—that may change existing taken-for-granted knowledge.

Gartner's research processes were designed and continue to be explicitly geared to generating particular kinds of knowledge. This is not simply about attempting to predict the future. As we will analyse in detail in Chapter 5, Gartner analysts undertake diverse kinds of future oriented assessment.

The Stalking Horse approach seems honed to picking up early signals and in particular, it would appear, to detecting changes in existing trajectories and patterns. Thus Elias Thomas, Gartner's Senior VP for Research, describes how Gartner are 'fast followers not leaders'. In this respect, their pronouncements tend to be fairly conservative:

> We react to success. If it succeeds and other vendors start piling in, we go 'right. Something is going on there' and we go after it. Now we might be tracking a tech for 8 years or 10 years before that or even longer in some cases . . . no analyst has kind of bet their career on one vendor just because they think it is cool even if they think it is genius, doesn't mean that it is commercial. Often what it takes is, you know, a change of management or something at that company, it starts to take off, other vendors pile in, and suddenly you get the trigger, and you get the analysts saying 'we're fast followers not leaders . . . (interview, Thomas).

2.2. GARTNER'S INNOVATIVE RESEARCH PROCESS

In establishing one of the first industry analyst organizations, Gartner set out to create a 'decision-support company'. Its staff are encouraged to demonstrate the value of their knowledge outputs and advisory services in helping its customers (technology adopters, vendors, investors) make practical choices. This goal shapes not only the ways in which they generate knowledge, but also the ways in which this knowledge is presented to the clients. We have seen how, rather than doing conventional (e.g. market) research, that applies large scale quantitative techniques to capture existing trends, Gartner evolved tools and methods honed to detect *changes* in patterns. Rather than producing long technical reports, new formats were developed that could convey findings rapidly, and could form the basis for advisory services. Finally, knowledge outputs have to be relevant. For example, as we will explore in the next chapter, before they are released into the world, outputs must be assessed and must pass a 'so what?' test.

Gartner's (2011) account of the 1980s Gartner 'research process' highlights six major elements: Surveillance, Pattern Recognition, Stalking Horses, Search, Document and Strategic Planning Assumptions. We explore the first three of these. Gartner (2011a) describes them as follows in Table 2.2.

Shepherded by Gartner, a distinctive mode of knowledge production and consumption gradually emerged. This novel mode of research differs from conventional large-scale market research surveys (e.g. as described by Ovum) and management consultancy. It involved what Elias Thomas, Gartner's Senior VP for Research, described to us as 'qualitative type research' established through 'subjective enquiries' (interview, Thomas). This exhibits a

Table 2.2. The major research elements according to Gideon Gartner

Surveillance	'We expected our analysts to be sensitive to all appropriate inputs . . . to read extensively, attend relevant meetings, visit with vendors, and pursue meaningful conversations with clients, peers and supervisors, all with the purpose of optimizing the preconditions for pursuing relevant research and documentation'.
Pattern Recognition	'A talent or skill . . . to identify "patterns," leading to more original and provocative research conclusions than our competition . . . most analysts understood that keeping their eyes open to the broad IT spaces they might recognize certain "patterns" which could lead to original interpretations, and of course to our goal: original conclusions!'.
Stalking Horses	'The idea was to create a graphic or tabular presentation, hopefully including quantification of the idea or concept which would then serve as a basis for further study . . . and inquiry . . . and discussion . . . perhaps finally resulting in an approved consensus view at our research meetings' (Gartner 2011a).

number of mutually reinforcing features that differ from previous models of technical expertise:

i) *A shift away from producing long and detailed technical reports, towards shorter and simpler reporting formats*

As Gartner told us: 'I wanted the notes to be very brief so I designed a one page format which everybody had to adhere to' (interview, Gideon Gartner), (though he also notes that to satisfy his analysts' preference for longer reports he introduced two part research notes comprising his short summary and a longer report). Elsewhere he notes:

Soon after we launched and unlike the relatively long reports our competitors wrote, I designed a standard two-sided format for what we simply called a "research note". It was designed to provide what I considered to be "incremental" information, broken into user-friendly categories, while being sufficiently brief to be completed within 1-2 hours (which would lead to attractive analyst productivity). Of course, we produced medium-size reports as well, but the one-pagers were quite appreciated by our clients. This was a victory on two fronts: analyst productivity, and client satisfaction (Gartner 2010b).

We note here the emergence of new formats (including graphics, notably the Magic Quadrant and lists) whereby information could be rapidly conveyed, and what Gartner describes as 'authoring principles': '. . . timeliness, relevance, meaningful and actionable conclusions, clarity, brevity where possible, and even decent grammar' (Gartner 2010b).

ii) *An emphasis on selling advisory services*

Paradoxically, though Gartner Inc. is famous for its short reports—especially the Magic Quadrant—the report is no longer the final deliverable but becomes an occasion for discussion with the client (as evinced by the aforementioned 'Stalking Horse' concept). Gartner's emerging business model focused less on sales of detailed technical reports, which had previously characterized the field, but upon growth in subscription services based on personalized advice.

iii) *Research and its analysis and dissemination become integrated*

Through these discussions, the analyst develops a network of players—primarily technology users, but also vendors and investors—with whom they engage. The hitherto separate activities of *data collection, analysis* and *dissemination* are undertaken in parallel:

> The interesting bit is that the enquiry is where the customer is asking us a question. In the process of asking that question I have to ask you what are you doing, what have you got, so I have to ask you a whole bunch of questions to get the context. So what it means is that I have got a free interview for the first ten minutes of an half hour conversation and then I am going to answer the question for 20 minutes to be helpful. But in there, there may even be more information that comes out where they go: 'Oh Yeah I forgot to tell you that . . . ' (interview, Thomas).

Queries received from clients and calls out, what Gartner described (2011b) as 'proactively collecting information from sources', become a key part of the knowledge production process.[6] In contrast to traditional sequential conceptions of the research process, involving data collection and analysis followed by dissemination, we find these operating *in tandem*. As Gartner analyst Toby Old stated:

> The whole thing about this Gartner role is that everyone wants to talk to you. The CIOs from the customer side want to talk to you, and the vendors also want to talk to you, and in the end you are kind of really just are in this nexus role where there is information coming together, and you just soak that up, and then you learn from the end customers, and you learn from them, and you are pursuing regular contact with the vendor (interview, Old).

Crucial to their role is the nexus of interactions the Gartner industry analyst maintains with a diverse array of actors. The Gartner analyst has been portrayed as a spider at the heart of a 'dense web'.[7] The diversity of these extensive interactions is one source of trust in the analysts' assessments. Another is their staggering intensity. Gartner analyst Paul Winter points out how:

> Well, you do talk to a lot of clients and you hear about things going well and things not going well. We have an average of 500 clients contacts, you know phone calls or meetings with clients every year. So, that is a good sample on which you can make more reasonable forecasts (interview, Winter)..

As one of Gartner's competitors notes, '[y]ou don't normally get paid by everyone you talk to in research...it is a great, great model' (interview, Governor).

There is also a different mode of knowledge aggregation beyond statistical calculation. Gartner analyst Thomas describes how he learnt that you could establish a picture within 10–15 interviews after which extending the number of interviews to 100 would not change this.

Central to the previous two points was Gartner's strategy of 'hiring senior professionals' who could 'demonstrate deep knowledge and articulateness in specific areas of IT' and who were 'peers of our clients' (Gartner 2010b). In this model, the expertise of the individual analyst is key. As Elias Thomas told us, discussing how he helps Gartner sell its services to clients: he is a 'walking talking product' (interview, Thomas).

The various features of Gartner's distinctive mode of knowledge production and consumption are clearly visible in the activities and organization of industry analysts today. According to Gartner, 'the firm's success was arguably based upon our unusual research methods. Simply put, some combination of processes which would be taken seriously by first our own analysts and subsequently by our client prospects' (Gartner 2011). This is by no means a static model. It was not invented overnight but was worked out over the first decade of Gartner's activities. Crucial elements of Gartner's current operations—and in particular its key current output, the highly influential Magic Quadrant—were not part of his original concept. And as we see next and will explore in detail later in the book, the process whereby Magic Quadrants and other Gartner products are created has changed substantially in the recent period.

2.3. GIDEON GARTNER'S 'TEN INNOVATIONS'

Though, in its early years, 'Gartner was a hodgepodge of ideas' (Gartner 2010b), it gradually established a novel and distinctive model of expertise: the industrial advisory service which is evident in the role of today's industry analyst. Gideon Gartner's blog summarizes his view of the innovations that Gartner Inc. achieved during its formative years in ten areas—see Table 2.3). We have already shown how this involved a distinctive research and dissemination process geared particularly towards assisting potential IT adopter organizations in their procurement decisions. These innovations also involved radical thinking in terms of the business model.

Central to these ideas was consideration of the value that analysts offered for their target clients. Running through Gartner's thinking about the key

Table 2.3. Gartner Inc.'s innovations during its formative years

Clients	'I proposed that our new firm would benefit from selling our services to three quite different constituencies simultaneously! Not only to "vendors" of computer products and services who were then the primary buyers of IT information services, but also to "users" of such products and services, as well as to "investors"'.
Hiring	'Unlike our competition we would hire senior rather than junior professionals, who were peers of our clients who could demonstrate deep knowledge and articulateness in specific areas of IT, and who would have to survive a rather lengthy and difficult group interview!'
Reports	'Soon after we launched and unlike the relatively long reports our competitors wrote, I designed a standard two-sided format for what we simply called a "research note"'.
Content	'Our content standard was meant to provide incremental decision-support rather than rehashed information. Many advisories preached this, but ours was documented in detail. This apparently unique "Research Process" was detailed, taught in analyst courses and preached by research management at all of our weekly meetings which involved all analysts and quite a few salespeople as well!'
Conferences	'When we had more than several different services (we began with only one) I designed a replacement for our initial conference format, which presented 5-year "scenarios" of each service sector. It listed the sector's macro trends followed by key issues to be faced and of course our projections'.
Sales	'We gambled on both quantity and quality of sales and marketing personnel. Most of our competitors had begun their business with relatively little capital, while we (by chance or intent) raised sufficient funds . . . to build a very substantial end-user sales organization'.
Culture	'The name we picked for one aspect of our research process was called the "Stalking Horse" . . . The name Stalking Horse later catalyzed my idea that we should have a mascot, obviously the horse!'
Business Measurements	'While all our competition measured its financial progress by measuring revenue, we changed the game from our early beginnings, focusing internally on both the "annualized" dollar value of our installed base at a given point in time, and more importantly on the growth of this dollar value during periods of time (monthly, quarterly, and yearly)'.
NCVI	'Our net growth was called NCVI (Net Contract Value Increase) and affected both 100% of sales commissions, and some much lower percent of the bonus awards. It was measured explicitly for every individual territory, region, sales team, research service, and industry. Of course our total NCVI was also used for bonus calculations, from senior executive functions down to the mail room. All sales commissions and company-wide bonuses were based almost entirely on appropriate growth increments, not on revenues for the period'.
Shareholders	'I must add that virtually all early Gartner employees were shareholders, all the way down through administration. We had a tough option program: 5 years linear vesting (four years vesting was and is typical) and when employees left the business for any reason, we could buy back all their vested stock at "Fair Market Value" (FMV)'.

innovations that underpinned Gartner Inc., and the management systems that he set up, is intense and sustained attention to the value proposition and business model. As Gideon Gartner told us:

> I just sat down with a blank sheet and I said how can I come up with a deliverable model and a cost model etcetera that is totally different than anything that is being done today and would be of more greater value. And I came up with a whole bunch of ideas and that became the basis for Gartner. And then during the first year I refined the model and developed it much further. And by the second year we were really rolling (interview, Gideon Gartner).

Rather than selling detailed technical reports or market surveys (like its established competitors) Gartner's emerging business model was focused upon growing its subscription services based on personalized advice. Gartner was keen to find ways to demonstrate the value these services would bring to their clients. Ensuring that customers would maintain their subscriptions was an immediate priority for Gartner analysts and their managers, requiring them to respond to queries and provide 'good advice that saves them money or reduce[s] their risk' (interview, Thomas). As well as access to large numbers of reports, the emphasis was upon personalized advice looking at the specific needs of clients: responding to queries from clients and also making calls out to clients, as well as access to conferences/teleconferences and to knowledge networks and contacts.

In the 'ten innovations' summarized above in Table 2.3, the sustained focus on client value that would drive growth and renewal of subscription services is backed up by detailed *Business Measurement*. Gartner's monitoring systems did not just measure revenue growth, the standard indicator in many organizations, but also growth in successive periods in contract value across the different parts of the business. *Net Contract Value Increase* was used for both bonus calculations and commissions and provided a very direct incentive for the performance of analysts, managers and sales staff. This was an approach that Gartner had observed first hand within IBM in its business leasing access to mainframe computing. As he states (Gartner 2011b):

> After all, this was essentially a rental business, and our obvious goal was to create client satisfaction so that clients would not cancel, and we took the position that while research shortfalls or the economy could cause dissatisfaction or cancellations for any reason it was the salesperson's duty to be on top of every shaky situation even if a combination of new sign-ups, positive renewals, but also cancellations, would result in small, flat or even negative "contract value" which would result in no commission at all![8]

A recurrent concern in Gartner's account is to increase research productivity, given the potentially high and escalating upfront costs of research. He describes the '80:20 Rule' that he articulated in the early days of Gartner Inc., proposing that analysts should reduce the proportion of their time spent collecting information in order to double (from 10 per cent to 20 per cent) the amount of time they spend on 'producing written output and initiating out-calls to our best clients' (Gartner 2011b). Gideon Gartner (2011b) explains the thinking behind this rule thus:

> Assume that average analysts spend 70% of their working time collecting infor-mation (reading the trade press, going to meetings, attending IT shows, travelling, attending GG conferences, and so forth), and 20% of their time on processing what they learned, in their heads... before spending the last 10% of their time devoted to producing written output and initiating out-calls to our best clients (as analysts on Wall Street did). To me, these numbers seemed to be reasonable approximations of reality. Next, assume that through stronger discipline (woops, a dirty word), the overhead could be reduced from 70% to 50%, and that the savings would be distributed equally between research and output. Result? The amount of original research (thinking, writing drafts, working through spread-sheets, proactively collecting information from sources...) would increase by a full 50%, and the visible output would improve by a full 100%!

The continued focus within Gartner Inc. on maximizing value generation is perhaps one key reason why it has outperformed its competitors. Noble (2013) notes that Gartner invests very heavily in marketing its services; analysts only account for 25 per cent of the total staff (significantly lower than its compe-titors; and revenue generated per analyst within Gartner, at more than $1.1m per analyst, is around 70 per cent higher than its nearest rival Forrester (see Figure 2.1).

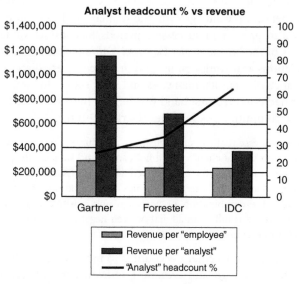

Figure 2.1. Revenue per analyst (of top analyst firms)
Source: Dave Noble Intelligen Analyst Relations[9]

2.4. HETEROGENEITY OF INDUSTRY ANALYSTS
AND THE HYBRID MARKETS THEY SERVE

Though Gartner Inc. took the lead in defining a distinctive approach—and there has been some convergence around this model,[10] the community of industry analysts continues to be differentiated. Various research and analyst firms exhibit more or less differing business models and different ways of creating and disseminating knowledge. Partly this reflects their different origins and the methods and expertise they bring with them. However, we must also note the continued differentiation of research organizations in terms of who they sell their advice to, their business models, their ways of producing knowledge and communicating it to their clients etc. As a former Ovum analyst told us:

> there are very different commercial models that one can operate. Crassly speaking one model is purely to provide advice purely to the vendors. And that advice is, well, based on the perception the analyst or the advisor understands something about the demand side . . . There is another model which is almost the polar opposite of that, which is we understand the vendor community, we understand everything they are doing and we advise buyers and we absolutely avoid doing any work with vendors because that will taint us and compromise our independence. And then there are hybrid models (interview, Ward Dutton).

These organizations are differentiated not only in terms of their target clients but also of the *value proposition* they offer to particular customer targets. Analysts gear their offerings to the information and advisory needs of particular types of organization, and may even target particular kinds of actor within these organizations. Creating knowledge services geared towards particular client needs is in turn associated with the development of particular models with regard to how they conduct both research and knowledge transfer.[11] For example, it shapes the internal organization of knowledge production as well as relationships with external players in terms of how knowledge is acquired as well as with how it is validated and valorized.

Though Gartner had identified the unmet information needs of organizational IT users, he had inherited from Oppenheimer a hybrid clientele that included investors (Gartner 2011d). He decided that he would continue 'to sell to three constituencies at once' (interview, Gideon Gartner). He saw beneficial links between these 'multiple constituencies: Wall Street clients (i.e. investors), technology vendors, and corporate users of technology, each with different (but overlapping) advice requirements' (Gartner 2011). As one Gartner analyst later put it: 'We are in the middle':

> We talk to users 80% of our time, 20% our vendors, and, we are in the middle, the users come to us because we know what is coming, the vendors come to us because well we know what the users want and what they are likely to want for the future (interview, Winter).

Gartner, however, presents its core business as being 'decision-support' for the IT user organization.[12] Though Gartner operates in 5 or 6 different markets, its core market was described to us by Elias Thomas Gartner Senior VP Research as qualitative advisory services. 'That is where we are king of the hill by a long way, where we have 75 plus, between 75 and 80% market share' (interview, Thomas).

Though, from the outset, Gartner has offered commercial services to vendors and investors as well as technology adopters, in their work they stress their independence from vendors (as we will see shortly). Amongst Gartner and other industry analysts, there is an informal convention that the term *client* refers to organizations adopting/using technology. Though industry analysts only make available a limited amount of information about their sources of income, most receive funds from vendors—though the balance of income between these varies and some organizations put a cap on this income (Bernard & Gallupe 2013). As the Wikipedia entry on industry analysts somewhat gnomically observes: 'This matrix of relationships presents opportunities where conflicts can arise—particularly over vendor funding... [which] may impair the independence/objectivity of analyst advice'.[13] As we see in the next chapter, the question of independence becomes a key feature in the organization of industry analyst work in terms of how knowledge is produced and assessed.

2.5. TEMPORAL DYNAMICS OF INDUSTRY ANALYST EXPERTISE

The key idea behind Gideon Gartner's vision of advisory services revolved around providing information that can support technology adoption decisions by organization managers. A key theme of this book is to investigate how these early ideas about decision support have been translated into actual contemporary knowledge products that can be useful for IT managers. These user organization managers are confronted by a 'sea of innovation opportunities' being promoted from a multiplicity of vendors and consultants. The number and range of proposals for business improvement continues to grow with the escalating supply of new technologies being proposed as solutions for ever-changing organizational prescriptions. Organization managers (and others, e.g. investors and product development managers within vendors) face acute difficulties in assessing the current strengths and future prospects of these solutions. However, they find themselves under pressure to make choices—to achieve best practice or secure competitive advantage—at a stage where the performance and prospects of these solutions remain relatively unproven. How can organization managers navigate this constantly changing sea of opportunities with its multiple tides and currents? How can they avoid wasting resources on unsuccessful procurements or avoid regret at failure to exploit upcoming opportunities? How can they provide evidence to inform and legitimate particular choices? The knowledge outputs of industry analyst provide important supports to these managers.

The final feature we will examine at this stage concerns the distinctive temporal dynamics of industry analyst expertise. Industry analysts would seem to face the same challenge (as do other groups like management consultants) in deploying knowledge about developments that are constantly changing. Studies of management consultant expertise, reviewed in detail in Chapter 4, suggest that their knowledge base is too perishable (Muzio el al. 2011, Fincham 2006) to be 'organizable as common resources' (Abbott 1988: 324) as might be done by a traditional professional community with slower knowledge cycles. This constraint would seem to apply no less to industry analysts. Indeed the continuing dynamism of the knowledge and the domains of activity it pertains to are central to understanding industry analyst work.

2.5.1. Gartner Hype-Cycle

To address these challenges, Gartner introduced in 1995 another instrument: the Hype-Cycle (see Figure 2.2). This simplified 'signature graphic' offers a graphic representation of the dynamics of emerging technology fields. It shows characteristic changes over time in expectations about a promising technology (Fenn & Raskino 2008). The pattern that Gartner analysts and others had encountered across a range of promising technologies, evolved through a number of phases (Feen 2007, Bresciani & Eppler 2008). The cycle starts with a 'technology trigger' that attracts attention to a new innovation, in turn mobilizing 'hyped' unrealistic expectations, which when not supported by initial experience drop off, prompting a shift from a 'peak of inflated expectations' to the 'trough of disillusionment'. Subsequent successful experiences provoke more positive perceptions, which gradually improve with experience (the 'slope of enlightenment'), which eventually levels off as the benefits become widely demonstrated and accepted ('plateau of productivity'). Gartner notes that hype-cycles for particular technologies may evolve quickly or slowly (Bresciani & Eppler 2008). They are intended to help managers take decisions, for example about whether to take the risk and win the benefits of early adoption of a promising technology or to wait until its prospects are more clearly established.

The Hype-Cycle has been criticized by Science and Technology Studies (STS) scholars for producing unduly generic accounts, that ignore variation between cases, and that unhelpfully convey a simplistic 'linear' view of the unidirectional

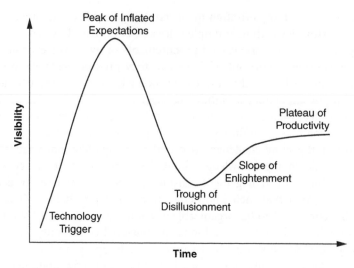

Figure 2.2. The Gartner Hype-Cycle
Source: Author depiction

trajectory of technological development, overlooking the ways that technology pathways often diverge from anticipated routes in the course of their development and uptake (Borup et al. 2006: 285). Alternative versions of the Hype-Cycle have been proposed that address the eventual collapse of expectations as a technology becomes obsolete and recognize that some technologies may be abandoned before the enlightenment phase (Bresciani & Eppler 2008).

Others have drawn attention to these cyclical processes in business innovations as new proposals emerge, and attract attention and investment before becoming superseded. Theories of the emergence of dominant designs (Abernathy & Utterback 1978), based on analysis of the maturing of industrial sectors such as automobiles, aerospace and electrical goods, have been extended to characterize the shorter life cycles of particular products. An initial fluid product phase of product innovation, involving experimental development of a wide range of designs, is followed by convergence of designs and the emergence of a dominant design. Initial product diversity is reduced as less successful products fail and suppliers withdraw from the field, which 'matures' around a smaller set of offerings broadly converging around the dominant design.

Institutionalist writers within Organization Studies have similarly drawn attention to the circulation and uptake of particular 'Management Fashions' (Abrahamson & Fairchild 1999).[14] Discussion of 'fashions' and 'bandwagon' effects has criticized rational choice models of management. Institutional theorists have drawn attention to the role of particular visions in reducing uncertainty for technology developers and adopters regarding which of the vast array of potential organizational and technological innovations they should pursue. Thus Swanson and Ramiller (1997: 460) highlight the importance of what they describe as *organizing visions*, defined as 'a focal community idea for the application of information technology in organizations' in three ways: producing an understanding of an innovation, in legitimating it and in mobilizing the resources needed to realize it. A later paper suggests that these organizing visions have a particular *career* (Ramiller & Swanson 2003): they struggle to gain ascendance and eventually are displaced. We find much of interest in this analysis, and the detailed empirical research it inspires. The work is perhaps held back by the analytical framework, which focuses upon the circulation of managerial discourses within a community.[15] Such a simple community communication model leaves underspecified the complex topology of IT product markets (a point we return to in Chapter 10). Here theory yet again lags behind industrial practice and was late to draw attention to the emergence of new kinds of players like industry analysts who exercise increasing influence within such 'communities'.

Our analysis in contrast seeks to address in detail the processes through which these communities are formed and to chart their detailed and changing structures. We go beyond the undifferentiated notion of communities to examine their particular topologies and we observe the emergence of third parties such as industry analysts that work to constitute arenas within the extended agora of technological and organizational change (Kaniadakis 2012). In a previous analysis of enterprise systems we characterized these arenas as 'technology fields' (Pollock & Williams 2009).[16] Though this terminology was adequate for a rather long-lived and stable domain with relatively clear boundaries, in other contexts these arenas are more ephemeral. Moreover, even well-established 'fields' are subject to continued reconfiguration and boundary changes as the technology and its users evolve (Meyer et al. 2005).

As fashions become established, they point towards areas of innovation that can be exploited. But eventually these areas of technology opportunity become exhausted (Rip et al. 2000). These technological and organizational visions are thus 'relatively transitory collective beliefs' (Abrahamson & Fairchild 1999: 709). They help constitute temporary social spaces: the diverse communities of players bound up with a particular vision. Suddaby and Greenwood (2001) suggest that competition intensifies the cycle of generation and exhaustion of new business ideas.[17]

This cyclical model, illustrated by the Gartner Hype-Cycle, which provides a way to unpick the community dynamics of innovation, also provides pointers to the multiple different kinds of future-oriented knowledge work that Gartner is undertaking. We provide a brief sketch here (and will also explore them in more detail in Chapter 5). Our research highlights how Gartner analysts see an opportunity to gain leverage for their knowledge—its robustness and relevance to their clients—by their various kinds of knowledge intervention. This starts when Gartner seeks to identify emerging arenas where its interventions, for example giving 'a name' to a product market, help catalyse their formation. Nevertheless, as a field matures, a small number of 'tried-and-tested' solutions may become established in the market. The uncertainties surrounding promising innovations, and the information asymmetries that they generate, will become weakened, as does the value of Gartner's expertise. This means that Gartner has a limited period in which its knowledge can be deployed to 'make a difference' for its clients. Gartner needs to stay ahead of the game, to identify areas where something is moving. Though it may be a major player, it faces a continual battle to retain 'cognitive authority'.

Naming interventions and other kinds of knowledge practices that seek to hold sway across a community seem to have particular import here. Elias Thomas, reflecting on many years of experience as a Gartner analyst observed:

> I think what we are doing is that we are looking for the naming of the market as it coalesces to a point where it makes sense, where we can mentally put bounds around it and say that's what it does, and then it moves on. Once you are down, once you are down to the ERP [where most big companies have got a choice of 3 or 4 to play with] is not that interesting, it is just about hanging on (interview, Thomas).

We can distinguish two general types of promissory work here i) *framing*—identifying significant promising opportunities for business advancement; and, ii) *discrimination*—helping would-be adopters to discriminate between offerings within a particular frame.

2.5.2. Framing the arena

The initial challenge in innovation is to understand the changing innovation landscape and identify the most promising opportunities amongst the flow of proposals for organizational improvement. Here Gartner analysts produce various long-term assessments such as 'Scenarios', which are five-year forecasts for market dynamics, winners and challengers and technology breakthroughs (Eppler 2006). We have already examined Gideon Gartner's Stalking Horse concept as one of a number of techniques crafted to identify whether there is a shift in thinking. Starting with 'a scenario and a hypothesis of where a market may be going' (Eppler 2006: 258) analysts probe their collaborative networks. We discuss in Chapter 5 how at this stage analysts have a certain level of autonomy in circulating thought-provoking positions (what we describe as 'visions let loose'). These provocations probe the world of business innovation, to detect whether there is a response across its networks (like a spider twanging its web, to use the analogy cited earlier).[18] Where these explorations yield a response they become the basis for Gartner to produce more targeted interventions—and in particular naming interventions.

Analysts run risks of incorrectly identifying trends i.e. of proposing a terminology and technology concept that is not taken up or that moves in different directions (as we will see in the case of Customer Relations Management [CRM] or what Gartner initially identified as Technology Enabled Relationship Management [TERM]). It may appear safer to wait until patterns are clearer, but this runs the risk of allowing others (vendors, competitor analyst firms, academics) to take the initiative. Through this proactive role, and in particular, naming interventions, Gartner analysts seek to maintain cognitive authority. This is the perception that 'we are always ahead of you, we are always more on the button about what is going on in our area' (interview, Thomas).

Naming interventions help constitute an arena in a number of ways. By focusing attention on a promising area, they help mobilize the resources needed to develop and exploit the innovation. In the early stages of a new area this kind of intervention may encourage swarming of offerings with multiple suppliers entering a field with diverse offerings, of uncertain utility and rather limited implementation experience (Williams 1997).

2.5.3. Discrimination

However, these arenas also create a space where another kind of promissory work can be undertaken—and particularly by those who have established cognitive authority over the field. Gartner analysts are also involved in helping define and develop shared understanding about a novel innovation ('sensemaking'). This involves placing boundaries around a field and naming it and bringing a new product market into existence. And as time goes on, solutions are further developed, more evidence is available about their effectiveness and, in particular, as implementation experience grows, successful solutions emerge. Here Gartner exploits its intensive links with enterprise technology buyers. Eventually Gartner analysts will produce 'lists' of suppliers in particular fields and ultimately Magic Quadrants that enable enterprise technology buyers to select between the main providers of that class of solutions. Though its origins remain obscure, the Magic Quadrant rapidly became a central element in Gartner's advisory services. As we will show, this is not a straightforward but a 'dividing knowledge' in that Magic Quadrants sharply split opinion about their effectiveness and accuracy, not to mention bias. Thus, Gartner are regularly required to robustly defend this knowledge (as described in later chapters). Latterly Gartner have started to produce another output, called the Gartner MarketScope, designed to offer advice about emerging product areas where a successful model had not yet been established, and where it is therefore not yet possible to draw a Magic Quadrant. As Gartner's website explains:

Understanding Emerging Markets: When markets are growing and IT solutions are stable, Magic Quadrants provide the best tool for understanding how the players are competitively positioned. But when new markets emerge and user requirements are in flux, solutions are often approached in wildly different ways, making a competitive positioning less useful. This is where the MarketScopes can provide critical insight.[19]

Later on, as an emerging application field begins to take shape, Gartner is in a position to develop tools to discriminate between different supplier offerings in a field. Here Gartner has achieved considerable leverage over the market through its Magic Quadrant (and competitors like the broadly comparable counterparts produced by Forrester). We will examine the circumstances in which the Magic Quadrant is seen to be most effective in terms of providing information that can assist clients in their procurement decisions. We will explore just when the Magic Quadrant is useful in terms of the number of offerings and ability to differentiate between them. In the early stages, when large numbers of suppliers may have been attracted to a promising application field, there may be too many players to make effective comparisons or to draw a useful Magic Quadrant. Much later, when a field is mature with some products prevailing whilst weaker offerings fail, and where applications are well characterized, procurement becomes less uncertain and there may be little need for a Magic Quadrant. Between these two points, the Magic Quadrant becomes what our informants described as the 'beautiful picture' (Chapter 9). When it is in this form it directly influences procurement choices and indirectly shapes expectations about technology vendors and their offerings.

2.6. FURTHER EVOLUTION OF THE INDUSTRY ANALYSIS MODEL

Over time, Gartner has elaborated a range of knowledge outputs that allow it to bear upon various moments in the evolution of a technology. Some of these can be seen to rest on the back of well-established software lifecycle and maturity models that describe how initial diversity in the early experimental/emergent stage of a product is followed by shakeout in the market as dominant models become established (Agarwal & Tripsas 2008). Thus the 'IT Market Clock', that Gartner Inc. announced in 2010, charts the progression from birth to standardization to industrialization and obsolescence. In this, it reproduces in only slightly modified form elements of Ward's (1987) software lifecycle model. Whilst the Gartner Hype-Cycle and Market Clock explicitly track the maturation of product lifecycles, other outputs are geared towards particular moments. The latest Gartner initiative has been 'Cool Vendor' awards geared not to established vendors but to up-and-coming suppliers who 'challenge long-held assumptions and . . . [transform] the way businesses operate and consumers engage with technology' (Gartner Inc. 2013). The recent proliferation of Gartner outputs includes Market Guides, Vendor Ratings, IT Scores, Market Share analysis and Market Forecasts (Gartner Inc. 2015). As Elias Thomas Gartner VP Research told us 'we have common sets of published documents where we can hold two or three hundred documents on a particular topic' (interview, Thomas). Gartner Inc. has even published a guide to their products and how they may be used, and its large conferences begin with a session entitled 'how to get Gartner' (Gartner Inc. 2015).

So we see that there is continued experimentation in the sector—with tools launched and less successful ones retired—though it may not be straightforward to modify or retire established knowledge products. Gartner encountered this in relation to its Magic Quadrant. The Magic Quadrant has been its most salient product. It is onerous and expensive to produce but it has proved its most effective tool to date.

Gartner has expanded its range of knowledge outputs and interventions to the point that it is today able to offer research and advice right across the information technology domain with products that engage with multiple moments in the innovation process. It would seem that Gartner finds it advantageous to make its 'mark' (see Chapter 7) in the information space (to leave a large footprint in what we have called the agora of technical and organization change) in its efforts to sustain and grow subscription income and exercise cognitive authority over whole technical fields and cycles.

In this introductory chapter, we have presented a brief overview of this new model of industry analysis expertise. However, this account leaves unanswered the specific ways in which this knowledge was generated and how it is validated (and we observe the exigencies arising from the need to produce defensible knowledge). We turn to this in the next chapter, where we start to draw on our detailed qualitative interviews of the strategy and practices of Gartner and other industry analyst organizations. This is to explore the methods and practices through which analyst knowledge is created. We then consider how analysts themselves come to be expert—their prior training and experience (how they are selected and how they develop their expertise and reputation).

NOTES

1. http://www.computerreview.com/design/aboutus.html. Accessed 11 September 2014.
2. http://www.yankeegroup.com/ENG_apple.do. Accessed 11 September 2014.
3. In January 2013, The Yankee Group was taken over by 451 Research. http://www.yankeegroup.com/about_us/. Accessed 11 September 2014.

4. http://en.wikipedia.org/wiki/Industry_analyst. Accessed 11 September 2014.

5. Gartner (Gartner 2011) traces his model back to two publications that he read during Gartner Group's first year (1979/80): The Tao Jones Averages: A Guide to Whole-Brained Investing by Bennet Goodspeed (1979) and David B. Montgomery and Charles B. Weinberg's 'Toward Strategic Intelligence Systems' (*Journal of Marketing* 43, Fall 1979). Goodspeed was an Investment Research consultant who co-founded the 'think tank' Inferential Focus. He complained about the lack of creativity in investment advice, reflected in 'herd' behaviour by investors, reinforced by the resort to quantitative methods, without reviewing the bigger picture. His concept of 'whole brained investing' proposes that effective investment requires both left-brained analysis, and right-brained creativity.

6. It may be unhelpful to overstate the differences between Gartner's research process and other firms. For example, David Mitchell, Research Director of Ovum Research, observes that Giga, 'one of the firms that got bought by Forrester . . . used to produce about 60% of their research volume through what they call CQA method. It was Catalyst, Query, Answer...60% of the volume of their research was driven directly by customer enquiry, and you aggregate and anonymize that' (interview, Mitchell).

7. 'German views: the analyst spider's dense web'. Post on Influence Relations, 21 October 2014 (edited by Duncan Chapple). This includes a translated excerpt from a German paper by Marco Pister. Pister states: 'The role of an analyst can be pictured as that of a spider in the centre of a dense web'. http://www.influencerrelations.com/3263/german-views-the-analyst-spiders-dense-web?utm_source=twitterfeed&utm_medium=twitter. Accessed 21 October 2014.

8. http://gideongartner.com/2010/04/gartner-innovation-during-its-formative-years/

9. We are grateful to Dave Noble of Intelligen Analyst Relations for giving us permission to use this figure here.

10. For example, though Ovum's core business is its technical reports, David Mitchell, Ovum's Research Director, pointed out: 'We then offer a customer enquiry service on top of that. So if someone becomes a subscriber they get an unlimited volume of enquiries into any of the analysts in the team. So if your enquiry is about where did you get that number from, what is that about, what do you think about 'x', you just pick up the phone to the analyst team and build the relationship directly. That is unmetred and unlimited in the contract, so as to just build that interaction. And then we do more consulting type work on top of there' (interview Mitchell).

11. For example, Noble (2013) reports that of the major industry analyst firms, Gartner has the lowest ratio of analysts as a percentage of total employees, at just over 25% compared to 63% for IDC, 35% for Forrester and 55% for Ovum, noting that 'these firms have quite different business models, research services, analyst types and client bases, so it is not unusual that the ratios should vary, but it is interesting how starkly different they are'.

12. This choice of a hybrid market puts Gartner analysts in a position of tension—e.g. between meeting user needs versus meeting vendor needs. Had Gartner adopted a user-only market their independence might have been easier to establish—but they deliberately decided against this. This puts it into an 'edgy' space. We return to this point below.

13. http://en.wikipedia.org/wiki/Industry_analyst. Accessed 20 March 2014.
14. Management fashions (Abrahamson & Fairchild 1999: 709) are defined as: 'relatively transitory collective beliefs disseminated by the discourse of management-knowledge entrepreneurs, that a management technique is at the forefront of rational management practice'.
15. Thus Ramiller and Swanson (2003) highlight in particular the differential (critical) reception of particular visions according to their perceived interpretability, plausibility, importance, and (dis)continuity from existing practice/models.
16. Abbott (1995) highlights the difficulties faced by institutional accounts in explaining how particular categories of actors and artefacts—technology fields—are constituted. Jørgensen and Sørensen (1999) use the concept of arena, defined as a line drawn in the sand, to discuss how fields may come into being.
17. As Suddaby and Greenwood (2001: 945) note: 'Commodification leads to hyper-competition'. Abbott (1988) illustrates this sequence with reference to the inability of computer programmers to effectively establish control over their knowledge product because of rapid commodification. Within the first three decades of programming capability, 'there have been four or five generations of experts in programming, each one rapidly outmoded by software that made its knowledge a commodity' (ibid: 241). Commodification of the capacity to programme intensified competition so much that the cycle-to-market for new programming techniques was reduced from cycles measured in years to cycles measured in weeks. There is considerable evidence that the pace of commodification is 'quickening' (i.e. the contact between players is more frequent) and is becoming more significant (i.e. more 'fatal'). The time lag between dominant ideas in management consulting is diminishing. Consultants speak of the need to 'get new consulting strategies to the market quickly', a practice which is viewed as a primary driver of the overall frenzied growth of the management consulting industry (Kennedy Research Group, 1997).
18. Swanson (2012) draws an interesting analogy of observing a 'ripple' amongst the innovation community. But this just reinforces our point about the flat ontology— a pool—of his presumed community.
19. http://www.gartner.com/technology/research/methodologies/research_markets.jsp. Accessed 23 October 2014.

3

The Organization of Analyst Work

In the previous chapter, we explored how the distinctive model of industry analyst expertise began to emerge. In this chapter, we draw on interviews with industry analysts to understand how this complex and intricate knowledge work is actually performed. We explore this work at four different levels: the form of knowledge that industry analysts deploy, the methods by which this knowledge is generated and validated, the process by which these experts are formed (i.e., their recruitment, induction and career evolution), and finally the day-to-day management of this expert labour.

3.1. FORMS OF KNOWLEDGE THAT ANALYSTS DEPLOY

3.1.1. From 'bottom-line advice' to 'what you are going to do about it'

Gartner as a 'decision-support company' must produce user-oriented knowledge that is practical and defensible. This form of knowledge creation is linked to Gideon Gartner's concern to *add value* to their customers and his view that Gartner should be a decision-support company rather than a market research organization (Gartner 2007). What is at stake is the ability of analysts to generate *practical knowledge* to inform the particular the choices facing their primary 'clients', namely organization managers considering adopting new technologies (see Figure 3.1).

We saw in the preceding chapter how Gideon Gartner moved away from the quantitative research methods that captured established trends in order to focus on possible shifts in opinion and emerging concerns (as evinced by the notion of The 'Stalking Horse'). This was one of the ways he sought to inculcate in his analysts an ability to propose 'original and provocative conclusions' (Gartner 2011a) rather than reinforce existing consensus. This is at the heart of what has come to be known in recent years within Gartner as 'The

"Gartner Group provides the distilled, bottom-line advice that top ● executives need to make decisions."

--Portia Isaacson Wright, Ph.D.,
Publisher and Editor, *Future Thinker* 1.2

A recent article from Associated Press says: "Gartner Group is one of the top computer-industry think-tanks in the country...clients pay up to several hundred thousand dollars a year to attend annual conferences, pick analysts's brains, and peruse the company's analytical bulletins."

Introducing Gartner Group's Catalog of Research Reports.

Our new FREE catalog describes Research Reports that present and summarize analysis of a wide range of high-tech subjects: Communications networks. Software. Office systems. Computers. DEC. IBM. And more.

Executives at over 900 companies worldwide rely on Gartner Group. Our analysts provide these clients with specialized research information, data, and in-depth analyses to help them make decisions that support and protect investments in information technology products and services.

Now, Gartner Group's series of Research Reports can also assist you in making these decisions.

Here's just a sampling of what you'll find in Gartner Group's Research Reports:

• Financial strategies to optimize the acquisition and disposition of equipment.

• New advances in computer-aided software engineering.

• The evolution of ISDN.

• Latest developments in T1 and T3 wide area network technology.

• Anticipated product strategies of IBM & ● DEC.

• IBM's high-end strategy for operating systems.

• Local Area Networking strategies in the 1990s.

Take the first step. There's no obligation.

For a free copy of the Catalog of Research Reports, call Jill Whitney at (203) 967-6855. Or write: Gartner Group, Inc., 56 Top Gallant Rd., Dept. FT, Stamford, CT 06902.

Please send me a free copy of the Catalog of Research Reports.

Name _____ Title _____

Company _____ Phone _____

Address _____ ●

City _____ State _____ Zip _____

Mail to: Gartner Group, 56 Top Gallant Rd., Dept. FT, Stamford, CT 06902. Fax to: (203) 967-6886

Figure 3.1. A 1989 Gartner advert describes the new service of 'decision support'
Source: *Future Thinker* Vol 2 No 9 (17 November 1989)[1]

Google Test' in deciding what knowledge products they create. Gartner analyst Paul Winter describes the criteria that surround the production of a Gartner report: 'We write what is called a Research Note. It has to pass the so-called 'Google test'. The Google test is, if the client can get it from Google, there is no point writing it. You have to write it some way that goes well beyond what Google says' (interview, Winter).

As well as not restating knowledge that may already be widely accepted, there is no point in producing work that might, in popular parlance, be described as only of 'academic relevance'. Thus as Elias Thomas, Gartner Senior VP for Research, points out 'The worst criticism you can make is "so what?"': 'The key thing Gartner does well, as a structure of how we present our research is that we are very driven by what we used to say was the bottom line. We now say "what you [the client] need to know". But it is like what you [the clients are] going to do about it'. (interview, Thomas).

Gartner's outputs are focussed on knowledge that makes a difference to its customers, and presented in such a way that customers can readily interpret and act upon it. This was accompanied by a shift away from the detailed market reports that had previously prevailed towards short reports and novel formats such as the Magic Quadrant. Analysts themselves must possess a much broader knowledge base than what is presented, including a level of detailed information that may not be directly relevant to its clients. The simplified reports were used as a starting point only for direct discussions with clients.

3.1.2. 'Pod of knowledge'

Gartner's services revolve around employing highly expert staff. To carry out their work, as Elias Thomas, Gartner VP Research told us, 'each analyst has to maintain their own pod of knowledge' (interview, Thomas). Therefore, every analyst will develop specialist knowledge and contacts around a particular technology field or theme. Gartner analyst Toby Old states: 'some guys cover financial applications, some deal with and cover CRM, and you know a couple of people covering CRM, to some other people covering HR, you know, databases, middleware, portals etc' (interview, Old). In this way Gartner analysts develop what Paul Winter described as 'the T-model of expertise' coupling a 'general knowledge of everything' with deep knowledge of their specialized area: 'You actually don't choose your area because the company wants basically a "T" from you. It wants a general knowledge of everything; and then a very, very deep knowledge on a specific thing' (interview, Winter).

This knowledge pod needs to be continually renewed. As Elias Thomas explained they must know more and keep knowing more than other people in constantly changing specialist areas: 'Our value is not that we know more than other people, it is that we keep knowing more in that area for ever and ever and ever . . .' (interview, Thomas). And whilst focusing on their core areas they also need to remain alert to other developments in related fields. Thomas drew our attention to the potentially difficult trade-offs faced:

> The more focused you are the better you are at your job in my view. But then you
> have got the trade-off that if there is a new area over here that is emerging you

have got to be willing to move into that if that is where the heat is and that is where the questions are coming. You just have to keep your ear to the ground about which direction should I be spending more of my time. So it is kind of like setting up a camp, trying to draw a boundary around it and slowly moving it all the time, trying to make sure you are capturing what is hot. And even [though] our company is huge and we cover most areas if you sat down with the analyst and said got any holes in your research, any gaps? Every analyst will say that yeah we are not getting enough of that, we need more of this. So there are huge holes all over the place in terms of what we are doing. So we are all, you are trying to trade off keeping it focused enough so you have got enough depth, and you are confident about what your knowledge is versus not missing something (interview, Thomas).

The crucial way in which analysts are able to renew their knowledge is through the networks they maintain, in the course of their advisory work, with a wide range of actors. A key part of the work of analysts is the frequent meetings and telephone calls with technology buyers, vendors and other specialists. It is through these interactions, which in frequency and intensity far exceed what, for example, an academic social scientist could maintain with their research subjects, that the analyst's knowledge base is renewed: 'We just talked to 20 people exactly like them every day...' (interview, Thomas).

3.2. METHODS FOR GENERATING AND VALIDATING KNOWLEDGE

So far we have only considered individual capacity development, but it is clear that analyst knowledge is developed through knowledge networks. Analysts draw on wide networks of informal exchanges with vendors, users and others. Nonetheless, their knowledge and information is refined and tested initially and most directly within Gartner. Here we explore the way that analysts internally are organized into various informal communities. We also note the adoption of increasingly formalized methodologies for the production and review of Magic Quadrants and other outputs, driven by a concern to ensure that their knowledge claims are robust and defensible.

3.2.1. Gartner analysts are organized into research communities

Gartner analysts are organized into various research communities. Elias Thomas described how analysts would sign up to take part in multiple series of research meetings. These include frequent (e.g. monthly) meetings with those with cognate interests as well as more occasional meetings with wider arrays of colleagues (see Figure 3.2).

Figure 3.2. Gartner's European HQ
Source: Author photo (NP)

> I meet the CRM team every week . . . every 2 weeks there is a business applications
> team meeting . . . 6 times a year, all software analysts meet together . . . And every
> quarter there is an all research meeting. It is an academic one, I say academic,
> I mean it is a discursive debate, argument type, present and argue your case type
> session (interview, Thomas).

Thomas notes how this was a continuation of the 'think-tank culture'
from the earliest days of the firm. Gartner analyst Winter makes a similar
observation:

> Gartner is organized by research communities. There are markets . . . so if you
> think you know about it, you sign up. This is very, very independent . . . You sign
> up for a research community and the research community will have a call every
> week, one or two hours, worldwide, and across time zones. Once you are in a
> research community you go the meetings and these things are debated quite a lot.
> It allows you to form your ideas . . . (interview, Winter).

These informal collegiate structures facilitate the development and testing of
knowledge (e.g. by crystallizing and refining views). Winter continued: 'What
Gartner is very good at is allowing all of this information to circulate freely.
None of us takes criticism in a negative way. As a matter of fact, criticism

makes your opinions stronger because you start debating them and you start to think' (interview, Winter).

These forms of knowledge networking have a certain resemblance to academic research networks. However, in academia it remains largely up to individual academics to choose their collaborations (Blau 1994). Whilst individual Gartner analysts also exercise some autonomy, their networking activities are collectively organized within and beyond the organization. This coordinated approach is particularly marked when it comes to deploying expertise in forms that go out into the public domain (which may thereby impinge upon the reputation of Gartner and even have legal implications).

Analyst and research organizations also maintain databases of the particular areas of expertise of their researchers and of their clients and research subjects. Thus, Gartner's skills database helps them to 'locate the right analyst, route them to a right call' (interview, Thomas). However, centralized databases and other kinds of formal coordination mechanisms are not very effective in such rapidly changing domains: 'we are not keeping volumes of information on each vendor because it changes so fast, to maintain it, it is usually just garbage most of what is in there' (interview, Thomas). Instead, they resort to the looser kinds of coordination enabled by the operation of multiple overlapping internal knowledge networks. The work of Gartner analysts is conducted in teams who work closely together:

> We work in teams where we are very tight in the teams, so we can back each other up and we know what each other is doing. Outside of that team, there is a bit of consolidation but at the company level it has to be driven almost top down to make us actually look up and say what is going on in your area. And we go to company meeting where we learn about each other's research areas but that is more an interesting background information (interview, Thomas).

Under certain circumstances, a more concerted approach to mobilizing knowledge and opinion is needed. Elias Thomas told us: 'The different analysts groups all very independent of each other. We do big initiatives where we try and pull things together across Gartner' (interview, Thomas). One example is when dealing with major vendors:

> For instance, if we are writing about SAP, and you want to write a big thing about SAP, you are trying to pool all the knowledge about SAP into a central view, you can't have every analyst having a different view. They may have their view on their little pieces but you have to then get some consistency across, and we have all these kind of structures and templates to make sure we plug in in a consistent format (interview, Thomas).

Toby Old, Gartner's Senior SAP Analyst, made much the same point:

> Now with the main vendors like SAP, Microsoft, IBM, Oracle you need somebody who coordinates that overall position on SAP and brings together those different

opinions across the breadth of the analyst community, and that is what I do. My goal as lead analyst was to try understand about 5 elements of every key area of SAP and then on each of those key areas I would have a colleague who was the real expert. But it was my goal to try and have that broad overall understanding of SAP (interview, Old).

Old also drew our attention to another feature of these arrangements. Gartner only allows people to stay in the lead analyst role for a major vendor for a couple of years; they are then 'rotated' to avoid any potential problems of independence. '[Y]ou do it for two years and then they rotate you. We don't want one person in that role for ever. We want to rotate people through that role so that they don't become too close to the vendor' (interview, Old).

3.3. PRODUCING DEFENSIBLE KNOWLEDGE

In recent years there have been a (relatively small) number of high profile court cases against Gartner (see Table 3.1). Here we encounter another exigency of the work of industry analysts—concerning the need to demonstrate the independence of their assessments. Producing knowledge outputs that make a difference brings its own contingencies. Gartner are often producing outputs like the Magic Quadrant, which are designed to allow potential customers or investors to discriminate between different offerings. Gartner

Table 3.1. The 'Gartner Tax'

In 2014 a lawsuit was filed against Gartner for the placing of a vendor on a Magic Quadrant. The technology vendor NetScout argued that Gartner's decision to rank it a 'challenger' as opposed to a 'leader' or 'visionary' in its market was potentially damaging for its reputation and standing. The lawsuit cites how: '[f]ailure to get a favorable mention in an analyst report could undermine years of product development. Acceptance, on the other hand, boosts a company's exposure and is essential for buyers drawing up short lists' (NetScout Vs. Gartner 2014: 16).[2] There was also mention that NetScout had failed to pay the so-called 'Gartner Tax' and that this was a partial explanation for its poor ranking.

The Gartner Tax is described by a commentator writing in an industry outlet: '[Gartner's substantial success is due to the worst kept secret in the IT industry: Gartner has a 'pay-to-play' business model that by its design rewards Gartner clients who spend substantial sums on its various services by ranking them favorably in its influential Magic Quadrant research reports . . . and punishes technology companies that choose not to spend substantial sums on Gartner services' (Carr 2014).

This comes hot on the heels of the case from a few years earlier where ZL Technology similarly took Gartner to court for the low ranking it received. In the lawsuit they wrote: 'The power of a positive ranking in Gartner is immense because it is often the case that large purchases of technology are based exclusively on the MQ Reports'.[3] ZL Technology were unsuccessful in their bid to sue Gartner. Most industry commentators think that NetScout's lawsuit will also fail (Carr 2014).

therefore needs to be able to defend many of its assessments, which, because they can have significant impacts on a vendors prospects in a particular market, are often contested by these vendors.

Gartner has adopted a number of measures to defend these kinds of assessments in the face of potential claims that their work lacks rigour or has been influenced by commercial relationships with vendors. We will explore how the methods and data by which Magic Quadrants and other outputs are produced have become increasingly formalized in Chapter 7. As Elias Thomas stated: 'You have to now document all the interactions with ['client references'] and how you collected it, and what information was collected, and the raw data, so if anyone escalates you can say here it is' (interview, Thomas). This was necessary as, if circumstances require, analysts need to be able to defend their claims in the face of (threatened) legal action. As we note in Chapter 5, where we discuss our taxonomy of promissory work, different kinds of knowledge claim are subject to different kinds and degrees of accountability. The Magic Quadrants are particularly tricky. As Gartner analyst Paul Winter notes: 'That sometimes gets very nasty, very nasty, you know. Law suits' (interview, Winter). For Gartner to operate it needs to be in a position to produce knowledge that is credible. This in turn depends on their perceived expertise, the rigour of their methods and their independence of view. The suggestion that Gartner analysts can be influenced by vendors provokes a very strong response:

If anyone says you are just being bought off by vendors then we just go nuts! We know that we are not. But we hate being accused of it. And at the heart of it is that [if] we were being bought off by vendors then we are dead. We are worthless. So, as long as we got the credibility and the knowledge in that area to draw a sensible box and we are not biased in the way we are working then, and we are clearly focused on the user, we are OK (interview, Thomas).

3.3.1. Increasing organization and accountability of knowledge production

Knowledge production within large industry analyst firms is becoming an increasingly organized process. Various factors, and in particular the threat of litigation and the need to maintain the quality of outputs and predictions, have led to increasingly elaborate methodologies and systems for producing and checking knowledge claims. Gartner analysts we spoke to harked back to the *think tank culture* that prevailed in the early days. Though the firm is today much larger, this tradition continues in the operation of internal research communities through which Gartner experts in particular fields who may be dispersed across different time zones periodically get together to debate developments. Today the collective organization of knowledge production and review is more formalized than the past. In Gartner and other larger industry analyst organizations, key public outputs such as its Magic Quadrant or its Strategic Planning Assumptions are subject to prior internal review by their peers:

> All the people in your group, at least 3 of them have to comment, it then goes through your manager. The manager has to comment on that. Then it goes to basically randomly to 3 other analysts around the research, generally around applications, and they have to comment (interview, Winter).

The knowledge produced is thus becoming subject to greater internal accountability. This 'internal peer review' involves rigorous debate within the analyst community. This process exhibits some similarities with the tenets of academic debates in science. Thomas describes quarterly research meetings to which all were invited as 'academic': 'I say academic, I mean it is a discursive debate, argument type, present and argue your case type session' (interview, Thomas), and in a later interview suggests that 'at the heart of it there is a sort of truth element to it' (interview, Thomas). Though sharing some similarities with peer review in academic research, there are sharp differences in that this remains a closed process operating within Gartner. Thomas was one of a number of analysts who characterized this 'pseudo-academic':[4]

> There is peer review but we not throwing it out for peer review in the general public. It is peer review behind closed doors. It is not transparent . . . There is a genuine pull by the analysts to be independent and . . . there is a pseudo element to it because it clearly isn't academia in the way we are doing our research (interview, Thomas).

Over the years there had been a 'drive towards consistency' within Gartner in terms of how key public outputs are generated: 'We all used different scoring mechanisms . . . we all had processes but they were all slightly different. Starting about maybe 5 or 6 years ago we started to really tighten it up to make it consistent across the company' (interview, Thomas). Given the rapid growth of the company over a few short decades, it was no longer feasible to get everyone together to agree the process. Instead: 'we have a methodology department for instance and their job is largely to standardize processes' (interview, Thomas). Thus in July 2005 Gartner announced updates to its Magic Quadrant Methodology and Process involving 'Standardized tools and templates' in order 'to increase transparency, consistency and predictability for Vendors, and to improve the value of these deliverables for our User Clients'. Analysts will now use a set of 'standard evaluation criteria, which ensures consistency over time and allows our User clients to better track the markets we cover' (Gartner Inc. 2005).

This standardization drive had led to some unease amongst analysts. Some argue that diversity of opinion and debate was a source of strength. Thus

Gartner analyst Alex Drow describes how analysts avoid adopting an off-the-shelf ('pastry cutter') view. Instead, 'everyone has their own view':

> But we always pride ourselves that we don't have a pastry cutter response to everything. So if you were to ask Gene [Alvarez] about his views on mobile and so on he might be a bit more pro than [Elias Thomas]. So we have the positions on major things but everyone has their own view on which shade of grey, and what are the things that folks need to be doing. So we all have slightly different opinions on things. And I think that is healthy (interview, Drow).

And even Nancy Erskine, who (as we explore below) played an important role in promoting standardization of methodologies within Gartner, flags the need to balance structure and freedom. Some analysts expressed concern that the emphasis on consistency might be at the expense of exercising expert judgement, that the motive was defending the company rather than adding value to customer. This could lead to tensions between analysts with their culture of independence and the concerns of managers to avoid the threat of complaints (escalations) from vendors and to ensure that they could produce an audit of how particular assessments were derived. There was a trade-off here:

> the definition of quality being used there is about consistency, repeatability and audit trail . . . But the question is, does it add value to the reader? . . . So it is an interesting trade-off really. Who is the value for? . . . I think a lot of this is to protect the company against vendors prosecuting them. So it is defensive rather than beneficial to the customer (interview, Thomas).

3.3.2. Formation of Gartner Office of the Ombudsman

An important development here has been the establishment in 2004 of the Gartner Office of the Ombudsman. Nancy Erskine, the first to hold this post, had previously been training Gartner analysts on methodology and running its Research Department. This was linked to the establishment of a formal 'escalation process', whereby vendors could raise their concerns about Gartner's assessments. Where complaints are raised, the Ombudsman would go back to the analyst to check how the assessment had been made. This, it was observed, provides an incentive for analysts to follow procedures. And the Ombudsman was surprised when it transpired that many of the calls coming in to the Ombudsman Office were not from vendors but from analysts concerned to pre-empt escalation.

> we've seen internal associates . . . come to us with, hoping to avoid kind of formal escalations so to speak. What has happened is, they are going wait a minute, where is my research, or where is this piece that I am writing, I am foreseeing danger ahead and potential conflict. Let me give these guys a call and ask their opinion about what's, am I missing something. Are there some facts I should be

considering here, is my tone overly negative, is, have I been complete in following the methodology and the process. Are there areas where I really need to make sure I am crossing all my Ts and dotting all my Is (interview, Erskine).

3.3.3. Importance of quality and independence of Gartner's advice

We have already noted the importance attached to the quality and independence of Gartner's assessments. Elias Thomas noted that independence: 'is our most critical thing' (interview, Thomas). As well as their general assessment of the prospects of particular technological fields, their specific comparative assessments of different products and their suppliers can have enormous impacts on the commercial prospects of vendors. Gartner's independence has been questioned in a context in which it is being paid by many of the firms it is assessing—and it does not disclose these payments (Snapp 2013). Critics of these arrangements told us of stories being circulated about 'disgruntled suppliers and vendors' who attributed unfavourable assessments to a failure to pay a so-called 'Gartner tax' on the grounds that 'we can't afford to pay the twenty grand we need to pay to get onto a Gartner Magic Quadrant' (interview, Ward Dutton). Our informant did not know if this was true or not but noted that this was the 'perception' amongst vendors and this was consequential:

> I don't know whether [the Gartner tax] exists or not to be honest. You know some particularly grumpy vendors who don't come out so well say: 'oh, we have to pay this whatever it is in order to get included, and if we don't pay it, we don't get briefings, they don't come and see us, and they don't bother including us in the research'. I suppose whether that is real or not is besides the point; the key thing is, is that there is a perception and that has an impact (interview, Ward Dutton).

There was, however, little direct evidence of corrupt inducements. Indeed the very experienced Gartner analysts we interviewed, despite being 'regularly offered kickbacks', noted that lack of independence 'gets you into trouble' and that analysts were expected to act 'with integrity'.[5] It was thus very rare for analysts to 'get things seriously wrong' and to lose their job (interview, Winter).[6] Elias Thomas from Gartner recalled two cases where analysts had been sacked: 'One was fired for plagiarism. Another one was fired for not being independent basically. For being too biased, for being biased. His colleagues didn't have any trust in him anymore. There is no evidence that money changed hands' (interview, Thomas).

Conversely, Gartner analysts repeatedly and strenuously stress their independence—which lies at the very core of their business.[7] Their decision to create a Gartner Office of the Ombudsman was motivated 'to instantiate the independence and objectivity of Gartner':

it was really to instantiate the independence and objectivity of Gartner which really were the cornerstones of the company since it was founded. And there was no kind of awful event that started the office it was really realizing that these were . . . things that were really part of the fabric of Gartner . . . We said you know, we want to put a stake in the ground. We want to demonstrate how important this is to us and so have a place for them to go . . . And we wanted to make sure that this wasn't just a place for clients so we said clients, non clients, vendors, users, governments, academians, and internal associates. If they felt I have a question about objectivity or independence or, you know, I have a concern, you know, they had a place to go (interview, Erskine).

The creation of the Gartner Ombudsman is thus portrayed as a reflection of the existing ethos and culture of Gartner culture, and not as a response to problems.[8] Gartner perhaps needs an Ombudsman because their size and influence means they are subject to critical appraisal. At the same time, their size means that they also had the resources needed to support this kind of internal scrutiny. Indeed Gartner's possession of an Ombudsman office is seen by Nancy Erskine, Gartner Ombudsman as *a brand differentiator*. Critics, however, have noted that the Gartner Ombudsman, although explicitly drawing on these models, lacks the kinds of safeguard found in journalism or public administration. Thus, as Snapp (2013) notes, there is no institutional independence between Gartner and its Ombudsman (the Ombudsman is an employee of Gartner, and the complaints and responses are not made public).

3.4. FORMATION OF EXPERTISE: DEVELOPMENT OF THE INDUSTRY ANALYST CAREER

3.4.1. Recruitment

The expertise deployed by industry analysts cannot be achieved simply by formal education; there is, as yet, no degree programme that will train people to become an industry analyst! Though analysts typically possess a first degree in computer science or related subjects, most of their knowledge is experience based, acquired over time and developed in the course of their work/career. Indeed the particular level and combinations of knowledge are learned through an extended journey that typically involves a series of jobs in different firms and industry sectors. To understand the formation of industry analysts we therefore need to develop a dynamic model of *the expert career*.

Our analysis here draws upon the concept of *formation of expertise* to signal that what is at stake is more than just cognitive processes of learning/skill acquisition; it involves experience-based learning and development of a personal and professional identity acquired through experience and 'an extensive

Figure 3.3. 'Walking talking products'
Source: Author photo (NP)

learning journey, which bears at least some of the characteristics of appren-ticeship' (Fuller & Unwin 2010: 217). Analyst expertise is embodied in highly reputed individuals. 'I am a walking talking product that has got value' (interview, Thomas) (Figure 3.3). Moreover, this expertise rests not only in formal knowledge and skills; it also includes personal characteristics (as we see shortly and explore further in Chapter 8).

The analyst's knowledge and skills, along with reputational and other indicators of capability and performance, are acquired and developed in the course of undertaking their advisory work. However, the formation of analyst expertise starts before their appointment. We explore how in recruitment and in induction of neophytes, Gartner seeks to select and develop staff with a demonstrated ability to perform in certain ways—conducting assessments, engaging with clients—that will build trust and reputation.

3.4.1.1. Prior experience

Industry analysts need to deploy an extensive range of technical and commer-cial knowledge of particular classes of IT applications, including knowledge of the strategies of their suppliers and the experience of organizations adopting them. Industry analyst firms therefore tend to recruit staff who already have extensive industrial experience. There is, however, no defined pathway for developing an analyst career. Indeed our empirical research suggests that the specific career pathways of individual analysts have been rather diverse. But within this, some broad patterns can be detected.

A minority strand of industry analysts come from a background in market research or other area that involved quantitative social research skills (interview, De Sousa).[9] However they all need to have a strong IT technical background, and the majority seem to have originally been information technology specialists working in industry, perhaps as consultants, who at some stage sought to broaden their role. Several respondents flagged to us that they had come across the idea of becoming an analyst by more or less accident. What seems to have been key for many analysts in their decision to take this radical career step was a desire to deploy their expertise in a different way.

Thus Paul Winter had 16 years prior industrial experience including 8 years working at a large IT supplier. He had had relations with Gartner as a client for some years before he applied to work for them. 'I had interactions with analysts, some good, some bad. It always intrigued me that, these people, they sit somewhere and they write things that everybody likes . . . or fight with them. So I said I'll give it a go. And that was about 13 years ago' (interview, Winter).

Jon Collins, Director FreeForm Dynamics, recalled how, after doing a computer science degree and working as a programmer, he got involved in technology management and consultancy before he encountered on the web an advert/job description from an analyst firm. He became excited as he read their requirements:

> . . . needs to have had a broad range of experiences in different technological domains; needs to have thought about things strategically as well as etcetera; needs to be able to work at all levels; needs to be able to write; and then presentations . . . and I thought my goodness, that is me! . . . And I banged off an email that evening without, little or no thought other than wow!. And on Monday, they offered me an interview and I have been an industry analyst ever since, about 3 weeks later I was doing the job (interview, Collins).

Such a strategic move from a more 'technical' to a consultancy/strategic management role seemed to be a recurrent feature in many analyst careers.[10] This industrial experience brought not only formal knowledge but also wider understanding of the IT industry and its firms and a network of contacts that were useful to the analyst role. Thus Toby Old, who became Gartner's lead analyst for SAP products, had previously spent 11 years working for SAP: 'So I had been in the industry for 15 years when I came in, so a lot of it is about your knowledge of the industry, your contacts, your network in the industry, that is a big part of it obviously' (interview, Old).

People also develop their careers *within* the industry analysis sector—often moving between jobs across different industry analyst organizations. Jon Collins, Director FreeForm Dynamics, had held five different jobs since becoming an analyst: 'I worked for Bloor for about 3 years . . . I set up my own firm . . . And then I was an associate analyst for QuoCirca, and then I was an associate analyst for MWD with Neil [Ward Dutton]. And then I was invited to be a director of FreeForm' (interview, Collins).

This diversity within the analyst community is partly a consequence of how the category of industry analyst was established. As we saw in the previous chapter, the advisory industry emerges at the interface between a number of areas (scientific journalism/publishing, market research, investment advice etc). Differences in individual backgrounds and career pathways are one source of variety within the analyst community. It provides a mix of skills and capabilities within analyst firms:

> . . . as analysts there are people [who] can articulate stuff very well. That is what they can do, they sort of look at stuff and eventually they can say no, often they have got a good journalistic background or whatever. There [are] people with a very strong technical background. And then there [are] people with a very strong research background . . . Then you've got people who come to the industry analyst from a journalistic background or just from a general 'I want to write about it' background. And then you got people who want to take their technical capabilities and just you know broaden (interview, Collins).

The role of the analyst is not uniform but differs within and between firms. People move around and tend to end up in positions that make best use of their particular strengths and aptitudes:

> I love the selling side of it. Some analysts hate that. They don't want to spend their time doing that, they like to stand on stage and entertain. So they spend their time just flying on planes all over the world being a great presenter. And other guys like to write lots. So what you end up with, on average you end up with a nice mix but in reality each individual analyst is a bit different (interview, Thomas).

Similar internal diversity was noted by respondents from other research and analysis firms. There are also sustained differences between industry analyst firms in terms of their target clients and their research methods (Bernard & Gallupe 2013). These differences are reflected in the kinds of people they recruit and deploy. As Jon Colllins explained, 'So there are companies that are very technically competent or very domain competent that actually are applying a level of expertise' (interview, Collins). We will see in Chapter 10 that these differences between analyst firms are an important feature of what is coming to be seen as an 'ecology' of industry research and advisory expertise.

3.4.1.2. Selection

Gartner and other industry analyst firms have developed distinctive recruitment processes geared to careful selection of candidates for this demanding role. We have already noted the formal skill requirements (experience in appropriate technological domains, writing and presentational skills). However, the selection process seems to be geared not just towards possession of particular (technical) skills, but also towards more personal characteristics. Elias Thomas drew our attention to an 'interesting' feature of Gartner's selection process: after individual interviews, you then faced *the group interview*:

> They do something called a 'group interview'. You are interviewed by everyone in your team first, individually, so you have about 8 interviews, face to face for about an hour, up to an hour, usually half an hour at a time, and they have to unanimously vote that you are OK. That you know your stuff. Once they unanimously agree that you are OK then you can go to the group (interview, Thomas).

What Thomas described as a 'cultural thing for Gartner', geared to establishing 'that you know your stuff', seems also to be searching for other characteristics—'that you are OK'. Also, it appears that one of the things that Gartner is looking to do is to recruit people with an ability not just to communicate effectively but also to *defend* their claims and to operate under pressure. This was most clearly revealed by what is known within Gartner as the *grace under fire test*. Those who get through the group interview are asked to prepare and present a report.

Elias Thomas still remembered very clearly what happened next: ' . . . you have to write a paper . . . and then they put you into a room and you have to present it, and then they ask you questions . . . Little did I realize that the game is nothing to do with the paper, the assumption is that you are going to write rubbish anyway . . . ' (interview, Thomas). Recruiters are apparently not so much interested in the analysis being made but the capacity of the individual to present and discuss their forecast:

> I will never forget, I walked in, there was 2 guys sitting beside me. I was sitting facing a video screen. And on the wall from America was 4 guys sitting facing me. And then there was 2 guys on the other side, so I was surrounded by 2, 4, 6, 8, 10 people around me. And they said, present your paper. And as I started the guy on the screen put it on mute, and they would sort of point at you and write stuff down, and do things like that. And you are . . . looking at that and sweating! It doesn't look good when they are doing that to you. And then the guy beside me started whispering, sort of looking at you . . . And that would carry on for a bit, they would let you go for about 5 or 6 minutes . . . (interview, Thomas).

It seems the practice was not to let the presenters finish but to interrupt them with a series of questions:

> I remember one of my first questions was something like, you said this about client-server computing, and you seem to be arguing this is the case, and I said no, no I am not arguing that at all, I am arguing this is the case. They said, well you did say that. No I didn't, I said that. So I stood up for myself. And the guy said,

OK, OK, you don't know what you are talking about at all, do you? (interview, Thomas).

The testers, apparently, were probing for equivocation:

> It is just a brutal exercise. What I didn't realize was that the exercise, they still do it today, the game that is being played is "will you lose your temper?" If you lose your temper you are haven't got a job. If you change your mind or back down, you haven't got a job, because you can't defend yourself. So you are trying to get this fine line of not losing your temper but not backing down, defending yourself in a coherent manner under pressure (interview, Thomas).

The prospective analyst who crumbles under pressure or changes their mind and is forced to retreat from a position seemingly does not pass the test. This is because the traits sought are confidence in a position even when there is much uncertainty surrounding it.[11] Recruiters are interested in identifying people able to present and defend a position clearly and concisely regardless of whether or not the position is thought to be the correct one. Though Thomas felt this to be 'a brutal exercise', it did prepare him for difficult encounters in his job with groups of clients: 'You do occasionally at Gartner get put in a position where clients, you are surrounded by 10 clients and they are all going "what the hell are you talking about, you idiot!" and they all have a crack at you. You have to dance basically. It is kind of useful for that' (interview, Thomas).

3.4.1.3. Induction

New recruits to Gartner then go through a protracted induction process. Depending on their level of experience, as described in the opening to this book, they go through an intensive training programme to immerse them in Gartner's specific tools, processes, methodologies and procedures. This was described as being more or less like a *Boot camp*:

> [new recruits] go to boot camp of course. That is more about . . . how the company works for tools, processes, procedures, how to work with sales. It is a weeklong course if I remember. Then there is a couple of specific courses on how to do a Magic Quadrant. There is a whole e-learning library, there is a whole database on tools on how to do one, the procedures you have to go through, and then there is a whole load on what are the official processes you must apply (interview, Thomas).

When Gartner takes over an existing research/advisory firm—and this has been an important feature in its development and growth—there is reportedly an intense process to align the neophytes with Gartner culture and procedures.[12] Some of the companies they absorbed had previously offered a service working for vendors that involved 'writing their marketing material for them' (interview, Thomas). This kind of activity was not compatible with Gartner's emphasis on being independent from particular vendors. Elias Thomas, Senior VP for Research, Gartner Inc., stated: 'That is the business Gartner didn't get into, got out of in fact. So every time we buy a company and they are doing that then we have to shut that part of their business down' (interview, Thomas). Although there is currently more emphasis on the provision of formal training for new recruits, from the outset an informal 'apprenticeship' system has been key to becoming an effective industry analyst: 'You learnt by being mentored, someone sat next to you and [said] "no, no, no"' (interview, Thomas). A recent recruit to Gartner, Toby Old, described how neophytes are given a light load, but gradually learn 'on the job' to undertake and become productive with different kinds of task: 'You have a mentor when you first come in. The first few months you are not expected to do a lot from a delivery point of view. And then the more experience you get, essentially what happens, your productivity goes up' (interview, Old).

The apprenticeship system plays a key role as new recruits take on the production of key knowledge outputs such as the Magic Quadrant. As Elias Thomas described:

> And then normally on the first one they will join forces with another analyst who'll . . . show them the way through. The difficult thing is dealing with the vendors. So being briefed by them is being easy, but when it comes to the calls where you are debating where the dot was, that's tough. It can be very, very tense; that is where you normally want a more mature analyst on the call saying 'this is the way it is and this is why' (interview, Thomas).

The role of the experienced analysts is to help the neophyte to convey their assessments to potentially hostile stakeholders in a in a way that does not end up with legal disputes! Elias Thomas continued: 'Junior analysts will then learn how to express themselves without [provoking], the issue is not putting across what they, why they think what they think, it is doing it in a manner that does not provoke, so you don't have lawyers being thrown at you' (interview, Thomas). It would appear that there is 'an art' to presenting the Magic Quadrant in a way that avoids litigation. What seems to be at stake here, as in the case of the 'grace under fire' test, is the ability to produce defensible knowledge.

3.4.2. Developing a reputation within the organization and within the sector

Through this apprenticeship system, analysts gradually develop their capabilities. This, we were told, takes about two years. The process is not just a question of acquiring skills but also of demonstrating their capabilities, showing their peers that they could be relied on. Analysts are competing within the organization to advance their reputation. Though their work may initially be supervised by their co-workers, they gradually become trusted and extend their remit—perhaps getting to the stage of having their own Magic Quadrant and making naming interventions. They advance their status within the internal market. Gartner assesses the performance of their analysts indirectly e.g. in terms of whether clients are renewing their subscriptions and directly by getting feedback from clients about the perceived value of advisory work. Through these activities, the performance of individual analysts can be ranked. Indeed, within Gartner, analysts are placed in a league table (see Chapter 8).

Expert status is not only developed internally. It is also developed externally. As experienced Gartner analyst, Paul Winter, observes, analysts need to develop a reputation in the industry, conceived in terms of 'your value, the things you bring to them'. He goes on: 'Working as an industry analyst it takes about 2 years to get your job going, because you have to be well known in the industry—people have to know about you. They've got to respect you for the things that you say. Like your value, the things you bring to them' (interview, Winter).

The predictions and other knowledge interventions made by analysts are increasingly formally tracked externally by third party organizations such as 'analyst relations' professionals. As Gartner analyst, Paul Winter, noted: 'Predictions are tracked. There is an independent company who takes what they call a strategic analysis of all predictions, and tracks them over time' (interview, Winter). (We return to this point in Chapter 8 where we discuss what happens when predictions go wrong). Similarly, David Mitchell, Research Director, Ovum Research, observed: 'There are firms who analyse the analysts . . . people whose job is to be analysts of the analyst sector' (interview, Mitchell). That there are such experts potentially changes how industry analyst knowledge is traded (a point we return to in Chapter 10).

3.4.3. Managing analyst work

Our earlier research on managing expert technical labour highlighted the challenges in organizing and controlling the work of highly specialized staff (Williams & Procter 1998). Can industry analyst managers understand what the technical specialists they manage are doing in a way that allows them to assess its quality? Can they maintain authority? We showed that managers need to be able to demonstrate some level of technical competence to legitimate their role in relation to technical specialists with complex skills that would be difficult for a non-specialist to assess (ibid.). These considerations are highly pertinent to Gartner industry analysts—experts with exceptionally strong reputations for possessing the highest level of expertise in relation to their domain. This gives them considerable authority. It also makes it very easy for skilled analysts to move and trade their knowledge elsewhere. They could move to another firm, or even go independent (see Chapter 10). These features make industry analysts 'hard to manage' in conventional ways. They have a high degree of autonomy. Elias Thomas used an analogy (one intriguingly often deployed to describe the difficulties in managing another traditionally autonomous, highly-expert group: university academics): 'Gartner is like a herd of cats, it is like herding cats' (interview, Thomas).

Difficulties in managing expert analysts are compounded by the promotion of characteristics that have been actively encouraged in the selection of these staff: ' . . . there is a sort of culture of independence by the analysts who don't like being pushed around by management or being overruled' (interview, Thomas). As Gartner analyst Paul Winter told us, 'Managing Gartner analysts is dreadful. You can't fob them off with stories, you know. Typically, you have little power. It is a desperate situation'. As a result, analysts have a high level of autonomy in their work: 'You are given a lot of leeway' (interview, Winter). Gartner has a very flat organizational structure, a corollary of the collegiate organizational structure, with large numbers of highly reputed expert staff at the 'bottom of the hierarchy'.[13] Gartner analyst Paul Winter explained: 'In research, the people—the famous people who people really listen to—are at the bottom . . . There is a very flat structure . . . Most of the analysts are at the bottom of the hierarchy' (interview, Winter).

A further consequence of this flat structure is the lack of an effective promotion ladder. There are relatively few managerial jobs to be had. Some analysts might decide they wanted to move into management (particularly given the intensive demands of the job). Paul Winter suggested that typically 'when you are sick of travelling' you 'want to become a manager'. However, analysts are not necessarily desperate to move away from the knowledge networks that underpin their standing and become a manager of these hard to manage experts:

> If you want to go into a management career yes you can do it. Then Chief of Research, most of the bosses are ex-analysts, most of them. Probably 100%. So, unless you want to go for a management job where you start managing people. Typically most of us are quite happy to stay where we are (interview, Winter).

More conventional market research organizations like Ovum seem to have had a stronger internal division of labour market, with a clearer organizational hierarchy/career pyramid (though this may be changing as a result of the offshoring of research).[14]

The difficulties of applying conventional management methods to technical specialist staff, favours what Friedman (1989) characterized as managerial strategies of 'responsible autonomy' rather than 'direct control'. This involves incentives and value systems to encourage active alignment between staff and organizational goals. In this case, the reputation and perceived value of individual analyst expertise and the Gartner organization are closely coupled. Gartner's earnings revolve around this perceived value. And top analysts are very well rewarded. This is not to say that the management of industry analysts arises spontaneously from this simple alignment of interest. Instead, we find a rather distinctive model of work organization and performance assessment. The work of industry analysts is subject to various forms of assessment. However, the goal of this scrutiny is not to achieve detailed direction over tasks and short-term goals ('direct control' in Friedman's [1989] terminology). In its place industry analysts find themselves bound up in a situation in which they need to be self-managing. And this is done in ways that orient analysts to the strategic and commercial goals of the company.

There is a comprehensive system of collecting information which includes direct feedback from clients about advice received and assessments of public performances. As we will see in Chapter 8, Gartner also collects information about activities at their conferences. There are also 3rd party organizations collecting data about analyst performance.

Various elements of analyst work are being scrutinized. One thing that is immediately visible within the firm is their published output. Their performance here is regulated in a system that was described to us as 'publish or die'. As Elias Thomas told us: 'The culture of the company is . . . a bit like publish or die. The only reason you will get fired is if you stop writing. It is pretty much it' (interview, Thomas). However, he noted that beyond this minimum level of output, there is considerable leeway about the volume of publications: 'Some analysts may only write 4 papers a year. Others will write 50. So there is quite a wide gap between the amount of volume you can produce in a year, so it is not like you have to write tonnes of stuff' (interview, Thomas).

Publication is only one part of a huge range of activities that analysts need to undertake. They must also make various kinds of presentations and participate in the numerous meetings and telephone discussions with 'clients' and vendors through which information is elicited and advice offered. Many of the activities that analysts undertake are subject to some form of assessment—not just their formal research outputs, though these seem to be most salient. The analyst is thus subject to (and must navigate their work in relation to) multiple assessment criteria: 'OK, we are paid to write research in that I am paid to do enquiries and I am paid to help the client and we get rated on how well the client is happy with our advice' (interview, Thomas).

This is a *highly competitive* setting in which their achievements are being assessed not only by peers and managers within the organization but also, critically, indicators are being developed and monitored regarding the satisfaction of external clients. As Gartner analyst Paul Winter told us: 'I talk with my boss every month, if I need to . . . I am assessed on the basis of feedback from clients. Number of downloads . . . of papers. General client satisfaction' (interview, Winter). Gartner analyst Elias Thomas describes the system through which the performance of analysts, collectively as well as individually, is reviewed:

> Every quarter at least, sometimes more, the Head of Research sits down with all analysts and we all have to . . . spend an hour going though what the financials look like, what the customers are saying, how we are performing in terms output and what are the metrics of the business basically: what does our retention rate looks like for our customers? How our product lines, each of our product lines, how they are growing, all that kind of stuff. That is very commercial I guess and rewarding a few people for being good and going above and beyond and working stupid hours or whatever if they had to (interview, Thomas).

What is striking about this system is that the criteria against which analysts are being assessed relate closely to the overall performance of the firm (business metrics such as sales, customer retention, rather than indirect indicators). These also feed in to annual review and reward systems. Analysts find their individual prospects coupled closely to the firm performance.

One consequence of the wide range of analyst activities is that demand for their services greatly exceeds their available time. And to survive analysts are forced to develop strategies to manage these effectively open-ended work-loads.[15] For example, Gartner analyst Paul Winter describes the various schedules through which he struggles to manage the huge volume of client and vendor calls (with contacts often in a different time zone), meetings and associated travel. Given that his assistants are organizing these schedules for him, he has found it necessary to generate effective heuristics to regulate how his calendar is scheduled. Thus, he will limit travel to alternate weeks and only travel to a place if he has a certain number of meetings in place (five if you are somewhere like Copenhagen or three in China where meetings are harder to schedule):

> We are pulled from one side to the other. We travel a lot . . . It is either a travelling day or it is not. A travelling day is difficult; your time is very, very tightly checked up. I have a practical rule that I never travel from home unless I have 3 meetings in the same place. Otherwise you travel. I have that rule. And typically, and depending where you are, if you are in Beijing you can only do 3 meetings in a day. If you are in Copenhagen you can do 5 or 6. So a typical travelling day, you wake up in some hotel, you have some breakfast and you can go. There is somebody waiting for you in reception, you have a car, you just follow the flow that has been mapped out for you. A day at home is typically like today. And there is an organizer that we have all got. I start working at 7, that's 4pm in Australia, so if I have some Australian clients I can still talk to them. All the calls are scheduled in advance (interview, Winter).

3.4.4. Note on gender

The challenging work-life balance that a Gartner industry analyst faces prompted us to enquire whether this might be a 'job for the boys'. We sought to discover whether analyst work, with its strong technical focus and with the selection of candidates able to present and defend positions with authority, was seen as predominately 'male' work. The role of industry analyst is, however, by no means a male preserve. A search of 5200 analyst profiles on the ARchitect Database in which the gender could be established indicated that 27.5 per cent of analysts are female.[16] Though the majority of analysts were male, women made up a significant minority. We have not been able to verify this through quantitative research but it was suggested to us that there were gender contours. Female analysts were not evenly represented across different sectors of analyst work, but were most frequently encountered providing advice to those sectors and types of organization with significant numbers of female staff. It would appear that the gender breakdown of analysts reflected the gendered contours of the sector from which they were recruited.

NOTES

1. We are grateful to Portia Isaacson Bass publisher and editor of the industry journal, *Future Thinker*, for giving us permission to reproduce this advert here. http://pcmine.com/P/FT/Future%20Thinker%20v2%20n8.pdf Accessed 1st March 2014.
2. http://www.channelweb.co.uk/digital_assets/8088/NetScout_vs_Gartner.pdf Accessed 5th March 2015.
3. https://technobabble2dot0.wordpress.com/2009/10/21/contentious-conversations-in-analyst-relations/Accessed 5th March 2015.
4. For example, James Governor from RedMonk states how 'the analysts are pseudo-academics . . . there are some, and we call them the ivory tower analysts, there are some who are really academic. I mean an academic with all the negative corollaries that has. You know, sort of, academic who has just gone off into a research room and spent far too long looking at one thing and not talking to anybody about it at all' (interview, Governor).
5. Paul Winter told us 'what people buy is our independence. So if you are too much lenient towards a vendor or not, can't see the opposite then that gets you into trouble. You have to be balanced in your opinions. We can't own any share of the companies that we are evaluating. So, we [are] also regularly offered kick-backs . . . so we need people with integrity' (interview, Winter).
6. Paul Winter described how 'you know, and if you get it seriously wrong however we lose our job. [Has that happened?]. Oh God, yeah. I think over 700 analysts there is an average of about . . . I hear about 2 or 3 cases every quarter. These

wouldn't be as much things that go wrong but something similar' (interview, Winter).

7. Elias Thomas described that 'people buy us partly through insurance to some degree, in that it is safe. Got the biggest provider in the market who is giving us advice. Sometimes they are doing it because they want to make a decision. Sometimes they are doing it because they want to save money... we know the list of reasons and why they buy us. Probably at the guts of it, and my personal belief at the heart of it, I think the real thing we have got going for us is independence' (interview, Thomas).

8. Elias Thomas from Gartner argued: 'it is not because we are moral or our governance structures or our ombudsman is more powerful it is just, I think the heart of Gartner's culture is if you think about it seriously, if you went up against say Gartner versus Deloitte, if we are not independent, then, we will say we will do your SAP project for you. [If] we are trying to compete against someone like Deloitte, then we are dead. Deloitte is a 20 billion dollar company and we are 1, 1.2. At that point, we are toast. But when they say 'we are independent' we go 'no you are not. You are quite willing to, you have to feed your mouths of your consultants but we don't. That is not how we work. We are *Which?* magazine' (interview, Thomas).

9. Particularly amongst firms such as Ovum, IDC and Inteco that emphasized market research surveys (interviews Ward Dutton; Collins; Thomas).

10. For example, Elias Thomas had spent 3 years working as Programmer and Analyst, Software Sciences/Data Sciences, followed by 3 years as a 'Research Consultant' at a market research firm.

11. In his ethnography of the work of weather forecasts, Fine writes that: [t]he dark heart of prediction is defining, controlling, and presenting uncertainty as confident knowledge. To forecast is to strip uncertainty, responding to the demand for surety, eschewing ambiguity' (2007: 103).

12. However, the induction or retraining process that those from newly acquired firms undergo seems rather unevenly applied. One analyst told us that shortly after having joined a small market research firm as a recent graduate, her firm was taken over by Gartner, which meant she went home on Friday only to find herself working at Gartner on the Monday without so much as a day of training (interview, De Sousa).

13. We must not forget that the analysts are very senior and well-paid staff in organizational terms. It is notable that our respondents, in discussing their work, only seem to notice themselves (e.g. the 810 analysts and 481 consultants at Gartner in 2011). They rarely mention other grades of Gartner staff (such as the 1268 sales agents at Gartner in 2011) let alone the other support staff that make up the bulk of Gartner employees (Bernard & Gallupe 2013).

14. Mitchell (from Ovum) described how: '[i]t used to be that there was a pretty strong pyramid apprenticeship model. So you would start, and you are a primary researcher doing some data gathering on a report as a team of maybe 3 or 4 looking at business intelligence marketplace. And once you had done a year or so there and you had your work critiqued and gone through an apprenticeship route, and there would be about a chapter of the report to write based on the ETL

[Extract, Transform, Load) tools. And maybe after 3 or 4 years you'd gone from your analyst, senior analyst, to principal analyst where you are responsible for that whole piece of research. So there was a learning model on the job. Now most of the lower level data gathering, initial analysis isn't done on shore. It is done by outsource teams in other parts of the world. It makes it much harder to develop a professional career model through that apprenticeship route in either of the UK or the US' (interview, Mitchell).

15. We anticipate that academics and researchers in research-active universities will immediately recognize various similarities between elements of this work system and their own highly competitive systems of globalized knowledge production and training, particularly from the increasing number of countries that have adopted formalized research assessment exercises.

16. We are grateful to Duncan Chapple for extracting this data for us from the ARchitect database. The Architect database is maintained by ARInsights (http://www.arinsights.com).

4

The Professionalization of Business Knowledge

Thus far we have examined how Gideon Gartner set out to constitute a novel and distinctive model of expert work. But how are we to conceptualize this expertise? Here, drawing upon writings from the Sociology of Professions and alternative perspectives from the Sociology of Science and its extension into the Sociology of Markets, we consider the extent to which industry analysts represent a novel form of expertise.

To address this we initially turn to the body of existing research into expert labour and in particular to the Sociology of Professions. Many studies examine how, over the last century, various groups of specialist labour emulated the mechanisms that had been successfully used by scientists, lawyers and medical practitioners to achieve professional status, autonomy and rewards. We find similar attempts by further groups (for example social workers or management consultants) as well as technical experts. Specialist occupations seeking to establish professional status need to make choices in terms of how their knowledge is produced and applied and how their efficacy is established. Science and medicine constitute one well-established, and culturally accepted model. However, other models are also available (e.g. from law, journalism, management consultancy). This begs the question as to which models have influenced industry analysts.

4.1. RESORTING TO EXTERNAL EXPERTS

Our initial exploration of expertise (Williams et al. 1998) noted the burgeoning number and range of specialist fields of knowledge and associated experts. This pattern has continued unabated into the twenty first century. Growth in the number of experts, and their perceived salience, has been accompanied by the proliferation of new kinds of knowledge expertise, including that of the industry analysts that are the focus of this book. In the industrial setting, the increasing complexity of computer-based systems and the search for improved organizational performance and responsiveness to 'the market' are just some of the factors seen to drive the growth of management consultants and other forms of business expertise. Moreover, 'lean firm' prescriptions since the 1980s have stressed the economic advantages, indeed competitive imperative, of outsourcing many functions, including specialist labour, that might previously have been undertaken by the organization. This process has now extended to include more strategic issues. As a result, today most firms must buy-in substantial parts of their technical and change management expertise.

The resort to expertise to resolve problems of uncertainty of decision-making in contexts of incomplete information in turn creates new uncertainties and knowledge requirements (Williams et al. 1998). In particular, how can organization managers assess the quality and trustworthiness of different experts and the pertinence and utility of their expertise to its business challenges? Some degree of knowledge is needed to assess the competing claims of different providers of expertise. This dilemma is reflected in the emergence of new classes of expert (individuals and organizations) that can offer firms advice on how to select and manage their relationship with key strategic suppliers of business knowledge (including providers of change management consultancy and of embodied expertise in the form of new technological systems). These complex domains and the capacity of experts over these fields are characterized by considerable ambiguity and uncertainty (Alvesson 2001).

4.2. PROFESSIONS

'Professionalization' has been held out as one way to resolve this problem of resorting to expert advice. Professionalization describes the processes whereby a specialist occupation seeks to achieve autonomy/control over the conduct of work and its status/rewards by exercising monopoly over the legitimate application of a body of specialist knowledge, 'organizable as common resources for a body of individuals' (Abbott 1988: 324), to solve client problems. Early writings on professions flagged the two-fold benefits of professional institutions: in protecting the autonomy of expert judgement from external political and economic influences and, conversely, in regulating the behaviour of experts by penalizing abuse of expert status and opportunistic exploitation of the unequal balance of knowledge between expert and client. A body of research over the last three decades from what has been termed the 'Sociology of Professions' has explored the wider uptake of this model, derived from the older professions of medicine, law and the sciences. But do these particular conceptions apply to business knowledge—and the new forms of expertise provided by industry analysts—that are emerging today?

4.2.1. Professionalization as solution to problems of expert knowledge

Professionalization has long been discussed as a solution to quality problems in occupations that require expert knowledge. As Freidson (1994) points out: 'In any large and complex community there must be some conventional way by which people can identify an expert without having to rely on word-of-mouth testimonials, on prior personal experience, or on time- and resource-consuming, risky, trial employment' (ibid: 59).

Experts by definition possess specialized, esoteric knowledge that cannot readily be evaluated by generalists applying everyday criteria (Mok 1971, Freidson 1994). Professionalization provides an institutionalized way of 'attesting expertise' (Gross & Kieser 2006: 72). As Abbott's (1988) classic study in the Sociology of Professions states:

> Professions were organized bodies of experts who applied esoteric knowledge to particular cases. They had elaborate systems of instruction and training together with entry by examination and other formal pre-requisites. They normally possessed and enforced a code of ethics or behaviour (Abbott 1988: 4).

This traditional view of professionalization can be traced back to Carr-Saunders and Wilson's *The Professions* (1933). The first generation of writings, informed by the 'functionalist' analyses of Parsons (1939, 1954) and Merton (1982), highlight the beneficial role of professional institutions in protecting the autonomy of experts from pressures from vested interests (e.g. of public administration or commerce).[1] Much of the early work of professions, accordingly, was concerned to define and differentiate professionals from other occupations through their possession of various attributes (see for example Raelin [1989]). The various accounts broadly share a set of 'core defining characteristics' of professions, including 'formal education and entry requirements; a monopoly over an esoteric body of knowledge and associated skills; autonomy over the terms and conditions of practice; collegial authority; a code of ethics; and, commitment to a service ideal' (Anleu 1992: 24). Though professional behaviour, initially, was seen to be rooted in conceptions of 'gentlemanly' behaviour, this definition of professionalism has become overtaken by the medical/scientific model (Fournier 2000).

4.3. SOCIOLOGY OF PROFESSIONS

The Sociology of Professions arguably became established as a result of the radical critique emerging from the 1970s that reacted against the above view, which it described as the 'functionalist' account, and the privileged status it accorded to professional expertise (Brante 1988). It can thus be seen to represent what we might call the 'second wave' in the analysis of professions. One of the earliest contributions (Freidson 1970) criticized (in the case of medicine) the prevalent functionalist theories of professions as 'scientifically-based, practically-efficacious, and socially altruistic' (Coburn 1992: 497). Larson (1977) in particular revisits Weber's idea that professional groups exercise social closure to advance their interests. Her concept of 'professional project' highlighted the strategies for sectional occupational advancement accompanying professionalism. Notwithstanding the diversity of currents in the Sociology of Professions, most of these accounts, in reaction to the functionalist account, share an emphasis on how expert communities exercise 'social closure'. This is to gain authority over an area of expert knowledge and to exclude others in order to increase rewards and, crucially to achieve autonomy/control over the exercise of their work (Gross & Kieser 2006). In similar terms, Freidson (1994) argues that professionalization seeks to retain control over the definition, organization, execution and evaluation of its activities. This encompasses control over who has the right to produce certain services, how such rights are acquired, and how these services are produced (Muzio et al. 2011).

4.3.1. Ecology of Professions

Abbott (1988) perhaps represents the most fully articulated contribution to the Sociology of Professions. He offers a dynamic analysis of professionalization as an interactive system. Expertise is not exercised by expert groups in isolation: the professionalization project takes place in an *ecology of professions*. Abbott highlights competition within and between different professional groups, which takes the form of 'jurisdictional conflicts'. Abbott's work has been highly influential in subsequent debates and it is helpful to review his framework.

Abbott's analysis explores the activities that need to be controlled in order for the profession to stay in command over its jurisdiction: the classification (e.g. in medicine, diagnosis), reasoning (e.g. inference) and remedying (e.g. treatment) of a problem. Across these three activities, jurisdictional control is maintained through legitimation, research and instruction.

Abbott addresses two key dimensions of the professional project: the *intra-professional* and *inter-professional*. In relation to the former he highlights internal stratification within a profession, i.e. the development of vertical divisions of knowledge and status, with some more routine tasks being delegated to lower status groups and perhaps ejected from a profession. At the upper end of the spectrum, he draws attention to *professional regression*. Issues of expert judgement—regarding both matters of substantive controversy and questions regarding the expert status of particular practitioners—are referred to members of the field with the highest status. The elite of the field become internalized within the profession and socially and linguistically distanced from clients.

As we will show, this represents one of the most striking differences between traditional professions and industry analysts such as Gartner Inc. There is stratification within the expert community, but this takes place *within* the analyst organization. And the elite of the field are not distanced from clients; quite the reverse, they become client facing 'stars' as we show in Chapter 8.

Central to Abbott's analysis is the concept of *jurisdictional work*—in their labour, professionals encounter members of other groups and take part in various kinds of boundary work and conflicts over authority with other professional groups. Abbott's dynamic model highlights a strategic dilemma facing professional groups—rigid professional organization facilitates validation of claims in competition with other groups but conversely limits flexibility of professional groups to colonize other problem areas. One corollary is that in areas where there is constant change in the domain of practice and thus of knowledge it may not be feasible to establish the professional structures around recognized bodies of knowledge needed to validate experts' status, performance and knowledge claims.[2] Abbott discusses the systematization of knowledge and how this may vary according to the insertion of a profession into the wider system of professionalization. For Abbott, a systematized, formalized and codified knowledge base may be viewed as an outcome as well as a prerequisite for professional action (Muzio et al. 2011). We will return to this point below in relation to business knowledge.

4.3.2. Professionalization competes with alternative forms of structuring expertise

With their focus on established professional models, this 'second generation' of scholars portrays professionalization as competing with alternative forms of structuring expertise. Various writers in the Sociology of Professions address the challenges to the professional model and the possibility of alternate forms of structuring expertise. Professionalization is by no means the only model for organizing expert labour; nor is its success guaranteed. Thus Abbott (1988: 324) argues that 'we have professionalisation . . . because competing forms of institutionalization have not yet overwhelmed it . . . Professionalism . . . competes with alternate forms of structuring expertise, in particular, with commodification and organization'. Freidson (1994) offers a similar formulation, portraying professionalization as competing with markets and bureaucracy: professionals seek autonomy rather than being subject to the dictat of consumers in the market or managers in public administration and large corporations (Gross & Kieser 2006, Muzio et al. 2011).

Abbott (1988: 324) analyses the competition between professionalism and commodification. This:

> arises in part because the commodities embodying expertise require develop-
> ment, maintenance and support that increasingly exceed the resources of indivi-
> dual professionals. The commercial organisations and governments that invest in
> commodified professional knowledge compete directly for client fees with profes-
> sionals, whether the commodities provide services directly or are simply used by
> professionals in practice . . . But nonprofessionals increasingly own and operate
> professional commodities, which makes the present more dangerous to the idea
> of professionalism itself.

Control over the production of commodified knowledge by large commercial organizations is seen thereby to threaten the professional model in which knowledge is 'organizable as common resources for a body of individuals' (Abbott 1988: 324). These challenges to established models of professionaliza-tion were seen as likely to both limit the autonomy of professional work and restrict the growth of the professional form of expert labour (Coburn 1992, Evetts 2006).[3] Fournier (2000: 68) draws attention to some of the inconsis-tencies in these debates, for example some portray the 'logic of the market' as leading to 'a "corruption" of professional practice' (i.e. a loss of autonomy) whilst others see it as 'intensifying the bureaucratic trend towards the com-modification of professional knowledge'.

These challenges to the professions figure in recent writings on health, welfare and social services and education. Here a range of specialist occupa-tions has, it seems, sought to extend the established model of professional work, derived as we have seen from medicine, science and law, to various other kinds of specialist work—and especially to that delivering certified quality of service in various public services and statutorily required functions.[4]

Social scientists have examined professional organization as a source of resistance to commercial pressures and other reorganization and rationaliza-tion efforts, in particular those arising in the recent period via 'New Public Management' initiatives. Writers in this category appear to revert to elements of the functionalist analysis through their identification with the traditional professional model coupled with an often unacknowledged normative com-mitment towards its 'public good' features in terms of the protection from external pressures it appears to offer. Under this model, expertise, profession-ally regulated, encourages self-discipline, protecting clients from the risk of being exploited, ensuring quality of service and protecting the autonomy and rewards for professionals in their work (Brante 1988, Fournier 2000).[5] This model of expertise seems to provide a solution to the problem of resorting to expert advice. But do these particular conceptions, derived from the older professions of medicine and law and the sciences, apply to business knowledge, and the new forms of expertise that are developing nowadays.

4.4. PROFESSIONALIZATION OF BUSINESS KNOWLEDGE

There is a substantial body of research into another, already well-established, group deploying business knowledge: management consultants. There has been a debate about the applicability of the analysis of professionalization to management and systems consultants and other business knowledge experts (McKenna 2006). The number of managerial consultants has grown rapidly by over 10 per cent per year over the last three decades (Gross & Kieser 2006). Public and private organizations are today spending large sums of money on external consultants. They buy-in expertise from a range of professional service firms and individual consultants. But how can they identify the most trustworthy experts? This state of affairs has been described as 'ideal grounds for professionalizing the consulting industry' (Gross & Kieser 2006: 71) as this provides a means to protect clients and fellow consultants from poor quality advice.

Writers from the Sociology of Professions have highlighted the extent to which management consultants and other information occupations have failed (Abbott 1988) or, more particularly, *have not sought to achieve* (Gross & Kieser 2006, Muzio et al. 2011) professional status in the sense described above. Thus Abbott (1988: 245), considering computing occupations and the other expert labour involved in developing and maintaining Management Information Systems (MIS), notes that '[n]o coherent set of people has in fact emerged to take jurisdiction in this area. It continues to be extremely permeable, with most training on the job, most expertise readily commodifiable and careers following wildly diverging patterns'.

Instead, Abbott (1988) notes the emergence and dominance of large interprofessional organizations that supply contractual services. He attributes their success to their efficiency in making available and integrating the range of specialist knowledge and experience needed to develop and implement computer systems:

> ... new social structures offering these information resources more efficiently ... [and] large scale consulting services that install complete information systems for corporate clients have become common only in the last 2 decades. Like many such areas this one was invaded by organizations whose common property was their ability to field the multiprofessional teams necessary ... " (Abbott 1988: 244).[6]

These MIS providers mainly arose from the large international consulting houses, which, in turn, were often based upon the (then Big Eight) large international accounting firms. So here we see an alternative to the classic professionalization model based on the ability of these large organizations to deploy multiple kinds of expertise, often constituted through internal training rather than externally validated training and certification.[7] Abbott (1988) observes that these groups may achieve a certain professionalization 'in the sense of creating a coherent occupational group with some control of an abstract expertise' (ibid: 154). However, their internal structure differs from that of conventional professions such as medicine and law: 'They are much less committed to rigid definition of jurisdiction or membership, since they must be flexible enough to move in directions that enable organisational survival' (idem.).

Gross and Kieser (2006) analyse how these big consultancy organizations resolve potential uncertainties about the capability of their experts. This is largely by establishing (as a proxy indicator of past performance) and maintaining (as a promise for clients and incentive for consultants regarding their future performance) their corporate brand (Alvesson 2001, Armbrüster 2006, Gross & Kieser 2006, Muzio et al. 2011). Perceptions about their capacity to resolve client problems is in turn supported by:

i) developing distinctive change management concepts (Fincham 1995, Kipping & Armbrüster 2000, Gross & Kieser 2006),

ii) emphasizing the selectivity of their recruiting processes as a guarantee of individual capacity (only the best get in and are retained) (Gross & Kieser 2006), and

iii) emphasizing the extensive experience of their consultants in resolving problems with other clients—exemplified by the number of successful cases they have been involved in (Gross & Kieser 2006) which becomes a kind of currency for valuing expertise.

We note that whilst traditional professional certification provides assurance of a requisite standard of performance, these proxies for quality give potential clients something else: a way to identify the *best* service providers to help them achieve competitive advantage.

The alleged 'failure' of the professionalization project in management knowledge has been attributed variously to the lack of state regulation of expert status (Gross & Kieser 2006, Muzio et al. 2011),[8] the consequent low barriers to entry (Glückler & Armbrüster 2003), and the variety of areas encompassed (information technology, management, accounting [Muzio et al. 2011]) which is seen to favour large firms able to deploy both the broad range of expertise and the skills in managing interdisciplinary teams. The latter points are also seen to underpin the strength of large management consultancy organizations. However, as Muzio et al. (2011: 818) point out:

> In these areas, unlike in the case of the traditional professions, large firms have predated and subsequently constrained the development of professional institutions. Firms themselves became the main locus of professional closure and regulation, shaping the development of this field and determining, to a large extent, the status and material conditions of practitioners.

Consultants thus seem to have been prevented from sustaining a traditional professionalization project—or perhaps more importantly, they may have *opted out* as they did not need it. The success of these firms in validating knowledge through their standing in the market meant that they had little need for external professionalization institutions to validate their expertise, and there is some evidence that they actually inhibited the development of professional institutions (Gross & Kieser 2006). 'Consultants have been able to establish themselves as widely acknowledged and sufficiently trusted experts. They have done so without professionalisation in the traditional sense' (ibid: 92–3).

The apparent failure of professionalization in the area of business knowledge can also be understood in terms of the character and distribution of the expertise involved. Whilst the traditional professionalization strategy revolved around the possession of a systematised, abstract knowledge base, some have suggested that 'consulting knowledge is too elusive, fuzzy and perishable to sustain a traditional professionalisation project' (Muzio el al. 2011: 807).[9] More pertinently, the need for business knowledge to be implemented and prove useful for particular organizational clients perhaps limits the abstraction of knowledge (generic models have to be translated to meet particular client needs).[10] Change management knowledge thus revolves around a combination of generic and specific knowledge, of formal knowledge and practical experience (Kipping & Armbrüster 2000, Werr & Stjernberg 2003).[11] Rather than offering universal solutions, firms want to validate the particular utility of their specific approaches embodied in proprietary methodologies and a distinctive brand (Armbrüster 2006, Muzio et al. 2011). These paradoxical features of business knowledge worked against the professional model (Muzio et al. 2011).

These arguments would seem to have particular pertinence to the case currently under examination (e.g., the IT applications domain). Knowledge of this domain is extensive and heterogeneous, reflecting the variety both of technology solutions and of (sectoral and organizational) application contexts. As a result, it is hard to codify and generalise it into the kind of 'abstract knowledge base' that could be appropriated, deployed and certified by a traditional professional organization. This knowledge is moreover under constant, and arguably accelerating, change as a result of the dynamism of the IT solution markets and of the strategies of their organizational users. Abbott (2005: 254) sees this as a key factor in the 'failure of the "information profession" to emerge as a stable and effective actor in the ecology of professions, despite the massive importance of information work in the current economy. The blunt fact is that knowledge turns over too fast for a real information profession to emerge'. Rather different solutions to the circulation and validation of these kinds of knowledge may be called for.

4.5. HOW THIS RELATES TO THE MODEL OF INDUSTRY ANALYST EXPERTISE

These arguments also appear to apply to industry analysts. In particular, it seems that these analysts do not need professional associations to validate their knowledge. Instead, reputational indicators and above all the brand of the analyst organization becomes a key proxy for quality of expertise (the 'quality' of the staff the firm employs, the 'rigour' of the methodologies they deploy etc.). In this respect, analysts exhibit some similarities with management consultants. There is of course substantial overlap in the areas of expertise and experience deployed by analysts and IT consultants. Their career paths may intertwine. And industry analyst organizations may provide consultancy services, for example in advising technology adopters in the course of their technology procurement or advising a vendor on product development strategy.

Yet Gartner analysts will often go to great lengths to distinguish themselves from management consultants. Indeed, they portray these consultants as *consumers* of their research. Hence, Gartner analyst Paul Winter told us that the big consultancy firms 'are not competitors, they are clients . . . Most of the research that they [need,] they will get it from us' (interview, Winter). The core of Gartner's business is its research base. Gartner analysts also distinguish themselves from consultants based on their *independence*. Thus Gartner analyst Elias Thomas observes that the big consultants are dependent on securing particular contracts: 'They will say that we'll give you independent advice. And we will say no you won't. Because they have got to pay for a whole load of consultants to keep them busy. We are paid to give advice and we get very, very upset if that independence is questioned' (interview, Thomas).

Gartner analysts strenuously emphasise their independence. As we saw from the last chapter, protecting their reputation for independence profoundly shapes the methods used by analysts and the character of industry analyst expertise. The independence of large industry analyst firms such as Gartner Inc. is rooted in their large client base, and in particular on their subscription based services (e.g. for technical reports and advisory services) provided to large numbers of organizations: 'The largest of the firms work on a syndicated research basis. So they try and have 80% of their revenue coming from repeatable annuity based subscriptions that you buy access to' (interview, Mitchell).[12]

Despite some similarities with the big management consultancies in terms of the reputational role of corporate brand for example, the distinctive model of industry analyst expertise established by Gideon Gartner was rather different to the existing management consultancy firms. The expertise of Gartner analysts was not limited to the efficacy of their advice for particular clients, but also rested in their ability to produce a wide range of outputs that could exercise wider cognitive authority over entire technical fields. This book will give a number of examples of how they exercise this authority:

- Chapter 6 will show how this included for example identifying and giving a 'name' to emerging technical areas
- Chapter 7 will discuss how it is through the construction and defence of 'signature' tools such as the Magic Quadrant that marks Gartner out from all others
- Chapter 8 discusses how the 'charismatic' analyst on stage is able to capture, mobilise and organise sentiment surrounding new innovation

In naming a field, for instance, industry analysts are conducting a very specific form of work. They are, as one analyst described to us, 'drawing a starting line' that everyone else lines up behind (interview, Thomas). These kinds of naming interventions, in theory, could emerge from academics or could be attempted by vendors, individually or in collaboration. However, as Elias Thomas (Gartner VP Research) observed, vendors do not have 'the clout' to do that themselves—unless they are so large that they can control the entire market but that is apparently rare (interview, Thomas). This 'third party' role highlights ways in which Gartner's knowledge outputs exhibit some elements of a 'public good'. Though targeted towards the technology adopters, their assessments help shape emerging application markets, including both the procurement choices of adopters and vendors' development strategies. Industry analysts, though often controversial, are highly influential.

Given these potentially crucial consequences, and in particular the potentially immediate implications for the sales prospects of vendors, Gartner may need to be able to defend their claims. Here our research has drawn attention to the increasingly elaborate and formal methodologies Gartner Inc. requires its analysts to use in the production of key knowledge outputs like its Magic Quadrant, together with increasingly systematic internal regulation within Gartner of the production of these public outputs, which go through an internal 'peer review' process.

Gartner also developed elaborate mechanisms to maintain, and visibly demonstrate, corporate regulation of the quality and independence of research. Its methods of knowledge production and governance drew some elements from the scientific/technical model of expertise. Though resembling the procedures of conventional technical specialists or medical and scientific professionals, they also differ in some striking ways. For example, Gartner's think-tank culture and debates bear some resemblance to academic review systems. Gartner outputs are increasingly subject to internal quality control (e.g. through standardised methods and review by colleagues within the firm). However, review remains internal to the analyst organization; we do not find the external peer review or scrutiny by a certificating professional body that characterises traditional professional communities or underpins the verification of scientific knowledge. Analysts themselves drew our attention to these similarities with and differences to technical or scientific expertise. They describe their knowledge production as similar to science, involving a 'truth element', but different, as *pseudo-academic* rather than *scientific*. Whilst Gartner's presentations may emphasise the pursuit of truth, in their work industry analysts prefer a more nuanced account.[13]

4.5.1. The establishment of cognitive authority

We have found Turner's (2001) typology of experts particularly helpful in clarifying these differences, highlighting, as it does *the establishment of cognitive authority*—a question that is also at the heart of our enquiry. Turner notes: 'Expertise is a kind of possession, certified or uncertified, of knowledge that is testified to be efficacious and in which this testimony is widely accepted by the relevant audience' (ibid: 130). He further notes that studies of (professional or scientific) expertise have tended to focus on established expert groups such as physicists—groups which can draw on credibility already established amongst its wider as well as its more immediate audiences. They have *already* achieved 'legitimate cognitive authority' (ibid: 131); the efficacy of their knowledge base and methods are widely accepted. For such experts, which Turner calls 'Type I experts', recognition is a corporate achievement: '[T]his corporate authority has achieved a particular kind of legitimation, legitimation not only beyond the sect of physicists, but acceptance that is more or less universal' (ibid: 131). However, as he observes, this begs the key question: 'How did cognitive authorities establish their authority in the first place? And how do they sustain this?' (ibid: 130). 'Establishing cognitive authority to a general audience is not easy' (ibid: 130). In the case of physicists, it was major achievements 'like nuclear weapons . . . and new technology [that were] the coin of the realm' (ibid: 133).

Though the Sociology of Professions has tended to focus upon established experts, 'Type 1 experts' in Turner's typology), industry analysts exemplify a rather different kind of expertise, resembling most closely Turner's '3rd type' of expert—that need to create an audience for whom they are expert. These are 'groups and individuals who create their own following' (ibid: 145) because they have 'proven themselves to this audience by their actions' (ibid: 131).

Here Gartner in particular managed to establish cognitive authority over a number of strategic IT markets and especially enterprise systems solutions. Their cognitive authority is sustained not through the operation of a wider professional community (for example through external peer review of their knowledge outputs) but through the reputation associated with the Gartner brand. We have noted the emphasis within Gartner on internal quality control and visible warranties of Gartner's impartiality: quality control resides with the brand rather than a broader professional community. As James Governor CEO of the analyst organization Red Monk observed:

> analysts are not even professionals, not in the strict sense of the word that we sort of understand in this country at least. You are not a professional until you have done at least seven years of study. There is no equivalent of that in the analyst business. You can come from any background. And really in some sense an analyst business is just something that certifies people as able to be analysts (interview, Governor).

And what is at stake here differs subtly from the means by which scientific veracity is established through the acceptance of knowledge claims across a scientific community amongst whom there is broad consensus about the criteria and methods by which the quality and validity of knowledge can be assessed. As we will see in Chapter 8 the key test of Gartner's expertise is not the enduring truth of its knowledge claims but its *utility* value. That is, it is assessed based on its relevance for members of client organizations needing to make decisions. For Gartner these are primarily potential technology adopters seeking to assess different supplier claims and also vendors planning the development of their products.

4.6. NEW APPROACHES TO PROFESSIONALIZATION AND EXPERTISE: A THIRD WAVE OF ANALYSIS?

Questions arise about how relevant the conceptual frameworks from the Sociology of Professions are for management consultancy and other business knowledge experts, and for a range of other new expert occupations that are subject to very different sets of exigencies/forms of validation. We have already noted that the Sociology of Professions took as its starting point the classic historical professions of medicine, religion and law etc., which were seen to provide a template for analyzing the wider spread of professionalization (and also, arguably, a template for analysing the professionalization strategies of expert groups). These exemplars have unhelpfully skewed analysis of expertise and professional work. For example, one consequence of this identification with the traditional professions, distinguished from other expert occupations, has been to draw a gulf between professions and other specialist occupations (and their strategies to attain expert status) even though these share many common characteristics (Evetts 2006). Various writers, noting this, have argued that classical professionalization should be seen as just one strategy of occupational power (Fincham 2006, Muzio et al. 2011).

The undue focus of the Sociology of Professions on professional institutions and their role in establishing closure has, we argue, held back understanding of the evolving landscape of expert work. It is something of a paradox that the Sociology of Professions, with its focus on social control mechanisms (e.g. jurisdictional competition, closure and boundary work), has paid rather little attention to the actual *content* of professional work and the know-ledge(s) involved. As Turner notes (2001: 130) 'these literatures have generally ignored . . . the problem of the origin of authority' because they have largely directed attention to those groups that have *already* established a systematised, formalised and codified knowledge base and for which 'legitimate cognitive authority' has already been achieved (ibid: 131).

This critique has informed recent discussions both of new models of professionalization and of new frameworks for analyzing the emergence of these new kinds of expert labour.[14] A 'third wave' of analysts has argued for a shift of the focus of enquiry away from professional institutions towards:

i) detailed examination of expert work and the processes by which expert status is achieved (Anderson-Gough et al. 2006);[15] and,

ii) more concrete analyses of the particular contexts, actor configurations and contingencies surrounding expertise formation. These include 'the wider historical context of professions and the role of other key actors, such as the state, employing organisations and competing groups in shaping their development' (Muzio et al. 2011: 807) as well as the networks through which new professionals achieve and demonstrate professional competence (Anderson-Gough et al. 2006).[16]

Following a similar pragmatic turn,[17] Preda (2009), analyzing the emer-gence of a body of expert financial knowledge, insists that: '[a]n account of the constitutions of jurisdiction should start from the content of this expert knowledge and its generation' (ibid: 150).

Issues of how to validate expert knowledge also arise in the absence of the social structures of professionalization (i.e. with groups that have not yet achieved cognitive authority). Homologous considerations arise when we examine these other forms of expertise as have been found in relation to established (e.g. techno-scientific) expertise. Preda (ibid) for example studies the emergence of a body of expert financial knowledge in the absence of professional or quasi-professional structures in relation to these experts. He examines the twentieth century 'Chartists', who offered investment advice based on the 'technical analysis' of charts of movements in share and other prices. Preda's discussion of 'chartism as expert knowledge' (ibid: 153) draws, like ourselves, on the Sociology of Professions and the Sociology of Scientific Knowledge and is a particularly interesting template for us to consider.

Preda also turns to Turner's (2001) typology of experts in terms of their legitimacy with target audiences. Preda sees Chartists as belonging to the 3rd group in Turner's schema, i.e., those who have not yet established wide recognition. Chartists did not have an audience for their work; they had to go about actively creating it:

> users were configured as depending upon a body of specialized knowledge which they cannot obtain by themselves, and as needing experts in the interpretation of price movements . . . [and] unbiased judgment. At the same time the technological apparatuses on which this knowledge depends are represented as requiring special skills and powers of interpretation which brokers, being too busy, have not developed (Preda 2009: 163).[18]

Achieving expert status also required demonstration of the efficacy of that knowledge. That is, Chartists had to persuade 'brokers and investors alike that [this new knowledge] was indispensable' (ibid: 153). He points out two elements to this process: 'the successful persuasion of users that they need a special form of knowledge in their activities' (ibid: 152) and 'controlling the distribution of this expert knowledge and making it more difficult to access' (ibid: 162). Preda's historical study provides a rich account of how his Chartists were able to create their own following. For example by publishing papers and books, they created a 'tradition' that legitimated their activities. In addition, Preda notes as important their circulation of various tools and devices, such as stock price charts or ticker tape machines, which together constituted what Beunza & Stark (2004) call a distributed 'socio-material apparatus' that would reconfigure the work of stockbrokers.

As Preda foregrounds, this apparatus quickly became key for those employed in stock markets. He discusses how the 'price ticker' produced a constant flow of prices such that it reconstituted stockbrokers' practices:

> The ticker transformed the character of price data: a continuous flow of data replaced the rather unsystematic price lists. Trust was shifted from idiosyncratic knowledge of transaction partners to a machine which could travel across social contexts. New modes of attention and observation were introduced, which brought individuals together into price monitoring activities, in public places (2009: 25).

With the introduction of these technologies, the importance of the outputs of the Chartists became central. Preda (ibid) describes how those working in stock markets switched from observing markets to observing 'the tape'. We find this focus on how material objects help in creating a following useful and will explore it throughout the book. We have already mentioned the Hype-Cycle, but Gartner were able to extend their influence through the creation of an array of such devices. We will return to this point in our discussion of the Magic Quadrant in Chapter 7.

4.7. INDUSTRY ANALYSIS AS A NOVEL AND DISTINCTIVE FORM OF EXPERTISE

Writers from the second wave of the Sociology of Professions have empha-sized the choices that expert groups need to make in terms of how their knowledge is produced and applied (Mok 1971). Abbott (1988) notes how, in making these choices, groups may seek to draw upon culturally legitimated modes of practice, and, particularly over the last century, upon the scientific model. As Mok (1971: 109) observes, '[e]very profession's members are con-fronted with the necessity of choosing a role model'. Mok suggests that particular professions adopt and institutionalize distinctive combinations of *producing knowledge* and *applying knowledge* to solve the problems of a lay clientele, with an emphasis on the latter given the potential credibility and financial rewards of meeting client needs.

We have explored the strategic choices pursued in particular by Gideon Gartner that underpinned the emergence of this new category of expert. Though the methods of knowledge production employed by industry analysts embody some elements that resemble conventional technical specialisms, they also differ in some striking ways. Here our research has drawn attention to the increasingly elaborate and formal methods used by Gartner for the production of key knowledge outputs such as Magic Quadrants, together with increasingly systematic internal regulation of the production of these public outputs. Though methodologies may resemble the knowledge creation and governance systems of medical and scientific professionals, the analysts themselves, as we saw in earlier chapters, describe their knowledge production as *pseudo-academic* rather than *scientific*. For example, Gartner outputs are subject to internal quality control *within the firm* (e.g. through standardized methods and internal review) rather than external peer review that underpins the verification of scientific knowledge.

Thus our analysis of industry analysts sees these as exemplifying a different kind of expert to the established expert groups that Sociology of Professions has tended to focus on, i.e. those who have already achieved wide acceptance of their knowledge base and methods. Industry analysts instead resemble those

Figure 4.1. An Everest Group analyst attempts to build a following
Source: Author photo (NP)

characterized by Turner (2001) as needing to create an audience for whom they are expert. This exigency pervades much of their activities (see Figure 4.1). Here Gideon Gartner, in establishing the first industry analyst organization, set out to create a 'decision-support company'. Its staff, as we show, are encouraged to demonstrate the value of their knowledge outputs and advisory services in helping its customers (technology adopters, vendors, investors) make practical choices. This goal shapes the ways in which they produce and apply knowledge; rather than doing conventional (e.g. market) research, applying large scale quantitative techniques to capture existing trends, Gartner evolved tools and methods honed to detect changes in patterns. Knowledge outputs need to pass a 'so what?' test (see Chapter 8). Rather than producing long technical reports, new formats were developed (Chapter 7) that could convey findings rapidly, and could form the basis for advisory services.

4.8. ALTERNATIVE MODELS

As well as established models of technical expertise, we can see a variety of models that may contribute to the industry analyst role, most pertinently that of financial analysts, journalists and management consultants.

4.8.1. Financial analysts

Foremost here is the role of financial analyst. In thinking about the possibility of establishing a market for this novel form of expertise, Gideon Gartner drew perhaps most immediately on his ongoing experience and links in Wall Street. Rather paradoxically, this influence is not always commented on in discussion of the industry analyst role. However, these experiences, along with ideas about marketing, pervade Gartner's thinking and provided a taken-for-granted template. Thus, in considering how industry analysts would allocate their time between functions (and the scope to allocate their time more profitably through the '80–20 rule', discussed in Chapter 2), Gartner took as his starting point the rough breakdown of a 'Wall street analyst's' time. Likewise, Gartner's decision to employ 'senior industry people, who were in fact "peers" of their prospective clients' appears to have been taken from Wall Street practice.

Financial analysts, also known as investment, security or equity analysts, today comprise a relatively established group. The market for technology investment advice has been around for more than a century (Preda 2009). They have been subject to enquiry from a range of perspectives, including econometric studies of their effectiveness as well as more recent sociological explorations of how they were formed (ibid.) and how they operate. The econometric research has for example looked at the limited evidence of efficacy of financial advice (Cowles 1933), while noting a bias in their advice which tends to over-estimate growth possibilities and underestimate risks (Wansleben 2012). This failing has been attributed variously to their resort to imitating their peers (Rao et al. 2001); to their personal economic interests; and to analysts' experience that positive assessments not only reward accuracy of earnings forecasts but also enhance their promotion prospects (Hong & Kubik 2003).[19] The sociological work has provided important insights for our study, most notably studies which discuss ways in which (sell-side) security analysts, in producing forecasts of a firm's future earnings, develop calculative frames to assess how corporate performance is assessed.

Chapter 6 shows how industry analysts, in constructing the potent product categories through which the potential of companies are assessed, act in a manner akin to security analysts (Zuckerman 1999, Beunza & Garud 2007, Wansleben 2012). This together with related ideas from the Sociology of Finance contributes to a more generic understanding of how these forms of expertise operate as epistemic systems of knowledge production and consumption. Thus Knorr Cetina (2010) has observed how financial analysts draw not only on formal information but also on direct contacts and site visits (which she characterizes as 'mini-ethnographies') to 'see through' performance claims (ibid: 189). We also share Knorr Cetina's (2010, 2012) interest in exploring the temporality of the worlds to which analyst knowledge pertains. The financial analysts Knorr Cetina studied operate in a world of investment and speculation in which assessments of future stock values are perennially vulnerable to events.[20] In such contexts, she argues, 'truth takes second place to news and rumor' (Knorr Cetina 2010: 190). We return to this argument in Chapter 8, in which we question her view that the accuracy of a financial prediction 'seemingly does not matter all that much' (ibid: 182).

However, it is instructive to explore the different temporalities of knowledge and the worlds to which they belong. Knorr Cetina (2010) contrasts the constantly changing ground of financial analysis data with the stability of the worlds that are the subject of natural science which underpin the rather long-lived character of scientific theories and methods. Our industry analysts also are seeking to exercise mastery over domains that are constantly shifting as a result of changes in technology and business processes, and in particular seeking to exercise cognitive authority over ephemeral promising technology fields. This was one of the factors undermining the scope to codify industry analyst knowledge into a generic form that could be exploited in the way that classic professionalization strategies—as described above— have attempted. Our industry analysts perhaps represent a mid-point between natural science and financial analysis. We return to the (varying) temporal dynamics of knowledge in Chapter 11, our conclusions, where we discuss how this might inform a taxonomic understanding of the Sociology of Business Knowledge.

4.8.2. Journalists

Another model that may be pertinent to our enquiry is that of the journalist. Gartner's Ombudsman role, for example, was explicitly lifted from the media rather than public administration. Nancy Erskine, Gartner Ombudsman told us: 'we modelled ourselves initially on the news media and the kind of the voice of the reader, so to speak, more than Government or internal or HR oriented ombuds-people' (interview, Erskine).

Journalists as professionals deploy an occupational ideology that emphasizes 'integrity' and 'objectivity' (Aldridge & Evetts 2003). Though the latter term incorporates multiple meanings, the main claim advanced is that good journalism is the disinterested search for, and weighing of, evidence. The 'good journalist' provides balanced and transparent access to the best informed/ most authentic sources. There are some obvious parallels with the industry analyst role here. Indeed, as we have already noted, one of the precursors for industry analysis was the publication of technical and market reviews. The industry analyst expert as conceived by Gideon Gartner, perhaps like journalists, exploit a wide range of contacts in searching for information but also, more like traditional technical experts they i) deploy specialized techniques to bring this knowledge together in consistent ways and ii) possess the expertise needed to make complex judgements. In emphasizing their impartiality, several of the Gartner analysts we interviewed portrayed themselves as the *Which?* magazine for the sector (see Aldridge [1994] for a discussion of the *Which?* magazine). They also noted ways in which they were not like *Which?* Magazine, particularly in their response to clients' calls and personalized advice. Gartner's Elias Thomas argues that what distinguishes analysts from journalists is their 'focus and persistence': journalists will shift their attention according to what topics are hot and newsworthy; they will 'learn enough about it and then find a story, write a story . . . so they are constantly flitting around' (interview, Thomas). Gartner's critics make a rather different comparison, pointing out that whilst newspapers and other commercial media make money from advertising, 'not every entity [they] report on is a potential revenue source. Over at Gartner, however, every entity they report on is either a current or a potential revenue source' (Snapp 2013: 41–2).

4.8.3. Management consultants revisited

Another relevant example that we have already explored is management consultancy. Here the failure of management specialists to conform to the traditional professional model had been attributed by writers from the Sociology of Professions to the success of large firms deploying a broad range of requisite expertise and skills in managing interdisciplinary teams. The strong brand identities of these big consultancies provided both a proxy indicator of past performance and presumed guarantor of future performance (Abbott 1988; Muzio et al. 2011). The big firms did not need professional status (Gross & Kieser 2006). However, the distinctive model of industry analyst expertise established by Gideon Gartner was rather different from the existing management consultancy firms. Gartner resembles the big management consultancies in terms of the reputational role of corporate brand. However, Gartner analysts distinguish themselves from consultants. They portray consultants as consumers of their research, and in particular see them as dependent on particular consultancy contracts. Gartner analysts in contrast emphasize their independence which results from their large client base and in particular their subscription based services (e.g. for technical reports and advisory services) provided to large numbers of organizations.

The cognitive authority that Gartner sought and achieved was rooted not just in the efficacy of their advice for particular clients—but also in their ability to exercise authority over a whole technical field. Their pronouncements, though often controversial, are highly influential. Their assessments help shape both the procurement choices of adopters and the development strategies of vendors. Gartner also developed elaborate mechanisms to maintain, and visibly demonstrate, corporate regulation of the quality and independence of their research. And here we saw how they drew some elements from the scientific model of expertise (e.g. the appointment of an ombudsman, elaboration of formal methodologies and internal peer review of findings). But, as already mentioned, the analysts themselves describe their work as similar to but not the same as science: as *'pseudo-academic'* involving a *'truth element'*. We traced this back to the distinctive model of industry analyst expertise articulated by Gideon Gartner in the first decade of Gartner Inc.'s existence. This was in terms of the kinds of knowledge produced and the manner in which it is generated, validated and applied:

i) Gartner sought to offer value to its customers by being a 'decision-support' company; its outputs had to pass the 'so what' test. Methods like the 'Stalking Horse' seemed honed to help analysts detect early signals, patterns and shifts amongst their client network

ii) At the same time Gartner's assessments needed to be credible, independent and defensible, and we will show how in recent decades their production is subject to increasingly formalized methodologies and internal review

iii) Whereas some market research organizations instituted a detailed division of labour and skills (i.e. between lower grade data collection staff, statistical analysts and experts) Gartner wanted its analysts to combine advisory activities with research in the course of their engagements with technology vendors and users, and therefore appointed highly versatile expert staff.

4.9. CONCLUSIONS: THE CHALLENGE FOR THE SOCIOLOGY OF PROFESSIONS

It would appear that the role of industry analyst offering advisory services has drawn elements from a number of domains of practice, including conventional quantitative and market research, academic, science and medical professions as well as others including journalism, and perhaps crucially, investment analysis and marketing. The Sociology of Professions has provided an interesting conceptual framework for our enquiry. However, its early writings drew narrowly on traditional (medical, legal, scientific) examples and offered rather static analyses that focused upon social control mechanisms and jurisdictional conflicts. In the course of the chapter we have moved away from those approaches that paradoxically paid relatively little attention to the content of professional work and knowledge. Our analysis instead focuses in detail upon the content of expert knowledge and how it is generated (Preda 2009), and how it achieves cognitive authority (Turner 2001, Muzio et al. 2011) through an array of interactions amongst diverse actors (Anderson-Gough et al. 2006). The challenge now is to examine these detailed knowledge practices which includes throwing light on how their knowledge work takes place through and is shaped by interactions with a wide network of players.

Whilst industry analysts must tackle similar challenges to traditional technical expert groups, which includes the ways in which they organize and regulate their processes of knowledge production resemble, that indeed explicitly draw upon some elements of the established medical/scientific expertise model, they also differ in a number of important ways. In particular, it seems that industry analysts do not need professional associations to validate their knowledge. Instead, reputational indicators and above all the brand of the analyst organization becomes a key proxy for quality of expertise. In this respect, industry analysts exhibit some similarities with another, already well-established group deploying business knowledge: management consultants. However, again there are differences. Gartner's assessments may have crucial consequences for suppliers and adopters, and they need to be able to defend their claims. As a result, the knowledge outputs of Gartner analysts have become increasingly subject to standardized methodologies and to internal review mechanisms. These bear some resemblance to academic review systems. However, analysts described these mechanisms to us as *pseudo-academic*. Review remains internal to the analyst organization. We do not find the external peer review or scrutiny by a certificating professional body that characterizes traditional professional communities. The importance attached by Gartner to the quality and independence of their assessments is also reflected in their recent appointment of an Ombudsman. What all this suggests is that the category of industry analyst is neither uniform nor static. In forthcoming chapters we will examine these processes empirically though our detailed qualitative interviews with a range of industry analysts as well as exploring other sources such as public and on-line where the knowledge practices of these experts are extensively discussed.

NOTES

1. Though these discourses often counterpose professionalism to competitive economic and political systems, this may be misleading. Freidson's (1994) classic early work portrays professionalism as the 'Third Logic' alongside market and bureaucracy. Likewise Dingwall (2008: 2) reminds us that Parsons departs from Weber's emphasis on the growth of rationality to counter economic self-interest. Rather than counterposing self-interest and altruism he observes that both are

interpenetrated, and that the capitalist economy and the professions/the rational socio-legal order they point to are both historical products of modern society.

2. As we alluded to in Chapter 1 there was an attempt to establish professional structures for industry analysts but this was opposed by Gartner, as described by an informant (interview, Collins). Why would Gartner 'allow it' he asked. 'A professional body is actually a . . . restricting mechanism. I think they [Gartner] are probably quite happy to make their own decisions as opposed to feel incumbent on other people for a code of conduct or whatever' (interview, Collins). Though as we will see in Chapter 10, the emerging community of 'analyst relations' specialists who advise vendors on how to engage industry analysts have sought to professionalise their role.

3. As Fournier (2000) notes, various writers emphasise how these forces may serve to undermine the professional model. 'Although the logics of bureaucracy and of the market are supposed to operate through different mechanisms—i.e. through the codification of professional knowledge for the former, and through direct attacks on professional monopolies for the latter—both have been declared to be fateful for the professions' (Fournier 2000: 68).

4. There has of course been an important shift over time in the character of professions including not least the medical profession. When theories of profession first emerged, medics were independent practitioners, perhaps part of private partnerships or employees of small enterprises. This model continues in general practice in the UK and elsewhere but has disappeared from hospital medicine which is provided by large public or private organisations. Today's professionals are often employees. Some provide services as labour only sub-contractors (e.g. change management or technology implementation consultants). More generally they are employed by larger service organisations or as specialist functions providing those services to larger organisations.

5. Brante (1988) makes the telling observation that, though this 'neoWeberian' perspective inverts the traditional functionalist model, both templates effectively reproduce the professional ideology of expert groups. Professional activities are not (allegedly) governed by self-interest, but by a body of objective and scientific knowledge which is used to inform decisions and intervention carried out for the public good (Fournier 2000: 76).

6. Consultancies develop mechanisms for circulating formal knowledge and experience. Larger ones have formal knowledge sharing technologies as well as complex a division of labour that rotates junior and mid-career staff through projects (Kipping & Armbrüster 2000).

7. Abbott (1988: 154) observes: 'Professionalisation—in the sense of creating a coherent occupational group with some control of an abstract expertise—is not impossible within workplaces made up of multi-professional bureaucracies . . . But the internal structure of a profession successful under such conditions differs strongly from that of a profession successful under the earlier arrangements of audiences for professional claims. Such professions are more inclusive than medicine and law . . . They are much less committed to rigid definition of jurisdiction or membership, since they must be flexible enough to move in directions that enable organisational survival'.

8. Various writers point to the role of the state in licensing many traditional professions and in requiring expert credentials/membership of professional bodies for those undertaking certain kinds of professional work. Such credentialism has underpinned the extension of the professional model that we have just noted into health, education, welfare and social services. It has not, however, been a feature of the new professionals in areas of business and information systems— though there have been attempts in some countries (e.g. Germany) to require certification of business consultants (Gross & Kieser 2006). Intriguingly financial/ securities analysts have been regulated, notably by the US Securities and Exchange Commission established in 1935 after financial crises were attributed to unrealistic over-valuation of stocks (Wansleben 2012). The requirement for certification of 'sell-side' analysts, who in the US must be members of the Institute of Certified Financial Analysts, has underpinned some elements of professionalisation in the field. Industry analysts, management consultants and other domains of business knowledge have remained a matter for the market to resolve.

9. We agree with Muzio et al. (2011) that it is unhelpful to propose a functionalist relationship here but instead seek to explicate the close interplay between organisational processes and knowledge generation/distribution processes.

10. And as we see shortly, especially Chapter 8, Gartner specifically seeks to generate knowledge that 'makes a difference' for its target audiences.

11. Werr and Stjernberg (2003: 884) note that management consultancy, as a knowledge system, involves a distinctive combination of theoretical and practical knowledge: 'knowledge as practice [is] generated, maintained and accumulated through action in a specific context'. It is 'tightly linked to a specific context and person'. Its 'accumulation is dependent on individual actors [and the] continual development of shared understandings among a group of actors sharing a practice'. Kipping and Armbrüster (2000) similarly highlight the tension that therefore arises between circulation and implementation of managerial knowledge.

12. Mitchell (Ovum) describes how: 'it is that recurring revenue that gives you the predictability and robustness of the business. Some of the smaller firms work on almost a consulting model, so they produce some IP, but their business model is essentially I'll do a speaking engagement there or a small project there, so economically they will look like consultancies' (interview, Mitchell).

13. Thus Gartner analyst Andrew White asks: 'Is it really possible to achieve a single version of truth?' Gartner Blog Network (20 February 2014). White observes that users look to them for 'truth'. Industry analysts who might be more comfortable with a formulation of 'a commonly agreed and accepted set of truths that operate as a foundation, on which we will each derive our own, interpreted contextually centric views' find this not to be a very marketable phrase, so we all tend to use 'single version of the truth'. Source http://blogs.gartner.com/andrew_white/2014/02/20/is-it-really-possible-to-achieve-a-single-version-of-truth/. Accessed 21 October 2014.

14. Various writers note that traditional sociological concepts are not capable of comprehensively explaining the expert status of such 'new professions' such as management consultants (Gross & Kieser 2006: 92–3). One response has been to 'modify theories of professionalisation so that they effectively come to grips with changes in expert work that have occurred in recent times' (ibid: 93).

15. From this perspective, professionals are those who are more proficient than other members of their occupation. The discourse of professionalism operates both as an occupational ideology and as a disciplinary mechanism (Gross & Kieser 2006, Evetts 2006). Evetts (2006) contrasts organisational professionalism—a managerial discourse of control based on standardization and performance review—with occupational professionalism discourse conducted within professional groups that involves discretionary decision-making in complex cases; occupational control of work; trust by clients and employers. This framework, though interesting, offers a somewhat simplistic, disembodied view of the performativity of discourses; and paradoxically reproduces a rather traditional view of professions.

16. Abbott has recently (2005) redeveloped his framework in ways that pave the way for such an examination of how professionalisation emerges as part of a system of 'linked ecologies', an idea that we find useful and which we will return to discuss more fully in Chapter 10.

17. Thus Mennicken (2010), in talking about professionalisation in an accounting context, argues [folio p7] 'that we need to redirect attention away from questions of professional association, towards instruments and activities of internationalisation and micro-differentiation to recognise the diverse ways in which audit expertise is organised, staged and legitimised'.

18. Preda analyses the Chartists' ability to collect and process voluminous data carefully. However, 'establishing expert status was not just a question of establishing control over arcane knowledge...this expert discourse claimed an epistemic monopoly over the observational apparatus and declared the validity of user judgment to be contingent on their services' (Preda 2009: 163). A paradox arises here because expertise is believed to be effective, but is not completely accessible to outsiders. As Turner (2001) notes 'it is the character of expertise that only other experts may be persuaded by argument of the truth of the claims of the expert' (Turner 2001: 129).

19. Gartner has similarly been criticised for a generic bias towards IT solutions and a specific bias (rooted in its complex procedures for engaging vendors) towards larger vendors (Snapp 2013).

20. Knorr Cetina (2010: 180) notes that '[i]nvestment and speculation thus involve what we may call time transactions, in which expected future outcomes determine present decisions, and the future begins to matter as a series of potential events that may affect this outcome and one's present financial position...As a result...reality becomes 'news'-indexed...[analysts] continually adjust expected future outcomes and current moves to reflect the new information. A time transaction, then, is not concluded in the present. It involves a moving horizon of things that may matter for the financial positions one holds'.

5

The Business of Technology Expectations

In this chapter we continue to build our initial understanding of industry analysts through conceptualizing them as 'promissory organizations' that produce future-oriented research. We draw particularly on the literature from the Sociology of Expectations and discussions concerning the 'constitutive' nature of expectations. We investigate the various forms of promissory work conducted by industry analysts and different forms of accountability attached to this work. We begin to map out a basic *typology* to characterize this promissory work according to differences in kind and effect. This does not yet represent a complete or systematic typology; it is instead an initial attempt to investigate the potential for an empirically grounded characterization of the different 'kinds' of expectations produced, their variability in 'effect', and the way in which they are subject to different 'webs of accountability' or 'validation regime'. We see this as the opening stage of what will become a much more complex characterization that we will develop as we progress through the various chapters of the book. We show how the Sociology of Expectations provides a useful set of concepts for articulating the dynamics and differences surrounding product-based expectations. But the approach also has some weaknesses. We thus supplement our understanding with recent developments in Economic Sociology and the Sociology of Finance where a theoretical framework is unfolding in relation to the 'performativity of theory'.

By tracing the work of 'promise builders' in the emergence of specific artefacts and innovation fields, the Sociology of Expectations has demonstrated how technological expectations influence the development of new artefacts and knowledge (van Lente 1993, Swanson & Ramiller 1997, van Lente & Rip 1998, Brown et al. 2000). The focus has typically been on 'innovation players' whose hopes and efforts are invested in the success of new technologies. However, as we demonstrate here, in recent years we have seen the growth of entire organizations dedicating themselves to the production, distribution and sale of future-oriented knowledge and tools (Firth & Swanson 2005, Burks 2006). Intermediaries such as 'industry analysts' draw up signposts about the state of the industry and its future development, and set criteria for assessing new innovations. Such assessments are often critically oriented towards vendors and their offerings, and turn out to fulfil a crucial role in shaping the development of technological fields and constituting markets for constantly changing supplier offerings. Scholars have yet to consider how technological fields may be shaped through interventions by these and similar types of market actors. What influence does the emergence of intermediaries such as industry analysts, specializing in the business of technological expectations, have on the development of new technologies?

Our general aim is to throw light on the important function played by these specialist players for mobilizing promises and expectations in supplier and user communities. In this chapter we analyse these actors as 'promissory organizations' to capture the predictive element of their work (e.g. how they systematically *mobilize* promises about new technologies) but also the wider evaluative, often critical, role they play (e.g. how they play a sustained role in the *organization* of the promissory space). Promissory organizations are defined as intermediaries, which are prodigious in the production of future-oriented research that not only represents the state of affairs in a particular marketplace but also contributes to shaping such markets. Our specific aim is to understand the extent to which their advice is 'performative'—suggesting that technological visions mobilized in the building of technological fields do not simply describe future technologies but also help to bring them into being (van Lente 1993, Brown et al. 2000, Michael 2000).

Industry analysts appear to be an ideal group to test and develop the emerging performativity thesis in that they exhibit complicated and highly uneven forms of influence. Current work on the performative nature of technological expectations is thought-provoking. However, we argue that, in the absence of tools for assessing whether and how particular promises will or will not be achieved, there is a risk of simply projecting outcomes forward from current expectations. This work needs to be strengthened through the addition of further analytical templates for tracking promissory work with respect to the differing ways it may generate and configure innovation and thus sustain and meet expectations. Thus to fully unpack the work of industry analysts we also draw on recent discussions of the 'performativity of theory' emanating from Economic Sociology (Callon 1998, 2007) and the Sociology of Finance (MacKenzie 2006, 2009), which include the basis of a framework for conceptualizing strong and also weak forms of influence, as well as successful and failing forms of knowledge. Inspired also by the argument that the nature, character and effect of promise-based assessments are best understood comparatively (cf. Borup et al. 2006), we begin to derive from our fieldwork a *typology of promissory work* that characterizes differences between various kinds of promissory behaviour.

5.1. SOCIOLOGY OF EXPECTATIONS

Scholars acknowledge how expectations are crucial to the development and shaping of new science and technology. Borup et al. (2006: 285–6) argue that innovation rarely '...can work in isolation from a highly dynamic and variegated body of future-oriented understanding about the future'. Promises are seen to be 'fundamentally generative' in the production of artefacts and knowledge. Expectations can help innovators mobilize support and funding for emerging artefacts. van Lente (1993: 187) developed the nostrum: 'by sketching a future, others will find reasons to participate' to characterize how expectations grab and direct the attention of actors. Stewart (1999) coined the homologous term 'poles of attraction' to explore how innovative firms (IT vendors) firms seek to mark out their plans and visions of future technology with various identifiable purposes. These purposes include mobilizing the expectations of potential customers and thereby building confidence in, and winning commitments to, an emerging technology, and, at times, warding off competitors, mobilizing 'fear, uncertainty and doubt' and thus frustrating a competing technology. Not only do expectations help enrol external actors (or ward off competitors) they are also seen to guide and shape the activities of technology development teams. They do so, as van Lente (1993) argues, by providing structure and legitimation to an inherently uncertain activity. Working within the field of Information Systems, as already noted, Swanson and Ramiller (1997) have highlighted the role of 'organizing visions' in information systems innovation, encompassing interpretation, legitimation and mobilization, all of which help to mobilize the material and intellectual resources needed for innovation. Such visions help build consensus about what to expect and about the nature of the various opportunities and risks that may lie ahead (Borup et al. 2006: 285).

Scholars have focused on the often 'hyperbolical' nature of expectations. Gregory, for instance, has developed the concept of 'incomplete utopian project' to describe the 'phenomenon of envisioning as constructed, evoked, and employed within an innovative intra- and inter-organizational effort, and to open up theorizing about innovation, work practices, and technology' (Gregory 2000: 180). The word 'utopian' draws attention to the influence of 'longstanding deeply shared desires simultaneously characterized by their unrealizability and their devotees' tendencies to over-reach reality in their pursuit' (Gregory 2000: 194). It has been suggested—though we are not sure how this can be measured—that expectations are becoming *more* unrealistic and levels of hype are *increasing*. Borup and colleagues (2006: 286) write that 'hyperbolic expectations of future promise and potential have become more significant or intense in late and advanced industrial modernity. This shift in intensity is probably connected with a number of tendencies in the contemporary character of science and technology'. These tendencies include but are not limited to the fact that 'processes of science and technology innovation have become more complex, with a significant increase in the amount of communication and interaction across institutions and epistemic borders' (Ibid. 2006: 287).

Challenges arising from the growing technical and organizational complexity of innovations, which drawing upon increasingly extensive arrays of formal and informal knowledge that may be dispersed across many occupations and organizations, are aggravated by the accelerating pace of innovation. Actors thus seek competitive advantage by improving the efficiency of communication between producers of complementary products and with the 'market' constituted by intermediate and final consumers (Howells 2006, Stewart & Hyysalo 2008). We see the emergence of active strategies to grapple with and manage complexity and uncertainty as well as attempts to improve the pace and efficiency of learning rather than simply 'waiting and seeing' whether an innovation succeeds through trial and error. There is, as a result, greater competition between expectations, meaning that more attention is placed on future knowledge and its coordination. Added to this, or perhaps because of this, new kinds of activities (road mapping, standardization, public policies, envisioning, etc.) and actors (industry watch bodies, consultants, academics and of course industry analysts) are emerging, designed to better regulate and systemize that competition between ideas. Consequently (and perhaps this is what Borup et al. [2006] refer to), expectation-building activity has been significantly augmented and has become increasingly proactive and oriented towards longer-term futures. However, we would argue that what is most interesting about these forms of expectation is not their imputed hyperbolic character but the fact that they are coordinated in a more organized way. For example Bakker et al. (2011) highlight the interaction between 'enactors' of particular technological variations and 'selectors', constituting 'arenas of expectations' around promising technology fields.

5.1.1. Accountability

There is an important body of research suggesting that the articulation of expectations and 'hype' about new technologies requires serious analysis, as they constitute an important medium for shaping innovation. The reason expectations are often overly optimistic, say Geels and Smit (2000: 882) is '... *not* that forecasters or futurists are ignorant or short sighted', but rather that '[i]nitial promises are set high in order to attract attention from (financial) sponsors, to stimulate agenda-setting processes (both technical and political) and to build "protected spaces"'. Brown (2003) provides a note of caution, arguing that '[i]n so many cases, the present fails to measure up to the expectations once held of it. This can have disastrous consequences for the reputations not only of individuals but entire innovation fields' (Brown 2003: 9). Along similar lines, Borup and colleagues (2006: 289) suggest that unrealisable expectations may damage credibility because, by making such promises, actors can potentially be 'held to future account'. Intuitively we feel this is right but think scholars could also be more nuanced here. It is unlikely that all expectations are accountable in the same way. Longer-term predictions, for instance, may project too far into the future and be couched in too many techno-scientific uncertainties for any group to be held responsible for their non-materialization. Conversely, there may be other shorter-term assessments that subject such predictions to more stringent scrutiny (and possibly sanction). Moreover, if it is true that expectations are subject to different forms of accountability, this begs the question of whether they also exercise different forms of 'influence'. This takes us to the topic of performativity.

5.1.2. Self-fulfilling prophecy

The notion that promises are 'performative' or even 'constitutive' of phenomena is a fruitful line of enquiry (van Lente 1993, Michael 2000, Borup et al. 2006) but also one that needs to be strengthened with the addition of new theoretical templates and further empirical work. The clearest example of how the notion of performativity has been applied in this context is the history of the microchip. In the 1960s, G. E. Moore predicted that the microchip would continue to increase exponentially in complexity and processing power. 'Moore's law', as it has become known, was widely judged to have been a successful prediction. Its success has been explained on the grounds that it was a 'self-fulfilling prophecy':

> This prediction turned out to hold so well that we may speak of a self-fulfilling prophecy. The fulfilling did not occur because it was a prophecy, but because actors have taken up the prophecy, and acted accordingly. The provided the reasons for other actors to accept the expectation and act accordingly, etcetera (van Lente 1993: 87).

It has become something of a commonplace within the Sociology of Expectations to analyse the role of expectations through a version of Merton's (1948) 'self-fulfilling prophecy' concept. Interestingly, as already mentioned, industry analysts themselves regularly mobilize a vernacular version of the self-fulfilling argument when accounting for their own influence (Hind 2004). How might we develop our understanding of this concept and thus throw new light on this area? The notion, as Merton originally formulated it, works on the idea that if an authoritative enough actor makes known its beliefs, and if these beliefs are taken up by others, then what was once simply an assumption held by this actor has a good chance of becoming a 'fact'. In other words, because industrialists and technologists were convinced by Moore's claim that increases in the density of circuitry on microchips would be persistent, they acted as if it was true and continued to fund research into the further miniaturization of this technology. The prediction was thus brought into being (see also MacKenzie [1996], who offers a similar view on the history of the microchip). Importantly, neither van Lente nor MacKenzie suggest that technologies are a simple or direct *product* of promissory work. This contrasts with some of the recent work from the Sociology of Expectations, which presents a rather linear or causal view of predictions. For instance, Borup et al. (2006: 286) write that expectations are both the 'cause and consequence of material scientific and technological activity'.[1]

However, the idea of a self-fulfilling prophecy is problematic because it hangs on the notion of 'beliefs'. The key aspect of Merton's argument was that the initial assumption does not have to be correct. It is enough that it is taken up and believed by sufficient people for it to become correct. The most problematic aspect of the notion of a self-fulfilling prophecy is that it invites the interpretation that *any* belief or vision, if handled and communicated by an adequate number of trusted actors, could become true. This is presumably the case for the most robust or insubstantial of facts or rumours: it is simply enough that people take-up a statement. Because the belief is widely shared by others then it makes little difference if the statement is well-informed or arbitrary; because it is believed by everyone the world comes to resemble it (MacKenzie 2006, Callon 2007). This interpretation, whilst widely held, is found wanting because it does not deal adequately with the 'content' of expectations or the work involved in their 'production' and 'validation'.

What is at stake when we ignore the content and production of expectations is that i) it presumes that the prospects of particular promises are independent of the extent to which they are underpinned by a knowledge base and ii) it ignores how the success of promises depends upon their insertion into a particular arena and the interactions that take place around them. Thus the formulation might allow for the reading that Gartner could literally throw darts at a chart when constructing its Magic Quadrant ranking and it would seemingly make little difference because as long as enough people were made to align with the view in the graph, it would become true nonetheless.

Practitioners and academics alike have depicted this form of business knowledge in such a way. For instance, one of the concepts advanced to capture the presumably unsubstantiated status of these kinds of knowledge claims is Rip's seminal work on 'folk theories'. Folk theories, he writes ' . . . are a form of expectations, based in some experience, but not necessarily systematically checked. Their robustness derives from their being generally accepted, and thus part of a repertoire current in a group or in our culture more generally' (Rip 2006: 349). Indeed, in one of the few papers we have come across on Gartner's work, Rip describes the Gartner 'Hype-Cycle' as an example of a folk theory. He notes that whilst it is highly influential it does not necessarily result from sustained forms of research:

> Introduced by the Gartner Group as the Hype-Cycle for information and communication technologies, it has become a folk-theory par excellence, because it is widely recognized, used to draw out implications, and *not an object of systematic research*. The visualization provided by the Gartner Group is widely referred to, and copied on websites . . . It shapes thinking about further developments and possible responses (ibid: 352–3, *emphasis added*).

As we see it, there is a problem with the notion of a folk theory when applied to the work of industry analysts. It places undue emphasis on the acceptance of this knowledge as opposed to its production. This lends weight to the idea that these tools could be more or less arbitrary and that they become influential primarily because of their diffusion. The other problem with the concept is that it is also indifferent to the fact there are various levels of work involved in the construction of folk theories. Our fieldwork tells us something different. Gartner's knowledge and its associated knowledge production processes are more developed and nuanced than is sometimes presented by its critics. The aim of this and subsequent chapters will be to assess the potential for an empirically grounded characterization of how industry analysts go about producing (and also managing the reception of) their outputs.

More generally we argue that scholars need to be more precise when talking about expectations. We need to say something about the various effects expectations might have (be they strong, weak or even 'temporary' forms of influence). Not all expectations influence technologies in the same way. Why is this? Current templates do not give us the ability to differentiate between 'successful' and 'failed' claims, except perhaps through hindsight (Geels 2007). This suggests that we need to reflect more carefully on the causal nature of expectations so as to be able to say something about their differential robustness and outcomes as well as to acknowledge the forms of work involved in their production. This also, we will argue below, involves addressing the broader set of relationships surrounding the production, distribution and consumption of these knowledge outputs.

5.1.3. New insights into performativity

Some of these issues have been discussed within recent scholarship in Economic Sociology and the Sociology of Finance. Two strands in particular might help us conceptualize more fully the market for expectations. In his work on financial markets, for instance, MacKenzie (2006: 16–18) investigates the influence of the Black-Scholes-Merton model on the derivatives market and develops a typology of different types of performativity. According to MacKenzie, some theories when applied have little or no observable effect on a setting, which he describes as 'generic' forms of performativity. Others 'make a difference' in some way when applied, which he deems 'effective performativity'. Still others bring about the 'states of affairs' for which they are good 'empirical descriptions', which he describes—after the Sociologist of Science Barry Barnes—as 'Barnesian performativity', similar to the notion of self-fulfilling prophecy. Finally, some theories change economic processes so that they conform *less* well to their depiction by theories, which he describes as 'counter-performativity'.

The second set of ideas is Callon's (1998, 2007) attempt to recast the success of economic theory as arising from a process of 'world making'. He describes how theories emanating from the academy are 'indexical', meaning that they can only be understood with reference to particular circumstances, time and space. If these theories are to have influence they must create the context or, to use the term he prefers, 'world' to which they point. Successful theories are those able to create some form of 'material reality' or 'obligatory point of passage' that others are then forced to take into account. Those unable to mobilize their world will fail. Importantly, this formulation draws explicitly on the idea from Actor Network Theory that agency is configured within a network of both human and non-human actors. To reflect this, Callon (2007) describes the theories and the world they create as a *socio-technical agencement*, the latter term depicting a heterogeneous collection of material and technical elements that act on and adjust each other (as discussed in Chapter 1).

These ideas can be applied productively to the discussion of industry analysts. We find MacKenzie's typology useful as it provides for more precision when talking about the differential outcomes promissory work might have. Whilst not directly adopting his terminology, it is a practical inspiration for the *typology of promissory behaviour* developed below. Callon's conceptualization is valuable because it enables us to begin to discuss the forms of work involved in the production of expectations, which includes identifying their success and failure: that is, how certain kinds of promissory activities become obligatory points of passage (or not) for those working within technological fields.

5.2. MARKET FOR TECHNOLOGICAL EXPECTATIONS

As we have already shown, the market for future oriented knowledge claims is a relatively recent phenomenon. It was only in the 1980s, for instance, that a few of the large management consultancy organizations began to collate and sell information about the new kinds of IT available. This was followed in the 1990s by the growth in popularity of specialist commercial research firms, which gathered and traded information on vendors (Firth & Swanson 2005). By the end of the twentieth century, however, a new, influential class of knowledge producer developed and proliferated, heralding a much more elaborate system of consultancy and advice that attempts to subject vendor statements about new offerings to a more systemized and formalized evaluation. These firms anticipate the evolution of new technical fields and of the business contexts that patterns their use and utility. Their work includes articulating and mobilizing support for generic technological visions (with some industry analysts aligning themselves with specific vendor visions). However, and importantly, a large number of these analysts try to subject the promissory work of specific innovation players to a certain level of scrutiny and accountability. Their work does not aim to generate specific promises, but to circulate different promises and expectations mobilized by others. It includes the production of expectations based on—and often critically oriented to—assessments about vendors and their offerings.

5.2.1. What are promissory organizations?

We introduce the notion of a 'promissory organization' to the discussion of expectations because we think there is a lacuna in existing understandings of the market for future-oriented knowledge claims, and also because it allows us to make sense of the key roles certain intermediaries play within marketplaces. This notion highlights how particular firms such as industry analysts both articulate generic visions of the evolution of a technical field and subject the promissory work of innovators to scrutiny. We define a promissory organization as an intermediary that routinely and continuously produces future-oriented knowledge claims. We suggest that these intermediaries do not simply reflect or represent the state of affairs in a particular marketplace, but actively contribute to its shaping. Industry analysts operating within the IT sector are the example focused on here, but further illustrations can be found in other domains, particularly those dogged by high levels of uncertainty and change (the life sciences [Tutton 2011, Morrison & Cornips 2012], energy [McDowall 2012], health and environmental domains, and so on).

Promissory organizations have numerous interesting characteristics for studies of technological expectations. Latour (1987) has written that the modern scientific laboratory gains its strength as a place where diverse instruments are gathered together. Promissory organizations create themselves as centres of power by building a wide and varied range of expectations and assembling the organizational machinery for disseminating them. This includes mechanisms and networks for developing and communicating 'successful' claims, but also those needed for dealing with more contentious, problematic and 'failing' knowledge.

One of the most interesting things about industry analysts is that they produce enormous amounts of research. Many of the larger firms make dozens of claims daily about a vast range of innovations. An internal Gartner document entitled 'Analyst Performance Measures: Activity & Impact' states how in terms of 'research written' each individual analyst is expected to write '20–40' research notes and to answer between '250–750' client inquiries per year (Jeff Golterman, Gartner analyst, presentation to the IIAR, March 2011). Gartner is not alone in this kind of productivity. A commentator on industry analysts writes, 'Each week, the top analyst firms will publish three or four hundred research reports' (Chapple 2007). Even the smaller firms are apparently 'maxed out': 'We have got someone inside the company who chivvies us all on to write more blog articles and so on and so forth. I think most weeks most of us write 2 or 3 articles in a day, and then to come up with a blog post' (interview, Collins). This is a lot of output by anyone's standards! This begs the question as to how such large volumes of 'envisioning' are sustained. Moreover, while it is commonplace to conceive of their assessments as products of individual analysts, the empirical material reported here shows that they result from a dense array of distributed, more or less observable processes and interactions. In what follows we discuss three examples of promissory work produced by Gartner, but before doing so we provide some detail on how we conducted this part of our study.

This chapter presents three 'vignettes'. The first episode introduced us to the influence of Gartner when one of us was conducting participant observation research on the procurement of an IT system at a local government office in England. At that time, for almost a year, we viewed Gartner's influence from the point of view of their consumers. As the procurement team debated the pros and cons of various solutions, we were able to observe (and collect material on) the influence of Gartner's recommendations and research. The second episode occurred a few years later, when we came across Gartner's influence while conducting another study on the design of large packaged software systems. At that time, we were able to observe how Gartner sought to construct one of its research documents (the Magic Quadrant). The final episode arose from our choice to attend international IT conferences and venues where we knew Gartner would be present, in order to observe Gartner's interactions with other participants.

5.3. INFRASTRUCTURAL KNOWLEDGE: PROMISSORY-WORK MADE DURABLE

The first vignette relates to how Gartner *classify* new types of developing technologies. STS scholars have shown classifications to be powerful because they can reinforce or create certain 'world views' (Timmermans & Berg 1997, Bowker & Star 1999, Berg & Timmermans 2000). We see classification as a powerful way for industry analysts to shape innovation; they name technologies in a way that anticipates their trajectory of development, the particular form and functionality technologies will take and categorizes the players who will enter the market, and so on. Technological classifications are similar to the 'organizing visions' identified by Swanson & Ramiller (1997), in the sense that they are subject to varying levels of support and momentum. When classifications are successful, as STS writers have noted, they often become something of an 'infrastructure' (e.g., a resource that fades into the background and only becomes visible upon break down [Bowker & Star 1999]). This kind of 'knowledge infrastructure' is a key theme in the book. We argue that industry analyst firms create a knowledge infrastructure that allows IT markets to operate. This point about infrastructure is also a further reason why the notion of self-fulfilling prophecy is found wanting when applied to expectations. Whilst 'beliefs' about a vendor or the potential of a new technology are important, there are alternative forms of influence that shape markets in ways that few outside these firms ever get to see. In particular, this is that the infrastructures developed by these firms have effects way beyond individual beliefs about them (MacKenzie 2006). We encountered such infrastructural knowledge when observing Gartner's influence in our ethnographic study of the procurement of a complex information system by a local authority.

5.3.1. New category of 'CRM'

'Melchester Council' (a pseudonym) was choosing a Customer Relationship Management system (CRM) system as part of its e-government agenda. This system is now a required feature of organizational landscapes, but when the fieldwork was being conducted there was uncertainty about its necessity and design. The procurement was a protracted affair and to speed things up Melchester engaged the services of Gartner to provide 'background' information on the suitability of one particular vendor. 'NewVendor' (a pseudonym) had done particularly well with its sales pitch and had the support of various staff from within the Council. However, some issues still needed to be resolved. The most pressing was that no one from Melchester had previously 'heard' of NewVendor, and this lack of knowledge was causing uncertainty within the procurement team. There were fears about committing such an important project to an 'unknown quantity'. One apparently easy way to settle the matter was to 'ask' Gartner for information about NewVendor. A Melchester IT manager (Ron) duly telephoned Gartner but was surprised to be told by an analyst specializing in CRM that he could not provide a formal vendor rating on NewVendor because no one in Gartner had *heard of them either*! This analyst said he would cross check with colleagues and call back, which he did so a few days later, but only to report how NewVendor were also unknown to wider Gartner colleagues. The IT manager circulated a note of the telephone conversation amongst the procurement team about how Gartner could 'not provide any research papers on the company or its products' (IT Manager's circulated notes). Some days later the particular Gartner analyst wrote to the Council summarizing the telephone conversations and drew the following conclusions:

> As a follow-on call we checked with two different CRM analysts in the U.S. Both belong to the call centre team and neither had heard of [NewVendor]. They take about 400–500 calls from clients per year. One focuses on call centre applications and the other on call centre infrastructure . . . The Bottom Line is that . . . we do not believe the [NewVendor] proposal is necessarily in the best interests of [Melchester] (letter from Gartner to Melchester).

What we see here is that Gartner cast doubt on NewVendor, going as far as to suggest that Melchester should *reject* this vendor. The episode did not finish there, but took an interesting turn when NewVendor, informed of Gartner's opinion, attempted to play down its significance by suggesting that the problem resulted from a 'categorization' difficulty. According to NewVendor the problem was not with them and the fact they were unknown but with Gartner's *classification* of the CRM market. Apparently, this was not broad or flexible enough to include the kind of innovative services NewVendor offered. To provide evidence of this they sent to the Council a detailed description of how their 'integrated framework approach' offering differed from the more conventional kind of CRM. Gartner responded by pointing out how a number of other more established CRM providers *already* offered the kind of innovation described. What then followed, however, was a complex and lengthy discussion between Gartner and NewVendor about the nature of CRM and the classification process (described in more detail in the next chapter).

Meanwhile the Melchester team became increasingly confused and certain team members enthusiastically embraced Gartner's critical comments and sought to marshal support from others to reject the vendor (see Pollock & Williams 2007). Indeed this is what happened. Shortly after the discussion with Gartner, the NewVendor solution was no longer considered a viable option for the Council.

To summarize, we have argued that Gartner shape innovation through proactively naming and defining new classes of emerging technologies. This is a process that does not simply allow industry analysts to represent the market/technology but also to shape it. Gartner project an initial definition of a class of technology, but rather than modify their definition each time they encounter a different case they expect vendors to conform to their existing category. Those outside the classification are seen as anomalies (Zuckerman 1999, Beunza & Garud 2007). Indeed, we can see how this kind of infrastructural knowledge (the classification) had a significant and enduring influence on the marketplace. In the case described, because of Gartner's view of what the technology should look like, this particular vendor was not able to enter the particular marketplace. Gartner's research thus demonstrated a strong form of performativity. This allows us to describe technology and market classifications as *promissory work made durable*.

5.4. VISIONS LET LOOSE

This second vignette investigates the intriguing issue of how those who trade in future oriented knowledge claims manage 'failure'. One might imagine such experts would have mechanisms for downplaying claims found to be inaccurate or that they would attempt to deal with failure in private (as do other knowledge providers [Shapin 1994]). This is because it is often assumed that failure is directly tied to authority and credibility (c.f. Brown 2003).

5.4.1. Demonstrations of failure

Purely by chance, we stumbled across a forum where Gartner dealt with failure in the most *public* of settings: in front of an audience of over 200 practitioners attending an annual international industry IT conference. One of the authors (NP) was listening to senior Gartner analyst Mark Zolo give his keynote address, which he gave each year to this particular conference, when the speaker pointed out how he wanted to do things a little differently this time around:

> What I have decided this year, because several of you have said, 'You know it would be fun to take a look at some of the stuff you have said over the years, and if it makes sense today, or, if it doesn't make sense. Or what it was, and what we talked about over that period of time'. So I went back even pre-Gartner when I was at CAUSE and picked out some of the slides. And I thought that I would start from about 1992, partly because that's as early as my PowerPoint slide went back, I didn't have anything that was in a form that I could use (Mark Zolo, presentation at Educause).[2]

What he was proposing to do was to go through his past predictions to see what had actually happened—if they turned out to be 'accurate' or not! He then set about reading through old PowerPoint slides, discussing his old predictions and continually stopping to insert anecdotes as well as to invite the audience to confirm the claims by raising their hands. The first claim was about e-learning and the future of traditional higher education:

> In my first year at CAUSE some of you asked 'What are some of your recom-
> mendations and some of your strategic planning assumptions? What do they look
> like?'. Here is some of them from 1996. That's really 10 years ago now.
> *'By 2001 distance learning will be a mainstream activity on 80% of the campuses'.*
> How many of you think that one has come to pass? How many of you [very
> few hands raised]. How many of you think it hasn't yet [many more
> hands raised]. Mainstream activity? Still not. OK (Mark Zolo, presentation at
> Educause).

With the first slide, most of the audience seemed to agree that what had happened was not that which was predicted. He then paused for a few seconds, before making a slightly different point: 'How many of you though have a large percentage of either hybrid or blended courses on your campuses today? [A few more hands are raised]. Yeah. OK. So part of it is coming there'. He then addressed another prediction that '*Western Governors University would have a dramatic impact upon higher education*'. However before asking the audience to verify this claim, he carried on: 'How many of you *remember* Western Governors University? [Laughter from audience.] Oh, yes! Oh, yes! [More laughter]' (Zolo, conference floor).

The Western Governors University, like many of the other new for-profit virtual universities at the time, was largely a failure (Cornford & Pollock 2003). Mark's acknowledgement of this and seeming irreverence towards his prediction was greeted with widespread laughter. He continued:

> Western Governors Association Initiative. At that time I was on the task force for
> the Western Governors, and I tell you, if you ever want to see panic in [university]
> Presidents' eyes, this one brought it about. The Western Governors, the idea that
> you have this group of states coming together in the form of a virtual university,
> *really* did have the attention of a lot of people. And I remember Presidents
> coming up to me and saying 'Am I really going to find myself in a situation
> where I am going to have to compete with universities around the world?' (Mark
> Zolo, presentation at Educause).

These institutions did not have the direct influence that Gartner had predicted but this does not deter Mark from qualifying and defending his claim by pointing to the wider effects they did have:

> The point is, Western Governors started to shake thing up. And at the time of
> this particular Gartner and EduCause update I said 'If they never offer a course,

Western Governors will be successful because they will have shaken up higher education to start thinking about technology and the role of technology in teaching and learning'. And I think that is true. The reality is that they haven't done too much from the point of view of offering course work and becoming an institution, although they were accredited (Mark Zolo, presentation at Educause).

From then on his presentation begins to follow a familiar pattern. We are introduced to a past claim: 'IT coupled with better business practices and co-operative arrangements can bring about both cost avoidance and significant savings'. The analyst then ironicizes the claim: 'Any of you *seen* any significant savings . . . ?' [laughter]. 'How about cost avoidance?'. Having questioned the claim's veracity he then attempts to convince the audience that the prediction contains elements of truth: 'Sometimes, yeah, we have. And there I have to say there are times when people see savings. The problem I find is that as we have done some of these savings *we* [the IT community] don't get credit for them'.

This episode is interesting because the audience is invited to evaluate Gartner's research and to look at what they said *would* happen as compared with what *actually* happened. Gartner are airing their claims for retrospective scrutiny. Of course, the particular analyst skilfully manages this process so that the fragilities surrounding this form of promissory work are never fully exposed and claims are not strongly contested. Rather, in some respects, he attempts to recast the claim in the present, so that both the prediction and present-day perspective are more closely aligned. We might read this episode as a set of unrealized promissory activities that are later discursively re-adjusted to match the setting and vice versa—a process Brown and Michael (2003) describe as 'retrospecting prospects'. However, while such a conclusion might be valid, we think the episode highlights a different point.

Callon (2007) has argued that theories are performative when they successfully bring about the 'world' to which they point: they create some form of 'material reality' or 'obligatory point of passage' others are forced to take into account (such as the 'infrastructure' described in the previous section). Applying this notion to this vignette, we might say that promissory work does not exist in isolation but has meaning and efficacy in the world it creates for itself. Successful promissory work would be actively engaged in constituting the reality to which it points. However, in this case, Gartner appeared to neither build upon nor defend this knowledge, but seemed willing simply to let the claim go. Thus we might say that promissory organizations sometimes produce and communicate a kind of knowledge that is not a priori defendable. The performative reading of this is that some types of expectations based knowledge have limited or 'temporary' effects. These expectations are simply launched into the ether: they are *visions let loose*.

5.5. STATEMENTS AND THEIR WORLD

In this final vignette, we turn our attention to the 'Magic Quadrant'. The Magic Quadrant is interesting to study as a form of promissory work because it is helping create a new kind of evaluative world or evaluative culture where technology adopters compare vendors against each other according to a mix of present day and future based criteria. The aim is to provide information to IT decision makers about the current and future performance of technology vendors, their behaviour, and their understanding as well as their vision of the future marketplace.

5.5.1. A new evaluative world

To give some indication of the evaluative world or evaluative culture developed we present an extract from a presentation given by analyst relations consultant Carter Lusher from SageCircle to an audience of fellow analyst relations professionals and IT practitioners where he talks about the Magic Quadrant:

> A quick bit of history: This was developed in the mid-80s and it's based on a very simple two-by-two graphic. And originally this was designed as a snapshot of the market and it was always coupled with what was called a 'Strategic Planning Assumption'. Now of course these were all done on paper, back in the 80s. You've got the Magic Quadrant as part of a piece of paper called a Strategic Planning Assumption, and it was intended as a single instant in time, and sometimes it was going to be updated, and if it was to be updated it would be updated on a frequent basis. And so this was a very, very simple concept when it first came out. But over time this has become very, very pervasive and very, very high impact, and because it has this really strong influence on shortlists for IT buyers, it has gained an awful lot of traction. It was not part of its original intention (webinar, Carter Lusher, SageCircle).

Coming in the form of a two-by-two matrix, the Magic Quadrant ranks vendors according to criteria authored and diffused by Gartner: a vendor's 'completeness of vision' and its 'ability to execute' on that vision. It is the former that is of particular interest to us here since it concerns how vendors envision the future:

> In the Vision, across the bottom, the most important question is: Is there a vision? Is there a roadmap? Is there a direction that this company is taking with this product or this technology? But a really key part of this is: is that vision aligned with the trends of the industry? And does it match what Gartner believes that the vision should be? And therefore: how complete is the vision as compared to what Gartner expects it should be? (webinar, Carter Lusher, SageCircle).

What Carter Lusher is describing is how Gartner are attempting to shift the way adopters typically assess technologies prior to purchase. Whilst in the past they might look directly at the technology and its functionality as well as fit to the organization amongst other things today Gartner argue that it is important to assess the vendor's perception and plan for the future. As Lusher describes:

> If there's a significant difference between the analyst's vision for the market and the [vendor] executive's vision for the market, then you are going to be in some trouble with this Magic Quadrant. Because remember, the completeness of vision is how well does your product or service match Gartner's view of the market? And then the question is can you change that? (webinar, Carter Lusher, SageCircle).

This will include efforts to anticipate future changes in a vendor's strategies and practices relative to other vendors. This suggests that the Magic Quadrant is transformative: it offers a new way to evaluate vendors in terms of qualities that did not previously exist—a process of transformation that we describe empirically in Chapter 7. However, the world that Gartner is attempting to set out also requires a research process. Depending on Gartner's assessment of a vendor's vision, it is then placed in one of four quadrants labelled 'niche player', 'challenger', 'visionary', or 'leader'. The same consultant describes the significance of this:

> The four quadrants that are then dropped into place are if you match Gartner's vision and you really are able to execute, you're considered a Leader. If you're not so much matching futures, but you've got a good solid product that is well received by the market place, they call that a Challenger. With those people who fall into the very visionary but they just don't have the company, the customers, or the product to really say they've executed, well they drop into the Visionary stage. And for the small vendor, maybe the start-up, somebody who's really new to this, they fall into what we call the Niche player (webinar, Carter Lusher, SageCircle).

5.5.2. Getting to the 'truth'

Gartner analysts produce new Magic Quadrants for particular markets or sub-markets each year, and each time they reassess the position of the various vendors operating in the markets. Gartner collect evidence for their ranking from a variety of sources that includes research on vendors as well as discussions with the users of the technology and various others. The tool is also viewed as 'problematic' in certain circles. There are those that are sceptical as to whether there is a serious research process behind it (Greenemeier & McDougall 2006). There are also concerns that the analysts are not entirely 'independent' of the vendors they assess. Gartner analysts themselves not only point to the complex research methods but also to their independence:

> We are paid by our company to do our job; but . . . there is a sort of . . . righteous-ness element to it. In other words, a sort of search for the truth. OK, we are paid to write research, in that I am paid to do enquires; and I am paid to help the client. We get rated on how well the client is happy with our advice. But at the heart of it, there is a sort of truth element to it (interview, Thomas).

We describe the research process that produces the Magic Quadrant in later chapters. What we want to highlight here is the way Gartner emphasize certain key research principles within their organization:

> We are pseudo-academic in the way we work. We have a very rigorous peer review. So if I write something, it takes me 42 days to get it out the door. I can't just write something, I can write it in a blog if I want, that is fine, but anything that is published within Gartner, I have to have two peer reviews followed by a manager, not a manager but a peer mandatory review, it is the kind of leader of that area who has to review. Then it goes up to a team manager, and then we can get down to things like editing etcetera. And if it is something real big and controversial then it will go through much more reviews like that. So up to 16, 17 different individuals will review it, give you feedback on it and kick it to bits (interview, Thomas).

Notions like 'peer review', 'research methodologies', 'data collection' and so on are an increasingly common aspect of the vocabulary of industry analysts. An ex-Gartner analyst we interviewed tells us that the mere fact Gartner have been taken to court several times for its placing of vendors on the Magic Quadrant and 'won' suggests something: 'The magic quadrant therefore has to be something that's auditable and trackable' (interview, Levin).

To summarize, we have shown how this form of promissory work has a strong but contested influence on the marketplace. Indeed the prime conten-tion pursued here is that the spread of the Magic Quadrant has created a new evaluative culture or world. This is with regard to the manner in which procurement should be conducted and the nature of the vendors involved in that process. This includes building a research process whereby Gartner can speak 'authoritatively' about the capacities and potential of IT vendors (we discuss the idea of an evaluative culture more fully in Chapter 7). Importantly, even though Magic Quadrants are contested, Gartner appear able to defend their assessments.

5.6. CONCLUSIONS: INITIAL TYPOLOGY

The *business of technological expectations* is increasingly commercial in or-ientation, product minded in ambition and potent in influence. Crucially, whilst there has been extensive research on the efforts of scientists and technology developers to mobilize *particular expectations* around proposed technical advances, much less attention has been given to intermediary organizations devoted to the production, communication and selling of expectations-based knowledge products and services. We have focused on the case of industry analysts who routinely produce various types of future oriented knowledge that has consequences for shaping markets and products. We have termed these actors *promissory organizations* to capture how they successfully mobilize support for *generic* promises and visions (deploying signposts about the state of the industry and its future evolution), and also increasingly 'organize' expectations within procurement and innovation markets (subjecting the *particular* promissory work of innovation players to scrutiny and accountability). In a context of growing competition between diverse technology suppliers, by articulating claims about the current performance and further development of their highly complex products, which are difficult for potential adopters to assess, industry analysts serve to regulate and systematize that competition. The increasing influence of this kind of intermediary is changing the nature and dynamics of the promissory space.

The substantive aim of the chapter was to throw light on how industry analysts shape innovation and markets, whilst our theoretical goal was to understand the extent to which their advice is 'performative'. How does this form of promissory work shape or nudge the direction of innovation and procurement choices? Arguably, current frameworks developed within sociological research on expectations do not allow us to answer this in a sufficiently comprehensive and nuanced way. The notion of a self-fulfilling prophecy runs the risk of treating emerging technologies as a direct *product* of expectations (van Lente 1993, Guice 1999, Brown et al. 2000, 2003, Rip 2006). Scientific and technological visions rarely demonstrate simple kinds of performativity. Even if seemingly stable beliefs are shared by relevant actors, one cannot ignore the possibility that other actors and factors may enter the field (Jørgensen & Sørensen 1999). Scholars interested in the Sociology of Expectations need to ask why some kinds of consensus or compelling vision materialize while others do not. Clearly, not all expectations constitute innovation in the *same* way. Why is this? Why do certain forms of promissory work appear to be more successful? These questions underpin our insistence that it is necessary for scholars to develop complex analytical registers in order to track the complicated and highly uneven levels of performativity associated with expectations. Richer analytical templates and rigorous methodologies are required. This challenge concerns whether it is possible to construct a *typology of promissory behaviour* that characterizes the unevenness of these commoditized forms of expectations.

Inspired by frameworks emerging from Economic Sociology and the Sociology of Finance, we use our empirical research to identify at least three different kinds of promissory work (see Table 5.1). The first is *infrastructural*

Table 5.1. Initial typology of the promissory behaviour of industry analysts

	Kind	Effect	Accountability
Infrastructural Knowledge	-definitions & classifications of technology markets	-organizing change in the marketplace	-advances in a slow & careful manner
	-strongly institutionalized (invisible until breakdown)	-strong and enduring influence (promissory-work made durable)	-authoritative
Statements & their World	-assessments of relative location of suppliers within product markets for different user sectors.	-strong but contested influence (dividing objects)	-brings about 'accountable' change
	-active attempt to make research successful	-creates winners & losers	-process behind tools robustly defended
Visions Let Loose	-signposts drawn up about the state of industry and future development (longitudinal predictions) -transient statements	-some influence but typically only 'temporary'	-speculative & low in accountability -not subject to close scrutiny or sanction -does not appear to damage reputation if inaccurate

knowledge, which typically attempts to classify technology markets. This type includes definitions of the technological field and maps of players within that arena. These classifications of technological markets are institutionalized, meaning that they exert a powerful and enduring influence. They endure because they are rendered invisible in the way Bowker & Star (1999) describe 'infrastructure' (as visible only upon breakdown). Secondly, we find more transitory forms of intervention that can be described as *visions let loose*. These are typically provocative signposts drawn up about the state and future development of the industry. These kinds of predictions appear not to be built in the same careful way as other kinds of research but are simply 'launched into the ether', resulting in relatively short lived levels of influence. Finally, there are what we call *statements and their world* through which actors generate assessments of the location and potential of various suppliers within the product market for different user sectors. These statements have a strong but contested influence on the market, as analysts attempt to make their research successful with world-building activity.

We also noted how different types of promissory work are subject to varied forms and standards of accountability and verification. Infrastructural knowledge, for instance, advances slowly and carefully as actors attempt to define the technological field (in some cases, to say what the next generation of technologies will look like) and to organize change in the marketplace. It is a form of boundary work (Gieryn 1999) through which analysts attempt to categorize technology vendors and markets in a very material way, according to existing classifications. Consequently, analysts who develop such knowledge may be blind to vendors who do not neatly fit their categories (Beunza & Garud 2007). Such assessments are 'authoritative': whilst they can be (and often are) challenged, the industry analysts tend to stick to original classifications (doing otherwise can diminish credibility—see Zuckerman [1999]). Similarly, statements and their world bring about 'accountable' change. This type of research must be accountable, indeed defensible, because it produces 'winners and losers'. Industry analysts try to be categorical about what is the right technology, in order to help technology adopters make purchases based on assessments of the current and future behaviour and competences of vendors. Visions let loose, by contrast, are more speculative and appear not to be subject to the same levels of rigorous accountability as other kinds of promissory work.

Our initial typology, which we will use throughout the book, suggests that there is a spectrum of promissory activity. At one end of this spectrum is a kind of research that is extensively and elaborately put together; where necessary this output is robustly defended and it appears 'to matter' a great deal to industry analysts and the others who use it or who are described within it. At the other end of the spectrum are kinds of promissory work that seem more like 'provocations' that attempt to capture interest. Intriguingly, it did not seem very important when these provocations failed, perhaps because such failures do not explicitly damage reputations. Contrary to what some have argued (e.g., Brown 2003), we found that mistaken predictions could be openly discussed in some public venues! And we return to consider why this might be the case and what exactly these predictions are doing in Chapter 8.

We sought empirical answers to the question of why certain kinds of promissory activities fail or succeed, but we do not necessarily think that the question should only be addressed empirically, especially if it is limited to hindsight. We advocate an empirical programme on the business of expectations, but with a theoretical orientation necessary to create a typology of promissory behaviour. In this chapter, we have identified three types of promissory behaviour, but there certainly must be others that a more complex typology would encompass. It is this that we attempt in forthcoming chapters. We will take each of the initial elements identified here and unpack them further. We are not attempting a 'systematic' typology, because promises and expectations are such all-encompassing features of human activity that it would seem presumptuous to generate an empirically-validated map of promissory processes. Moreover, whilst there may be generic similarities between expectations, industry analyst organizations operate within particular contexts as we discuss in Chapter 10. The aim of such a typology is not to improve our ability to decide on the accuracy of promissory work—we are not suggesting that our analysis provides privileged access to the future (Barben et al. 2007).

Notwithstanding such limits, we think we should be able to say something about the promissory process (Geels 2007), and provide some insights into the different moves and strategies that industry analysts use—insights that may provide an understanding of the potential strength or weakness, robustness or fragility of particular claims. The upshot is that such research allows us to delineate some of the underpinnings of their success or failure (Barben et al. 2007, Geels 2007), as can be seen most clearly in terms of the various 'webs of accountability' or what we will describe, in later chapters, as a 'validation regime'. Surrounding certain claims (statements and their world, for instance) there appear to be dense arrays of knowledge linking players together, as well as formalized and highly distributed processes through which data are gathered (resonating with what Callon & Muniesa [2005] call a 'calculative network'). Moreover, this formal process is increasingly exposed to external scrutiny and comment. Whilst clearly not governed by the strict controls of independent 'scientific' or 'academic' knowledge, this kind of assessment is subject to its own forms of accountability, which deserve further study. Alternatively, visions let loose reveal a much less dense web of accountability and fragile links with little in the way of defensible knowledge.

NOTES

1. We suggest that a prediction is not causal because we cannot presume stable trajectories and the continuation of existing sets of expectations (Fleck et al. 1990). As Jørgensen and Sørensen (1999) remind us, even where apparently stable sets of beliefs are shared by other relevant actors, one cannot rule out the entry of still other actors and confounding factors into the arena. In such an environment, there is every opportunity for beliefs to be challenged and reworked in the arduous process of creating artefacts and making adequate linkages with the organizational and institutional practices of intended users. Various analytical frameworks within Science & Technology Studies (STS) have argued that the achievement of a new technology takes place in a heterogeneous landscape, involving a diverse and unevenly malleable array of human and nonhuman elements.

2. CAUSE is a US non-profit organization that has as its mandate the promotion and increased diffusion of information and communication technologies (ICTs) within higher education. It is today known as 'EduCause'.

6

Who Decides the Shape of Product Markets?

Names matter. As we have seen from the previous chapter, the ways in which new technologies are 'categorized' is a matter of fundamental importance. As anyone who has studied the digital economy for any length of time will tell you, there appears a compulsion within this domain to rename technologies (Swanson & Ramiller 1997, Currie 2004). IT vendors periodically (and repeatedly) designate offerings differently from those of previous generations or from competitors. Between 1990 and 2002, for instance, industry application software vendors used nearly 400 *different* terminologies to describe their products (Pontikes 2008). There is a proliferation of terminologies—often encapsulated in their (typically) three letter acronym. The conventional explanation for these naming practices is that competition pushes vendors to differentiate their products from those of a rival (Teece et al. 1997). No one wants to be seen to be emulating a competitor and a new name would appear to constitute one important way to distinguish a difference.

Yet, despite this compulsion, certain designations appear able to colonize wide areas of activity. Some technologies may be given a standard nomenclature that can then prevail for a significant period of time (as evidenced by the recent examples of MRP, MRPII, ERP, CRM etc.). These names refer not to a specific homogeneous product but to a more or less heterogeneous collection of artefacts (software, management techniques) which then go on to link a community (or, rather, several overlapping communities) of suppliers, intermediaries and adopters (Pollock & Williams 2009). Such terminologies propose a boundary that links a group of (often quite various) artefacts while differentiating them from others. This begs an important question that scholars interested in information systems have yet fully to answer: *Who decides?* Who determines the boundaries around a product terminology? By this we mean who judges whether or not an individual technology instance is included as part of a wider terminology. In other words, who, if anyone, is naming and categorizing technological fields?

Current scholarship has tended towards a *communitarian* framing of this important issue. Who shapes a name? *The community does.* The overall conception of a product market is seen to be moulded not by any one specific individual or group but by vendors, adopters, journalists and consultants together, in what Wang and Ramiller (2009) have described broadly as the 'innovation community'. Terminologies gain traction within a community precisely because no one group or actor has the final say on their shape and meaning. Their role seems similar to Star & Griesemer's (1989) concept of 'boundary objects'. Passing through many hands, a name becomes a hook that can facilitate a variety of understandings and interpretations. Indeed, such diversity and ambiguity in meaning is seen to lead to richness and robustness in the process of innovation around a terminology (Swanson & Ramiller 1997).

This kind of formulation seems less adequate today. It represents a rather imprecise way to characterize what this book is arguing has become a more organized process. One has only to look back at the recent history of information systems development, for instance, to see that, although the early stages of recent major innovations were characterized by initial ambiguity, later developments were pursued in a more structured manner (Pollock & Williams 2009). This was because at the outset of today's modern corporate information systems, the 'knowledge infrastructures' of information technology were often rudimentary and inchoate (and early accounts of these categories resembled the communitarian account above), but, over time, the institutional framework surrounding these technologies have become more established (Abrahamson & Fairchild 2001, Wang & Swanson 2007, 2008, Swanson 2010). Comparing the development of information systems today with the development of systems from just a couple of decades ago, we are struck by the number of specialized intermediaries that now surround workplace information technologies.

We suggest that the communitarian view might be strengthened by foregrounding the emergence in recent years of new *knowledge infrastructures of information technology* that attempt to draw up and police the boundaries that surround new technological fields of activity (Swanson 2010). Clearly, vendors and other members of the wider community still feature centrally in the designation of a technology. However, the consensus surrounding an emerging field can often nowadays be steered *inter alia* by 'industry analysts'. We are not alone in noting this important development. Wang and Ramiller (2009: 20) have pointed to how it is industry analysts who are often the 'originators' of new terminologies or, if not the authors, the body at least which attempts to 'provide the first public articulation of [an] innovation' (see also Swanson 2010). What we want to do here is to develop this insight further through describing and conceptualizing in detail the work of Gartner in naming technologies.

Our argument is that it is industry analysts, and Gartner in particular, who have established the cognitive authority to exercise control over the labelling of a technology and subsequent interpretation of that name. They do so through making continuous 'naming interventions' within the IT domain and then attempting to control how that name is carried forward through episodes of 'categorization work'. We explore this by examining particularly Gartner's role in shaping the development and evolution of Customer Relationship Management (CRM) technologies.

The empirical part of this chapter is presented in four 'acts'. The first discusses in more detail how the analyst firm critically assessed a new vendor seeking to enter a market—for which it had no experience or reputation and where it was proposing to offer a novel CRM product. The second describes the various factors that shaped the analyst firm's judgement—what we describe as its 'knowledge frame' (Beunza & Garud 2007). As well as focusing on the capacity of industry analysts to shape technological fields, we also attend to the constraints on how they proceed. We find them to be operating in a highly complex environment where their interventions can be, and often are, contested. Thus, thirdly, we describe the opposition that can swell up around assessments, which can then force the analysts to have to *defend* their position. Contestation also reveals the internal disagreements that can emerge around these naming/categorization practices. We show how individual analysts within Gartner were at odds with each other about whether or not the particular vendor was part of the CRM field (or indeed to which field it belonged). We conclude by discussing the ambiguity that has now grown up around CRM and what this means for the shape and direction of this particular technological field.

Conceptualizing the classification of markets is not straightforward and requires the bridging of a number of disparate bodies of literature. This includes supplementing our conceptual toolkit with ideas from Economic Sociology on 'critics' (Zuckerman 1999, Rosa et al. 1999, 2003), the 'finitist' perspective from the Sociology of Scientific Knowledge (SSK) (Barnes et al. 1996), and recent Science and Technology Studies (STS) investigations into economic and financial markets (Beunza & Garud 2007). The chapter is based on a longitudinal study that includes ethnographic research conducted on the eve of the birth of contemporary CRM and interviews carried out more recently as part of our ongoing study into industry analysts.

6.1. COMMUNITY VERSUS COMMODITY

A number of scholars have argued for the need to pay attention to the nomenclatures of technology supply and associated commentary as a site where technology futures are worked out and promises articulated and validated. In this respect, the new terminologies emerging within the IT sector have been conceptualized variously as 'technological visions' (Webster 1993), 'organizing visions' (Swanson & Ramiller 1997), 'practice-based imaginaries'

(Hyysalo 2006), 'technological imaginaires' (Flichy 2007), 'fashions' (Baskerville & Myers 2009) and 'IT innovation concepts' (Wang 2009), to name but a few. We focus here predominately on the notion of organizing vision as it offers perhaps the most comprehensive account of this phenomenon in the IT application sector.

Swanson and Ramiller (1997: 460) define an organizing vision as a 'focal community idea for the application of information technology in organizations'. They developed the notion to show how the constant proliferation of 'buzzwords' in the information technology sector was not specious or hollow, as some had argued, but played an important role in mobilizing the material and intellectual resources needed for innovation. One of the key aspects about organizing visions is that they are shaped not by specific individuals or groups but the wider IT innovation community. Terminologies are essentially seen as discourses that gain traction precisely because no one group or actor has the final say on their shape and meaning:

> The organizing vision is developed by many different storytellers, who modify and embellish it to suit their own and their audiences' tastes and interests, and only more or less fully, never in complete and definitive detail. It necessarily changes and grows over time in the re-telling, as the community finds its way (ibid: 463).

The analytical concept of an organizing vision has given impetus to others to investigate the work names do in processes of innovation (Currie 2004, Wang & Swanson 2007, 2008, Swanson 2010). Relevant to our empirical focus, for instance, Wang (2009) has similarly theorized the rise of Customer Relationship Management (CRM) as an 'IT innovation concept'. He underlines how the term CRM was interpreted and understood differently across a diffuse and heterogeneous group of actors:

> ...the customer relationship management (CRM) concept was created and developed by the CRM community. The once leading vendor, Siebel Systems, despite its dominance in that community, never owned the concept; anyone interested in CRM can read, hear, write, and talk about the concept. Members of the CRM community may agree or disagree on certain aspects of the concept and, thus, promote or discredit the concept accordingly (Wang 2009: 6).

We find particularly useful the literature that draws attention to the wide range of constituencies involved in the shaping of a new field and the resultant interpretive flexibility that can often surround an emerging technology. However, its focus on the 'diverse interoganizational community' (Swanson & Ramiller 1997: 458) may not sensitize fieldworkers to the presence and influence of the kinds of market actors described here. Moreover, whilst we acknowledge that the development of a technological field is not a space *owned* by any particular group of practitioners, vendors, users or analysts, it is also (increasingly) true that certain institutions now exert particular influence over it. The IT innovation community (Wang & Ramiller 2009), whilst it is *a community*, is not open and equal in the way in which we might conceive of 'scientific communities', say, operating under the Mertonian ideal (Mulkay 1976).

In some of the first large-scale packaged workplace information technologies, for instance, the main institutional repositories were practitioners: user organizations, management professions and professional associations (Swan et al. 2003). However, we also note a pattern familiar from other innovations: the establishment of a division of expert labour. From the 1970s onwards, we have seen the increasing influence of management consultants, and by the 1990s, consultancy organizations were beginning to collate information about supplier offerings, while by the twenty-first century we find a much more elaborate system of consultancy and advice, and the emergence of specialist industry analysts, making available formalized and systematized assessments of particular vendors and their offerings (Swanson 2010). Analysts are attempting to make comparative assessments of vendor technologies on a more commodified basis, a prerequisite for which is the definition of vendor systems and the application goals to which they are geared. What we witness is that a market is being built for new kinds of knowledge-based products. We would point to how, today, the development and evolution of technological fields are increasingly shaped by processes of 'specialization' and 'commodification'. This imparts particular sets of dynamics to the community. As Adler and Heckscher (2006: 30) suggest, whilst commenting on the ineffectiveness of new kinds of markets for supplying knowledge, 'individuals get the output of specific expertise but not the ability to interact with it and improve it'. We think there is an important point to be made in relation to how new kinds of actors and forms of knowledge constitute markets. Unpacking this further requires that we combine insights from Information Systems research with relevant scholarship from Economic Sociology on 'mediated markets'.

6.2. MEDIATED MARKETS

Economic Sociologists describe mediated markets as the places where 'critics' (as in 'food critic', 'theatre critic', 'wine critic' etc.) play a pivotal role in shaping the nature of transactions between consumers and producers (Zuckerman 1999, Rosa et al. 1999, 2003). Critics are said to shape *demand* through endorsing certain products over others. They also shape *supply* because whereas vendors are said to strive to differentiate themselves from competitors they are, through the presence of critics, seemingly forced to conform their goods in line with the main characteristics of other offerings in the *product category* targeted. Critics will seemingly only review those products that fit comfortably within the areas they cover (Zuckerman 1999). Those that do not fit within a particular category—because they are unclear, overly complex or 'too novel'—will be 'screened out' of consideration (ibid). Products that fail to attract reviews and endorsements are, according to this argument, seen as 'illegitimate' (ibid.).

From the point of view of Economic Sociology, the product category becomes the central aspect in a mediated market. It is described by Zuckerman (1999) as a 'social screen'. This screen is 'not designed by the actor but external to her, given in the categories that comprise market structure' (ibid: 1404). Actors therefore are forced to take this form of knowledge into account but are not necessarily able to shape it (cf. Adler & Heckscher 2006).

The advantage of the work of Zuckerman over other more narrowly con-fined Business Studies (e.g. Teece et al. 1997) approaches is that it brings into view not only single product classifications but the presence of a whole context of work related to the screening of products. The analysis of market critics provides useful insights into how product categories can shape product development through exerting (often isomorphic) pressures on vendors. However, we see two weaknesses with the approach as it is currently set out. First, whilst reading this literature, we learnt little about the complexities and possible disagreements that may exist around categorization work. Critics appear able to apportion vendors within the confines of *stable* classifications and according to *fixed* vendor product properties. The process itself remains black-boxed and lends to the reading that the screening of vendors is a routine and unproblematic activity—a view with which sociologists interested in classification would almost certainly take issue.

The 'finitist' perspective within the Sociology of Scientific Knowledge (SSK), for instance, portrays the creation and maintenance of classifications altogether differently. For them, the categorization of an artefact cannot be fixed in advance (Barnes et al. 1996). Deciding whether something counts as a particular instance of a wider classification requires a *decision* to be taken and a *process* to be carried out. This is often a difficult and ambiguous process, which can be delegated to various forms of 'categorization work'. In this delegation, Barnes et al. (1996) note the central role of individual and collec-tive 'judgement' in deciding. Moreover, even when a choice is made, there is every possibility of contestation: 'No act of classification is ever indefeasibly correct' (ibid: 56).

Second, in weighing up the work on market critics, there are also obvious opportunities to bring in scholarship from Science and Technology Studies (STS), especially from those who have turned their attention to economic and financial markets (Callon 1998, 2007, MacKenzie 2006). These include scholars exploring the various *material artefacts* and *intellectual equipment* necessary for markets to operate (MacKenzie 2009). Researchers here have been seeking to recast and widen the debate on markets from one that focuses predominately on the 'interpretative' capacities of actors towards the tools and devices underlying and facilitating market-making processes (Callon et al. 2002). Extending this analysis to the work of critics, it might be suggested that conceptualizing product categories as purely 'social' (or cognitive) would imply that they have a rather weak influence. An alternative way to explain the constitutive effects of product categories might be to focus on the *equipment* involved in the screening processes. An exemplary instance of this latter ambition is a recent discussion of how securities analysts evaluate the issue of firm profitability (Beunza & Garud 2007).

6.2.1. Critics construct frames

Beunza and Garud (2007) attempt to broaden the lens of Economic Sociology by suggesting that market categories are only one of the factors shaping the work of mediators. When securities analysts, for instance, attempt to value the potential profitability of a firm their view is shaped by what they call, drawing on Goffman, an 'analytical frame'. An analytical frame is made up of a range of socio-material devices. Once constructed, these frames are said to focus the security analyst's attention onto a specific set of circumstances to the exclusion of other market information, directly suggesting how a new phenomenon should be judged. Interestingly, they note how frames are susceptible to 'controversy'. Indeed there can and often are 'frame disputes', which as Goffman (1974: 323) notes are 'endemic to framing'. These disputes arise because, once committed, securities analysts tend to persevere with a frame. To do otherwise, would seemingly diminish their 'credibility' (Beunza & Garud 2007). This commitment inevitably leads to disparities between different securities analysts, particularly between those reviewing the same phenomena whilst using a *different* frame. A controversy can lead an analyst eventually to *abandon* a frame in favour of another.

In what follows, we employ several of the above ideas. We bring together the work on 'organizing visions' with that of 'product categories' (for new designations are surely also attempts to redraw the boundaries around classes of technology). We show how the industry analyst firm studied attempted to evaluate one particular vendor's CRM offering, how this was complicated and fraught with disagreements, but also how analysts appeared to have established methods and tools for seemingly resolving such matters, which, influenced by Beunza and Garud (2007), we describe as their 'knowledge frame'. We find useful Beunza and Garud's (ibid) suggestion that frames can lead to disputes. However, our focus differs from theirs in the important respect that

---

Box 1. Research note

Context of the study

This chapter discusses specifically the role of Gartner in classification. The influence of Gartner in classification processes has been noted within Information Systems research (Ramiller & Swanson 2003, Firth & Swanson 2005, Burks 2006, Swanson 2010), in their authoring and subsequent shaping of the Enterprise Resource Planning (ERP) terminology attracting most comment. The successful designation of ERP by Gartner is widely acknowledged as a key development in the recent history of information systems. This was also a moment in which this group of experts appeared to gain a certain amount of cognitive authority. It was in their scenario document *ERP: A Vision of the Next-Generation MRP II* (Wylie 1990) that Gartner first coined the term 'ERP', proclaiming it the 'new information system paradigm'. Mabert et al. (2001: 69–70), for instance, noted that Gartner not only created the term but set out what functionality it should contain:

> The Gartner Group coined the term 'enterprise resource planning' in the early 1990s to describe the business software systems that evolved as an extension of MRP II-type systems. They stipulated that such software should include integrated modules for accounting, finance, sales and distribution, HRM, material management, and other business functions based on a common architecture that linked the enterprise to both customers and suppliers.

Soon after, other players (most notably vendors and consultants) began to flesh out what ERP was and how it worked, followed by adopter accounts of the organisational benefits of its adoption (Wang & Ramiller 2009). Outwith this initial involvement, Gartner appeared to exercise a hold over the activities of ERP vendors, in particular through the production of various 'research tools'. This included, for instance, their 'vendor briefings' that worked to consolidate the existence of this domain of technological activity. Vendor briefings constituted particular vendor offerings—a technology such as SAP's R/3 system, for example— as an instance of ERP (Pollock & Williams 2009).

Gartner continued to chart ERP's future development trajectory (Mabert et al. 2001, Judd 2006). In 2000, for instance, they boldly declared ERP 'dead' and mapped out a transition to the next phase (described as 'extended ERP' or 'ERP II' [Bond et al. 2000]). However, on this occasion, Gartner's death sentence turned out to be premature. This evidences how these organisations wield complicated and highly uneven kinds of influence. Not all interventions are able to sustain themselves. This throws up questions in relation to how we understand the prominence of these actors—an influence characterised by demonstrable moments of success but also equally failure—in subsequent technological fields.

Research Approach

We have been able to map out the changing dynamics of CRM and Gartner's role in shaping this technological field over a period of several years. The benefits of a longitudinal approach are that it will reveal how the capacities of the various knowledge infrastructures to control and police the boundaries surrounding CRM are not static but changing over time. This has been possible through

(continued)

Box 1. **Continued**

---

conducting studies at different stages in the development and maturation of CRM. We carried out an initial study at the turn of the century where we were able to witness Gartner's role in advising potential adopters of the benefits and disadvantages of particular CRM packages (Pollock & Williams 2007). We were able to return to this study through conducting further fieldwork almost a decade later on the more general influence of industry analysts. Here, as well as collecting new data, we were able to gain particular insights by re-examining with the benefit of hindsight our initial findings.

Fieldwork for our first study was completed on the eve of the emergence of contemporary CRM (early 2000s). At that time, there appeared to be little doubt that Gartner (just as it had done a few years previously with ERP) would have a strong hand in influencing the direction of this new field. All of its early writing indicated this would be the case. For instance in *Top Ten Trends in CRM for 2001* Gartner fired a warning shot over the heads of any IT vendors who might have been thinking of simply rebranding their existing solutions as CRM systems: "About 500 enterprises claim to sell CRM software, but only 200 actually do so" (Gartner Inc. 2001: 2). Our later fieldwork, however, reveals that in this context Gartner did not have anything like the same kind of influence. There now appears to be a number of industry analysts or equivalent organisations speaking with authority about this field (Wang 2009). This observation highlights the importance of a longitudinal perspective in understanding the evolution of technological fields. It also reminds us that whilst certain market actors can exert influence, the achievement of a new field takes place in an extremely heterogeneous landscape, involving a diverse and unevenly malleable array of social and material elements.

The First Study (2000)
Our interest in Gartner grew when one of us conducted a year-long ethnographic study at a public organisation. This large institution (described in the previous chapter as 'Melchester') was attempting to complete the procurement of a new CRM system and had contacted Gartner for help in the evaluation of a number of prospective vendors. The procurement team were finding it difficult to assess critically the various options, and thus an IT manager telephoned a Gartner analyst specialising in CRM. The advice received was then fed back to the wider procurement team (he would type up notes of his various discussions and circulate these at meetings of the wider procurement team). However, rather than clarify the situation, the analyst's intervention created further confusion. It led to a hotly contested debate between Gartner and one particular vendor about the nature and novelty of their offering. This contestation is discussed below.

One of the authors had good access to Melchester for over a period of a year. He was able to attend and observe the various meetings concerning the procurement, to collect material such as email communications and official correspondence, and interview the various players involved in the selection process. In total, the fieldworker attended more than a dozen such meetings and conducted over twenty interviews.

The Second Study (2009–2011)
Our second viewpoint on Gartner was when we returned to study their role in shaping CRM several years later as part of a further investigation of the nature and

role of industry analysts. Here we conducted interviews with Gartner as well as with a range of other players in the industry analysis field. In terms of which Gartner analysts we chose to interview, these were not chosen randomly but we deliberately singled out those we had witnessed in our earlier research at Melchester. The aim was to see whether (and how) Gartner's view on CRM had developed in subsequent years. Two analysts in particular had been influential—one based in the UK and the other in North America. The American analyst has now left Gartner and is no longer an industry analyst and—thus was not contacted. The UK analyst is still highly active in the field and we have interviewed him twice as part of our current study. We have also interviewed and had informal discussions with three other members of the CRM team.

we give greater attention to how industry analysts vigorously *defend* their frame. Before turning to the empirical material, we provide some detail on how we conducted our study.

6.3. ACT ONE: YOU'RE NOT ON OUR LIST

We begin by discussing Gartner's intervention during the Melchester procurement. Gartner had been asked to provide the organization with information on the various CRM systems under consideration. The 'vendor briefing' is one of the most common research tools used by Gartner and other industry analyst firms to scope out the market. It is the principal vehicle whereby IT vendors present offerings and business strategies to analysts covering their particular product market (Gartner Inc., no date). The idea is for analysts to collect information about vendors, which then forms the basis of later assessments or recommendations. Gartner purportedly conduct more than 12,000 briefings with vendors every year (Drobik 2010). It is also common for Gartner's clients to ask for briefings to be undertaken on their behalf. Alternatively, vendors (especially newcomers) may contact Gartner in order to brief them. Whilst Gartner advertise their coverage as extensive, it also acknowledges that no analyst firm can cover *all* vendors in a market (ibid).

6.3.1. Providing an assessment of vendors

Gartner was sent the names of the vendors and the basic description of the kinds of solutions offered. A Gartner analyst based in the UK ('Elias Thomas'), responsible for providing research specifically on the CRM market, responded with his view on each of the possibilities. These were then summarized in a document by a Melchester IT manager before being circulated within the wider Melchester procurement team. The analyst's comments were described as follows:

> LAGAN has done a good job in Birmingham and Belfast. They are very specifically working in the Local Government marketplace, they know the business well and [Elias's] view is that they should be on the list of products to be considered. ONYX is a US company and . . . work mainly in the private sector. Their products are good, but there would be some concern over scalability if we expected the operation to extend to hundreds of users in the front-office. . . . [Elias] has a list of some 500 vendors of CRM, many of which he meets on a regular basis to track the development of their products. [NEWVENDOR] is not on the list, he had not heard of them. He took an action to speak to a colleague based in America and come back to [Melchester] on what the US Analyst knew of them. SIEBEL has the largest share of the commercial marketplace, but he felt that in a few years, ORACLE will have emerged as the leading supplier to the Local Government market. This is not because it has the best products, but because it is better at selling to Local Government (note circulated within Melchester).

Prima facie, there was nothing particularly surprising about these reviews. Only one vendor (Lagan) appeared to receive an unqualified endorsement. The remainder were seen to have both a number of strengths and weaknesses. It was only through paying close attention to the detail of the document that one finds the bombshell. The vendor we are calling 'NewVendor' appeared to be something of an anomaly in Gartner's eyes. It did not appear on any of its 'lists', meaning the analyst firm could not provide specific commentary on this vendor. The analyst stated how he would check with Gartner colleagues based in the US as to whether they could provide more detail. In the meantime, he provided some preliminary comments based on his analysis of the documentation sent:

> They speculated that the [NewVendor] product was a toolkit rather than a full solution. In this case their concern would be how much expertise [the 'joint venture partner' working with Melchester] had with the product. It was explained that [NewVendor] staff would be likely to be involved in the installation as well. [Elias] would then be concerned about the ongoing support once the [NewVendor] specialists leave the site. He felt that [Melchester] would be the Guinea Pigs for this solution and in our position he would not be prepared to take the risk (note circulated within Melchester).

Based on limited information, the Gartner analyst was able to raise a number of concerns about NewVendor, consisting mainly of the fact that it appeared not to have a 'complete' local government CRM solution available. Since previous customers were all from different sectors (telecommunications and banking), this meant it would have to carry out extensive redevelopment of its existing system. Melchester would potentially therefore be 'guinea pigs' for this work. In the analyst's view, it was not worth taking the 'risk'. Later the same week the Gartner analyst gets back in touch to say that he had spoken to his US colleagues and they too were *unaware* of NewVendor. The Gartner analyst 'has been in touch with his colleague in the US, but [NewVendor] were unknown to him as well. Gartner can therefore not provide any research papers into the company or its products' (note circulated within Melchester). This latest news caused some disconcertion amongst Melchester employees. NewVendor had attracted many complimentary comments about both its technical ability and the willingness of its technical staff to address the needs of Melchester—for many people it was their 'preferred option'. This was now seemingly being challenged.

Melchester thought it necessary to give NewVendor the opportunity to respond to the (potentially damaging) review, which it choose to do and in a robust manner. NewVendor pointed to a number of issues related to the status of its software (this included the fact that whilst its solution was 'new', the various components going into it were 'tried and tested products' already running in various other sites around the world). It also raised some objections to the kinds of research produced by industry analyst firms.

> Their [NewVendor's] comment when it was pointed out that they were unknown to Gartner was that in the two years the company has been in existence it has not spent any time or effort in making itself known to industry analysts. This is because at present these companies do not have a category for what they are offering (what NewVendor called the 'integrated framework approach') (IT Manager's circulated notes).

When informed about NewVendor's comments, Gartner, in turn, sought to defend its own position. The analyst pointed out how it was not *him* problematizing NewVendor but the Gartner client base. He describes how one important way Gartner gets information was not simply through 'being briefed' by technology vendors but through contact with their own clients. He goes on to add how the CRM team had conducted over 150 CRM vendor briefings in the last year alone and only a small number of these had been initiated at the request of vendors. The bulk came through requests from their clients. The important point, he notes, was that in all these requests '[n]o client has asked us to ask for a briefing from [NewVendor]', which he thought was something of a 'surprise'.

To summarize, the industry analyst firm Gartner has thrown into question a procurement choice through casting doubt over one particular vendor—the newcomer that had emerged as the favourite. In the eyes of Gartner, NewVendor was an unknown quantity. As they saw it, they were *not* part of the CRM field. They thus provided a potentially critical review of this particular offering, one that later leads to NewVendor being *removed* from the user organization's list of possible options (see also Pollock & Williams 2007). This begs the question: Why was this vendor problematized in this way? Answering this requires investigating Gartner's research process.

6.4. ACT TWO: GARTNER'S KNOWLEDGE FRAME

6.4.1. Making sense of a bit of chaos

The enterprise system market is extremely complex. It is fast changing with the constant arrival of innovations, concepts and terminologies (Swanson & Ramiller 1997). Through conducting their research, industry analysts see their job as 'trying to make sense of a bit of chaos' (interview, Thomas). They are attempting to provide some 'clarity' to those paying for their services. Here we want to show that they have established means for doing this. This includes the methods used to scrutinize the claims vendors make about technologies. This task is facilitated by a wide range of social and technical components. Perhaps another way to say this is that these analysts have established 'frames' (Beunza & Garud 2007) through which they view developments in the market. Let us look in more detail at the nature and form of these frames.

6.4.1.1. Naming interventions

An essential part of Gartner's framing of an emerging technological field is the various 'naming interventions' it makes. Gartner are prolific in designating technologies, the successful naming of ERP being only the tip of the iceberg (Mabert et al. 2001). Here an industry analyst reflects on why firms like his have emerged to perform this role:

> ... often they [IT vendors] don't have the clout in their own right to name ... They haven't got the independence to be able to; unless they are so huge that they dictate, determine what the market is called. But that is rare. Normally somebody wants a third party to make that 'naming intervention'. It could be academia that does it; sometimes it is. It could be a group of vendors who get together and start using common terms. But normally the vendors are desperately trying to use different terms because they don't want to be seen to be copying or following a competitor. So what happens with us is we [Gartner] are in effect drawing a starting line saying: 'there is the line'. And everybody lines up behind it... (interview, Thomas).

Naming interventions are the analysts' means of sorting the world for its clients. It is not just their expertise and knowledge that makes them well placed to do this; it is also because, and apparently unlike other commercial actors, as the analyst goes onto describe, they have no 'axe to grind'. They seemingly have the 'independence' and 'credibility' to name a technology. They are the only ones able to draw a 'sensible box' or 'starting line' from which others can build. A Gartner analyst talked us through what he thought his firm was doing in coining new terms:

> When something like CRM comes up or ERP or whatever, you'll find that what was going on there was that analysts were going: 'Look there's a pattern. There's a trend. It's consolidating. This is coalescing or whatever. This vendor has bought that one. This is going to go in that direction. It's all going to end up like that. And that's going to be called [pauses for effect] 'ERP''. We are doing that for the users. The vendors then go: 'Great. That is where we are going. Boom! We're an ERP vendor'. They do it because they can see that we have drawn a box around a market that they are slap right bang in the middle of and they feel that they can dominate it or have a serious part to play (interview, Thomas).

Gartner is attempting to make sense of developments for *users*. The particular analyst is clear about this. He repeated it several times during interviews and discussions. However, he also notes how these interventions affect the activities of vendors—who will often align themselves around a new terminology. He explained this (constitutive) effect through describing how Gartner had been influential in classifying some of the technologies related to CRM:

> . . . we coin[ed] . . . acronyms like 'MRM', which is Marketing Resource Management in about 2001. EFM [Enterprise Feedback Management]—I think we came up with in about 2005 . . . So, for example, in marketing, we used to talk about MOM . . . which is like Marketing *Operations* Management. We decided we would prefer the term Marketing *Resource* Management. I can't remember exactly why, but it was about the resourcing, staffing and operational issues, and it is interesting now you will hardly ever see the term MOM. It just got *slaughtered* by MRM. And every vendor says 'We are an MRM vendor'. And it got its own momentum and off it went. That is kind of how it works (interview, Thomas).

According to the analyst, their terms acquire their 'own momentum' and that seemingly 'is kind of how it works'. Of course, just *how* it works is the issue that needs to be explained. When pressed for further detail on what Gartner did when coining terms, the analyst talked us through an example that he and a colleague had recently been involved in:

> I can tell you the story of EFM very clearly, because I have been involved in that with one with my colleagues. . . . [He] and I were looking at it and saying . . . 'well wait a minute. There is an elite group of Feedback Management vendors here who are giving multi-channel, real time, and they are doing analytics, and they are handling multiple different processes with one tool, and they are pitching themselves as a means to consolidate, a bit like ERP, down to one tool for handling all inbound and outbound feedback between themselves and the customer'. So we said it is: '*something* Feedback Management'. And we noticed that there is a

company up in Boston [who] started to use the term 'EFM'—Enterprise Feedback Management—and we went 'that's the term we like'. So we basically stole it and started using it. We said . . . 'this is EFM and this is FM. This is Feedback Management and this is Enterprise Feedback Management and these are the players in the market and this is what is going on'. We started that about . . . 2005. And if you look around now, any Feedback Management vendor who is of any decent type will have EFM slapped all over their website because that is the term (interview, Thomas).

Interestingly, as the analyst (perhaps unintentionally) lets slip, Gartner are not always strictly the authors of the terms. However, it is the organization that further develops and gives increased impetus to them; they help *shepherd* terms (Wang & Ramiller 2009). And the analyst thought that Gartner's seeming ability to successfully promote terms is related to 'timing' and its extensive connections to the wider community:

If Gartner steps in at the right moment—and it is coalescing; and no term has got dominant position—with Gartner getting in and stamping it, with the right timing, then that is what the term becomes. Because Gartner has got a rough contact with so many customers; because that is where we get our information. Yet we know most of the vendors. We are a big organization. We can get organizations to agree that is the term. Because we in effect draw a box around something and say: 'That is the market. There's the definition of it. These are the elements. These are the players. This is how you evaluate it. This is how you compare' (interview, Thomas).

Gartner (more than any other industry analyst firm) has been successful in naming technologies. However, whilst it appears to have had continued success, there has also been a number of 'failures'. What is interesting to note is that the majority of these are not public failures because most naming interventions tend to 'die internally':

More difficult is where you try something out and it doesn't fly. What tends to happen there is that it tends to die internally more often than not. In other words, an analyst becomes an advocate of something . . . there's a team of people who created it, but the key issue is that there is a team of people involved but there is one leader who is passionate about it and relentless. That is the key thing. It is partly the intellectual curiosity and the intellectual exercise of 'that's the way things are going', 'that's the trend', and being right! It is a combination of that but also being an absolute heavy, marketing it to death—internally first, because unless it flies internally it will never get outside. So normally by the time it has got outside it has got 20 or 30 analysts behind it, going 'yeah. That's the term we are going to use. That's the term. That makes sense. That's the term I'm going to use. I'll make sure that I'll reference that in my work'. And so it has got momentum in it. And Gartner will hammer away at it for several years often, till it gets enough momentum to get it going (interview, Thomas).

Conceiving of and shepherding a name is not simply an 'intellectual exercise' but equally involves enrolling and convincing others. If a terminology is to get out of the Gartner offices, it must already have mobilized an internal community of support. This means that individual analysts must become 'passionate' about a concept such that they can persuade others of its benefits ('marketing it to death—internally first'). Here we get a glimpse of both the internal community that must be mobilized within Gartner but also of the organizational machinery that needs to be set in train to help shepherd a term out into the world.

6.4.1.2. *Organizational machinery*

Thus far, in common with the notion of organizing vision (Swanson and Ramiller 1997), we have talked primarily about new terminologies as 'discourses'. However, in the last section, we also introduced the notion of 'organizational machinery'. By this, we mean that the frames of industry analysts are both symbolic *and* material. Names are aided in their operation with various kind of 'knowledge infrastructure' (Edwards 2010). We saw this quite vividly in the case of NewVendor, where a classification worked to problematize this particular actor (a classification is what MacKenzie [2009] might term 'intellectual equipment'). Gartner's definition of CRM was not simply a theoretical construct but one supported by various kind of listings, as we will see shortly, including lists of players and their products' core characteristics.

That said, it should be noted that many of these lists appeared to have a particularly 'local flavour'. We describe what we mean by this through discussing Gartner's attempts to computerize their lists (see Leyshon & Thrift [1999] for a discussion of the automation of lists). In principle, lists could be held on enterprise-wide electronic databases within Gartner, such that information belonging to one analyst could be made available to colleagues elsewhere, especially those located in different geographical locations. However, as we saw in the discussion of NewVendor, even those analysts specializing in the same area did not appear routinely to share information with each other. The UK analyst, for instance, had to check via the telephone with US colleagues as to whether anyone in the US offices had information on NewVendor. It seems the computerization of lists occurs but only in a rather limited way. An analyst explains why this is so:

> We've got skills databases: 'who knows what'. Client services team uses that, so it is to route the call to the right analyst. Each team has knowledge bases. They tried these glorified schemes of having a centralized knowledge base. There are *some* company wide ones...But we are not keeping volumes of information on each vendor because it changes so fast, to maintain it. It is usually just garbage most of

> what is in there. You look at it, and you go: 'Where the hell did this come from? It is about 3 years old'. Hopeless! So it's got to be maintained frequently. So what you are really seeing is that each analyst has to maintain their own 'pod of knowledge' and the job will be to find the analyst with the knowledge (interview, Thomas).

The analyst notes the problem of how information stored within centralized information sources quickly becomes 'garbage'. Obviously, as noted at the outset of this book, this is a world that is changing quickly, where knowledge is contextual and contingent. It thus appears that analysts do not work with formalized (centralized) kinds of information but keep control of their own individual 'pods of knowledge'. Lists and knowledge are attached to particular (groups of) analysts. We return to this point in Act Three, where we argue that a corollary of this is that analysts can often end up employing different frames when analyzing the same vendor.

6.4.1.3. Frames are entangled within the wider user community

Discussing these local forms of knowledge begs the question as to how analysts form their views (or compile their lists). Where does their knowledge come from? There appear to be three main sources: talking amongst themselves (for instance, where they 'peer review' each other's reports); meeting with (and quizzing) the actual vendors that are being assessed (the 'vendor briefings' discussed above); and interacting with their clients (who are often the actual users of these technologies). In all our dealings with Gartner, these latter interactions were said to be the primary opinion-forming source for analysts (and this was evidenced by the discussion of NewVendor above). A Gartner analyst expresses the scale of the interactions analysts might have over a 'normal' year:

> ...some of the analysts last year were doing a thousand enquires, that's a thousand calls a year, 200 working days doing five calls a day, that's five hours on the phone a day just talking to customers... Then face to face like I am doing here, there might be another 150, 200 conversations like that in a year so, [then] 700 face to face conversations of 20 minutes up to an hour. That's a lot of data in just one area. So as long as you are narrow enough in your focus, you would have to be an idiot, I personally believe you would have to be an idiot not to work out what is going on in that area (interview, Thomas).

Thus built into a frame is this process of interaction with clients. This can involve relatively simple interchanges, for instance the number of times an analyst is asked about a particular vendor. It can also—and perhaps especially—come from more qualitative forms of dialogue: such as continually hearing comments of a certain type about a vendor. An analyst describes how most of these comments cropped up when they were explicitly searching for feedback on particular vendors (as when they called up the 'references' supplied by vendors) but also in other interactions where it was common for their clients to be candid about their experiences with vendors. An analyst gives an example of typical kinds of feedback:

> 'Oh yeah, I forgot to tell you that they were complete idiots. They did x,y,z'. And you go 'Right. Why's that?' 'Oh, they did this. They sent this guy along and his name is', that sort of thing. Sometimes you can even get down to which individuals in which companies are screwing up (interview, Thomas).

To summarize, what we are arguing is that, in order to make sense of the IT domain, Gartner builds knowledge frames. These frames then go onto create boundaries within the marketplace (primarily but not exclusively through 'naming interventions'); they generate certain kinds of problematics amongst technology vendors (through episodes of 'categorization work'). The frames of industry analysts are supported by various market and knowledge infrastructures (lists and databases); and are shaped by the interactions analysts have with wider communities of users. The next section shows a further aspect of frame making which concerns the ability of industry analysts to 'defend' their frames. We examine this by returning to Gartner's encounter with NewVendor and showing the further forms of contestation that emerged between these actors.

6.4.2. Gartner defends its frame

The discussion around NewVendor's system was characterized by two starkly contrasting positions. NewVendor saw itself as an innovative player, offering more than a simple CRM solution. The problem, in their view, lay with Gartner's rather narrow classification of CRM. Gartner strongly disagreed. Everything in their frame pointed to the fact that NewVendor would be 'a risk'. They were not, in their view, part of the CRM field. The issue came to a head when NewVendor were asked to say what exactly was unique about their proposal. Gartner, in turn, was invited to comment on these claims. The episode was played out when NewVendor produced a document describing how their solution differed from those offered by competitors. We reproduce the main parts of the exchange here. NewVendor begins by outlining the novel features of their system: '[NewVendor] is the first vendor to provide an *integrated framework approach*' (NewVendor document, *our emphasis*).

The 'integrated framework approach' is NewVendor's own terminology. This seemingly provides a more connected type of CRM solution. Gartner's repost, however, is that NewVendor's claims are exaggerated and that their approach is similar to that already being offered by other vendors: 'Loud Cloud, Graham Technologies and several others have said the same in the past' (Gartner Comments appended to NewVendor document).

NewVendor sets out the details of how its offering differs from others, emphasizing particularly the disconnected and 'patchwork' nature of competitor technologies:

> With other vendors, [Melchester] would be buying separate products for CRM, Portal front-end, CTI [Computer Telephony Integration], workflow and document management, email automation and rules engines. While individually these might compare favourably with the [NewVendor] components, this would be a patchwork solution and it would be very difficult getting these components successfully integrated (NewVendor document).

NewVendor states that competitor systems are made up of distinct components that have to be brought together through laborious (and potentially risky) forms of programming work. They point to how their solution already contains important integration functionality that other vendors would be required to bring in from elsewhere. Gartner refute this, noting how there are already systems on the market with most if not all of these capabilities. As Gartner see it, other vendors could market their systems in the exact same way:

> The majority of vendors in this space will provide some form of portal front-end, call management, eService, workflow, email automation and rules engines plus CTI integration (but not CTI). Usually this is achieved through partnerships with a small number of partners (e.g. Interactive Intelligence with Onyx and Siebel with Avaya) (Gartner comments appended to NewVendor document).

Gartner then focus on the similarity between NewVendor's system and that of one other vendor:

> It is interesting the degree of overlap with eGain. We would see eGain as a vendor that already competes in the eService, email, workflow and a portal front-end but not in the area of CTI or call management. Software vendors have not traditionally crossed the boundary between application and infrastructure but Avaya with Quintus and Altitude would make the same arguments as those made here (Gartner comments appended to NewVendor document).

Here they concede a novel feature of the NewVendor system—that it has 'crossed the boundary between application and infrastructure'—but also point out how other vendors might make the same claim (see Rao et al. [2005] for a discussion of the difficulties this kind of 'boundary crossing' within product categories brings). Gartner also refutes the suggestion that integrating the various components in one system would be problematic, highlighting how NewVendor itself might suffer the same kind of integration difficulties:

> We disagree that all combinations are very difficult to get them to work together—it depends on the combination of products selected and whether that combination has been achieved before. [NewVendor] is not exempt from

integration with the ACD system and the existing eGain applications (Gartner comments appended to NewVendor document).

This exchange highlights further aspects of Gartner's frame, in particular the issue of *commensuration*. Espeland and Stevens (1998) suggest that powerful actors attempt to maintain existing classifications (and resist enlargement to account for more variability) to preserve their ability to commensurate. That is, to maintain comparability amongst vendors (Lounsbury & Rao 2004). In other words, their methods are fundamentally relative: they assess vendors not as stand-alone organizations but always in relation to others. The result is that Gartner is able to point out that the apparently novel features of NewVendor's Integrated Framework Solution are already contained within existing offerings.

To summarize, what we have shown is that when contested Gartner will robustly defend its frame. It does this mostly through processes of commensuration, which, as argued by Espeland and Stevens (1998), can appear a highly robust mechanism to defend seemingly controversial decisions. It is one that seemingly puts decision making on a 'neutral' plane (everyone can see the characteristics of competing systems, such that individual bias is apparently pushed out of the frame). Act three continues this focus on contestation but this time through discussing a face-to-face meeting between Gartner analysts and NewVendor employees. Here we ask: If a frame shapes the way industry analysts assess a vendor then what happens if a vendor is viewed through different frames?

6.5. ACT THREE: INTERNAL DISSENT: NOT ALL IN GARTNER VIEW THINGS IN THE SAME WAY

6.5.1. Different reactions to same data

Since the confusion surrounding NewVendor was growing rather than declining, and because there were no available research papers on the vendor, Melchester decided to ask Gartner to conduct a vendor briefing on their behalf. (As a Gartner client, they had the possibility of commissioning a number of briefings each year). Thus, several weeks later, a US based analyst [whom we call 'Dr S'] finally sat down with NewVendor employees to quiz them about their technologies. A Melchester document describes how:

Gartner conducted a supplier briefing in the USA with [NewVendor] on 26th March, following our queries. This discussion was to get feedback from that briefing. [Dr. S] was one of the analysts involved in that briefing and [JT] is our account manager who arranged the call. [Dr. S] was first given a brief summary of our current position and what our plans are (note circulated within Melchester).

The meeting appeared productive for both parties. One Gartner analyst feeds back her thoughts and assessment to Melchester:

> [Dr S] covered [NewVendor's] reasons for not making themselves known to Gartner before, i.e. an emerging company whose product doesn't fit neatly into existing categories. They see themselves as providers of business process utility solutions/service providers rather than simply software suppliers. They customize their products for a particular industry sector and aim to share the cost across the customer base to reduce costs. [Dr S] felt they had a very theoretical way of presenting themselves and had found it difficult to find the appropriate analyst (note circulated within Melchester).

This comment appears double-edged. On the one hand, Dr S points to the problem new vendors experience when starting out (they are an 'emerging company' and their products do not neatly fit into existing industry analyst categories). She identifies how NewVendor thought itself 'residual' (Star & Bowker 2007) in relation to the way Gartner categorize and define CRM. On the other, she also indirectly criticizes them for failing to understand the role and influence of industry analysts (how to relate to them, how much effort to invest in interacting with them, how to present its strategies and products, and so on). However, Dr S then goes as far as to suggest that Melchester should *not* give too much weight to the initial assessment of her UK colleagues:

> She advised not to read too much into the fact that they were not known to Gartner. It was in [NewVendor's] interest not to be classified with other CRM vendors as they offer broader services. They did not want to be seen as simply a software vendor. They had perhaps failed to take a more pragmatic approach to this (note circulated within Melchester).

Indeed the analyst explicitly points out that it was advantageous for New-Vendor *not* to be compared with other CRM vendors since they were offering something different/more. She then lists further (mostly positive) aspects about NewVendor that had not surfaced in the initial assessment:

> Analysts attending the briefing had been impressed with [NewVendor's] knowledge of their marketplace and their understanding of software evolution . . . [NewVendor] have a legacy of customers in the Insurance, Banking and Telco sectors both as [NewVendor] and former companies. Less so in the Government sector. The client list is impressive (note circulated within Melchester).

The analyst commented positively on their 'knowledge of the marketplace' and their 'understanding of software evolution', two of the important criteria by which Gartner rates and evaluates vendors. She also passes comment on their impressive 'client list', which, as already mentioned, was another of the criteria by which vendors are judged. When the conversation turns to some of the more thorny issues, the analyst gives her view of the 'risk' of going with an unknown quantity:

> Asked for comments about it being risky going with a company we had not previously heard of, she said that it is not necessary always to go with a big name, but the risk has to be managed. A key question is who is responsible for delivery. It was explained that [a joint venture partner] is the prime contractor and [Dr S] said we then have to ask how we will be protected by [the joint venture partner] against non-delivery (note circulated within Melchester).

What this analyst does is bring into the frame other factors, in particular, the fact that NewVendor is not acting alone in supplying its systems but supported by a joint venture partner organization—a very large British telecommunications company with a recently established software and systems integration division. It is made clear that it is the joint venture partner that is ultimately responsible for delivering a successful project. The analyst also points out that it is also in NewVendor's direct interest to ensure the project is a success: '[NewVendor] is still an emerging company and has to build a list of satisfied clients. [Dr S] would therefore expect them to ensure that projects were a success' (note circulated within Melchester).

Comparing this assessment with the previous one, we find that the analysts are focusing on the same vendor but coming to different conclusions. In concluding, the US analyst makes a point that goes some way to explaining these contrasting assessments. Her area of expertise is not strictly speaking CRM solutions; she specializes in 'Business Process Outsourcing' (BPO):

> [Dr S] said that she was not a CRM specialist; Business Process Outsourcing was her speciality. It had been [NewVendor's] choice not to go into the CRM category. She emphasized, however, that [NewVendor] is not a Business Process Outsourcer. They work with partners, perhaps the most significant being a recent project in Australia with EDS as the partner (note circulated within Melchester).

A way to conceptualize this, perhaps, is to suggest that the analyst is not committed to the same frame as her UK colleagues. She is investigating Melchester from a different modality. It could be argued that vendor qualities are being constituted through two different frames, and because these organize responses, they each create different kinds of problematic. Viewed through the initial 'CRM frame' NewVendor is compared to other CRM vendors (and is seen to be replicating only what is already in the marketplace). There is the use of particular kinds of equipment and interactions ('lists' constituted from community engagement). The problems raised include NewVendor's absence from 'lists', that they are 'not known' to the community, that there is not a complete system available, which means there is a high level of 'risk' involved, and so on. Alternatively, the 'BPO frame' appears more diffuse. It is one that includes but is not limited to CRM (there are multiple overlapping technology suppliers who have a potential claim to be involved in this area). When constituted through this frame it is recognized that NewVendor is offering 'broader services'. Here the equipment includes 'lists', but this time of 'impressive clients'. The issue on which the vendor is assessed is the fact that it is backed by a significant 'joint venture partner'. Further, the US analyst reinterprets the problems raised by the earlier analyst (unknown, risk, etc.) and concludes that these may not necessarily be reasons for concern. They could equally be understood as reasons why to *choose* NewVendor.

6.5.2. COMPETING FRAMES

What does this example of competing frames tell us? It suggests that this large industry analyst organization is not a 'unity'; there is no single Gartner-wide community view. Frame building appears to be an idiosyncratic 'craft' (as opposed to a standardized scientific) model of knowledge making. Analysts are highly reputable individuals trading in the Gartner realm—and attempting to further their own reputations (authority). Indeed, and recalling the discussion above about how analysts work not with centralized but with *individualized pods of knowledge*, an analyst revealed that one of the main difficulties Gartner has is getting its people to speak with one voice:

> ... Gartner's like a herd of cats. It's like herding cats. The different analyst groups are all very independent of each other ... We work in teams, where we work very tight in the teams, so we can back each other up, and we know what each other is doing. Outside of that team, there is a bit of a consolidation but at the kind of company level it has to be driven almost top down to make us look up and say 'what is going on in your area?' And we all come to meeting where we learn about each other's research areas. But is more of a kind of interesting background information. It is not going to help me do my job (interview, Thomas).

Interestingly, the passage above points to the difficulties of regulating this kind of knowledge and actor. Gartner regularly attempts to establish a more corporate view but analysts are seemingly pulled in alternative directions. This perhaps explains (in part) the internal contestation that exists around understandings of new technologies. Different 'teams' continue to read developments in different ways. They have their own knowledge infrastructure ('lists' and 'pods of knowledge'). Centralized knowledge repositories have given way to distributed and individualized resources.

Those located in different geographical locations, for instance, and specializing in the study of one or other related technologies, came to differing conclusions.[1] To make sense of this we argue that these analysts applied a different frame to the same vendor and this produced contrasting results. It turns out that there were often 'competing frames' at play within the analyst firm. The example is telling because it shows how the technological field Gartner is attempting to shepherd is contested *internally*. What we want to do now is show how the field was also contested *externally*. This brings us to the final act where we consider how frames are 'adopted' but also how they can be 'abandoned' (Beunza & Garud 2007).

6.6. ACT FOUR: FRAME TRANSFORMATION

6.6.1. Adopting/abandoning a frame

Gartner are widely seen as the coiners of the CRM concept (Norton 2000). However, whilst it was an early player in CRM's development, it was not the originator of the term. This is identified as the work of marketing academics who were talking and writing about the importance of 'customer relationship marketing' during the 1980s (Firth & Lawrence 2006). Gartner's interest is said to have begun in the early 1990s when they noticed a growing interest in new kinds of software. One analyst described this early involvement:

> In . . . 1993 Gartner created a Sales Leadership Strategy Service . . . And we created a Sales Leadership Strategy Service, and a Customer Services Support Strategy, and an NKT service to focus on the marketing director. And that was between '93 and '95. So we were quite early in looking at the technologies for sales marketing, customer services completely separately. Then with about you know probably only 2 or 3 analysts in each team . . . . That is amazingly early from a Gartner perspective. It is about '93, '95 we set up those services. I think only about '96, '97 we decided to put them together into a common group (interview, Thomas).

Once this emerging field was identified (and in keeping with its practice of performing naming interventions) Gartner set about *re-designating* it. Even though already widely identified as *Customer* Relationship Management the analyst firm attempted to re-label the field as *Technology Enabled* Relationship Management:

> And around about, just after maybe '98 or probably '98, I guess, '98, '99, [Gartner] came up with the term 'TERM'. Because [Gartner] said it's '*Technology Enabled* Relationship Management'. So we were pointing out that we're only going to look at technology not the strategy aspects of it. Our job is to look at the technologies that companies use. So they put the three teams together under one bucket called 'TERM' (interview, Thomas).

Recalling the logic behind this new terminology, the analyst notes how the existing designation was founded on an interest in the 'strategic' aspects related to customer relationships (the interests of its academic founders). Gartner's proposed change instead was said to reflect an interest in purely the 'technologies' of CRM. This naming intervention did not enjoy the same kinds of success as earlier ones (the ERP terminology, around this period, was just reaching the heights of its popularity). Whilst Gartner attempted to extend the notion amongst their industry contacts, using all of its organizational apparatus and community networks, the name simply failed to 'ignite':

> What we were defining as TERM was what most people would understand as CRM today. But nobody bought into the term TERM. It just didn't catch. It didn't ignite with people...In effect, the industry itself decided it was CRM. That was the term they were going to use. So it was one of these, it comes to a point when it is no good pushing against the tide. Even though technically we were more accurate, it didn't matter (interview, Thomas).

The analyst puts it quite starkly, stating how the notion 'went down like a lead balloon' with the rest of the industry. Had the term been constitutive? Had it affected how vendors labelled their products? The analyst was certain that it had not: 'No, not really. There might have been the odd one using it in their literature but they weren't saying "we are a TERM vendor". It didn't work. It never took off' (interview, Thomas). The result was that Gartner was forced to abandon the term TERM: 'We [Gartner] probably killed that in about 2000. It lasted probably only about a year, a year and a half, between about '99 and 2000' (interview, Thomas).

What, if anything, does this failure tell us? It is a demonstration of the contingency surrounding the work of a powerful market actor. The industry analyst Gartner plays a crucial role in mobilizing consensus around emerging technological fields. But this example shows that it is not always able to impose its view. Even the seemingly most influential of industry analysts can still fail to mobilize others around its vision of the world. We labour this point because we think it significant in terms of the shaping of a major organizational technology. We speculate that Gartner's failure to impose its frame had important consequences for the CRM field: CRM has not seen the same kinds of stability that one finds in earlier fields (like ERP). The biography of CRM appears to be different and perhaps more diffuse because of this.

6.6.2. Result of abandonment: Increase in ambiguity?

Shortly after the turn of the century, CRM technology had begun to resemble the 'organizing visions' described by Swanson and Ramiller (1997). The notion was being pulled in many different directions by various players. A Gartner analyst notes some of the transformations that CRM has experienced: 'CRM has been called Customer Interaction Management, Technology-Enabled

Relationship Management, Enterprise Relationship Management, Demand Chain Management and Customer Value Management' (Maoz 2001).

During this period, one of the only things that commentators appeared to be able to agree on was the level of confusion that had now developed around the technology. A Gartner analyst interviewed in the practitioner press makes the following point:

> Well, I think the people that are confused are analysts, journalists, vendors and, perhaps, consultants. I don't think the organizations that are involved are that confused about what they're trying to do. I've called it the 'flag-of-convenience' problem, in that they have a name for the program, the project, the initiative, the 'whatever they call it', internally. And, the term 'CRM' lost its shine in about 2001, so they renamed it in many cases, or they shut it down or repackaged it or refocused it, whatever (Thompson 2004).

Here the analyst points to how CRM has become nothing but a 'flag of convenience', a term that could be 'shut down', 'repackaged' or 'refocused' depending on a player's interests and circumstances. Interestingly, despite their loosening grip on the field, this does not prevent Gartner from making periodic attempts to make further interventions. During the period, pushed by the apparent discord, but also the fact CRM was caught up in the fallout surrounding the bursting of the dot.com bubble, Gartner continued to set up meetings with the idea of getting the major players to agree a new name:

> It is interesting, around 2001, we talked to companies. We were talking about CRM strategies to people and they were saying: 'We would rather call it Customer Strategy supported by CRM technology'. So around 2001, when it got discredited with the 'bust', in 2001, 2003, there were a lot of companies saying that they don't want to call it CRM anymore. In fact, we had meetings with all the major integrators, consultancies to say: 'Shall we come up with a new term?'. The problem was nobody could agree a term. Everybody tries to fragment in different directions... CRM ended up having this double meaning: it means something to do with business strategy... which is the original meaning; and it means to do with the technology. So it has this, it is confusing to people... (interview, Thomas).

What this suggests is that the framing capacities of industry analysts change over time. Despite its organizational machinery and extensive community connections, Gartner were seemingly unable to get the players to agree a common term. Thus they move from a rather rigid position to a more encompassing and open one. As a result, a certain amount of disorganization becomes evident in the sector. Indeed a Gartner analyst interviewed in the practitioner press describes how he advocates, when talking to clients, that they should now develop their *own* understanding of the term:

> About 1998 Gartner sat down and wrote a big definition, which starts with the word, 'CRM', and defines it specifically as a business strategy, and we've stuck

with that definition now for about—well, ever since '98. But, since 2002, our message has been pretty straightforward, which is: Ignore our definition of CRM, and in fact, ignore everybody else's definition of CRM and come up with your own definition.... In fact, something we're doing right this moment is questioning not the definition of CRM but whether the term 'CRM', itself, should still be used. And, we're wondering whether it's finally coming to an end as a useful acronym. Gartner had TERM up till about '99. And, since then, we've stuck with the industry phrase of CRM (Thompson 2004).

We have argued that the knowledge frame industry analysts apply to an area of activity allows them to inform and regulate the various goings on in that area. However, the frame that appeared applicable back in 1998 now no longer seemed to apply. Where at the beginning of the century Gartner was attempting to regulate the offerings of vendors, it had, just a few years later, as one analyst pointed out, become 'less dogmatic than [it was] back in '98'. Gartner appears no longer to be the sole actor attempting to shepherd this particular field.

To summarize this section, what we have shown is that the industry analyst firm studied was not able to impose its view on the CRM field in the same way it had done in earlier years. CRM was now being understood and interpreted in many different ways (in this respect the work of Swanson and Ramiller [1997] shows itself still to be highly relevant). However, whereas these scholars suggest that (a certain amount of) ambiguity can aid the proliferation of a new name, we would argue that it is precisely this ambiguity that industry analysts are attempting to police. If a technological field cannot be defined then it becomes difficult to regulate vendors within it. Thus, the increase in ambiguity meant that Gartner was forced to modify its position—or, in other words, to 'break frame' (Goffman 1974).

6.7. DISCUSSION: HOW INDUSTRY ANALYSTS FRAME MARKETS

We join scholars interested in making sense of the abundance of new terminologies that continue to proliferate within the information system domain (Swanson & Ramiller 1997, Wang 2009). Our particular entrance point has been to note the way certain standard and stable designations emerge and come to be applied to broadly similar, or, in some cases, differing set of artefacts. A more or less similar collection of rapidly evolving artefacts can be given common nomenclatures that then go on to endure for prolonged periods of time. We have sought to answer the question as to *who decides* whether or not a particular vendor technology is part of a wider terminology. Who, in other words, decides the boundaries around different nomenclatures? We have pointed to the effort of the 'knowledge infrastructures of information technology' that shepherd the consensus around new and emerging techno-logical fields. This is the particular role of industry analysts—and specifically of Gartner Inc.—who attempt to decide not only a name but the interpretation of that designation. Below we outline the various ways in which they do this (i–vii).

Gartner is well known for its *(i) naming interventions.* The designation of a technological field of activity is not trivial. If successful, such interventions can go on to provide crucial resources *and* constraints within which vendors and management and technology consultants' articulate offerings. We have drawn on the 'communitarian' perspective to show how new concepts achieve wide currency in a process catalysed through the activities of certain key players—in the case of Customer Relationship Management (CRM), notably vendors, consultants and industry analysts—but are also ultimately sustained by the activities of wider communities of organizational users and others (Swanson & Ramiller 1997, Wang & Ramiller 2009, Wang 2009, Swanson 2010). Naming interventions can reduce uncertainty for adopters and developers alike. The establishment of a new field draws boundaries around a set of artefacts and their suppliers and thereby creates a space in which some sorting and ranking may be possible. This often paves the way for a comparative analysis by adopters of the relative advantages of particular offerings for their specific organization. Clustering new kinds of offerings together may also serve to reinforce expectations about what functionality should be included and where the technology will go in the future. This also allows vendors to assess their products, their promotion and enhancement in relation to the features of broadly comparable products and their likely future development trajectories (in some case differentiating their offering).

However, just as a name can include it can also preclude: it is something that 'prevents' and 'constrains'. This can generate controversy, especially amongst those that become marginalized by it. Industry analysts can be seen to police the boundaries that they and others have previously set out through performing various kinds of *(ii) categorization work,* where they are able to say whether or not a particular vendor solution is part of a technological field. They can do this because, as the work on 'critics' informs us, they view the world through 'product classifications' (Zuckerman 1999). In this view vendors that fall outside this lens 'are penalized not simply because they raise information costs for consumers but because the social boundaries that divide product classes limit the consideration of such offerings' (ibid: 1404). This perspective usefully flags how the IT innovation community (Wang & Ramiller 2009) is not an entirely open and equal community, as there are forms of knowledge that actors are forced to take into account but which they are not necessarily able to shape (Adler & Heckscher 2006).

We have also made use of the 'finitist' argument that categorization is not straightforward but involves 'a decision'. Reaching a decision can lead to various forms of 'contestation' and, as Barnes et al. (1996) suggest, experts can often categorize the same object in contrasting ways. We saw how the seemingly novel technology produced by one newcomer was problematized and then how, in turn, it disputed the negative reviews it received (going as far as to call into question the industry analyst firm's research process). The newcomer appeared to fall between different 'frames' or infrastructures within the same industry analyst firm, each of which brought different problematics and qualities to the surface. This was damaging for the vendor's immediate and longer-term future: it not only lost out in the procurement contest described here but it also, as far as we know, has not been able to enter this specific geographical and sectoral specific market; nor does it continue to position itself in the same way in relation to other CRM vendors. (Even though it was at odds with how the industry analyst firm and others conceived of CRM, it has since come into line with the prevailing definition).

One other issue we raise with regard to the critics perspective is the suggestion that it is 'social' boundaries that limit the consideration of particular vendors. Zuckerman (1999) suggests that actors employ categories to *interpret* the offers set before them. Yet we are frankly sceptical that, by themselves, product terminologies can perform this role (particularly, as we learn from the finitist analysis, there can be much complexity and confusion surrounding classifications). Something else must be enabling these screening processes. One reason why the work of industry analyst is 'authoritative' is that their frames are shot through with various forms of *(iii) market infrastructure.* The particular infrastructure we observed during fieldwork was 'lists'. We might go as far as to suggest that one of the prime roles of industry analysts is filling out emerging technological fields with lists of varying description. List making appears to be rife within industry analysts firms. In all of the Gartner presentations and workshops that we attended the audience was treated to various kinds of lists: lists of 'Cool Vendors', 'of the priorities of Chief Information Officers', 'of the various kinds of functionality found in systems', 'of ranked vendors', etc. (see Bowker & Star [1999] for the importance of list making). Moreover, lists turn out to be particularly effective in sorting vendors. Whether or not someone appears on a list is (generally) not thought to be a matter for interpretation. A vendor's absence from a list can have an effect even if people disagree about the accuracy of the associated categorization process.

A further reason that the work of industry analysts has influence is that, when necessary, they will vigorously *(iv) defend their frame.* It is here the chapter adds (in some small way) to Beunza & Garud (2007). Industry analysts are not only frame builders but they have also established ways to evidence and shore up their boundary work (meaning they are 'frame defenders'). Indeed when making claims and interacting with clients we found there to be different modalities at play: they were times when industry analysts sought to signal quite clearly to adopters their (often critical) assessment of specific vendors, as well as contexts in which they were less candid as they sought to protect and shield themselves. This was because, attached to recommendations, was the issue of liability and responsibility. Industry analysts need to make their views accountable in terms of presenting them as the result of systematic process and in being able to defend their judgements. The principal ways in which industry analysts appeared to do this was through commensuration as well as by pointing to the provenance of assessments. Commensuration appears to provide industry analysts with a means to smooth away possible contestation (Espeland & Stevens 1998). The literature on product classifications suggests that placing a vendor in the context of others is an attempt to weaken its claim that its offerings are novel (Kennedy 2008). It is through comparing the offerings of different vendors that it seemingly becomes 'obvious' to everyone how things really stand. As for the provenance of their views, industry analysts claim that assessments are developed out of their many interactions with their client base. They rely on the testimony of these wider communities of users and decision makers. It is not *them* casting aspersions; they are simply reporting back (and aggregating) what their clients are reportedly telling them. In this respect, we might consider that the frames of industry analysts depend on these kinds of interactions. In other words, that they are *(v) entangled with wider communities of users.*

A way of capturing all these various points (i–v) is to say that new terminologies are often coupled to the practices, artefacts and communities of those who produce them (Hyysalo 2006). This conceptualization attempts to capture the role these market experts play in shepherding terms and also the way in which they are simultaneously attempting to realize and regulate the various boundaries proposed by the designations they and others deploy.

We have been careful to draw attention to the limits on how industry analysts proceed. These actors *have* become highly influential in drawing the boundaries around technologies but they are *not* able to impose their view. This was best exemplified, internally, when we saw how two teams of analysts failed to agree on the nature of the vendor technology they were both examining and then, externally, when the analyst firm was not able to convince others of the merits of a particular terminology ('Technology Enabled Relationship Management'). This evidences how industry analysts have limits in relation to their capacity to organize and speak about the events they come across. These experts are attempting to organize the consensus surrounding a technological field. It should perhaps be no surprise that they come across areas where the boundaries have already been drawn (or have been drawn differently to the ones they are proposing). When this happens, the industry analysts may *break frame* (Goffman 1974). In other words, these *(vi) experts do not always stick to their frame.* This contradicts Beunza and Garud's (2007) suggestion that, once committed, analysts necessarily persevere with a position because to do otherwise would seemingly bring into question their credibility. However, our fieldwork suggests that this may not be the only element here. Industry analyst firms recognize (and will at times openly acknowledge) 'misframings'. In other words, they are not afraid to withdraw a term that is competing against an incumbent terminology, especially if it appears only to be adding further confusion.[2]

We also suggest that *(vii) the framing capacities of industry analysts may change over time.* When Gartner coined the Enterprise Resource Planning (ERP) terminology back in 1990 (Wylie 1990), for instance, the firm had already been in existence for more than a decade. Whilst it had a number of rivals (Computer Intelligence, Dataquest, IDC, Input and Yankee were all well established by then) it had managed to develop the cognitive authority to make this important naming intervention. Few other organizations at the time could mobilize the organizational machinery and community connections necessary to draw and maintain the boundaries around a new technological field of activity. Ten years later, however, during the period when CRM was taking off, Gartner found itself competing with many other industry experts. Today, there is a large active body of industry experts and consultants writing, blogging, and selling ideas about technology. It appears that not only has a market for this form of boundary work been created but also that competition between various intermediaries has helped foster the ambiguity that we now find surrounding discussions of CRM. Since no one player dominates, this means that all attempts to define the particular technological field may have an effect. We return to this point in Chapter 10.

6.8. CONCLUSION: NEW KNOWLEDGE INFRASTRUCTURES OF INFORMATION TECHNOLOGY

We conclude by calling for increased attention to the knowledge infrastructures of information technology. Through their appearance, we have seen a shift from a relatively simple market of ideas to a more organized and structured one. Industry analysts, and Gartner in particular, play a crucial role in shaping technological fields. Their work may have immediate consequences for technology vendors and more broadly for the direction and pace of innovation within the wider IT arena. One implication of their work is that it may stifle novelty. Vendors who offer something different may find their products do not conform to standard product definitions and thus may fall between classification schemes (and be problematized). This conjecture alone deserves further attention, and we return to this point in the concluding chapter when we consider the policy implications of our research. Furthermore, we speculate that, in a context of accelerating technological innovation, that throws up new challenges and uncertainties to potential innovators or adopters, and where the normal processes of decision-making are deemed to be inadequate, there will be a growing number of experts of various types attempting to shape emerging technological fields. Clearly not all these actors will influence innovation in the same way or to the same extent; only a small number will produce terms able to designate actual fields; only some will be in a position to categorize vendor technologies. Indeed, as we have shown here, even the apparently most powerful of actors will fail to command the same level of influence over time or from one technological field to another. However, there is a need for scholars to develop the analytical tools and frameworks to allow a systematic and sophisticated study of their influence. Our research also suggests we may need to address a possible spectrum of knowledge institutions with, at one end of the scale, powerful bodies such as the industry analyst firm described here, which explicitly sees itself as organizing and shepherding technological fields, and, at the other end, actors and organizations that may be less central and may not necessarily even recognize their role as such. The recent upsurge of 'technology bloggers' (Davidson & Vaast 2009), for instance, is particularly pertinent in this latter respect. We have produced a study covering one part of the spectrum, where one group has managed to command the centre of attention, but there are many other kinds of organization and actor deserving of study.

NOTES

1. This appears a well-known problem in the industry that some put down to Gartner's lack of internal integration. Duncan Chapple describes it thus: 'The reality is that analyst houses are not the great knowledge sharing communities they claim to be. Look at the most extreme case: Not so long ago many of Gartner's customers saw it as a network of competing businesses [Research, Dataquest, Datapro, Consulting, Tech Republic] that stole revenue from each other by fighting over customers and hoarding knowledge. As much as Gartner encouraged its staff and customers to have single points of contact, the reality is that information never flowed smoothly across divisions and countries at Gartner [or at many other analyst houses]. Information and client contact are highly distributed at Gartner and most other analyst houses, like peer to peer computing. Don't think that unloading your ideas to the central office will lead to the data drifting out to where it needs to be. That's how a mainframe server works, not an organization where knowledge hoarding can be a way to keep your job' (Chapple 2002).
2. We found other examples where Gartner withdrew frames. For instance, in one such designation episode they coined the phrase 'Software Oriented Architecture' (SOA). A couple of years later, and even though adopters were apparently still

'confused with the idea of SOA' (interview, Ward Dutton), they released further research identifying a new development: what they called 'SOA 2.0'. This led to one of the smaller industry analyst firms setting up a 'petition' which generated enough negative publicity that Gartner were then forced drop what its critics see as this 'fundamentally flawed' terminology from its publications.

7

Marketing of Quantifications

with GianMarco Campagnolo

7.1. LABOUR OF COMMENSURATION

Earlier we quoted from Karpik's (2010: 14) thought-provoking book *Valuing the Unique* that 'the market is "equipped" or it does not exist'. Here he was referring to the seeming difficulties of choosing between certain products where the consumer cannot really know the qualities of these goods until after they have consumed them. Whilst he was talking about consumer products like wine or music, he could easily have also been talking about the extremely complex enterprise systems described in these pages. Indeed, the difficulties faced by the consumer in choosing between these large-scale industrial technologies are on another scale altogether in terms of the level of complexity and the costs of discovery. These substantial (often business-critical decisions) about what may be major strategic investments (costing several millions of pounds) are carried out infrequently and businesses often lack the expertise and experience needed for effective decision-making (Tingling & Parent 2004, Pollock & Williams 2009). The major difficulties faced are that would-be adopters are assessing not just technical properties but also intangible issues such as the future performance of a technology vendor (will it survive into the future?), its direction (will it continue to invest in the particular market in coming years?), its behaviour (can it fulfil its promises?), etc. Another aspect of this difficulty is that very different kinds of vendors and technologies have to be compared before a choice can be made. These are not insignificant problems.

Just how consumers are 'equipped' to make such comparisons is beginning to attract attention from scholars in Science and Technology Studies (STS), Economic Sociology, Information Systems, Organization Studies and beyond. Some have gone as far as to conceptualize the economy (Callon et al. 2002, Karpik 2010) and society (Espeland & Stevens 1998) in a way that puts *comparison* as central to its organization. Callon et al. (2002), in their 'economy of qualities' thesis, highlight the shortcomings of social science approaches that take for granted the 'assessment criteria' that play a role in mediating the choice of one product over another (Pollock & Williams 2007). Their interest is in how incommensurable artefacts are brought together and the relationships between them standardized, so that they can be compared in the same space (Callon & Muniesa 2005, Karpik 2010). This is the process that Espeland & Stevens (1998: 313) describe as 'commensuration': the 'comparison of different entities according to a common metric'. According to Espeland and Stevens (1998: 323) commensuration can 'radically transform the world' through bringing into being new categories and reconfiguring existing 'relations of authority'.

Within this view, there have been calls for greater attention to be given to the experts who measure and classify technologies and products. Scholars argue that the failure to capture or to explain how particular forms of assessment are brought into being and adopted may miss a key shaping element of the economy (Callon et al. 2002). Without the devices or measures to establish equivalence, Karpik (2010) queries how different objects can be brought together, compared and purchased.

It is precisely in this context of the marked asymmetry of access to information between vendors and purchasers and of difficulties of comparing and sorting complex information products that we see the emergence of industry analysts. There are dozens, if not hundreds, of such players attempting to direct and shape IT procurement markets through assessments of the relative capacity and standing of vendors (Firth & Swanson 2002, 2005). And it is Gartner which has emerged ahead of all others to mark its influence on how key technology selection decisions are made. Through the various innovations described in previous chapters—its 'Magic Quadrants', 'Hype-Cycles', 'IT Market Clocks' etc.—it has been able in important and direct ways to set the 'rules of the game' (Bourdieu 2005).

In this chapter we show how Gartner has done this by (i) redefining the measures by which technology vendors and their products are judged and ranked and (ii) how it attempts to visualize and compare the position of vendors and technologies according to the specific measures on its Magic Quadrant. This tool generates comparisons and contrasts that did not previously exist. It brings all the 'relevant' actors together into the same space. Given how potential adopters of large IT systems are drawn to assess and compare the features of vendors during procurement (Schultz et al. 2001) it seems to play an important role in mediating choice.

The substantive interest in the chapter is to understand the history, construction and contemporary use of the Magic Quadrant. We examine how its unique way of evaluating and positioning vendors seems to have become rooted in the practices and thinking of technology producers and technology buyers alike. We show how it both derives from, and has led to, deep transformations within corporate computing—changes that have gone largely unnoticed by Information Systems scholars and others. However, the

Magic Quadrant is not without controversy and difficulties. The tool is surrounded by constant discussion about its 'legitimacy' and its 'provenance'. Vendors may dispute which product characteristics should or should not be taken into account. It is also described by some as wielding 'substantial power' and by others as nothing short of 'simple marketing'. However, given these divergent assessments social scientists have been rather slow to examine these kinds of tools and explain their influence. The conceptual aim of the chapter is to discuss what the Magic Quadrant might mean for the discussion of 'commensuration'. Is the Magic Quadrant powerful because it is a ranking and therefore puts all vendors on an even scale, as some would argue (Espeland & Stevens 2009) or is it influential for some other reason? We make some suggestions in this latter direction through exploring the 'marketing of quantifications'.

7.2. 'THE MAGIC QUADRANT IS TRULY A REMARKABLE PIECE OF MARKETING CRAP. I WISH I'D INVENTED IT!'

This quote comes from the social media site Twitter. We chose this from (tens of) thousands of statements on the internet with regard to the Magic Quadrant because it points to two seemingly contradictory aspects of this tool.

The Magic Quadrant is described as Gartner's 'signature research' piece. Even though a number of industry analyst firms produce similar kinds of graphs—the Forrester Wave, the Ovum Decision Matrix, the IDC Marketscape, to name but a few—it is the Magic Quadrant that stands head and shoulders above the rest in terms of power, popularity and notoriety. It is an attempt to compare and rank software vendors according to a number of predefined measures. In the words of its authors, these are '... graphical portrayals of vendor performance in a market segment which summarizes a given market and its significant vendors at a point in time' (Gartner Inc. 2000: 2). It comes in the form of a box with an X and Y axis labelled as 'completeness of vision' and 'ability to execute' dimensioning a two-by-two matrix with four segments into which one can see placed the names of several vendors. Vendors are not randomly placed. Each of the segments are individually labelled as 'niche player' (bottom left), 'challenger' (top left), 'visionary' (bottom right) and 'leader' (top right). The position of a vendor in a particular segment signifies something regarding its current and future performance as well as its behaviour within their particular target markets (Burton & Aston 2004). Those placed further to the right are seen to have more 'complete

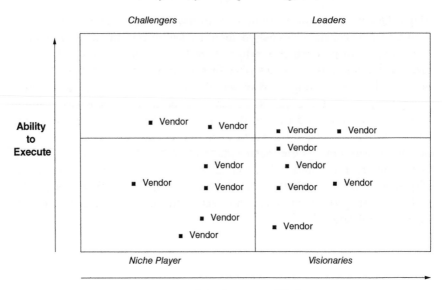

Figure 7.1. The Magic Quadrant

Source: Author depiction

visions', whilst those placed towards the top an elevated 'ability to execute' on that vision (see Figure 7.1).

But, as indicated by the quote above, the Magic Quadrant also divides opinion. Indeed, we came to think of it as a 'dividing object'. That is because it is acknowledged as having the power to influence a sale. Some argue that a high ranking on a Magic Quadrant guarantees a vendor more attention than its rivals (Hind 2004). There are those who go as far to argue that it can 'make or break' a technology vendor (Violino & Levin 1997). Because of its influence it has been described as the 'most famous and enduring analyst signature research' (Sagecircle 2008); it is seen as the 'most powerful'[1] and 'most highly visible' (ibid) piece of research within the whole information technology arena; and even considered as the most identifiable piece of business research across any industrial sector (Chapple 2015).

At the same time, the Magic Quadrant is described as a simple 'piece of marketing' (Howard 2004). One industry commentator talks about Gartner's output as a 'marketing product . . . disguised as research output' (Snapp 2013: 27). Another writes how 'The MQ truly is magic . . . for Gartner. The MQ is branding, marketing and selling magic for Gartner' (Sagecircle 2008). It has also been denounced in certain quarters as a 'low status' form of expertise that is devoid of 'intrinsic value' (Keiser 2002). Its assessment criteria are depicted as 'highly simplistic', 'flawed' and 'overly subjective' (Columbus 2005, Greenemeier & McDougall 2006, Whitehorn 2007).[2] Even analysts within

Gartner complain about it but see it as a 'necessary evil': a required but not particularly valued part of their role:

> It is a necessary evil. It is a strong branding thing. But it is not a high status thing, no. It is not, everybody works on them at some point . . . In fact, I would argue that the elite analysts don't want to be on them . . . if you took the top 50 analysts in the company, 30 plus of them don't do any Magic Quadrants, and you couldn't put a gun to their head and make get them involved in one again (interview, Thomas).

However, and rather strangely, this does not seem to have dampened enthusiasm for this particular industry analyst output. It is still appears to dominate procurement discussions, despite what is written or said about it. As one Gartner analyst points out, '[t]here is no stopping it. I will give you an idea. A good magic quadrant will get fifteen hundred downloads every month; a Hype-Cycle will get around six or seven hundred' (interview, Winter). Furthermore, much of the criticism directed at the Magic Quadrant appears to come from those who are also its users. The consumers of this research seem to be amongst its biggest critics! These contradictory features are widely acknowledged and discussed. An analyst relations consultant notes: 'No analyst relations (AR) manager will deny that Gartner's Magic Quadrants (MQs) are influential, partially due to the fact that they are graphical, yet they are one of the most controversial research deliverables ever created' (Gyurko 2009). How then can we make sense of an object with such seemingly dividing qualities: that is seen highly problematic but still widely used; that is controversial, but also seen as effective in comparing the performance of vendors; that is described as a simple piece of 'branding' but which also seems capable of influencing choices in the market?

7.3. WHAT'S THE MAGIC IN THE MAGIC QUADRANT?

Despite the prevalence of these and similar apparently simple market analysis tools there is as yet no specific 'sociology' or 'sociological template' to help us make sense of them. Reviewing various literatures, one finds a number of prompts that seem to offer guidance. Many of these however, would seem to leave unexplained many of what we would see as the pertinent issues surrounding the Magic Quadrant (its dual qualities for instance). Let us briefly review how existing schools of thought might approach this tool before discussing how we actually went about analyzing the Magic Quadrant.

Despite the success of market analysis tools within the business domain— one only has to think of the 'Cost Benefit matrix', the 'Product and Market matrix', the 'BCG Product Portfolio matrix' to name but a few (Lowy & Hood

2004)—there is still nowhere near an adequate set of concepts to describe how or what influence these tools have over the domains in which they are used.

One reason for this is that there has been a tendency by critical social scientists to 'debunk' them (see Thrift 2002). It is after all a version of the classic two-by-two matrix much beloved by European and American Business Schools (Lissack & Richardson 2003). Whilst there has been some focus on the 'interactional' (Pels 2003) features of these tools, how they might operate as 'boundary objects' (Star & Griesmer 1989), or how they might 'frame' complex organizational problem solving (Morrison & Wensley 1991: 112), the common response has been to ignore or, worse still, dismiss them. They have been described as 'simplifications' (Lissack & Richardson 2003), albeit 'powerful oversimplifications' (Ghemawat 2002). Because these tools are seen to reduce and hide complexity, some even describe them as 'unethical' (Lissack & Richardson 2003). We think this an understandable but unsatisfactory response. The research challenge is to take these tools seriously and to analyse the ways they are produced and the kind of actions they foster. There is more to these devices, we argue, than just reducing information to manageable dimensions. The notion of a simplification fails to capture or appreciate their important transformational characteristics.

Espeland & Stevens argue that every professional community has its own unique kinds of 'numerical pictures' (2008: 423). The industry analyst community is no different in this respect. Ghemawat (2002) discussed how towards the latter part of the twentieth century there was a profusion of figurations attempting to depict complex strategic and managerial decisions in relatively straightforward ways. Writing about the most famous of these, the 'Boston Box', Morrison & Wensley note how the benefits of this device are that the '. . . reader is informed *at a glance* of what may take several paragraphs to explain' (1991: 114, *original emphasis*).

What we attempt in this chapter, through exploring this characteristic of the Magic Quadrant, is to develop Espeland & Stevens' (2008) point, that is, to investigate whether the tool provides for unique kinds of commensuration in business settings, as compared to the formats used by professional communities and disciplines elsewhere. Our strategy is to open up this particular 'black box' to see how these processes of commensuration are arrived at and how vendor positions emerge from this contested socio-technical arrangement. Our thinking is influenced by scholars sensitive to the role that theories and devices play in constituting economic markets (Callon 1998, MacKenzie 2006). In doing this, we set in train a specific line of inquiry. We show how the Magic Quadrant is 'constitutive'. That is, it does not merely describe the state of affairs that already exists in the IT marketplace. Rather, in offering a new means of comparing and positioning vendors, it is also interacting with and modifying its object of study, such that it helps to create the world for which it is seen to be a good empirical description. In what follows, we analyse the

Magic Quadrant to show how it implies and gradually enacts a new world. This includes how Gartner set out an alternative way to describe and think of vendors as well as a research process that enables comparison and ranking. Using the arguments of Callon (1998, 2007) given in Chapter 1 we can say that the Magic Quadrant is successful (i.e., performative) when it is able to bring about the world that it points to (i.e., actors come to think of others and themselves according to these terms).

There is a further addition we need to make to the performativity approach and that is to capture the puzzling aspect of how this dividing knowledge has amassed such a large audience. In chapter 4 we extensively reviewed the literature on the Sociology of Expertise, particularly Turner's (2001) distinction between those experts for whom there exists a predefined audience and those who actively have to *create a following*. We found useful how Preda (2007) employed Turner's framework to study the birth of the 'Chartist' movement. These were experts who persuaded initially sceptical stock market traders that the new 'stock forecasts' they produced would be a useful addition to existing financial instruments. Preda (ibid) suggests that Chartism diffused because these new experts actively *reshaped* users' perceptions of how they should go about their work. Interestingly, Preda analyses the Chartist knowledge products as 'persuasion devices' to capture how it was the shape of the outputs themselves that seemingly convinced adopters seemingly of their benefits. He does not say much about persuasion devices other than how they could seemingly help in the 'reciprocal tuning' of the interests of its users towards those of producer groups.

There is a body of work from Economic Sociology on 'judgement devices' (Karpik 2010) that is also useful here. This is Karpik's term for commensurations such as rankings. What Karpik foregrounds in his discussion of these devices is how above all else they are 'commercial objects'. That is, they are in *competition* with other rankings for the attention of audiences. These devices compete 'to increase their hold on customers' (Karpik 2010: 51). They are constructed entirely with the aim of making things easier for the consumer. Each ranking therefore will offer consumers an 'oriented knowledge', they 'compete among themselves to make the products [displayed on the ranking] more visible and more desirable' (ibid: 52). Though neither Preda nor Karpik use this language, it might be suggested that these devices succeed because they enter the realm of another economic modality: marketing. But this begs the question as to how we might conceive of a ranking that invites and captivates its customer, without losing this important focus on commensuration?

A potential template can be found from within the work on commensuration itself. Espeland and Stevens' (2008) develop the argument that quantifications either 'commensurate' or they 'mark'. They locate commensuration and marking on two opposite ends of the same scale. At one end, there are numbers that value or measure different objects within a common metric, that is, a set of metrics that 'transforms all difference into a quantity' where '[d]ifference or similarity is expressed as a magnitude, as an interval on a metric' (Espeland & Stevens 2009: 408). At the other end, there are numbers that mark. In terms of marking, they write:

> Numbers often are used to identify particular persons, locations, or objects. Some numerical marks are simple and even arbitrary. Numbers printed on football jerseys are clear instances of numbers that mark, distinguishing particular players from all others on team rosters and television screens. Such numbers can take on the character of names, as when announcers referred to Michael Jordon as "Number 23," or when luminary numbers are "retired" to honor former recipients. Numbers can also be used as names, like the popular American whiskey called "Old Number 7". Used as marks, numbers distinguish one object or person without quantifying (ibid: 407).

This bifurcation is valuable because it allows for the proposition that numbers do more than quantify: they can also 'distinguish' one thing from another; and, to repeat the words from above, they can 'take on the character of names' (ibid). It is not such a large leap from here to suggest that quantifications could make a distinction to the extent that they become a 'brand' (Lury 2004, Kornberger & Carter 2010) or what Karpik (2010) calls an 'appellation'. Though Espeland and Stevens (2009) do not develop this line of enquiry, it is a clear implication of their work. To make sense of this, let us briefly note a few key elements of the idea of marking.

The idea of a 'mark' or 'marking' has a long history, going back several thousand years to Roman artisans, who would mark pottery so as to identity themselves as its producer (Lury 2004). The practice made its way into pre-industrial crafts (stonemasonry, printing, goldsmithing etc.,) and was used predominately in an effort to indicate 'value' but also to facilitate 'identification' and to 'distinguish' products from one another (ibid). Today some use the idea of a 'mark' and a 'brand' interchangeably (Kornberger 2009). A brand is often thought of as a 'mark of ownership' that builds trust in the consumer through the suggestion of 'an origin' (Karpik 2010). Brands are also seen to 'mark' relations between products (Lury 2004). Further, there is the notion of a 'trademark', which is seen to create a monopoly for the use of a particular mark with the joint purpose of protecting the producer from competitors and the consumer from uncertainty concerning the genesis and quality of a product (Lury 2004).

We now turn to our empirical discussion where, through discussing our fieldwork, we demonstrate how the Magic Quadrant is a form of both commensuration *and* marking. We define marking in relation to the way certain numbers are able to discriminate—as in producing particular 'names' or 'locations' on graphs or lists that have meaning and use way beyond the specific quantification (e.g., 'top right', 'top ten', 'bottom four' etc.) and that others find valuable for various reasons (either to advertise, to measure themselves against, to strive towards, to communicate to others, to defend choices etc.). Their point is that they can quickly signal the outcome of the commensuration ('leader', 'top right') without the necessity to go into the details (or complexities or controversies) of the quantification that give rise to it in the first place.

We want to develop an understanding of how the Magic Quadrant appears to allow for effective, albeit contested, forms of comparison in the (enterprise software) market. At the same time, we want to investigate how it has been able to attract an audience—though in our analysis we prefer the term 'community' since it suggests a more active engagement. We argue that it is able to build a community because the various marks it creates have sense for and can be understood by a wide range of actors (such that it becomes a reputable benchmark).

The chapter is divided into a number of sections. We begin by describing the assessment criteria that led to the Magic Quadrant. We describe the 'Matrix Community' that has been established around this tool. We show how the Magic Quadrant is used by those choosing between technologies. Through discussing the 'research process' behind the Magic Quadrant, we show how Gartner interacts with two main groups: technology vendors and technology adopter organizations. We discuss how technology vendors respond or 'react' (Espeland & Sauder 2007) to the marks created by the Magic Quadrant. We then examine the set of interactions between one particular Gartner analyst and an adopter organization as they attempt to shape the position of a vendor on the Magic Quadrant. The chapter concludes with an exploration of how the linking of commensuration with marking might throw light on an aspect of the performativity of quantifications that has not yet been given much attention by scholars.

Box 2. Research note

Researching objects such as the Magic Quadrant is extremely difficult and this may be one reason for the paucity of studies. It is not so much that the firms producing them are guarded when talking about their work (they can be, which is perhaps not surprising since many of them have been the subject of much criticism, especially from the practitioner press) it is also that it is difficult to know 'where' to study these actors. Magic Quadrants are not shaped in one specific place but across what Callon & Muniesa (2005) describe as a 'calculative network'. Thus during fieldwork the most insightful way to study this phenomena proved to be by examining the interactions of industry analyst firms with other players across organisational settings. This meant we conducted our fieldwork in inter-organisational nexuses rather than within the confines of particular sites. Indeed, this explains where our

---

(*continued*)

Box 2. **Continued**

---

initial interest in industry analysts was born. We had been conducting a long-term research project on software vendors and their interactions with user communities and various others (reported in Pollock & Williams 2009). We had chosen to study the supplier/user nexus and the complex web of relations that existed between them, which, in turn, alerted us to the important role of these kinds of intermediaries. Having achieved a good relationship with one particular IT manager (described here as 'Roy') working at a user organisation (described here as 'Langdon'), we were observing him when he subscribed to the services of Gartner and began to interact with them on a regular basis. Before long Roy had established what looked like a strong working relationship with one particular Gartner analyst Mark Zolo and in doing so appeared to have become an important factor in the shaping of the Magic Quadrant in that industry segment. It was mostly through our observations of Roy that a window onto the world of industry analysts was first opened up to us. Importantly, in the first instance, it meant we could follow the shaping of the Magic Quadrant for one particular market sector over a period of a year. Later, and based on this initial study, we would return to carry out a full-blown study of the Magic Quadrant described in Chapter 9.

We gathered most of the insights presented here during ethnographic research where we were able to view Gartner from a number of different analytical viewpoints. There were three main sources of data. Firstly, we found observing industry analysts 'in action' (Latour 1987) by attending a number of IT forums to be very fruitful. We supplemented this method of data gathering with informal discussions. NP was able to interview and question a number of Gartner analysts, the vendors subject to these assessments, as well as the clients and users of the research. Whilst this was a demanding and often intrusive form of fieldwork, it gave us access to what would normally be 'private' discussions that included very sensitive topics. Secondly, we conducted formal interviews with vendors and IT practitioners to ask them about their involvement and relationship with Gartner. Thirdly, we had access to Gartner documentation and reports (some were available freely on the internet and others were sent to us by one of the Gartner clients we were observing). One of the most important sources of data we drew on was electronic mail exchanges between Roy, Gartner analysts and the large software vendor SAP. Much of the discussion about (and interactions with) Gartner took place via email which meant we had unfettered access to the important effects this kind of assessment was having on vendors and users alike and the way in which these actors attempted to shape Gartner's view. Roy helpfully provided us with direct access to his email account over the period of a year giving us the ability to accumulate hundreds of emails (when completely printed out they had to be contained in two large ring binder folders).

7.4. WHERE DID THE MAGIC QUADRANT COME FROM?

Articles in the practitioner-focused press have attempted to discuss the aetiology of the Magic Quadrant but always reach the same conclusion—'no one is really sure'. Something of a mythology has grown up around this object (Whitehorn 2007). It is said that Gideon Gartner and his colleagues borrowed heavily from the 'Boston Box' when they constructed the Magic Quadrant (interview, Thomas). Whilst the potential to foster insights 'at a glance' is not confined particularly to the graphs belonging to industry analysts (see Coopmans 2014), it is a vision that Gideon Gartner appeared to instantly recognize. Gartner was also influenced by writing on 'decision theory'. Citing Montgomery and Weinberg (1979), he describes how he was interested in created provocative 'thought experiments' (Stiennon 2012) that might create further discussion internally. The Magic Quadrant exemplified what he termed a 'Stalking Horse' graphic. From our own discussions with Gideon Gartner and Gartner employees, we know it was first discussed within Gartner around the mid-1980s but interestingly, and something that helps sustain this mythology, our Gartner informant was also uncertain about how and when it was first presented externally. As Gideon Gartner stated (Gartner 2011a):

> around 1987/88, I was working on further enhancing the Gartner Group Research Notebook, and happened to introduce the 'stalking horse' graphic as one technique which our analysts could occasionally use when presenting at research meetings to support a conclusion. This initiative was meant to be for internal discussion only, because the method seemed an oversimplification (yet an interesting starting point for certain confrontations which would be challenging and educational at our meetings). I do not recollect ever allowing the publication of an MQ, but during the mid-'90s and well after I left Gartner, the MQ feature grew to be a major deliverable for many of its clients![3]

Whilst even Gideon Gartner is unclear when or how the Magic Quadrant first began to be used with clients, one of our Gartner informants identified this early usage as linked to the work of two particular analysts. However, she was unsure as to when this was and even suspected it to have begun its life with a different name:

> We believe the first presentation use of the quadrant (though it wasn't called that at the time) was in 1986 at Gartner's Scenario conference . . . We looked through our Scenario conference binders from 1985 to 1987—did not find any Magic Quadrants in the 1985 binder, one in 1986 and 1987. The analysts who used it at that conference were Mike Braude and Peter Levine in their Software Management Strategies Scenario—again, though it wasn't formally called a Magic Quadrant. Given our rigid discipline back in the 1980s of limiting Research Notes to two pages, we suspect that the Magic Quadrant appearance in presentations most likely predates their appearance in a Research Note, but are uncertain. Nor can we be certain that it wasn't used at another 'theme' conference earlier in 1986 (email correspondence with Nancy Erskine, Gartner).

Apparently, certain Gartner managers disliked the name 'Magic Quadrant' because it was 'neither a quadrant nor magic' (Sagecircle 2008) and thus started to use an alternative. Despite continuing to ask, we were unable to uncover what this name was so can throw no further light on the issue. (All Gartner's early research is now housed in a storage facility to which our informant did not have access). However, the new name did not last long, as the removal of the name 'Magic Quadrant' seemingly 'caused an uproar throughout Gartner Group, especially in the Sales force' (Sagecircle 2008). This was because '[e]ven in the early '90's it was becoming legendary' amongst IT managers (ibid.). There is still discussion today about changing the name. A Gartner analysts tells an audience why they have decided to keep it:

> In terms of the name, this comes up from time to time and while . . . The Magic Quadrant goes back many, many years, today it is such a preeminent methodology and research tool and so used, if there is one thing that is synonymous with Gartner it is the Magic Quadrant and the value of the methodology to our clients is so high, the readership is so significant that really with my brand marketing hat on I would say why would you change something that has visibility around the globe, even before a prospective client knows much about Gartner, they know about the Magic Quadrant and because it's become so widely used and so incredibly popular for all the reasons that you would care for and shepherd a brand carefully, it's been our thought to keep the name as is (Julie Thomas, Gartner analyst, presentation to the IIAR, July 2013).

In terms of the ideas behind the Magic Quadrant, we were able to observe a long serving Gartner analyst, Mark Zolo, discuss early thinking on how adopters should go about procuring new technology and specifically what criteria they should use when choosing between different vendor systems.

7.4.1. A new set of marks: 'Completeness of Vision' and 'Ability to Execute'

We originally approached our study of the Magic Quadrant using traditional forms of analysis. We had initially conceived of the tool as a 'convention', thus we were genuinely surprised to listen to a talk that pointed to a rather different story: that Gartner were setting out a distinctive new evaluative culture or ontology with regard to procurement. That is, they were not simply introducing a new kind of figuration but were identifying different presuppositions about what should be taken into account during procurement and what 'good performance' from IT vendors consisted of. To give some indication of this we present an extract from a presentation given by a Gartner analyst to a large audience of IT professionals. This analyst delivered the keynote speech each year at this particular conference. This time he had decided to reflect on the history of decision-making within corporate computing procurement. He begins by discussing the means by which people traditionally assessed systems prior to purchase:

> ... we put together [in the 1990s] an outline of how you should evaluate admin-istrative applications... And, we looked at *functionality, costs, service, support, technology, vision of the company* and *ability to execute*. And what we said was that in a stable environment you would look at *'functionality'*... That was pretty much what we were looking at. Why? Well a mainframe is a mainframe so *technology* wasn't that different from one to another, it was basically a vendor's box that you were buying but it was built around a common architecture.
>
> When you looked in terms of *cost*, that was the driving factor for us. And *service* and *support?* We really didn't think much about *vision of the company* or their *ability to execute* we just bought what they had to offer... So, we had some need but it was kind of focusing on *functionality* and *cost*.
>
> What we said in '97 was change. You need to look at *functionality* but most vendor packages are mature enough to where there is at least common function-ality, so it is a matter of *goodness of fit* that you are looking at... And we started seeing that trend in the early '80s... (Mark Zolo, presentation at Educause, *our emphasis*).

This extract involves a number of moves. Firstly, the analyst problematizes the conventional approach to assessment. The measures traditionally used, 'func-tionality', 'cost', 'service', etc., were, in this Gartner analyst's view, no longer effective in sorting vendors out. How might an adopter select between vendors using the criteria of 'technology' when the technologies in question were no longer significantly different from one another'? How effective was 'function-ality' as a deciding measure when vendors offered 'common functionality'? He goes on:

> ... that said, we had ageing of systems, people were using these systems ... whether they were proprietary or home-grown for 15, 20, 25 years... And, the point is that you had to look at buying software as being a partnership with a vendor, and that's a long-term relationship. It's not something short term. And so, the *vision of the company*—do they understand the business of higher educa-tion? Do they know where you were going?—and *the ability to execute*, those are still crucial. We still say it is about half of what your criteria should be. Now, if I am a... Chief Financial Officer... I am probably going to look at functionality as being crucial. That's fine. But somebody better look out for the good of the [institution] as a whole. Because your institutional perspective is the one that we're responsible to look out for in IT (Mark Zolo, presentation at Educause, *our emphasis*).

The analyst also thought it necessary to find new measures to capture how adopters tended to use the same solutions for long periods and were thus building longer-term 'partnerships' with vendors. He advocates studying the 'vision of the company' and 'ability to execute' on that vision. The second move is thus the advancement of a set of distinctive criteria or marks. We do not think it is overstating the point to talk about the Magic Quadrant in this way. A vendor's completeness of vision or ability to execute did not exist prior to Gartner's intervention. These ways of seeing and measuring were established only in recent years. It is for this reason that we argue that the tool is transformative.

The third move was the emergence of completeness of vision and ability to execute as a way to undertake comparative forms of assessment over others. They mark out particular vendors and products. That is, they give form to 'ordinal' characteristics as opposed to those that establish commensurability with individual adopter sites (Espeland & Stevens 1998). For instance, in the earlier decision-making frame, vendors were assessed on measures that were effective in detailing how a potential system related to the needs and shape of a specific user organization. By contrast, the new frame renders vendors commensurable with each other (Burton & Aston 2004). Thus, we can say that the Magic Quadrants generate visible comparisons that do not exist elsewhere (Callon et al. 2002), in that they mark vendors in a variety of ways (as a 'Leader', 'Challenger', 'Visionary' etc., or as we will show below, as 'top right', 'moved North' etc). In the next section, we want to show how what was originally meant to be just an 'internal' innovation has become highly influential in the spaces outside Gartner's offices. Today people more broadly treat the measures within this tool as real and consequential.

7.5. BIRTH OF A 'MATRIX COMMUNITY'

Espeland and Stevens (2009: 426) argue that the 'most successful numerical pictures influence the ontology of what they represent'. As they see it the 'picture becomes its own subject, replacing, in the comprehension of observers, what it originally was intended merely to depict' (ibid: 426). In making this point, we wish to highlight the performative aspect of this mark in that there are feedback loops between the Magic Quadrant and the world it is attempting to describe. The Magic Quadrant has transformed how large numbers of people view the IT market. When thinking about the procurement of IT, for instance, adopters find it increasingly difficult to conceive of selection without some form of reference to the Magic Quadrant. Large numbers of people now see and act in the world according to this simple figuration.

We want to go further and suggest that not only has the Magic Quadrant replaced previous modes of assessing technology, but it has also helped create an attached community—what we call, for want of a better word, a 'Matrix Community'. We use this to foreground the heterogeneous range of actors

Table 7.1. The matrix community

Actors (in)formed by the Magic Quadrant	Examples of how they interact with it
Industry analysts (who create the matrix)	'the success [of MQ] is because of the repeatability. People have learned how to use it. It's predictable' (interview, Lebber).
Procurement teams (that construct shortlists)	'it helps them understand the particular vendors where those ones are in the landscape' (interview, O'Hara).
Chief Information Officers (that justify procurement choices)	' . . . very simple tool to defend or make a quick evaluation' (interview, Muller).
IT Vendors (assessed by the Magic Quadrant)	'you don't really market yourself to Gartner as they are very focused on the communications they have with corporations' (interview, Smith).
Influencer relations professionals (that coach their colleagues within IT vendors on how to establish 'completeness of vision')	'Vendors spend anywhere from 60 to 200 hours to influence their position in a single MQ' (webinar, Carter Lusher, SageCircle).
Client references (that provide evidence of a vendor's 'ability to execute')	' . . . Mark Zolo [from Gartner] has been very negative to Campus Management. He has never called. He has never visited our site' (interview, Hale).
Analyst relations consultants (who advise IT vendors on how 'to move their dots')	'One of our clients was getting involved in a Magic Quadrant and . . . we tried to understand what the analyst thought about [the] company' (interview, Bentwood).
Investors (looking to buy up promising 'niche players')	'If you are a M&A responsible you always ask Gartner: who are the guys that are small, have a high momentum?' (interview, Muller).

who now interact with or through this tool. This community is made up of Gartner clients, those buying new technology, technology vendors, and a range of others that includes 'analyst relations professionals' and technology investors (e.g. those looking to buy up 'niche players'—one of the new Magic Quadrant categories). The full list of actors and their activities is described above (see Table 7.1). This is not a 'coherent' community (and one goal in Chapter 10 is to explore the asymmetry of this community/the typology of the ecosystem). People want different things from it (which fits with our conception of the Magic Quadrant as a 'dividing object'). But if the notion of a Matrix Community is to be useful then we should be able to demonstrate more than just an interest or investment in this tool but also the mechanisms of interaction between the various players listed. What follows is, first, a discussion of how the Magic Quadrant has become embedded in the practices of technology adopters, and second, the various interactions that occur within this community.

7.6. TECHNOLOGY ADOPTERS APPEAR ATTRACTED TO IT

7.6.1. Adopters build immediate choices on the Magic Quadrant

The main purpose of the Magic Quadrant is to support adopter organizations in selecting and adopting large-scale software systems or hardware. Procurement is a complex, multi-step process. It is complex because adopters have to make decisions on hard-to-assess factors. There are not only many possible offerings available but also adopters are rarely able to inspect or compare these products directly (Pollock & Hyysalo 2014). The aim of procurement therefore is to whittle down the many possible (in some cases hundreds of) vendors to a 'shortlist'. Shortlisted solutions will then be given more intense scrutiny. The first obstacle, however, is in arriving at the shortlist. Another is that Chief Information Officers (CIOs) and procurement teams often lack the necessary up-to-date technical and market knowledge to construct these lists (Pollock & Williams 2007).

It is in this context that the Magic Quadrant appears to provide adopters with specific information. An ex-Gartner analyst, now working for a technology vendor, told us how it helps give a picture of where particular vendors are in 'the landscape' (interview, Muller). An IDC analyst described this similarly as a picture of the 'battlefield' (interview, Doorly). As the ex-Gartner analyst put it, '[t]hese are very simple tools to communicate to executive management. For example if a CIO wants to buy a new ERP or CRM . . . this is a very simple tool to . . . make a quick evaluation' (interview, Muller). Others noted how procurement teams would discriminate between different parts of the Magic Quadrant when compiling shortlists. Those placed further 'to the right' are seen to have more complete visions whilst those placed 'towards the top' an elevated ability to execute on that vision. The Magic Quadrant is made up of four quadrants. One unwritten rule of good procurement, an informant tells us, is that those procuring 'should have 1 or 2 or 15% of these guys [pointing to the top right of the Magic Quadrant] in their evaluation list and invite them to a tender' (interview, Muller). Carter Lusher, analyst relations consultant for SageCircle, describes how it is common for adopters to choose from one quadrant only: 'We have examples of situations where, for example, a government contract will go out and the request for quote will begin by filtering and saying 'We're only going to consider people in the "upper quadrant" of the Gartner Magic Quadrant' (webinar, Carter Lusher, SageCircle).

Indeed, there is now a sophisticated vernacular understanding of the Magic Quadrant and what each of the marks say about vendors that sits alongside Gartner's own account. For instance, Carter Lusher talks an audience through the significance of each of the four quadrants:

Well, first of all, if you are a *Leader,* you are a company that has brains and bucks and so I should add them to the shortlist. And as a matter of fact, I might only consider people in this shortlist because obviously, these are the people that really get the market and have the market and are the leaders and therefore it's a safe bet. The *Challenger* is somebody, well they've got lots of bucks, but since they're not visionary, they're not going to grow with me, so maybe I want to not consider them in my purchase. The *Visionary:* brains, but not bucks, means, well, I am not sure that this company is viable over the long term and so maybe I do not want to put my trust in them. And, lastly, the *Niche* category: no brains, no bucks. Maybe they are the losers (webinar, Carter Lusher, SageCircle).

The Magic Quadrant can be used *before* a procurement choice has been taken, to help frame the decision and to facilitate the drawing up of the shortlist, and it can be useful *afterwards* to 'rubber stamp' a decision (interview, Doorly). 'Imagine a CIO wants to buy a new CRM system for a large organization costing...£15m', says Muller, 'and then he [sic] makes a decision, and he has to justify this decision in front of the board where...the CEO has no idea about IT' (interview, Muller). An industry analyst from IDC tells us how the old adage about 'never being sacked for buying IBM' has now been replaced:

> There's a lot of stages to this and MQ, Forrester Wave, IDC Marketscape are used in all of those processes to a greater or lesser degree, for all sorts of purposes. Sometimes it's as simple as, 'we never got fired for using a MQ or using a Marketscape'. It rubberstamps this group that's been selected. Look, they're on this chart therefore it's fine; the vendor validation that's gone into this. Right down to, we're deciding between two, they appear in here..." (interview, Doorly).

7.6.2. Magic Quadrant is 'too good'

There is a surprising downside to the Magic Quadrant that we were unaware of when we began this research. According to one Gartner analyst, it is 'too good' (interview, Old). What is meant by this? There are two aspects. On the one hand, this appears a positive comment and relates to how technology adopters require very little time to decode it. There is no need to 'sit down and discuss in detail these charts' one Gartner client tells us (interview, Vale). People find them 'easy to read'; indeed, they can be read and understood in the time it takes to point a camera (see Figure 7.2). They are (too) effective because people have become familiar with and know how to read the format. As another Gartner analyst tells us, 'the success [of the Magic Quadrant] is because of the repeatability. People have learned how to use it. It is predictable. It's the same each time, so it's easy to go back to it and not have to figure out what the analyst is trying to convey' (interview, Lebber). An IDC analyst tells us that graphs like the Magic Quadrant and the IDC Marketscape draw on basic mathematical understandings that 'up and right is good':

Figure 7.2. Magic Quadrants rapidly mark 'the landscape' for the reader
Source: Author photograph (NP)

> All of it I suppose goes back to Cartesian, if you really want to be fundamentalist about it, things that are top and right are going to be generally bigger on both axes aren't they? So that's the fundamental mathematical process that you, it's sort of human intuition based on a mathematical thing that up and right is good (interview, Doorly).

On the other hand, there is also a downside to the tool in that they seemingly encourage *quick* decisions. As one analyst put it, they invite adopters to jump to conclusions 'too fast'. Why is this problematic? Industry analysts 'warn' clients against taking procurement decisions by only looking at the Magic Quadrant: 'Our clients tell us ... things that we find scary, like we've just narrowed our shortlist down to anyone who's in the latest quadrant. We say: "don't do that"' (interview, Lebber). Industry analysts complain that even though Magic Quadrants come with research notes that provide further details on criteria used as well as caveats, these notes are seldom read. 'The problem with the Magic Quadrant is that the document is about 50 pages. What people want to see is the quadrant. They don't want to read the document' (interview, Winter). Another practical reason why these research notes are not read is that they often become separated from the Magic Quadrants because the vendors post only the figurations on their websites:

> ... vendors often promote these as part of marketing. If I'm in the leaders' quadrant, I'm going to promote that. So you're going to find that these pieces of signature research wind up being available in a lot of different ways. Many, if not every, Magic Quadrant is available for free on the web because somebody has reprinted it ... (webinar, Carter Lusher, SageCircle).

This can cause numerous problems, according to one commentator, because without the research note the Magic Quadrant can be 'misinterpreted':

> [The] graphic is the thing that people are looking at, but in reality the criteria on how that graphic is created may often appear in separate research notes. So the result is that the research note that explains the Magic Quadrant and all of its information is going to be one thing, and then you've got the actual Magic Quadrant, which started out in that research note, but sometimes becomes detached from it (webinar, Carter Lusher, SageCircle).

Another way the Magic Quadrant can be misinterpreted is that adopters may 'infer' the overall standing of a vendor, including products not assessed, from a single Magic Quadrant:

> One Magic Quadrant actually has the ability to impact overall perception, because in some cases, if you are on a Magic Quadrant but that Magic Quadrant isn't even about the product or service that people are really looking to buy, but they see you on a Magic Quadrant, they may infer the position on one Magic Quadrant as being equal to your situation with a product where you're not even ... maybe there is no Magic Quadrant. So it's important to understand that putting your name, your company name or product name, onto a Magic Quadrant can impact overall market perception (webinar, Carter Lusher, SageCircle).

Apparently, once released, despite yearly updates, a particular Magic Quadrant can float around for many years: 'Even if it's been withdrawn, or if it's been replaced with a new one, it tends to be out there in either print form or cached somewhere on the web ... And this dated Magic Quadrant might not reflect what the analyst currently is believing, and what they're currently recommending' (webinar, Carter Lusher, SageCircle). This can be problematic, because, as the informant notes, they may inevitably contain an out-of-date conception of a vendor's performance.

In summary, we have presented a range of (contrasting) views concerning the role of the Magic Quadrant. Our aim was not to discuss its appropriateness or otherwise for procurement but to foreground how, in practice, it has become one of the tools used to help arrive at a decision. We now turn to show how technology vendors and client references interact with the Magic Quadrant. We highlight their involvement through discussing how both groups have become an integral part of the research process sitting behind the tool.

7.7. 'RECURRING SIGNATURE RESEARCH HAS CLOUT AND IT DEVELOPS GREATER CLOUT OVER TIME AND WE KNOW THAT THERE'S A METHODOLOGY'

This is a comment made by an analyst relations consultant (Carter Lusher) during a presentation to IT vendors about the importance of the Magic Quadrant. We note it here because it points to how the Magic Quadrant is influential, partially because of how it is put together. The placing of vendors on Magic Quadrants results from interactions both internal and external to Gartner. The internal construction is discussed in detail in Chapter 9 where we show how the information gathered is turned into numbers that can be input into a spreadsheet. In this chapter here we go on to investigate how analysts gather information about vendor performance through interacting with different parts of the Matrix Community. These interactions are with technology vendors and a geographically dispersed network of vendor customers called 'client references'. We discuss how the former respond or 'react' (Espeland & Sauder 2007) to the tool and how the latter are organized into what might be thought of as a 'calculative network' (Callon & Muniesa 2005). We describe the information flowing within these networks as 'community knowledge' and discuss Gartner's attempt at objectifying and commodifying this insight.

We spoke to many Gartner analysts about how they constructed Magic Quadrants. Several talked us through the details of their work. Common to all these discussions was (i) that Magic Quadrants resulted from a long period of research (they were put together over periods of months rather than weeks or days) (ii) that they involved the work of different Gartner analysts (iii) that these analysts directly interacted with the vendors assessed; and (iv) that the analysts talked extensively with the customers of these vendors.

The formal process has (in recent years only) been described openly and publicly. For instance, a Gartner report describes how '[d]uring the research process, we may ask for new information and briefings from vendors. We often gather information from vendor-provided references, from industry contacts, from unnamed clients, from public sources ... and from other Gartner analysts' (Burton & Aston 2004: 4). Whilst conducting fieldwork we were able to interview a number of vendors subject to Gartner's assessment and also some of these so-called 'unnamed clients' or 'vendor provided references', as well as observing Gartner's interactions with these people.

7.7.1. Not simply 'marketing' to Gartner

We spoke to several vendors about their relationship with Gartner and other industry analyst firms. Sungard, a US based software vendor, has been consistently well placed on the Magic Quadrant, and when we spoke to them, they had once again been marked out as a 'Leader'. Unsurprisingly, they made every effort to publicize this. After being contacted for an interview the Marketing Director sent us (unsolicited) the recently published Magic Quadrant to show us how they had maintained their position. During the meeting, we took the opportunity to ask him about this positive placing. We broached the subject rather simply, enquiring whether they 'marketed themselves to Gartner'. He responded:

It takes a lot of work, actually [laughing]. And, you don't really *market* yourself to Gartner as they are very focused on the communications they have with corporations. So what they do, if you want to be considered for coverage on the Magic Quadrant, they send out a questionnaire in advance of the Quadrant. And it ends up being like a 50 page response that is required from a vendor, from, you know, the high-level product strategy down to the feature and functionality and architecture. So we make an investment to respond to that as thoroughly as possible. And, that's . . . where our placement in the Quadrant comes from (interview, Smith).

This exchange was instructive. The respondent (politely) chastised us for the suggestion that they 'marketed themselves'. The manager was replying to a tacit derogatory definition of marketing as 'selling' something irrespective of its quality. Instead, he made the point that responding to Gartner required much internal 'investment' and 'work'. He went on to insist that there needed to be substance behind the claim. Interestingly, other vendors made similar points, often explicitly refuting claims they did anything other than provide 'real information'. This was seen in an email exchange between a different vendor (SAP) and one of its closest customers (which was also a 'pilot site' for the development and launch of one of its new systems): 'We have spent quite a lot of time bringing Mark Zolo [from Gartner] up to speed on what we have achieved in terms of development and successful projects. I don't mean just "marketing" to him—I mean real information on real achievements, which have not been visible to him' (email between SAP and a customer).

In thinking through what this 'investment' and 'work' might mean we imagine a dual process whereby a vendor has to disentangle itself from the existing ways in which it conceives of itself, and then reframe this according to the measures set out by Gartner. Apparently, this turns out to be a common practice. Vendors systematically respond to powerful rankings such as the Magic Quadrant. Another informant, an ex-Gartner analyst and now an analyst relations consultant, describes this response:

Normally it's more about bending the way I talk about things. At the end of the day, these people [Gartner analysts] are smart so if I'm working with the analysts and they say, we're seeing an opportunity over here, you're stupid if you don't listen to them. It's not necessarily that you're bending things to meet the requirements of the assessment, in some cases maybe you are, but equally you should be listening and if you think that the analyst knows their specs and they're saying to you we're hearing from end users that this is becoming increasingly important and you've not got it on the radar, well then you should have it on the radar (interview, Levin).

This informant is clear. Whilst they might 'bend' some of what they say when they present themselves to Gartner, they are also 'listening' and taking what the analysts say into account ('you're stupid if you don't listen to them').

'Marketing' in this context is about providing 'real information' and investing time and work in the interaction. In other words, our reading of this and the other similar discussions we had with technology vendors was that they took these tools very seriously indeed. We came to see how the subjects of Gartner's research were 'on the move' so to speak, that they were remaking themselves in terms of the new world that Gartner was attempting to set out (Espeland & Stevens 1998).

7.7.2. Client references

The second group from which Magic Quadrant placings were derived are Gartner's interactions with 'unnamed clients' or 'vendor provided references' (which we describe here for simplicity as 'client references'). When completing the Magic Quadrant documentation, vendors are asked to nominate a number of 'client references' who can speak about their experiences with the vendor. Gartner's relationship with client references was particularly interesting. We observed how one particular Gartner analyst had built up and was managing a large network of client references with whom he interacted on a regular basis. These people would continuously feed back comments and experiences on particular vendors. We observed how vendor placings seemed a direct result of interactions within these networks. We describe this network in more detail below, but for now, we simply sketch some of its features. It was 'selective' in that analysts kept themselves close to certain client references and seemed to exclude others. It was 'reciprocal' in that the client references recognized the importance of these relationships (and sometimes used them to further their own goals). Interactions in the network were often highly 'informal' (typically based on telephone calls or quick chats at conferences, etc). Knowledge gleaned from conversations was often 'anecdotal' (i.e. informants would not provide formal reports as such but highly situated accounts of their experiences and predicaments with technology vendors).

Finally, these insights were seen as 'authentic', and of more worth and substance than the comments provided by vendors. For instance, a Gartner analyst describes how he assumes when talking to vendors that they are 'lying to him' and that the only ones actually telling him the 'truth' are the client references: 'Most of us trust what the users say to us' (interview, Thomas). The industry analysts we talked to presented a nuanced account of client references, with one IDC analyst going as far as to introduce the interesting category of 'captive reference':

> They'll interview references, some of them do user surveys as well because it's very important not just to take vendor references but to have a kind of systematic

view of users' comments as well. All vendors will tell you everything is great and if they provide references, they're hoping that they've got captive references. That's not always the case either but IDC does do quite an extensive user review, probably rather more extensive than Gartner's in terms of validating what the vendors are saying (interview, Doorly).

We might conceive of the client references who continuously feed back information to the analysts as 'satellites' and Gartner which, in turn, translates these judgements into positions on the Magic Quadrant, as a 'centre of calculation' (Latour 1987). Further, we can characterize the information within these networks as 'community knowledge' to emphasize both its anecdotal and distributed status, as well as its shared provenance. When challenged by vendors, for instance, Gartner would often deny it was in fact *them* acting but rather they were merely collating knowledge originated by others elsewhere: the client references. There are obvious parallels here with the more formal and technocratic processes of knowledge-making of science: both seek to make their knowledge claims 'objective'. Scientists tend to validate their claims in terms of 'objective nature' (Shapin 1994); Gartner, however, continuously pointed to the community of vendor customers from where the claims originated, and, as we will now describe, to a number of research protocols and 'qualitative rules' that sit between this community knowledge and final assessments.

7.8. QUANTIFICATION OF INPUTS OF CLIENT REFERENCES

What we are arguing is that Gartner is managing parts of the Matrix Community in such a way that this anecdotal evidence or 'community experience' is no longer highly particular and local but translated to a form that can travel the world. That is to say that this informal knowledge can be quantified and commodified and fed back to the market. However, these kind of 'judgements' were not easily objectified (Porter [1995] argues that judgements do not fit straightforwardly into quantification/commensuration). During fieldwork, for instance, we noted how Gartner often struggled to account for the provenance of community knowledge and how there was a certain amount of ambiguity surrounding the methodological status of the tool. In the early stages of the Magic Quadrant's career, the early 2000s, for instance, we found the more 'quantitative' aspects of the Magic Quadrant foregrounded; and then some years later, in the late 2000s, without any explicit recognition of this change, it was described as resulting from 'qualitative research'. Today, it is typically described today as having a mix of both these aspects: 'Gartner analysts use a combination of objective and subjective criteria to evaluate individual vendors...' (Soejarto & Karamouzis 2005: 5).

But what are these 'subjective criteria'? Rather than informal and impressionistic forms of research, as the term 'subjective' might indicate, these enquires constitute a highly sophisticated method to capture and translate the situated knowledge of informants. Drawing on the Matrix Community in this way was, we imagine, a response to a practical problem. One analyst may be monitoring the activities of many dozens of vendors across an entire sector. These vendors will be operating in countries across the world. If the analyst is to remain informed about these activities then they are reliant on this distributed and informal knowledge network. How else can oversight of this market and insight into the situated practices of the vendors be maintained?

Yet, this was also seen as one of the weaknesses of the tool and led to a situation where industry analysts would find themselves challenged internally: 'Our primary research guys are always very sarcastic about the way we do our research—this qualitative type research' (interview, Thomas). But the analysts are quick to counter their quantitative colleagues: '[W]e are always ahead of you; we are always more on the button about what is going on in our area. But we are doing it all through rather subjective enquires' (interview, Thomas). It is indeed the subjective nature of the research—and the fact that it is based on hundreds, if not thousands, of hours of qualitative discussion—that apparently gives these experts purchase on contemporary and future technology markets. It seems these methods shore up other forms of research that may be outflanked by the pace and complexity of IT markets or the 'marketing' of vendors. Indeed one might think that incorporating this kind of knowledge increases the tool's credibility, for instance giving weight to the argument that Gartner analysts are 'close to the action' or have their 'finger on the pulse' so to speak. It is this community knowledge that Gartner is attempting to objectify, to bring into the calculation these customer anecdotes which are seen as important but which have till now remained outside the frame.

7.8.1. Partiality and bias

Another issue appeared to be the obfuscation that existed around this community knowledge. That Gartner refused to make the names of their sources public, for instance, was a cause of much concern. There was also much uncertainty about whether Gartner contacted *all* the client references provided by vendors. The analyst relations consultant Carter Lusher describes how:

we've heard situations from some of our clients, where a particular analyst has required a certain number, let's say 20, customer references, and then they don't call any of them. And in other cases, a vendor analyst will require something like

3 or 4 customer references and they get called in detail. So it's very important to understand that that firm-wide standard for the criteria doesn't exist (webinar, Carter Lusher, SageCircle).

There was also little information on which client references they chose to speak too and on the weight given to their views. During fieldwork, for instance, we spoke to one IT manager who was critical of how, despite the claim that Gartner consult widely when conducting their research, they had never solicited *his* views. He was the IT Director of a large US organization and active in the wider software community, having until recently served as president of a SAP User Group for his particular industry sector. We interviewed him initially about this presidency but the topic of Gartner came up. He described how he thought the particular Gartner analyst responsible for his sector had not been completely even-handed when assessing SAP's solutions:

> ... he [Mark Zolo from Gartner] has been very negative to Campus Management [a new SAP system]. He has never called. He has never visited our site. SAP wants me to be on a conference call with him, but I really don't want that. He just knows everything; he never listens ... There are just some people you know that, I took an immediate dislike to him and that is because of that arrogance. But he does know a lot and Gartner is important ... He is not against SAP, he just thinks that they are a bit player and they are not serious. That is what I gather (interview, Hale).

Despite being well informed about SAP, and thus someone who might expect to be contacted, he was not part of Gartner's network. It seemed Gartner discriminated between client references when gathering information and that contact with these networks was unevenly distributed (Callon & Muniesa 2005). Indeed the issue of 'bias' implied in the above account was an aspect voiced several times during fieldwork. It was, for instance, the focus of an email exchange between one SAP Solution Manager and a customer:

> Up to now, I perceived [Mark Zolo], their chief analyst, being pretty vain—it is hard to turn his mind around just by facts. For the last Magic Quadrant we proved him being wrong in every single sentence of his comments to his (bad) assessment of SAP, but I believe this has made him more negative about SAP than before (email from SAP to IT Manager, Langdon).

Others at SAP made similar points. One of the most striking features of the various criticisms we came across was their identification of 'attachment' and 'authorship'. Gartner is a large, global organization with many hundreds of analysts but nonetheless our informants identified one particular analyst as the source of 'negative' assessments. We mention this because it contrasts with the strategies that Gartner itself employs in an attempt to 'objectify' their knowledge. Whilst certain practitioners and vendors highlighted the 'particularized' nature of expertise, Gartner was pushing in the opposite direction through attempting to demonstrate how Magic Quadrants resulted not from individual but from collective expertise and common research methods. On their recently established Ombudsman Blog, for instance, a 'code of ethics' was published which explicitly refutes the claim that Magic Quadrants embodied bias and emphasizes how, by contrast, they resulted from a 'collegiate' style research process:

> Each piece of Gartner research is subject to a rigorous peer-review process by the worldwide analyst team. Sign-off approval by research management is required prior to publication. This process is designed to surface any inconsistencies in research methodology, data collection and conclusions, as well as to use fully Gartner's collective expertise on any research topic (Gartner Website).[4]

The objectification and commodification of community knowledge includes a process of 'purification' (Power 2003), whereby Gartner was attempting to detach specific contributors from tools through emphasizing the formal research protocols and 'qualitative rules' that mediate between individuals and final assessments. Magic Quadrants resulted not from individual but global expertise; assessments were not simply 'discretionary'; analysts are strongly committed to certain 'academic' principles ('peer review', 'research methodologies', 'data collection' etc). Gartner have also published the specific criteria by which they measure vendors; the two components of the Magic Quadrant ('ability to execute' and 'completeness of vision') have been broken down to reveal a detailed list by which a vendor was measured (they can score between 1 and 3 points on each of the particular sub-measures). This was an effort to convince that calculation was less about 'personal discretion' and more about the following of qualitative rules (Porter 1995).

7.9. A MARK TO BE AIMED FOR

We have focused on how Gartner gathers information for its Magic Quadrants through engaging with IT vendors and client references. We want to develop this latter point by discussing how one particular client reference sought to exploit his closeness to Gartner for his own organization's benefit.

7.9.1. Magic Quadrant at Langdon

'Roy' was an IT Manager at a user organization we call 'Langdon'. Langdon was also a SAP customer. Sent the latest version of the Magic Quadrant by a SAP executive keen to report the 'good news' that their rating was finally improving, Roy, in turn, circulated it among his colleagues, careful to add his own interpretation of what *he* thought the Magic Quadrant was actually saying:

> See attached an e-mail from SAP with some positive news that Gartner have
> improved their rating of SAP products within the HE [Higher Education] sector.
> The diagrams are worth looking at because they show that SAP have improved
> since 2004 but also that they have a long way to go before they overtake their
> competitors (email from Roy to colleagues).

Although SAP was keen to highlight a change in position, Roy qualified the
improvement through highlighting the ordinal nature of the tool. This meant
that even though SAP had moved position, so too had all the others. Thus,
SAP still lagged behind its rivals according to Gartner. In a further series of
emails, Roy discussed with a SAP executive what *he* thought were the specific
problems that Gartner found with SAP. He received a reply to his email in
which the vendor appeared to accept the assessment: 'Yes, we need to move
"North" in the execution axis and "East" in the vision section. We really need
to push across the line into the "Leadership" Quadrant. Implementation
(speed, cost—same thing, to some extent) remains a challenge' (email from
SAP to Roy at Langdon). Here, we simply note how the properties of this
vendor appeared to be settled and adjusted to those of the Magic Quadrant.
The various actors present seemed to agree that Gartner had 'correctly'
identified that SAP had a poor 'ability to execute'.

However, this was not the end of the matter—not by a long way! What then
developed was a fascinating and quite unexpected series of events. Rather than
simply accept the assessment, Roy discussed with the vendor how he might be
able to *improve* SAP's position:

> ...I think that the [CRM] final result will help move things much further. If we
> can then exploit BW [Business Warehouse] to include financial and other in-
> formation then we should help to move the SAP position further in the right
> direction. I think that it is important for Gartner to realize that SAP are building
> up momentum as they move across the Magic Quadrant (email from Roy to SAP).

The 'CRM' project was a Customer Relationship Management system being
built by SAP and implemented within Langdon. It was seen as a significant
flagship venture since it brought together and integrated several previously
unrelated Enterprise Resource Planning (ERP) modules. What Roy was suggesting was that, once the CRM project was successfully implemented, news of
this could be fed back to Gartner to provide evidence of both their improving
vision and their ability to execute that vision.

7.9.2. Langdon becomes a 'client reference'

At this stage of the fieldwork, we were intrigued with how this might happen.
How could the CRM project be linked to the Magic Quadrant in this way? We
watched with interest as the IT manager attempted to gain Gartner's attention.

Having recently become a Gartner client, Roy had access to their analysts and his main point of contact was 'Mark Zolo'. We observed as Roy deepened this relationship with Mark: they began to conduct regular telephone conversations and to participate in lengthy email exchanges (which we had access to). Roy would engineer meetings with Mark in various places around the world (some of which we were able to observe). Roy discussed this blossoming relationship with one of his colleagues:

> He, [Mark Zolo], is coming to [Langdon] in early November to a . . . conference. I tend to speak to him approximately every two weeks. He is really interested in seeing what we have done in Langdon. He is also watching [Portdean] and [Tynecaster] at the moment. I think that he will also watch [Kingsbay] in the UK as well to see whether SAP can hit implementation dates. I am sure that we can generate some really good publicity from our CRM project (email from Roy to colleague).

According to the email, Gartner were watching a number of other client references from around the world from which it would gather evidence about SAP's ability to execute. Moreover, Langdon had become part of this calculative network. This raised a number of issues, not least as to why Roy might go to such effort to improve SAP's rating.

7.9.3. Improving SAP's placing on the Magic Quadrant

During the same period, Roy was also in regular contact with a number of SAP executives, continuously reminding them of the influence Gartner was developing among decision makers. The following message was typical of these kinds of interactions:

> I would suggest that SAP need to be aware of quite how much influence Gartner are developing amongst the HE community in the UK. This could actually be good news, given Gartner's comments about SAP and Oracle . . . But I suggest that your HE team should become well aware of Gartner's comments because they will certainly be known to HE IT Directors (though whether we would agree with them is something else!) (email from Roy to SAP Executive).

There is a sentence here that is important for our argument: 'though whether we would agree with them is something else!' Through this comment, Roy called into question the accuracy of Gartner's assessment of SAP. However, even though he appeared to be sceptical of the assessment, this was not necessarily important, because he still sought to influence it. The vendor executive replied to the manager and appeared to be grateful for the work that Roy was doing with Gartner:

> I appreciate your on-going dialogue with [Mark Zolo] of Gartner. As you know, we also have a parallel dialogue with [Mark]. I agree that he is looking for SAP to

'execute' on the 'vision' (in Magic Quadrant terms) in terms of key projects such as yours and [Tynecaster's] (email from SAP Executive to Roy).

Roy was more explicit still in later messages, outlining the specific interest Gartner had taken in his project, as well as the work he was doing to encourage this attention:

> Gartner (Mark Zolo especially) are following every twist with great interest. He wants to spend much time with me in [the US] before and during [a forthcoming conference] (he's invited me on to a User Panel on the Sunday higher education Symposium to discuss the question 'What message would I like to give to my ERP vendor?'!!). He also intends to visit [Langdon] during his trip to [UK conference] (being held in the [Langdon] area at the beginning of November). I am giving him very positive messages—he is very interested in the timescales of the project—possibly, because he is looking for evidence that SAP can implement good/solid implementations in a short time-scale. He is looking for similar evidence from [Portdean] and some other critical US implementations (email from Roy to SAP).

Roy outlined to the vendor how their position on the Magic Quadrant was now becoming directly linked to their performance at Langdon. What Roy hoped to achieve was to exert pressure on SAP to continue to devote further resources to his CRM project—the development had started well but had been floundering in recent months. In turn, SAP needed to improve (not worsen) their ranking. Roy thus anticipated that Gartner's interest would have a positive effect on the vendor. In another email to a colleague, Roy described the success this strategy appeared to be having:

> Things are getting ever more interesting for me and the SAP relationship. They are really moving into a 'partnership' role—throwing in highly competent resources to ensure that we go live on 10th October. Though I guess it helps that they realize that Mark Zolo has told them that Gartner are watching SAP's ability to implement at each of 3 universities in the world ([Langdon], [Portdean] and [Tynecaster]) and that their results will materially affect whether SAP move from the lower left quadrant to the top-right! (email from Roy to colleague).

To summarize our observations on this episode, the Magic Quadrant had two principal effects. Firstly, it framed the setting so that the means by which vendor rankings can be improved has been defined. No longer an abstract or difficult to measure notion, vendor performance was translated into the most tangible of things: to repeat Roy's words, the implementation of its systems in the three organizations 'will materially affect whether SAP move from the lower left quadrant to the top-right'. Secondly, the fact it tied in vendor rankings with the success of these projects opened up the possibility of new kinds of action. In particular, the Magic Quadrant became a 'resource' for actors to calculate and *act on* in different ways (Miller 2001). Let us now turn to the CRM project, for if SAP was to improve its position, it was essential the implementation continued smoothly!

7.9.4. SAP are currently not in the top right quadrant!

As the go-live date of the CRM project approached, everything appeared to be going well. Despite initial problems, SAP had now 'pulled out all the stops' to ensure the implementation was a success. Overnight, however, serious problems emerged and some amongst the internal IT team at Langdon were asking Roy to postpone the go-live till later in the month. Yet Roy was reluctant to do so, seeing any delay as damaging. It was exactly the kind of evidence that would underwrite Gartner's (poor) assessment of SAP's ability to execute. This presented Roy with something of a dilemma: to follow the advice of his team and postpone the go-live date or to soldier on as planned and hope things would work out. Roy spelt out the nature of the problem in a message to his internal IT team, suggesting they should carry on:

> I'm trying everything to ensure that we do not delay the go-live. It critically depends upon SAP resource availability. Gartner are watching closely because they have severe questions about SAP's 'ability to execute' within the HE environment. They have no problem with SAP's 'Vision'. Their views of these two parameters result in SAP's position in the Magic Quadrant. They are currently NOT in the 'top right' quadrant (email from Roy to his IT team).

Roy knew a delay would be potentially ruinous for the particular SAP team involved; not only would their position on the Magic Quadrant be affected but also he suspected that further Gartner criticism would negatively influence SAP's decision on whether to continue investing in this particular industry sector. Thus, he decided to push ahead with the go-live, fully aware the software was not properly tested (and that it would introduce risks to his own organization). Nevertheless, and despite his efforts, further problems mounted up and, several days later, the realization dawns that they were *not* going to meet the go-live date. The project therefore was postponed. A second go-live target was quickly set, and when the new date arrived, and though many problems had still not being resolved, the system was implemented. However, a few days passed and it became apparent that, in the rush to implement, everything was not as it should be. There were numerous difficulties and it was decided to *shut down the live system* whilst problems were rectified! This was as close to a full-scale disaster as one can get for a modern organization.

This presented Roy with a difficult issue: how should he break the news to Gartner and Mark Zolo? There were major 'issues' with SAP, and Langdon were left without an external facing system for several days. In an email to Mark Zolo, about a different issue, he added the following postscript:

The [CRM] project at [Langdon] is continuing to go really well. I have decided NOT to risk going live on 10th October but to delay until later in the month. We will still have succeeded in going from project mobilisation to go-live on a raft of SAP modules in 8 months—I just don't want to risk things by implementing without exhaustive user testing. However, I will be able to demonstrate to you what we have done in a 'QA' environment, if you wish to see it (Roy's email to Gartner).

What Roy did was to put to one side the various problems in favour of the more positive message. Gartner would *not* be told of the 'chaos' that ensued at Langdon. How are we to understand this? This was also a kind of calculation that made vendors comparable, though it may not typically be phrased in that way (since it could just as easily be described as a ploy or game). However, there was more to this than the notion of a ploy or game suggests (Callon & Law 2005). The Magic Quadrant is supposed simply to describe vendor behaviour and competence but, as we saw, it is interacting with these entities and those connected to it, 'encouraging' Roy to stick to the original implementation strategy, inviting him to conform to an ideal (a demonstrated ability to execute). Thus, Roy drew a boundary around the things that would go forward to Gartner, meaning that SAP's failings would not be taken into account.

7.9.5. How Gartner defends its marks when challenged

We have argued that, in compiling these tools, Gartner hands the discretion over to others in the Matrix Community to comment on the capacities of vendors. As they are keen to emphasize, it was not Gartner but the wider community providing a judgement. In effect, these others had the power to say whether a vendor could execute or had vision. We describe this process through analyzing how one adopter reported back to Gartner and in so doing how the site forced Gartner to defend its position. The particular episode took place in the US to coincide with Gartner's Symposium.

The IT manager from Langdon, Roy, travels to the conference, one of his aims being to update Gartner on progress of his CRM project.

At the conference, one of the authors (NP) was sitting conducting an informal interview with Roy when Mark Zolo from Gartner approached. Mark straightaway begins to tell Roy how he has just heard that SAP was already having difficulties with one of the other client references that Gartner was watching (Kingsbay):

MARK: Chris [from Kingsbay] and I were just talking, she has put some ultimatums out with them—SAP.

ROY: Yeah, the real problem with them, [Kingsbay], is that they have always written their own systems and they have gone for [best of breed] but

> when they start hitting sort of a PeopleSoft or a SAP they think that it is
> going to be straightforward . . . .So she has got problems?
> MARK: She said that they are £2m over budget and they haven't *even* started
> implementation.
> ROY: Oh, I think that a lot of that is going be, the guys from SAP, the ones
> that I have been talking to. It is just that the account manager of the
> Germans is bloody useless.
> MARK: But that is a key . . .
> ROY: . . . what's absolutely critical, what SAP have been doing, is that in the
> UK they have been recruiting, and they have been recruiting some really
> good people. But *those* guys, I don't see them at [Kingsbay] yet . . .
> (exchange between Roy and Mark Zolo).

This interchange is interesting because Mark Zolo begins by highlighting SAP's
failings through invoking the 'community' view (it was not him but Kingsbay
criticizing SAP). In contrast, Roy attempts to defend SAP through shifting the
focus back onto Kingsbay's lack of experience with the particular technology.
He also suggested that things were improving since SAP has just recruited
'some really good people'. This exchange went on for some in this manner with
both providing contrasting evidence. Roy was forcing Mark to both explain and
defend his assessment of SAP, which Mark appeared able to do—*and in a
robust manner*. This confrontation continued and eventually Mark has to be
less guarded, telling Roy what he thought were the real problems with SAP:

> I told them SAP seven or eight years ago that they needed to start investing in the
> Higher Ed sector. We have a saying: 'do something or get off the pot'. Have you
> ever heard that? (Roy: yeah). In essence what I told them, it's like 'You put your
> toe in Higher Ed but you really haven't committed'. They said 'We just hired! We
> got 10 people writing the HE system' [Roy: Gosh]. I said 'Are you kidding me?'
> I said 'how *can* you? I mean, that's embarrassing!' I said 'The smallest software
> companies in the US and Higher Ed would have 50 or 60'. I mean, DataTel have
> got 50, 60 people. PeopleSoft have 100, 150. Oracle have 150. You know 10 people
> is just nothing! They are up to, I don't know, 20, 25 now but still it is not what
> I would call for the size of the company, I mean they have the resources to be a
> global leader in higher education if they want to be. It is just that they have just
> never made the commitment. And that is what you are saying? (exchange
> between Roy and Mark Zolo).

What we had here were two actors opposing each other through offering
contrasting accounts of the qualities of a vendor. Roy openly challenged
Gartner's assessment of SAP and Mark was forced to defend his position.
Whilst the critical evaluation could have centred on a range of issues, the
point of Mark's analysis was to get at the 'vision' and 'execution' of the vendor.
What constitutes vision and execution in this particular context? They are
determined by a number of factors, but one in particular is flagged by Mark as

crucial. Whilst Roy stated that SAP *was* improving, it was clear to Mark that they were not sufficiently 'committed' to the particular sector. As he saw it, they were being opportunistic in this market ('they could be the global leader if only they wanted to be'). For Mark 'commitment' was the most important variable, since it is the clue to the vision and execution of the vendor. This particular thread of conversation ended when Roy was forced to fall into line with Gartner's assessment. Despite all his previous efforts, Roy has to concede the territory to Gartner and accept their placing of SAP on the Magic Quadrant.[5]

7.10. DISCUSSION: RANKINGS ARE NOT JUST ABOUT COMMENSURATING

Callon et al. (2002) suggest the market can be understood in terms of the regimes of expertise, devices and practices that measure, classify, and draw boundaries around the properties of products and technologies. In this view, metrical comparison or commensuration have come to be seen as providing the foundations for the organization of the economy (Callon et al. 2002, Karpik 2010) and, in certain aspects, society (Espeland & Stevens 1998). We agree with this direction and attempt to build on the suggestion that to understand the economy we must analyse just how 'equivalences' between vendors are constructed (Espeland & Stevens 1998, Callon et al. 2002, Karpik 2010). Industry analysts would seem to be an ideal form of expertise on which to base and develop this suggestion in that one of their founding concerns is to create such comparisons within the IT sector. What we have attempted to do is add nuance to how one particular form of commensuration—the Magic Quadrant—can entice and create an audience (Preda 2007). But the Magic Quadrant is difficult to study, as it inhabits an interesting grey space.

This high modern form of business acumen splits opinion. Just as it has a large group of apparent followers, there is also a wide-ranging (and increasingly vocal) community of detractors. Even those who might be thought of as its consumers rarely adopt this knowledge unquestioningly. They would point to how its influence was consequential but also characterize it as an imperfect form of knowledge. They recognize its power and influence, but equally see it as a simplification—a form of mere 'marketing' or 'branding'. The task of this chapter has been to make sense of both these aspects—these dual qualities, if you like. How can we account for the seeming disproportionality between the simplicity of the Magic Quadrant and its effects?

Our argument has been that to look at the Magic Quadrant solely as a form of commensuration would be to ignore crucial aspects. We have thus attempted to combine the different disciplinary viewpoints from Science and Technology Studies (Callon 1998, 1999, 2007), the Social Studies of Quantification (Porter 1995) and Marketing (Lury 2004, Kornberger 2010). We have made extensive use of the notion of performativity where it has been suggested that economic theories and financial models play a crucial role in making up the economy. In particular, adapting this argument to the case of industry analysts, we asked to what extent their tools could create processes of commensuration. This is how scholars might explain what Espeland & Stevens (1998: 331) describe as the 'formidable force' of a ranking and its power to alter the 'people and places where it intrudes'.

We found, in many respects, that the Magic Quadrant's success stems from its enactment of a comparative machinery. It is through rolling out this comparative apparatus that Gartner, in part, has found itself at the centre of IT procurement markets. We saw how the Magic Quadrant could reshape how people made decisions when choosing between IT vendors. The tool could bring vendors together in the same space (Callon et al. 2002) and put previously incommensurable technologies onto a (two-dimensional) scale (Espeland & Stevens 1998). It could do this because it has marked the dimensions of this scale and created the possibility of ordinal assessment and ranking of vendors, through establishing a number of new realities. 'Completeness of vision' and 'ability to execute' did not exist prior to Gartner's intervention; nor were vendors seen as 'leaders' or 'visionaries', etc. Today, if not completely taken for granted, these are nevertheless some of the primary measures of vendor performance that people use. The same is true for positions across the Magic Quadrant—'top right', or moving 'north and east' etc—which are widely recognized as targets to aim for.

Part of its acceptance is also related to how Gartner has created the means to carry out research on these measures. We have described the actualization of this new common metric through the construction of a research process whereby industry analysts could speak (with some precision) about these marks (the vision and execution of software vendors etc.). The analysts have in addition established extensive calculative networks through which they could draw on the views and opinions of those actually using the technologies under scrutiny. This knowledge was seen to have an unusual quality (informal, contingent and subjective) when compared to other (more quantitative) industry analyst research. But through the activities of the analysts, this 'community knowledge' was no longer the highly situated form of insight it once was, but was turned into a form of more robust—'quantified'— knowledge that could travel the world.

But there is arguably more to this tool than (just?) comparison. We found useful Espeland and Stevens' (2009) suggestion of a scale where quantifications either 'commensurate' or they 'mark'. It would be easy to locate the Magic Quadrant firmly at one end of this scale (i.e. to argue that it gets its power because it commensurates), but we take issue with their suggestion that it is numbers that commensurate that are the 'more socially transformative form of quantification' (Espeland & Stevens, 2009: 403). Our discussion of the Magic Quadrant would suggest that what is more transformative or what actually alters people and places should not be presumed at the outset. The aim of the chapter has been to show how successful commensurations appear to be entwined with or encouraged by 'marking'. It could be argued that the Magic Quadrant is just as much about marking (or 'mark(et)ing') as about commensurating. In some respects, we might even suggest—especially when talking about the Magic Quadrant—that it is marking that is the more trans-formative form of quantification. We make a number of tentative points in relation to this:

i) *The Magic Quadrant marks Gartner out from all others.* The quantifi-cation is distinct from tools of the same ilk. It is 'the most famous and enduring analyst signature research' (SageCircle 2008). It marks in the same way as a 'label' or 'brand': it is a '(trade)mark' (Lury 2004). The conventional understanding of a trademark is of a graphic representa-tion that is 'distinctive', where distinctiveness means 'recognisable by consumers in the marketplace' (Lury 2004). The Magic Quadrant is the output that everyone recognizes as pertaining to Gartner. Individuals only need to glimpse the numerical picture to know that it is Gartner (and not Forrester, Ovum, IDC etc.). We could go further here. There are even those who suggest that the Magic Quadrant is the most recognized piece of research across *all* business sectors (Chapple 2015). In other words, it marks this form of expertise out from similar groups. It is through this marking that people recognize the research as belonging to industry analysts and not consultants or academics.

ii) *The Magic Quadrant mark(et)s itself to readers.* As Karpik (2010: 49) reminds us, what is important for a commensuration is the 'conquest and keeping of customers'. Commensurations 'compete among themselves to make the products more visible and more desirable' (ibid: 52). Whilst most commentary has focused on making things commensurable—i.e. putting them on the same scale—the need to make decisions requires discrimination (a choice between competing options). In this respect, we have seen how the Magic Quadrant gives its readers an immediate impression of the market: it is purposely designed to *leave its mark* on technology adopters; there is no need for them to sit down to study these graphs because the 'landscape' or 'battlefield' appears to be (instantly) described.

iii) *The Magic Quadrant marks a choice as valid.* Once the procurement decision has been made, we saw how this quantification could mark (as in seal, affirm or 'rubberstamp') the decision. If you are making commitments to various choices (of artefacts, of sources of advice), you also need to signal these and the practical reasons for these selections. So marking needs to be communicated in such a way that others will adopt the same signification. Reading the Magic Quadrant seemingly meant that those outside the narrow confines of the procurement team, and without specific knowledge of the IT market could also appreciate that the decision was a valid one.

iv) *The Magic Quadrant creates marks to be advertised.* We saw how the vendors who make it onto the Magic Quadrant (and most do not—see Chapter 9) are 'marked' or 'badged' as part of an exclusive community (the 'Matrix Community'). Such vendors will pay Gartner for the right to circulate this graphic to potential customers. Importantly, the vendor is not simply listed on the Magic Quadrant. We have shown how the numbers (the quantification) take on the character of a name. The calculation carried out entitles the vendor to be identified as a 'leader', 'visionary', 'challenger' etc., or they are given the designation 'top right' or 'moved North' etc. This is *the mark*. From then on, this is how they will want to be known. Vendors will make every effort to advertise the fact, to tell as many others as possible—to *market the mark*. The commensuration becomes an 'advert' that is put onto their website ('If I'm in the Leaders quadrant, I'm going to promote that') or sent out to customers ('see the e-mail from SAP with some positive news that Gartner have improved their rating of SAP products').

v) *The Magic Quadrant creates a mark to be aimed for.* Just as it can distinguish vendors as above their competitors (*on the mark*) the Magic Quadrant can also place them *below the mark* ('SAP are not currently in the top right quadrant') or *wide of the mark* ('[SAP] have the resources to be a global leader ... [i]t is just that they have just never made the commitment'). Our informants were clear that if Gartner designates a vendor in a particular way ('not in the top right') that they should take this into account ('these people are smart', 'you're stupid if you don't listen to them'). Interviewees made similar points ('you don't really market yourself to Gartner'), and pointed to how they made 'real changes' to better synchronize with Gartner's view of the world. We saw that certain vendors and users alike went to extraordinary lengths to achieve these marks. In certain cases, the commensuration was less like a mark to measure oneself against and more a 'target' to be aimed for (Espeland & Sauder 2007). We saw an IT manager who attempted (unsuccessfully in the end) to push his vendor 'across the line into the Leadership Quadrant'.

vi) *The Magic Quadrant creates a (brand) community.* We have shown also how a community—the 'Matrix Community'—has been created around these marks. This community is a diverse, heterogeneous group held together through their joint investment in the Magic Quadrant, despite their often sharply diverging perceptions and interests. We saw how Chief Information Officers (CIOs) and procurement teams routinely incorporate the tool into decision-making. Vendors increasingly describe themselves according to this new comparative machinery and make an investment to respond to it, to 'take it seriously', so that it begins to mark much of what they do. The device also conditions the activities of vendors and those connected to these vendors (such as 'client references').

vii) *The Magic Quadrant marks the economic space.* The quantification is important because, like a brand, it can extend across space and time. It has what marketing scholars sometimes call 'brand extension' (Broniarczyk & Alba 1994). Adopters would reportedly extend the position of a vendor ranking to other vendor products, even when no such Magic Quadrant existed for that product. Likewise, a mark can endure for years. Even if a vendor performance has been re-quantified many times since the original mark, an old Magic Quadrant may still be out there ('cached somewhere on the web') to be found by a prospective customer.

7.11. CONCLUSION: (TRADE)MARKING OF NUMBERS?

We have looked to add nuance (but also in some respects to fight back against) the now growing chorus that commensurations are powerful because they rank. The dominant school of thought has been been to consider powerful rankings as metrical comparisons (Callon et al. 2002, Callon & Muniesa 2005, Espeland & Sauder 2007, Espeland & Stevens 2009), but this has not been matched with a broader interest in these tools as 'mechanisms of persuasion' (Preda 2007), 'commercial objects' (Karpik 2010) or 'trademarks' (Lury 2004). This is a pity, because as we have tried to show, the Magic Quadrant as a commensuration scheme (where differences are transformed into quantities) cannot be disentangled from the Magic Quadrant as a marking scheme (where numbers distinguish because they [trade]mark), that is, in other words, where numbers are turned back into 'qualities' (Lury 2004). People need only to glance at the Magic Quadrant to know immediately that it is about Gartner and not one of its competitors. They grasp with little hesitation—because the space has already been marked out for them—that 'up and right is good', and that this or that vendor is currently 'not in the top right quadrant', etc. Just as we need to analyse the performative role of common metrics, we need also to understand the ways in which quantifications can become endowed with a significance (marks) that means their influence may extend well beyond other (rival) metrical counterparts (see Kornberger & Carter [2010] which also points towards this argument).

We have argued that the performativity of this simple market analysis tool has been helped by and resulted in the creation of a '(trade)mark' commensuration. We conjecture that marking is *as* important as commensurating in the success of a ranking. In some circumstances, it may well be that marking is more important than commensurating. Quantifications that mark(et) seem unlike others. A commensuration that is able to distinguish itself from all others seems able to dominate a particular market at a particular point in time. Numbers that transform difference into quantities appear to attract less attention than those that (trade)mark. Commensurations that turn back into qualities seem able to organize spatial and temporal activities within the market in a way that ordinary quantifications cannot. In this respect we add to Espeland and Stevens (2009: 431), for it is not simply the tendency of quantifications, but quantifications-that-mark, 'to remake what it measures'. We want to develop this last point, as it seems to offer an explanation for the commercial success of the Magic Quadrant.

Marketing a commensuration. The Magic Quadrant emerges at the intersection of two 'communities' or 'disciplines' within Gartner. The first—industry analysts—we have already heard a great deal about in this book. The second, about which we know rather little, are the 'marketing' and 'sales' staff. Right from the outset, Gideon Gartner appeared to realize that industry analyst research would not shine by its own light. Thus he ensured that the size of the Gartner marketing and sales team was close to those of the research group. Today the marketers and sellers outstrip the producers of the research by some number (Snapp 2013). This is not a coincidence, but was one of Gideon Gartner's original 'ten innovations'.

In terms of Sales Gideon Gartner writes, 'we gambled on both quantity and quality of sales and marketing personnel. Most of our competitors had begun their business with relatively little capital, while we...raised sufficient funds...to build a very substantial end-user sales organization...and the resulting powerful large force was critical to our growth' (Gartner 2010b). In mentioning this, we want to foreground that what must be borne in mind when conceptualizing this expertise is the importance of the marketing effort. Our argument is that Gartner has made its mark, been able to 'hold the ropes' (Bourdieu 2005) of IT procurement markets, because it has created a tool that is an object of both commensuration and mark(et)ing. It is not simply raw quantitative data; it is linked to practices of enticing, capturing and keeping customers (Karpik 2010). To conclude, our analysis draws attention to the ways mark(et)ing knowledge and practices penetrate every aspect of this quantification. A crucial dynamic of the framing of the economy by quantifications is missed if the focus is only on one of these aspects. The 'magic' in the Magic Quadrant is surely then this heady mix of marking and commensuration.

NOTES

1. SageCircle blog. Is There a Need for a Magic Quadrant on the Analysts? Available online at: https://sagecircle.wordpress.com/2008/11/14/is-there-a-need-for-a-magic-quadrant-on-the-analysts/ Posted 14 November 2008. Accessed 21 July 2015.
2. The Magic Quadrant is also viewed sceptically on the grounds that the experts who compile it are not thought to be independent of those they evaluate (Greenemeier & McDougall 2006). There are seen to be 'sticky' relationships in their construction because Gartner analysts often end up assessing their own clients (a factor that regularly leads to accusations of 'partiality' and 'bias' [Cant 2002]).
3. Gideon Gartner, in talking about the history of the Magic Quadrant, goes on to say: 'I acknowledge that I had left money on the table, as MQs grew in external popularity (and considerable dislike). In a future post, I expect to discuss the damage which this tool can create, sometimes leading to questionable corporate decision-making'.
4. Gartner Office of the Ombudsman: (undated). Guiding Principles (subtitled: *Here are some key questions about our Guiding Principles on Independence and Objectivity: Protecting the Gartner Brand*). Available online at: http://www.gartner.com/technology/about/ombudsman/omb_guide2.jsp. Accessed 21 July 2015.
5. In the final stages of writing this chapter, the latest version of the Magic Quadrant was posted to us by a vendor (Sungard, once again the leading vendor!). We excitedly opened the envelope to see whether SAP's position had changed. Had Roy's activities had any effect on the position of his vendor? We found SAP placed more or less as in the previous year (though our ruler tells us there was indeed some 'creep'). It had moved slightly 'northwards' on the ability to execute axis but there was no change in its ordinal position. However, the text accompanying the tool did make interesting reading. There was mention, for instance, of how 'SAP is gaining valuable experience from ongoing implementations at [Kingsbay] and [Langdon]' and how these would be used to judge the position of SAP in the near future: '[w]hile there are ongoing projects at other institutions, SAP's future success in higher education will rest on its ability to implement the Campus system at these two universities . . .'. There was an also indirect mention of Roy at Melchester and the success he had in persuading SAP to take his project more seriously: 'The higher education product development team works closely with its current customers, and the user group is active and influential, including areas such as higher education CRM and business intelligence'.

8

Venues of High Tech Prediction

An industry analyst at a large banking conference considering technologi-
cal developments makes the prediction that within a few years a significant
amount of the financial organizations present in the room would move
from exchanging paper based invoices to predominantly electronic ones.
The speaker works for the well-known industry analyst firm Gartner Inc.
and his reason for making the claim appears simple: "My job as an analyst
is to make predictions. If they come true", he adds, no doubt for theatrical
effect, "I get rich and famous. If they don't, I lose my job" (interview,
Winter). However not everyone at the conference seemed to agree with the
keynote: "Your predictions are worse and more difficult to understand than
Nostradamus's prophecies," replied a banking executive. Gartner predic-
tions, it seems, attract similar comments across forums. In an editorial on
software security, a computer scientist writes: "Gartner's prediction was far
off base . . . This alone attests to how naïve whoever made this hideous
prediction is. I, for one, think I would rather imagine a world in which
there were no more Gartner Group predictions" (Schultz 2003: 463).

What are we to make of the peculiar form of business knowledge known as the
information technology (IT) prediction? What about the industry analyst
firms who produce them? Virtually non-existent two or three decades earlier,
there are now dozens of such firms, with the larger of these organizations
making predictions on an almost daily basis (Chapple 2002, 2007). Is this
impressive expansion, which has seen the assembling of an entire 'predictions
industry', evidence of the growth of some special form of expertise able to
predict the future? Whilst there is little systematic data surrounding just how
these claims correspond to actual events, it is widely understood that a number
will fail to live up to expectations (Bott 2012, Leonhard 2013). If the vignette
above is anything to go by, then this could be quite a large number! Are we to
dismiss these predictions as unfettered forms of knowledge (Bloomfield &
Vurdubakis 2002) and the firms who produce them as part of the 'cultural
machine that churns out ideas like there [is] no tomorrow' (Thrift 2002: 19)?
To our mind, to do so, would be to misconstrue this particular form of
business knowledge.

Despite questions concerning their veracity there has been no let-up in the numbers of predictions made, the appetite for this kind of insight, or the standing of those who produce them. If anything, the reverse appears the case (Sherden 1998, Bernard & Gallupe 2013). This begs the question: How does one account for the growing attraction of a form of knowledge that, at face value, regularly turns out to be 'wrong' (c.f. Evans 2007)? Perhaps the assumption that a prediction relies on its accuracy to spread is too crude (Schnaars 1989). We need to think more carefully about how industry analysts come up with these claims, who or what shapes them, how they persuade others of their efficacy, how people evaluate them, and the value found in them.

An important factor in their spread, we argue, is the shift a couple of decades ago from the dissemination and communication of predictions as mostly a 'literary activity' (Fine 2007) to one today where they are predominantly presented at specially designed industry conferences. This shift turns out to be important in building the acceptance of this knowledge. It also provides crucial insights into the distinctive forms of knowledge production and consumption at play here. To anticipate our argument, we find predictions to be less about forecasting the future and more about helping practitioners take immediate, practical choices (Mallard & Lakoff 2011). As such, predictions are judged not solely with regard to accuracy but have become subject to more plural forms of accountability and evaluation—such as their 'utility' for practitioners. This makes industry analysts highly dependent on understanding the responses their predictions generate at conferences. We show how they gauge the utility of their claims through interacting with and provoking reactions from the audience. We develop this argument by analyzing these venues as a space for the simultaneous production and validation of predictions and the role of the audience as offering a new form of 'public proof' (c.f. Shapin 1988).

This chapter is organized as follows. We build the case for considering the spatial organization of prediction work by discussing and integrating work on industry conferences with that on the 'social study of public demonstrations'. This is followed by our empirical material, which is based on interviews with industry analysts and observations of Gartner conferences over several years. We discuss this material and show how these events have reshaped a number of key aspects of the industry analyst knowledge making process, which includes reconfiguring the character and shape of the expertise producing these outputs, together with the format and content of actual predictions.

8.1. NEW FORM OF EXPERTISE?

Understanding the future is of utmost concern for organizations (Tsoukas & Shepherd 2009). Shapin (2008) argues that recent years have seen the proliferation of new kinds of experts with the capacity if not to predict the future then at least to help others operate in and manage the conditions of high uncertainty that surround the world to come. Along similar lines, Fine (2007: 100) suggests most societies will establish 'ritual specialists' whose responsibility it is to 'explain what the morrow will bring'. Whilst there is a small but growing body of work that considers these experts, we limit our attention to discussion of just three groups—meteorologists, financial analysts and economic forecasters—chosen because they provide important contrasts regarding the status, outcomes and forms of accountability surrounding industry analyst predictions.

8.1.1. Judging accuracy

Meteorologists are an apt case for analyzing the problem of judging accuracy. Their work is not only 'plagued by error' but the forecasters produce claims about future events that are checked and evaluated as a matter of occupational routine (Fine 2007). Fine describes meteorologists as operating under a special kind of 'scientific model' and much of his account of their work is given over to their production of what he calls 'verification statistics' (Fine 2006). They operate under a special model because lay people experience the weather in ways seldom found in the other sciences in that they demand to know whether predictions turn out as forecast. Formal verification of the outcomes of predictions becomes crucial for demonstrating the legitimacy of this expertise, argues Fine.

In contrast to this formal type of knowledge production and evaluation, Knorr Cetina (2010, 2012) discusses the financial analysts who sell investment information to speculators in investment and trading markets. She observes that there are no processes similar to those found in science that document 'research results as true or at least as the best available knowledge' (ibid 2010: 175). This is because, in her view, the accuracy of a financial prediction seemingly 'does not matter all that much' (ibid: 182). It is the arrival of new data that 'continually excites a market into further trading' (ibid: 182). People in these domains have little or no incentive to rake over old claims. The market is always looking forward to the 'next piece of information' (ibid: 182).

Economic forecasters produce macroeconomic models predicting the future state of production and consumption. According to Evans (2002, 2007), the important feature of predictions is not their accuracy but the unique and privileged *space* they create for discussion and interaction. The forecasts Evans studied were consumed in specially arranged 'forecasting clubs'. The business executives attending these meeting were apparently '...not paying for the pseudo-precision of numerical predictions' but the 'maintenance of a social space within which the consequences of policy choices can be examined'

(2007: 697). Most subscribers seemingly appreciated the inherent uncertainty of predicting and were less interested in specific numbers. They were confident that the predictor 'generally gets the important things right' (2007: 696), though they could at times challenge the direction of claims.

The IT predictions of Gartner and other industry analyst firms we describe below are not subject to the direct and formal science-like evaluation processes described by Fine (2006, 2007). But nor are they devoid of accountability altogether (Knorr Cetina 2010). We are sceptical of Knorr Cetina's (2010: 187) claim that modes of verification can be completely or simply 'suppressed' or 'turned off'. We thus argue the need for more complex understandings of the processes by which actors evaluate and build the acceptance of future oriented knowledge. We find useful in this regard Evans' (2002, 2007) prompt to give greater attention to the space and occasion of a prediction. We develop this point through considering approaches to the spatial organization of knowledge and public participation.

8.2. HOW VENUES PROVIDE FOR 'PUBLIC PROOF': FROM WITNESSING TO INTERACTION

This chapter shows how the venues where IT predictions are discussed are systematically organized to include external audiences in their construction and ratification. In doing this we find useful discussions from Science and Technology Studies on the role of the public in the evaluation of scientific and technological knowledge. We trace in particular a shift in initial interest in what has become called the 'social study of public demonstrations' (Marres 2009, Rosental 2013) by which publics are seen to move beyond simply *observing* knowledge production to more active *engagement* in its production.

Shapin (1988) has described how the invitation of the public into the private rooms of 17th Century scientists to witness live experiments was important for the spread of early scientific knowledge. It was significant because those observing the demonstrations could offer a 'public evaluation' or 'public proof' of what had gone on in these rooms. There are few thresholds as important as that between the public and private, Shapin argues, when it comes to the evaluation of knowledge. When outside we have to take on trust what is told to us by those with access to the inside. Yet once we cross the threshold, we no longer have to rely on what we have been told, but can judge for *ourselves* (see also Shapin & Shaffer 1985).

We find useful Turner (2001) in this regard who, in the more contemporary example of those who provide consultancy or advice services, has similarly argued the need to have witnesses over an otherwise closed world, able to offer testimony to the efficacy of expertise. Preda (2009) too discusses the private spaces deliberately laid out to foster exchange between experts and the public (and gives the examples of open kitchens, hospital wards, courtrooms etc., as places where the public can not only observe but also interact with experts going about their business). The desire to be observed and interact becomes particularly important when there are problems concerning the legitimacy of a professional group, he argues. Thus enhanced interaction across this threshold can be an attempt to 'persuade' or 'attract' followers to this expertise.

Barry (2001), talking generally about staged venues and public experiments, argues that not only observation but 'interactivity' has become a potent device in engaging audiences and legitimating technological expertise. Marres (2009) too shows how a dependency has developed whereby experts rely on securing the active involvement of the public for the domestication of science and technology. Public forums, she argues, should not be seen simply as a mechanism for the 'socialization' of knowledge but rather, because these venues have their own specific affordances, the *reconfiguration* of the knowledge and those things that surround its production and appropriation.

These points have relevance for how we conceive of industry analyst conferences. Attending such an event can be like glancing through a window into a private sphere. Or, for those running them, it can be a means of offering a public face to the outside. There is an embryonic literature on industry conferences or what has been called 'field configuring events' (Lampel and Meyer 2008), the name given to describe the places where business people meet temporarily in large numbers to discuss matters pertinent to the shaping of technology and product markets. The importance of these events is seen to stem from their ceremonial and affecting nature—how audiences can be seduced by or persuaded of the virtues and benefits of whatever is on show, often through highly charged 'dramaturgical presentations' (Garud 2008). Others have noted their specific interactional features as they allow professionals from different organizational and geographical circumstances to interact at close quarters to share knowledge and experience etc. (Lampel and Meyer 2008). What we want to focus on is how these venues are specifically organized to foster interactions between the experts and the audience and the consequences this has for reconfiguring a number of key aspects surrounding expertise.

Box 3. Research Note

As described at the outset of the book, Gartner produces research to help executives in large organisations to understand emerging technological trends (Firth & Swanson 2005), to help construct IT strategies, or to facilitate choices when procuring IT equipment and software (Burks 2006). We note that whilst clients can receive and view these predictions by reading paper reports or via email, the trend today is to access them via the conference. It seems that rather than 'reading' this research people nowadays appear to prefer to watch and listen to them (there has been a movement from 'eyes' to 'ears').[i] In terms of conducting fieldwork, these conferences offer unparalleled opportunities for empirical access in that they bring producers and consumers into close proximity for unstructured interactions (Lampel & Mayer 2008). Studying conferences also helps disrupt the popular conception that predictions are constructed solely by individuals (where their origin and evaluation can be put down to the vagaries of individual imagination and discretion) (Guice 1999). Our own fieldwork suggests that predictions result from more observable social and distributed processes. There are frequent interactions at the intersection between the production and use of this knowledge that contributes to its shaping. As we describe below, the creation of this form of knowledge is highly dependent on 'feedback'. Thus, its creation necessitates a high level of interaction and networking. These interactions are often mediated (through telephone, email or webinars) or take place in transient settings (industry conferences or workshops). This presents particular problems for traditional ethnographic research designs, located in particular moments and organisational settings. When observing these groups one often has the sense of never being in the right place at the right time (Law 1994). To help overcome this we acknowledge Marcus' (1995) point of the need to be 'strategic' during ethnography in order to capture phenomena that overflow the single site. This includes making explicit choices about the places to be studied. Influenced by provisional theoretical and empirical understandings about which sites and nexuses might be interesting, as well as pragmatic exigencies, we thus focused our attention on industry conferences.

Data gathering for the current study comprised attendance and observations of a number of industry analyst conferences and in-depth semi-structured interviews with industry analysts. We participated in three 2-day conferences in London and carried out more than 60 hours of observations. Whilst participant observation is a demanding and often intrusive form of research, these occasions turned out to be a particularly fertile ground for research. Here we could observe the formal presentations made by analysts and also approach them informally afterwards. Since the meetings were run in a similar fashion to academic seminars it was easy to engage analysts in conversation or to simply hang around and listen whilst others quizzed them about the thinking behind predictions. We were also able to chat informally with other conference goers, take-part in various structured activities (lunches, roundtables, one-on-one chats with analysts etc.). Whilst we benefited from these spontaneous discussions, we were also able to conduct formal interviews as described in Appendix 2. The collection of data at the conferences was facilitated by the service that Gartner offers to conference goers where it video records sessions and makes them available to participants after the event (for a further fee, of course!). This meant we could re-listen to conference presentations once back in our university offices.

[i] As Huczynski (2006: 244) writes whilst talking about consultant presentations: "Not only do managers appear to prefer to be told things, rather than having to read them for themselves, but also they appear to place the responsibility on the speaker to entertain them while communicating the information".

8.3. DRAGGING PREDICTION WORK FROM THE PRIVATE TO PUBLIC ARENA: FIVE ELEMENTS

We organize our empirical material around what we identify as the five key elements involved in dragging prediction work from the private offices of the analyst firm to the public arena of the conference. This is a discussion of (i) the *establishment and extension* of the conference (ii) how the conference could *reconfigure the kinds of expertise* involved in prediction work as well (iii) *how* predictions could be produced and *where* they could be discussed and communicated (iv) how the conference allowed analysts *the capacity to manage some of the contradictory demands* related to prediction work and finally (v) how the conference was used to *multiply interactions* between those producing and consuming this knowledge to help in its validation.

8.3.1. Establish and extend the conference

Today the 'conference' and 'prediction' appear natural bedfellows. The discussion of predictions in conference spaces appears an obligatory move in setting up this form of knowledge as reliable and useful. But it was not always thus. The analyst conference is a relatively recent innovation. Up to a few decades ago, prediction work was predominantly a 'literary affair' (Fine 2007) that involved the writing and dissemination of lengthy research style documents. It was one where the production and consumption of this knowledge was mostly separated. Reports would be read by clients back in the comfort of their own offices. Although they could telephone analysts to discuss the details of claims, they reportedly rarely did so (Gartner 2014). The gradual erosion of the disjunction between those who produced and consumed this knowledge began to occur during the 1990s. Gartner (and others) moved to create an alternative model for the production and dissemination of this research.

We have described in Chapter 2 how Gartner's founder, Gideon Gartner, talked of the 'ten innovations' that set his firm apart from the established players of the time (Gartner 2010b, Gartner 2014). The first of these innovations included the decision to stage conferences more frequently and on a much larger scale than had previously been the case. These early events were relatively modest compared to those today but they quickly began to gather status and attract a following. Gideon Gartner describes how the first conferences grew to become what today is called the 'Gartner Symposium' or just 'The Symposium' for short, as it is known more widely:

> . . . we had events every once in a while. In those days, we had very few events but we innovated dramatically in our events. I have I think one story of one little innovation that we did, but you know the Gartner Symposium today is my design [and] at every step I improved the design, I modified it. But at all times the press felt it was a leading innovator in designing new forms of how you present information at meetings (interview, Gideon Gartner).

What Gartner sought to do was define the nature of the new conference venue where they would publicly discuss a form of prediction called the '5-year scenario' and then later 'Strategic Planning Assumptions'. This space did not as yet exist; it had to be created. He recounts how in setting up the conference he borrowed from existing domains like the 'World Economic Forum':

> I designed a replacement for our initial conference format which presented 5-year "scenarios" of each service sector. It listed the sector's macro trends followed by key issues to be faced and of course our projections. We constantly improved but mainly expanded our format to include competitive challenges, new technologies to expect, and so forth. The point was to create an evolving structure which clients could get used to, and hopefully grow to love. I was most proud when once after attending the WEF (World Economic Forum) I was inspired to design yet a new format, this time called the Gartner Symposium, evolving again to be Gartner's IT Expo (Gartner 2014).

The Symposium attracted hundreds and thousands of IT professionals on a regular basis. It has become a fixed part of the industry calendar and an obligatory point of passage for managers and technology vendors alike.[1] Former Gartner employee Kathy Kane describes its importance:

> ...little did we know at that time (when The Symposium was designed) that I...was part of something very big that would become a true 'Industry Defining' event and would carry so much clout and weight that it would bring in many, many luminaries, that at its height would attract over 13,000 people to Orlando plus over 500 exhibitors, that it would become an international brand with events in Japan, Australia, France, Spain, South Africa and other locations...that it would have a community of over 30,000 people annually... (reported in Gartner 2014).

The conference has moved from the margins of what Gartner do to the centre. Gartner devotes an entire wing of its organization to running events. Self-described as the 'largest IT conference provider in the world', Gartner Events will begin planning events several months in advance and will conduct them down to the last detail. These events are carried out in existing spaces (often luxurious hotels) especially modified for the purpose. It is not unusual for these firms to turn up and install their own sound and lighting systems (and in some case the 'stage' itself as well as other dramaturgical props) (interview, Drow).

Once a particular conference is over this is not the end of it. Not by a long way. Stages and props will be dismantled and shipped to some other part of the world, as conferences are organized as recurring events in space and time. The Symposium (and the various connected summits, forums, workshops etc.) run throughout the year and the same conference can be recycled across geographies. An analyst at one of the events we attended describes how they managed this recycling process:

> We will have a few months rest and then we begin to think about the next one. We have one in the States coming up, so we will heading over there to the US. So,

quite a lot of the content we have here also appears in the US. But obviously dialled into a US based audience, and US examples and so on. And there are some new presentations just for that audience. So it is quite a workload to actually avoid the trap of old comfortable titles. You know, some of the messages are the same. But you have somebody who comes to an event and goes 'I saw that slide last year'. And, OK... there would have to be cross checking (interview, Drow).

We note how in tandem with the rise of the conference—or perhaps *because* of it—there has been a change in the character of the expertise within these firms and the format and content of predictions. Let us consider first the skills demanded by the conference.

8.3.2. Reconfiguring expertise: Skilled in engaging the audience

During the early conferences, analysts would simply walk out onto stage, greet the audience, and then proceed to read from a previously prepared paper (interview, Levin). The audience would follow the talk by looking at a folder containing papers handed to them on registering for the conference:

> When you were on stage you... didn't have any PowerPoint or any kind of backing. Literally, everyone had a binder in front of them. It did have slides that were crafted in power point inside, full of notes, and you would basically say 'now let's turn now to page number 2'. And they would talk about it. Then they say 'now let's turn to page 3'. You know, some analysts would be all over it, 'so now let's go to page 21. Now back to page 7'. They would use it as a reference (interview, Levin).

Binders were a necessity because talks would cover complex technical detail: '... it would be very detailed: diagrams or architecture or whatever it was. And then a whole page of notes underneath it... [s]o they were more like I suppose, academic notes' (interview, Levin). The present day conference could not be more different. The typical arrangement is one where an analyst is accompanied onto stage by very loud music (a kind of 'Gartner rock') and enthusiastically greets the (often very large) audience (numbers could vary between 15–20 up to 4–5 thousand people at a time!). A talk is fast paced, supported by vibrant visual graphics and above all else 'entertaining' (Huczynski 2006). Below, one of the author's fieldwork diaries records the moment one of these conferences begin:

> The large room full begins to fill up. There are over 300 people already in the room and more are piling in. The large screens placed around the room that had previously been listing 'interesting facts' now spring into life with quick changing dynamic images. The electronic music that had been looping in the background is now replaced by loud (extremely loud) rock music. The lights are dimmed. The audience begin to sit up in their chairs expecting something to happen. And here

they are appearing on the especially prepared stage. Not the entertainers or musicians one might expect but the 'Gartner analysts'. "We are the rock stars who will be on stage performing for you over the next couple of days", says one Gartner analyst (Jim Davies), without any obvious trace of irony, as he opens up a two day conference in London. And the event begins . . . (fieldwork diary).

If in the past the work of the industry analyst was a literary activity, nowadays it is an event-based one, shaped by the affordances and demands of the conference space. One consequence is that the original analyst figure from the 1990s is being overtaken by a new kind of analyst able to perform on stage. Whilst we do not want to push this point too far—since not all analysts turn out to be good presenters, see below—there is a sense that the conference performance has become a key feature defining these experts. We discuss this by exploring what analysts themselves feel about the conference—how it can raise various forms of emotion, from passion through to fear—and then look at some of Gartner's organizational mechanisms aimed at maximizing and measuring performance on stage.

8.3.2.1. From 'B-player' to 'star analyst'

Many presenters interviewed were enthusiastic about the conference. One analyst describes this vividly: 'It is something I love . . . [it] is one of the reasons I do [the job]. I love doing it' (interview, Ward Dutton). Others were more ambivalent, pointing to the demands it placed on their time: 'Another thing we do a lot is writing presentations. One fifth of our time we stand on podiums in front of an audience. We do our own events. We do vendor events. I will conduct our London conference next year' (interview, Winter). Another makes a similar point, but also notes how the size of the audience can create added pressure. He recalls a recent conversation with non-analyst friends:

> So they said 'how many times do you present a year?'. And I said 'maybe 60 . . . times a year. At least once a week, up on my feet in front of an audience'. And they said: 'it is like around a table with 10 people?'. I said: 'oh yeah, it is small. And the big ones will be about . . . 5,000'. They are like: 'right, OK!' So I said 'you learn to conquer your fears in front of . . . 5,000'. It is quite scary (interview, Thomas).

If in the past the analysts would build their reputation based on the quality and perceptiveness of their writing, nowadays it is stage performance that creates hierarchy. There are analysts reported to be 'exceptional' in this regard and then there are those seen as offering different sorts of skills. Let us start with the former:

> We have got a couple of guys here who are really, really good. And Gartner charges some ridiculous fee. It charges something like $15,000 . . . to have an

analyst for a day. And the reason for that is generally the standard of presenting is quite high. And you want someone to talk about ERP for the day, and you want them to stand on a conference, you know, lectern and attract people in with the Gartner name, you will charge for it (interview, Thomas).

Another interviewee echoes this description:

> ... some are exceptionally good presenters, can hold an audience, can take a couple of simple concepts and spin them into something that is memorable and sits in people's mind. The nature of the rigour of their research is pretty limited in some of those places. But again some of the ... highest profile researchers in all industries are those that can get that concept right, that enables people to remember it, and buy into it, and follow it through (interview, Mitchell).

These analysts were good in constructing and communicating predictions, but apparently less concerned with the rigour demanded by this form of knowledge making.

This contrasts with a second category that whilst evidently well qualified to produce the research, purportedly lacked the capacities of their counterparts in other regards:

> There are different sorts [of analysts]. So if I think of one of the analysts in my team, he is not very flamboyant, he is just a very, very thorough, rigorous analyst. You might say that he is a really solid 'B player'. But based on the thoroughness of what he does, rather than the presentation, kudos, or the nature of his writing, or being in the press, he is very well respected by the group of people that he serves. But that is just based on the thoroughness and rigour of his research. Again, a bit like some academics that are respected on their thoroughness or rigour but there is no real strong insight or blinding flash of light ... They are a different type of researcher, not necessarily good and bad (interview, Mitchell).

Whilst careful not to denigrate either category, our informant points to a division emerging within this fledgling expertise. He contrasts the so called 'B-Player' with the rise of what has become known more widely 'star analyst' who is valued for their personal and charismatic qualities (Fincham 2002). It seemingly did not matter that one group were less research oriented: it was just that they could perform better on stage and this catapulted them into the increasingly important public arenas of the analyst world, whilst relegating others to the private backroom spaces of the firm.

8.3.2.2. 'I'm 20th best in Europe'

Individual analysts know very well on which side of the divide they sit. Each time they appear at conference the audience are handed evaluation forms and asked to rate the speaker according to their 'performance' and the 'usefulness' of the content presented.[2] There is ample evidence to suggest that these evaluations matter. In one conference we attended, the presenter with the lowest feedback score was made to wear a red and white striped top hat—the conference was themed on a Dr Seuss book—for the remainder of the event as a very visible form of punishment.

Analyst evaluations go well beyond the theatre of the conference. Feedback is collated and made available throughout the firm, meaning that each analyst will know exactly where they stand in relation to colleagues in local and international offices:

> We stack rank every analyst, every conference, and at the end of the year they stack us top to bottom in terms of how we present. So you know exactly where you sit in terms of what the customers, the clients, the attendees have voted, giving you a score, a stack ranked score. So you know exactly on every event. You look where you are and see how your content was better than everyone else's content. And your speaker score, which is your ability to present, and you can see over the years whether you got better or worse and how you are doing' (interview, Thomas).[3]

A poor showing at conference is important because it could determine whether analysts are invited back to present at future events.[4] It could also influence progression within the firm (promotion) or access to company rewards (sabbaticals). It may even affect whether you remain *in* the firm (and we were told the story of an otherwise gifted analyst who had recently left the profession because he could not 'handle', no matter how hard he tried, presenting in front of large audiences). We return to the issue of conference feedback in a moment but first we want to discuss how the conference began to reconfigure the format and content of predictions.

8.3.3. Reconfiguring the how and where of predictions

The 'ten innovations' introduced by Gideon Gartner that we described in Chapter 2 included changes to the research process. Analysts were given directions about how and in what way their research could be reported. Gideon Gartner promoted the use of simple formats. Gone were the 'lengthy', 'academic' style reports. From then on all documents were to be 'very brief'. Gartner designed 'a one page format which [all analysts] had to adhere to' (interview, Gideon Gartner). He also initiated a distinction between the types of research that were to be circulated as documents and that which would be discussed and communicated *only* at venues. This included predictions known as 'Strategic Planning Assumptions' that would become 'primarily for conferences' (Gartner 2010b). Below we discuss why there were thought to be benefits to dividing research up in this way.

8.3.3.1. Strategic Planning Assumptions

Strategic Planning Assumptions (SPAs) are simple two-part-contrasts—as in 'today' versus 'tomorrow'. Here the existing state of affairs is presented, supported by figures, which are then extrapolated forward 4 or 5 years into the future (see Figure 8.1). It is perhaps no coincidence that two-part-contrasts have their history in the political rally where the personal virtues of a speaker have utmost importance (Grady & Potter 1985). The two-part-contrast allows the presentation of potentially complex arguments in a way that is both easy for the presenter to convey and easy for the audience to remember.

If this first example speaks of a linear transition from one state to another then the second type of SPA is a little more complicated. An analyst describes to the audience the thinking behind the SPA:

> A Strategic Planning Assumption essentially is an informed set of assumptions that Gartner is making about what is going to happen in the future. We try to make them very real by putting numbers behind them. We put a timeframe behind them. We basically use it as a 'Stalking Horse' to see whether or not the technologies and the business processes and the adoptions that we see are clients are going through are actually aligning with that SPA (Fletcher, conference floor).

The notion of a 'Stalking Horse' is central in the construction of a prediction (Bernard & Gallupe 2013). Gideon Gartner describes how the thinking behind the Stalking Horse was to create an 'idea or concept which would then serve as a basis for further study . . . and inquiry . . . and discussion . . . perhaps finally

---

Digital Marketing Will be Marketing's Priority for the Next Five Years

Today

1.8 billion internet users and growing

Mobile advertising in the U.S. reached $877.2 million in 2010, up 138% from the $368 million spent in 2009.

Social CRM application spending reached $600 million in 2010. Marketing departments were more likely to launch social CRM projects than other departments in the same company.

Tomorrow

By 2014, 6.7 billion will be connected to the Internet.

By 2013, mobile marketing applications will influence over 15% of online sales.

By 2013, spending on social software to support sales, marketing and customer service processes will exceed $1 billion worldwide.

By 2015, Internet-supported social marketing processes will influence at least 80% of consumers' discretionary spending.

Figure 8.1. Today versus tomorrow

Source: Gartner Conference Presentation

Table 8.1. Strategic Planning Assumptions (SPAs)

Strategic Planning Assumption
By 2015, 30% of Global 200 companies that focus on improving lead management processes will increase revenue 5% to 10% through better qualification, prioritization, distribution, augmentation, allocation, tracking and closing of leads from multiple lead-generation sources.

Reasons why SPAs will be true:	Reasons why SPAs will be false:
Growing investment in BoB lead management technology and process	Tactical KPIs and basic lead mgmt. metrics still the norm
Lead mgmt. KPIs and analytics identified as spending priority for 2011	Multichannel lead management proving difficult to implement: <20% success rate with >3 channels
Multichannel lead management becoming a necessity in social, mobile, digital enabled world	Consolidation of lead management market, multiple vendor 'packaging' options will delay the market

Source: Gartner Conference Presentation

resulting in an approved consensus view at our research meetings' (Gartner 2014). It often happened that the presenter was Janus-faced when talking about the future. Analysts would flip between talking about the positive aspects of a technology to then discussing the difficulties that can exist around an otherwise optimistic projection (Tutton 2011). Its presentation was seen as an occasion to provoke further enquiry and discussion and to solicit the opinion and experience of the audience (Gartner 2014). For instance, one presenter listed some of the reasons why a prediction might come true and then went onto give reasons why it might not (see Table 8.1)!

This form of SPA is interesting because we found these formats to be deployed during the discussion of 'mature' technologies, or where technologies had already been extensively discussed at previous conferences. In terms of the latter, there may be adopters sitting in the audience who not only remember the prediction from previous years but who may have direct, perhaps negative, experience of attempting to get the technologies to work as promised. In taking different sides of an argument there was a visible attempt by presenters to assure the audience that they had deep knowledge and understanding and were not suppressing or ignorant of difficulties, but also to spark a discussion. This begs the question: if analysts were developing specific forms of research solely for the conference venue, what sorts of understanding were they attempting to build?

8.3.3.2. Reframing content: What to do on Monday?

Relevance is an important issue for this firm, so much so that it has reorganized much of its research process in order to construct particular kinds of insights. In producing Stalking Horses, the analysts were not attempting to simply brainstorm or invoke far-flung futures. They wanted to produce predictions that that were 'relevant and actionable' (Montgomery & Weinberg 1979 cited in Gartner 2014). To unpack this further we discuss the internal research process and show how analysts, if wishing to make it to conference, were made to run the gauntlet so to speak. Before a new idea could see the light of day an analyst would have to submit it to colleagues in the same 'Technology Group', who would, in turn, provide comment. An analyst describes how a prediction could be subject to what appeared to be fierce internal critique:

> There is a tough, disparate bricks [that] . . . block your prediction. All the people in your group, at least three of them have to comment. It then goes through your manager. The manager has to comment . . . Then it goes to basically randomly to three other analysts around . . . applications, and they have to comment. And the predictions often change quite a lot throughout this journey (interview, Winter).

There was comment also from those across the wider Research Community. This community allows you to:

> . . . form your ideas, because when you come out with a prediction sometimes you just understand that either it is too risky, so you don't want to stick your neck out; or, maybe it doesn't make sense at all. You can only do it because maybe a colleague of yours has told you something which you didn't know before. What Gartner is very good at is allowing all of this information to circulate freely (interview, Winter).

This form of peer review has an effect. It meant the analysts considered themselves to be highly 'conservative' (interview, Thomas) and not wanting 'to stick their necks out' (interview, Winter). They also rarely ignored the input of colleagues. To do so would mean that a prediction could be 'blocked' and not make it to the conference. Various reasons were given as to why a prediction could be obstructed. It could be that it points to something that has *already* happened: 'The vast majority of predictions that do not make it out is because . . . our predictions are not predictions. We state something that is true already. Or possibly that is too close and that is just a silly consequence of what is happening' (interview, Winter). Another is where analysts cannot characterize the projected change in a simple and clear way—as a two-part-contrast, for instance—or they 'can't quantify [it] properly' (interview, Winter).

Apparently, the 'worst' critique that an analyst can receive, however, relates to its immediate utility and relevance to the conference goer. An analyst describes how when predictions are debated internally there is a strong pressure to develop research with practical implications:

> So when we challenge each other internally, the key . . . question we are always asking . . . It's a big trend . . . blah de blah de blah, cutting all of that out—what do we propose to do on Monday? 'Oh, not much. Doesn't really have impact for 5 years'. 'Well, who cares then?' It is not of any interest (interview, Thomas).

> **Actionable Advice**
>
> **What to do on Monday:** Create a business-led team to determine the impact of mobile technology and Web 2.0 on your current e-commerce capabilities and CRM plans
>
> **What to do next Month:** Answer the question "What's in it for me?" from a customer perspective for each process
>
> **What to do within the next year:** Engage vendors or resources who can quickly build capabilities for you in an iterative process. Be ready to stop or change any project.

Figure 8.2. Final slide of every presentation
Source: Gartner Conference Presentation

If a new 'big trend' has been identified but there is no immediate or practical outcome then it will not be presented:

> Unless you tell me [the client] what to do on Monday when I go back to my office and talk to my boss about the event it is of no use. So we . . . might set the context [say] where it is going and this is the big trend or this is the direction, but the end of each page is basically the same. This is the action we are advising you to take. It has to be pretty much a couple of bullet points (interview, Thomas).

Predictions are meant to have practical consequences for the client. They should be structured in such a way that leads to the initiation of some kind of response, to help the client make a decision:

> We are very driven by that, which does sort of focus your thinking a bit when you come to the end of it. The worst accusation you can have internally is 'so what?' which is the, 'yeah, it is brilliant but 'so what?' Good point! I'm embarrassed. So what does this actually mean? So what does a customer actually do? (interview, Thomas).

The goal it seemed was to help participants to reframe the future from something distant and abstract to something close and actionable (Mallard & Lakoff 2011). This focus on practical outcomes permeates all aspects of the conference and there are various rhetorical devices that ensured this requirement was visibly actioned. For instance, every presentation finishes with a slide titled 'Actionable Advice' which includes a section on 'What to do on Monday', 'What to do next month' and 'What to do within the next year' (Figure 8.2).

8.3.4. Conference allows capacity to manage contradictory demands of prediction work

Envisioning what new computer architectures will look like in the next five years or which particular breed of marketing technology will emerge over a rival one is a highly uncertain business (Fine 2007). Error is a common and inevitable aspect: 'We sort of take for granted that we are going to be wrong', says an analyst with many years of experience (interview, Winter).[5] Just as some analysts are better on stage, there are also those better at avoiding or managing failure. It is relatively common, for instance, to see a *caveat* at the conference. One analyst begins his presentation by telling the audience not to hold him 'accountable' for anything he was about to say whilst another drew a parallel between his presentation and the work of 'witches and fortune tellers'.[6] These examples are meant to amuse as much as deal with the difficult task of discussing accuracy. But since a prediction could 'fail', many analysts had developed strategies to avoid the public perception of failure.

One of these strategies was to be *ambiguous* on stage. In order not to be left with difficulties further down the line, analysts were intentionally vague. This could be temporally (as in *when* it might happen) or specificity (*what* exactly is happening and to *whom*). Another practice was to *revisit* predictions at specific intervals (e.g., to try to get it right second time around). Thus, an analyst might decide not to simply wait a prediction out but recast it based on recent developments and further information. Talking about quantitative indicators, one analyst reveals how:

> it is never forecast and forget. Forecasts are continually refined. So we tend to update ours once every 6 months at the outside. For some of the more volatile areas, it is once a quarter. And it is like any set of forecasts, if you get it widely wrong, tune your heuristics based on how wrong you've been, so as your forecasts get more accurate over time by the nature of your tuning (interview, Mitchell).

Through an iterative process, the prediction is continually refined and re-launched so that it gradually becomes more accurate. Typically an analyst is pushed to revisit a claim every 3 or 4 months (which coincides with the finishing of one conference and the planning for the next) and at this point, the analyst would be contacted and asked to revisit the slides.

8.3.4.1. Conferences make it come true

A further aspect that could militate against error was the possibility, once presented, that a prediction could *become* true. Those interviewed often talked about how others would be swayed by what was said during the conference. The analyst discussed at the outset of this chapter discussing electronic invoice adoption in banking describes how: 'if we say . . . electronic invoice[ing in banking] will grow 20% in the next—I think I say 5 times in the next 3 years, which is spectacular—if I do that, quite a lot of vendors would invest in invoicing solutions. So, to some extent, it becomes a bit of a self-fulfilling prophecy' (interview, Winter). This analyst was by no means unusual in stating it in this way. These experts are reflexively aware of how they can come to shape the things around them (as discussed in the Prologue of this book). But do they really encourage the phenomenon? Not everyone believes this of course. Or perhaps they find that predictions can have uneven effects. The analyst discussing banking contradicts his earlier statement: 'But nobody really listens to Gartner! I think there is a corner you turn in your life as an analyst in which, when you think you can drive the industry as opposed to predict. When they [technology vendors] say "we haven't gone into that yet", you don't' (interview, Winter).

8.3.5. Multiply interactions: Build real time validations

In this final section we discuss the extraordinary enthusiasm for 'interactivity' at these events (Barry 2001). All aspects of the conferences appear designed to encourage exchanges between presenters and the audience (c.f. Preda 2009). Gartner expect the audience to participate in the proceedings, rather than simply play the role of passive observer. We give two examples of the kinds of interactions that go on.

8.3.5.1. Hands up!

When presenting an SPA an analyst would almost always seek confirmation from the audience about its validity. An analyst sets out a two-part-contrast and then invites the audience to agree or disagree with what he is saying:

> I want to put two statements to you today and see if you agree with me. In 2 years time more than 35% of all customer service interactions will be via self-service. Currently it is around 20%...those of you that disagree with 35%. You think it will be lower? Put any hands up. Those who think it will be more? (Jacobs, conference floor).

The key method of creating an interaction was for the analyst to ask for the raising of hands—usually encouraged by the analyst first who raising their own hand—and then (in a somewhat theatrical manner) to scan the room, counting out loud to demonstrate that the audience view is being registered. If fewer hands are raised than anticipated then what ensues is something like the scene from an auction where the level of anticipated change is negotiated up or down: 'Ok. 50% [of hands raised]?...Fine! So I am more or less in the ballpark there. Bottom line there is that there is a huge push of transactions towards self-service' (Jacobs, conference floor). The analyst attempts to create the audience as interaction partners and flags the possibility that they might revise a prediction based on feedback. It is the audience who either confirms or denies the claim being made. What this points to is how the conference allows not simply for the communication of this knowledge but also its validation. This interactivity-aided knowledge validation is perhaps not new in the world of prediction making but we would argue that it is being made anew. This is seen most clearly in this second example where we see the development of a novel dramaturgical template borrowed from another area of socio-cultural activity.

8.3.5.2. Game show

The Game Show is the latest innovation within the conference. We witnessed it on some of its first ever outings. An analyst talks about how and why they came up with this particular format:

> I sat there with my colleague, because the two of us chair the conference, and we were ... very worried ... we had to do a panel, because we have to have our sponsors on stage. It is part of the package we sell for the vendors sponsoring the event, the Events organization were organizing that. We were bored sitting there interviewing 3 sponsors. It was just dull! So we did it like a 'Game Show' instead. We were like, 'this is not going to fly'! We were meticulous in our planning and the organization and execution and it worked really well. It went down a storm, and they loved it, the audience. We were like: 'we got away with it!' (Thomas, interview).[7]

The idea of the Game Show was to contrast the opinions of the different actors present: the analysts, the conference sponsors and audience. An analyst compèring describes this format to the audience:

> In a minute, I am going to invite up our 4 premier sponsors who will form a panel for us. And what we are going to do is ... give them 30 seconds to think about the answer to ... 8 questions ... They are going to write their answers on a board. They are going to turn them around without conferring ... And we are going to see how they have answered the questions. Then we are going to see if there are any difference in their questions. We may ask *you* [the audience] what you think. And then we are going to show you what the analysts think ... there are no wrong and right answers. So this is all looking futuristically, looking out into the future (Davis, conference floor).

The game starts and the panel of conference sponsors are asked: 'What percentage of sales marketing and customer service processes will be executed on a mobile device in 2015?' The panellists are more or less in agreement that there will be a large-scale shift towards mobile use (more than a 60 per cent shift).

The compère then reveals what the analysts think (only a 20 per cent shift): 'And the analyst view to compare that against. Much, much, much lower. . . . Yeah we [the analysts] are a lot more cynical, pessimistic maybe' (Davis, conference floor). The compère then turns to the audience, who have been given coloured voting cards and asks them to decide who they agree with '. . . if we do red is pessimistic and green is more positive like our panellists. I would like a vote ... are you with the Gartner analysts in terms of score? . . . Are we down in the 20, 30% range. Or are we more positive with the greens.

Hands up now. Vote now' (Davis, conference floor). The bulk of the audience agree with the panellists, to which the compere shouts 'The panelists win! The panelists win! I think that is about 70% I would say. 80% green. You're with the panelists! The analysts are too negative' (Davis, conference floor).

The quiz moves on and a similar response emerges once again, such that the compère begins to mock the position of the analysts: 'What did the analysts think? We thought "C", completely different, on average! So having established in Track 2 that the analysts are lunatics' (Davis, conference floor).[8] A pattern in the game begins to be established: 'Oh, that is excellent. That is really confusing. I would say that that is mostly green. There is not much yellow... analysts are lunatics. Let's see what the lunatics thought' (Davis, conference floor). The analysts are established as mavericks: 'Once again we are pessimistic. A little bit conservative'. Another question: 'The analysts think 15%'. 'Pessimists again'. The compère closes the game show: 'What we have learnt from this is that the panellists are very optimistic. You [the audience] are very optimistic and positive. The analysts are cynical, sarcastic and unpleasant individuals but we knew that anyway' (Davis, conference floor).

What are we to make of this? Is this just entertainment? Or does it demonstrate something else? The temptation, which should be resisted, is to dismiss it as a frivolous event—a bit of fun or entertainment. Clearly, there is a humorous element as the analysts play something of the role of 'court jester' (see Välikangas & Sevón [2010] for a discussion of the role of consultant as jesters) and set about a rather self-deprecating performance of how opinions differ. Yet there are reasons why we should take it seriously. The Game Show certainly carried with it a sense of indiscipline that was quite unlike the other (more tightly choreographed) parts of the conference. The analysts hardly had full control of events. There was a risk. They did not know what the audience or sponsor reaction might be. It could have been a failure. Indeed, it was not clear what constituted success or failure in this context. The aims appeared rather open-ended. Once finished there was a visible sense of relief on stage that the analysts had indeed 'got away with it' (Thomas, interview). All but the most minor things the analysts had predicted had been contradicted and in the most public of circumstances. Yet seemingly, it was not deemed a disaster. Rather, according to the analyst above, it 'went down a storm' so much so that Gartner now regularly run the Game Show at other conferences (Thomas, interview).

8.4. DISCUSSION: FROM PAPER TO STAGE

Our aim has been to make sense of a pervasive but complex form of business knowledge known as the 'IT prediction'. Whilst these future oriented statements regularly turn out to be 'wrong', this seemingly makes little difference to their uptake, the interest they attract, or the authority of those who produce them (Bott 2012, Leonhard 2013). What we have attempted to investigate is how, if the continued growth of IT predictions is not fuelled by their veracity, we might explain their spread. We have been interested in the processes by which industry analysts come up with predictions, the people and practices involved in their shaping, how they and others evaluate and establish the efficacy of this knowledge, and the value it has for those who consume it. To help throw light on this we have focused attention on the *venues* where this knowledge is presented and discussed. We have attempted to link the widespread circulation of predictions to the decision by the pioneering analyst firm Gartner Inc. to set up and run conferences and to dedicate the development of certain kinds of research and processes to these venues. This move turned out to be crucial.

In shifting predictions from paper to the stage, Gideon Gartner turned predictions from outputs into 'actions'. In that way he seemingly got around the problem of 'accuracy'. Rather than judging whether predictions were actually right or wrong they were judged as 'activities'. Siting prediction work in physical venues meant that a number of activities from then on were carried out in public as opposed to back in the private offices of the analyst firm. These events were not simply an add-on to the prediction. They were capitalized upon to become an integral part of the prediction process. We find, today, there is a specific interactional and locational aspect to the conference. It involves a particular form of engagement between those who produce and consume predictions. Those constructing predictions were brought together for a sustained and intensive period of time with those potentially using them. The analyst firm could then use these spaces to set out and promote claims and also utilize the audience to help in guiding choices about the kinds of predictions made.

In making these arguments, we have drawn on growing scholarship on the 'social study of public demonstrations' (Marres 2009, Rosental 2013). In particular, Shapin's (1988) analysis of how the public, invited into early scientific events, were not the *mere* audience for knowledge but had become an integral aspect in its spread through offering a 'public evaluation' or 'public proof' of claims made. Shapin argued that early public demonstrations allowed processes traditionally thought to be distinct—namely, the production *and* validation of knowledge—to be carried out in the same space. We have sought to develop the idea of public proof through foregrounding the notion of 'interaction' (which is more active than the rather passive notion of 'witnessing' found in Shapin's work). Industry analyst conferences are analysed as venues to engage (Barry 2001). They are what Marres (2009) calls 'engagement devices' that secure the involvement and contribution of the audience. We have developed a number of points in relation to this.

The conference was important, we argue, because it promoted confidence and acceptance of this knowledge. It promoted confidence because the analysts were simultaneously stating *and* legitimating knowledge. These venues were deliberately organized to encourage the audience to discuss and evaluate the knowledge presented. Predictions formats were structured in such a way as to provoke a response. The complex academic style prediction ('now turn to page . . . ') has given way to new formats which are easier to deliver and easier to remember. The simple two-part-contrast meant the audience could take a position ('those who disagree . . . put hands up'). Novel templates—like the Stalking Horse and the Game Show—were deployed to foster reactions from the audience ('are you with the Gartner analysts?'). On leaving the auditorium participants were invited to rate the 'performance' of the speaker and asked if they found the talk and the content 'useful'.

We are arguing that the value and confidence in predictions has become inextricably tied to the conference. This begs the question where does the value and validity of the conference come from. Dragging prediction work from the private backroom offices of the analyst firm to the public domain of the conference space also led to a shift in the character and form of the fledgling expertise producing this knowledge. At the birth of the industry, these experts were identified according to traditional 'research' characteristics. Nowadays different qualities have come to the fore. The 'personal' and 'charismatic' have become as important as the once celebrated notions of 'thoroughness' and 'rigour'. It is no longer enough for analysts to be 're-spected'; these experts must also be invested with charismatic features (Fincham 2002, Shapin 2008). The authority of these experts is tied to their performance on stage. All analysts can produce research, but not all are flamboyant, talented, able to turn a phrase, etc. It is also entirely feasible for people to 'read' these predictions back in their offices but today they predo-minately insist on 'watching' and 'listening' to them, through attending the conference. This is because, argues Shapin (2008), when people are confronted with or are forced to make decisions in contexts of high uncertainty, it is 'judgement' that comes to the fore. In exercising judgement, it is personal and familiar qualities that become important in evaluating and making sense of knowledge. And whilst the personal and charismatic can be exercised by repute or at a distance through documentation, it is more powerfully exercised inter-personally and through co-location.

Importantly, whereas in the past these analysts were accomplished in *engaging the data* today they are skilled in *engaging the audience*. Presented at close quarters with the charismatic figure, the audience were encouraged into reacting and contributing (cf. Barry 2001), to provide much needed feedback. Contrast this with the situation from just a few years earlier (the 'literary model') where there was a disjunction between the analyst and the client, between production and consumption, and between the production and assessment of this research. Not only was knowledge produced mostly 'in private' but also there were few mechanisms or occasions to solicit input on claims. The feedback so crucial for this process of evaluation would arrive slowly and sporadically (if it arrived at all). This had problematic implications for a knowledge producer dependent on understanding the public reaction to its claims (Were people in agreement with what was being said? Did they find it useful?).[9]

We further suggest that participants at the conference were validating knowledge and also contributing to its production. There is no better example of this than the Game Show. Initially, as we sat and watched this (rather bizarre) episode, we struggled to make sense of it. Later we realized that we were being given an important glimpse into how this form of knowledge production could sustain itself. The organizers were creating a number of future oriented tropes ('Stalking Horses') to draw in the audience, and then asking people to align or disagree with them. And what better way to test an idea than to contrive an entertaining experiment wholly about generating a reaction and augmenting the level of audience feedback. We thus came to see it as an important mechanism by which interactions could be multiplied (Shapin & Schaffer 1985). It offered further opportunities to include those from outside in this prediction work, allowing Gartner to simultaneously produce and test its predictions in real time, in the relatively protected space it had created for itself. The Game Show allowed a mutual (but not necessarily antagonistic) probing of each other's point of view (and the drama and humour of the event clearly helped Gartner create this protected space).

Building on Shapin (1988), we argue that conferences are significant in the evaluation of knowledge because they make things visible and accountable. The use of dramaturgical templates like the Game Show, the Stalking Horse, the hands up interactions, the feedback forms were not just entertainment or bureaucracy but provided for various forms of accountability and legitimation. Our interest here is how presenters could be held to account by various communities—the audience raising hands or filling in evaluation forms, the internal analyst organization collating these forms, colleagues in the peer review process 'blocking' predictions, and so on—and also, in turn, how being held accountable begins to shape what an analyst says or does whilst on stage. We were struck by how these charismatic specialists could on the one hand excel in front of an audience but on the other, also be cautious and afraid to 'stick their necks out' (interview, Winter) for fear of distancing themselves from the opinions of colleagues or people present. Foregrounding these more 'plural' modes of accountability also allows us to problematize assumptions that present predictions as unfettered or unbridled forms of knowledge (Bloomfield & Vurdubakis 2002, Thrift 2002).[10] In her work on financial analyst forecasts Knorr Cetina writes that '[t]here appears to be no process of consensus formation that would result in a community-wide recognition and validation of knowledge claims—no process that "certifies" research results as true or at least as the best available knowledge' (2010: 75). We are sceptical of the suggestion that a body of knowledge can be completely free of any form of assessment when our own fieldwork (on a related body of expertise) detected a rather complex ecology of accountability and verification that could establish confidence around these claims (we return to discuss the 'validation regime' at play in the concluding chapter).

We do not think it an exaggeration to suggest that not only does the audience actively participate in the production and audit of these predictions, but also to a certain extent, their reaction at the conference *is* the object of investigation. We noted how, during the conference, analysts would attend the talks of colleagues. Their involvement, it seems, was not just to listen to the speaker but to watch the audience. Moreover, such was the importance of taking notice of and accounting for audience feedback that it had become a key element of the internal research process. For instance, it was acknowledged by analysts that not all the predictions were good ones. Whilst all the analysts could produce research, not everyone had the capacities to produce the *right* kind of claims. Exposing ideas as early and frequently as possible to feedback and to conference audiences was therefore seen to be one remedy for these limitations. Transforming analyst opinion into what was seen as robust knowledge in this domain was to be via the conference. To understand this point fully we need to say more about what is being evaluated during internal peer review and at conference.

Predictions are not necessarily assessed for 'accuracy'. What is being tested is whether they have *practical purpose* for the conference audience. Analysts create credible futures designed to enlighten the *present* rather than to predict the future based on present trends and models (Mallard & Lakoff 2011). Their goal is to help enable others to make specific choices under contexts of uncertainty. They are a driver for reorientation and action; they should initiate some kind of a response or decision. A successful prediction in this context was one that could present the future not only as an object for reflection but of immediate *intervention* (ibid). The prediction should put contours on imminent change and tell the audience what to do once they are back in their offices on Monday. Hence, every conference session finishes with the slide: 'What to do now', 'What to do next month', 'What to do next year' etc. This begs the question as to whether the accuracy of predictions should be a concern. Can relevance for action become a replacement or supplement for accuracy?[11]

This discussion of the prediction as a form of intervention brings us to the final example where knowledge claims are simultaneously reported and *enacted*. Predictions are meant to be descriptions of the world. Indeed the weather forecasts described by Fine (2007) are just that. No matter how confident one is about a forecast this will not make any difference to how the actual weather plays out. But this static view of the prediction does not hold in all contexts. Industry analysts' present IT predictions with the explicit understanding that what is said on stage *may* go on to alter what those sitting in the audience do once they leave the confines of the conference venue. If an analyst says that a specific technology will grow, technology vendors in the audience, on hearing that prediction, may then invest in that type of solution and the technology will indeed grow as predicted. It follows that the analysts often know that what they say will be correct because, in many respects, they are 'actually influencing what is coming next' (Mitchell, interview). This form of enactment provides striking evidence of the further erosion of the disjunction between the production and validation of this knowledge. It is not only that activities at the conference occur in the same space they also regularly happen in the same *timeframe*. That is, it counters the assumption of a distinct temporal break between the stating of a prediction and acceptance of that claim. We expect things to stay the same long enough to decide whether they have turned out as projected (and not for the prediction to provoke the actual change before we have had the opportunity to evaluate if this is the case or not). But these venues of prediction make these assumptions (and disjunctions) increasingly hard to sustain.

8.5. CONCLUSIONS: PREDICTIONS DON'T TRAVEL (AS WELL) WITHOUT CONFERENCES

It is the conference that breaks the ice between the production and consumption of this very particular form of business knowledge.[12] Predictions are seldom launched into the ether or left to their own devices. Through the extension of the conference, there is a continual and simultaneous process of production and validation in operation, the stating of a claim and the provoking of a reaction first at one conference, and then another. Individual conferences are part of a regular circuit of events around the calendar and around the world through which analyst claims are generated, refined and distributed. These predictions do not result from some special form of expertise but are the culmination of this cycle where public feedback is sought and included right from the outset (see Hennion [1989] who makes this point about a further type of art form, music). If there was any further doubt that taking the conference as our point of entry was advantageous we need only note the interactions created and organized by the analysts themselves. These kinds of predictions require no legitimation other than the audience reaction (these real-time hands up interactions provide all the information needed). The analysts deliberately open a window onto their research process and do not seem put off when the reaction is negative or, when having tried things out, the scores on the evaluation forms come back low. This is because this is the best way to see (and literally 'seeing' the audience reaction turns out to be the thing desired) whether the prediction is any 'good', whether it is 'memorable' and 'sits in peoples mind', such that clients 'buy into it and follow it through' (interview, Mitchell). It is not that audiences are invited into these conferences simply to witness knowledge or validate that the experts actually do what is claimed of them (to offer a 'public proof' as Shapin [1988] might put it). There *is* a 'public demonstration' but it is the public and not just the prediction that is on show. They are not just 'witnesses' but actors just off stage so to speak (the public is the 'proof'). The analysts today are permanently obliged to take account of audience opinion. The experienced and charismatic analyst will know how to create a public reaction. They cannot prove their work without first going through the process of provoking and capturing sentiment at the conference. It is not enough to provoke sentiment; they have to demonstrate (to peers and managers) that they have the public with them. The various aspects of the notion of public interaction developed here need to be studied symmetrically. The incorporation of the public into a prediction is the same whether we are talking about its production or circulation. There is little difference between provoking public sentiment to validate the *production* of a prediction and provoking public opinion to help in the *circulation* of a prediction. In other words, the simultaneous production and consumption of predictions must be analysed together, and not as disjointed phases, which would inhibit our understanding of either one. The conference provides such a setting and we would thus commend its study.

NOTES

1. See Skov and Meier (2011) on the strategic importance of the industry event calendar and how entry into that calendar can create a particular conference as an obligatory point of passage.
2. Conference organizers insist (politely but firmly) that these forms are filled in (and large queues form at the exit to auditoriums as people are pressed into quickly rating talks before they hurry off to grab a coffee before the next talk begins).
3. This particular interviewee, who we thought was a rather gifted presenter, turns out, on his own account, not to be 'brilliant' within the firm but only 'not bad': '. . . somebody once asked me about presentation skills and presenting, and they said "you present quite well". And I said, "I am OK" . . . "I am about 20th best in Europe out of about 140 people . . . Worldwide I am probably in the top 50 out of the 700 analysts or so". "That is very good". I said, "no not really. Not in Gartner. In Gartner that is OK but it is not brilliant. I am not bad"' (interview, Thomas).
4. A Gartner analyst flags how past evaluations are important in choosing speakers: 'We use surveys of last year's and prospective delegates as to what topics are

important, as well as delegate speaker evaluations' (Jeffrey Mann, Gartner Blog). http://blogs.gartner.com/jeffrey_mann/2009/08/31/how-gartner-symposium-happens/. Accessed 12th August 2014.

5. There is no obligation for analyst firms to publish information about the accuracy of predictions and, as far as we know, there is no comprehensive or systematic data available. Some industry analysts will, as we saw in Chapter 5, occasionally reflect on things that did not work out as predicted. In the past, Gartner would occasionally release papers that reflected on predictions. As described by an analyst: '. . . there is this document that is called "Gartner Predicts" . . . and on the end of this document there is always a section on the predictions that come true, and how good we were in predicting patterns in advance, and a section on the things, you know, that we unfortunately didn't get right, and were completely lopsided. You know, there is a list of pathetic excuses why we got it wrong' (interview, Winter).

6. Recounting a recent Reuters press release, he tells the audience how: 'a month after the authorities began taxing Romania's witches and fortune tellers on their trade, [the Romanian] parliament is considering a new bill that would subject them to fines or even prison if their predictions do not come true' (Maoz, conference floor).

7. The conference sponsors were contractually entitled to 'floor time' but had previously just used this time as a sales pitch for their products, which, from the point of view the organizers, did not fit with the rest of the conference. Since their participation could not be dispensed with, the analysts came up with a format to funnel their input in an alternative direction. See Simakova (2013) for a discussion of the role of corporate sponsors at industry conferences.

8. Occasionally the compère would note a lack of consensus amongst the analysts about a particular claim or that not all of them were negative: 'If you look at the analyst view here there are two analysts that stand out. One is Michael Maoz and Adam Sarner again. So at least 2 of the 15 of us agree with you. That is a starting point' (Davis, Conference floor).

9. See Czarniawska's (2011: 182) discussion of the problems that News Agencies undergo because they do not receive regular feedback from audiences.

10. Balnaves et al. (2011), writing in the context of media ratings, see audience surveys as a form of 'audit' or offering a type of 'accountability'. As they see it, audience ratings have become a form of 'currency' which decision makers use to publicly demonstrate success and to justify choices. Ratings are also used to analyse and shape current offerings through identifying areas of weakness.

11. See Millo & MacKenzie (2009) who ask a similar question in relation to 'inaccurate models'.

12. An interesting feature of this knowledge is that it is the conferences and not the predictions that circulate. Because conferences are organized with a view to being reproduced in time and space, and predictions depend on these venues, this means that they have become the primary vehicle for the distribution of this form of knowledge. This contrasts with discussions within Science and Technology Studies—such as Bruno Latour's 'immutable mobile' (1987) and 'circulating reference' (1999) concepts—on how knowledge might

escape its locality. In discussing these ideas, Latour backgrounds the local features or contextuality of knowledge and foregrounds instead the conditions that allow for its effective travel. By contrast, we would argue that it is precisely these contextual aspects that allow this knowledge to move so effectively.

9

Give Me a 2×2 Matrix and I Will Create the Market

with Luciana D'Adderio

The previous chapters of this book have showed how rankings represent an important mechanism shaping markets. Such is their influence that scholars have labelled them 'engines' within the economy (Espeland & Sauder 2007, Karpik 2010). To depict a ranking in this way is to imply that it is not a passive portrait of the world but 'an active force transforming its environment' (MacKenzie 2006: 12). This is indicative of a growing consensus about how we should theorize the power of formal measures of performance and reputation (see Argyris 1954, Cooper & Hopper 1989, Lapsley & Mitchell 1996, Kornberger & Carter 2010). Despite highlighting a key area for empirical and theoretical inquiry, which has attracted much support, this conceptualization also carries unquestioned assumptions about the way we understand their constitutive role. In particular, the influence of a ranking is seen to reside predominantly in how it encourages 'mechanisms of reactivity' (Espeland & Sauder 2007) amongst market actors, as we saw in Chapter 7. What this suggests is that rankings are intrinsically 'social', at the same time raising the question as to whether there are further agential aspects that might extend this social mode of analysis. Are there additional agencies (other than how people respond to them) to be found in the makeup of rankings?

A useful prompt is found in tracing the idiom of the term 'engine' itself. From seventeenth century English science, for instance, we learn how instruments, artefacts and diagrams—combined with the 'ingenuity, craftiness and inventiveness' of gentlemen scientists—could function as generative engines in producing early scientific knowledge (Carroll-Burke 2001: 599). To capture the nature of this intervention, however, one also had to consider the tools and devices' hard, physical, material, engineering, and 'artificial' aspects (ibid: 600), which were key features of the artifacts involvement in everyday practices. Whilst the first view presents the intervention of engines as a social form of 'manipulation', the 'products of ingenious minds, clever contrivances and artful designs' (ibid: 599), the second places them squarely in the domain of practice, matter, method and constraint.

We see value in bringing both aspects together to capture how the abstract, generative capacity of a ranking can result from, and be shaped by, the interplay of a heterogeneous range of sociomaterial constraints and practices. To this purpose, and building on recent discussions of market devices (Callon et al. 2007), we develop the idea of a *ranking device*. This focus on objects is warranted because at a basic level a ranking cannot exist without some kind of device (ibid). The idea of the '100 top restaurants', '10 leading law schools', or '20 best cities to work and live in', for instance, would be impossible without the device of 'the list' (Goody 1977). Analytically the notion of device is useful because it captures how a ranking is an 'artifice', an 'artifact', the product of a practice (Oxford English Dictionary). In can also be used to describe an object that offers certain affordances and constraints, while at the same time capturing the aspect of 'clever contrivance' and 'artful design' (rankings are clearly devised in the sense of something manufactured or contrived) (ibid).

Here we build upon the discussion in Chapter 7 because we want to show that devices do more than simply facilitate the production and communication of a ranking; they also actively participate in their shaping. The specific argument developed is that it is these sociomaterial aspects, together with how people respond to them, that can account for the influence of a ranking. We would go as far as to argue that, in certain cases, the constitutive potential of a ranking resides in its affordances and constraints as much as any other complementary aspect (like the 'calculation' or 'commensuration'). The chapter draws on observations and interviews conducted over a period of several years on the construction and use of the 'Magic Quadrant'.

To show this influence we draw on and integrate a number of schools of thought from Science and Technology Studies (STS) as well as interdisciplinary Accounting research. The first is Miller's 'governance of economic life' framework, which studies the interactions between 'programmes' and 'technologies' as domains are made 'calculable' (Miller 2001, Miller & O'Leary 2007, Miller 2008). The second is the Accounting literature's focus on 'graphic inscriptions' (Robson 1992, Chua 1995, Bloomfield & Vurdubakis 1997, Ezzamel et al. 2004, Dambrin & Robson 2011, Qu & Cooper 2011). Whilst scholars have linked the issue of how a figuration might facilitate and mediate a financial decision (Miller & O'Leary 2007), they have not yet considered how calculations might be shaped by and result from the specific sociomaterial features of a graph. Finally, to demonstrate how a visualization might offer affordances and constraints to those producing a ranking, we draw on a range of studies from Science and Technology Studies on how material artefacts and economic markets mutually constitute one another (Callon et al. 2007, MacKenzie 2009, Vollmer et al. 2009) and the use of graphic inscriptions in Science (Latour 1986, Lynch 1985, 1988) and other domains (Espeland & Stevens 2009, Quattrone 2009).

9.1. RANKINGS ARE *ENGINES* WITHIN THE ECONOMY

Responding to the proliferation of rankings is said to be amongst the most important challenges facing organizations today (Espeland & Sauder 2007). Few aspects of the economy and society remain untouched by potent reputational and performance indices of one form or another. Some of the oldest and most impactful rankings include the credit ratings of institutions and states (Boot et al. 2006). Nowadays rankings evaluate the quality of art (Becker 1982), theatre (Shrum 1996), restaurants (Blank 2007), films, music (Karpik 2010); the past or projected performance of hospitals, schools (Wedlin 2006) and universities (Free et al. 2009); the standing of a company in relation to competitors (Schultz et al. 2001); the top consumer products to buy (Aldridge 1994); the best cities to live and work in (Kornberger & Carter 2010); and so on. The challenge today is that rankings are both broadening and deepening their coverage. Fuelled by new kinds of formats and technologies, it is common for organizations to be assessed many times over by different measures. Yet public and private organizations alike have little choice but to take these evaluations seriously. Research shows that irrespective of whether online or offline a ranking can have immediate and decisive impacts upon prospects (Karpik 2010). Being positioned below a rival, or failing to appear on a significant measure, can directly affect standing (Schultz et al. 2001), decision-making (Blank 2007) and market position.

Speaking about one of the most well-known rankings, the Red Michelin restaurant guide, Karpik (2010: 77) writes: '...this veritable paper engine [has] the rare ability to create the conditions of large-scale comparisons of incommensurable entities while thoroughly respecting their particularisms'. In their discussion of the global league tables of cities Kornberger and Carter (2010: 333) similarly suggest that league tables are (in MacKenzie's [2006] words) 'engines and not simply cameras' that create comparisons between hitherto unrelated places. The resulting competition between global cities, they argue, is not a natural fact but has been brought into being through the circulation of rankings. League tables now, in their words, 'form the battle-ground on which cities compete with each other' (ibid: 236); for example, they have actively encouraged city administrations to change behaviours and to develop strategies that set them apart from other metropoles (ibid).

Covering a plethora of devices as used in a variety of industries and contexts these studies address how rankings, as ordering systems, intervene in shaping the reality they attempt to monitor. One nuanced discussion of this kind, setting out in detail the means by which rankings are generative, is Espeland and Sauder's (2007) report on university Law Schools. They suggest that: '...rankings are reactive because they change how people make sense of situations; rankings offer a generalized account for interpreting behavior and justifying decisions within law schools, and help organize the "stock of knowledge" that participants routinely use' (ibid: 11).

Espeland and Sauder (2007) suggest that rankings do more than simply grade or describe: they also offer new interpretations of a situation. Actors then adapt their behaviour to conform this altered understanding (in a formulation that has much in common with Hacking's [1983] notion of representing and intervening). To evidence how a ranking can intervene, they cite the words of a respondent. A university manager notes how '[r]ankings are always in the back of everybody's head. With every issue that comes up, we have to ask, "How is this impacting our ranking?"' (ibid: 11). Their thesis is that ultimately rankings can become self-fulfilling:

> One type of self-fulfilling prophecy created by rankings involves the precise distinctions rankings create. Although the raw scores used to construct [Law School] rankings are tightly bunched, *listing* schools by rank magnifies these statistically insignificant differences in ways that produce real consequences for schools, since their position affects the perceptions and actions of outside audiences (ibid: 12, *our emphasis*).

This leads them to suggest that '[r]ankings are a powerful engine for producing and reproducing hierarchy since they encourage the meticulous tracking of small differences among schools, which can become larger differences over time' (ibid: 20). Whilst changes in interpretations and perceptions are obviously important, this view seems to suggest, however that a ranking is an entirely 'social' phenomenon that resides primarily in the 'heads' of actors. This would tend to overlook additional inherently material agential features. Espeland and Sauder (2007) hint at (but do not develop) the importance of material format in facilitating particular interpretations. To paraphrase their words, the *list* magnifies small differences that produce real consequences. Kornberger and Carter write that the power of a ranking 'rests in its capacity to shape people's *cognitive* maps and that it takes on material forms through translations into charts, models, graphs, documents, brainstorming techniques and other elements . . . ' (2010: 330, *our emphasis*). Building on Espeland and Sauder (2007) it could be inferred that a list does more than simply *magnify* a particular aspect of the ranking. Kornberger and Carter (2010) explicitly flag the role of artefacts but foreground cognitive dimensions, such that whilst devices figure in their analysis they are not necessarily seen as party to interactions.

Hacking (1992) provides a useful guide in his later formulation of the representation and intervention couplet where he acknowledges the centrality of 'instruments'. Representations should be studied alongside (not apart from) 'instruments', he argues, because it is these that produce particular kinds of intervention. In Hacking's view, representations and instruments co-produce one another. Miller and O'Leary (2007: 707) apply these ideas through addressing the interactions between 'programmes' and 'technologies'. Programmes refer to 'the imagining and conceptualizing of an arena and its constituents, such that it might be made amenable to knowledge and calculation' (ibid: 702). Technologies denote the 'possibility of intervening through a range of devices, instruments, calculations and inscriptions' (ibid: 702). The key aspect of their work is that processes of calculation can only be extended through the interaction between programmes and technologies. As Miller and O'Leary (2007) observe, it is not simply a case of 'implementing' a set of ideas within a device. Rather, devices come to mediate and shape conceptualizations and vice versa.

We enthusiastically adopt this terminology both for the ways it focuses attention on the 'calculation' involved in the production of a ranking (see Kornberger & Carter [2010] and Jeacle & Carter [2011] for this reading) but also because it flags the fact that this calculation results from a process where 'social' and 'technical' elements are brought together. Scholars working within this framework, however, have only begun to specify the process by which we might study and theorize interactions between material objects and wider calculative conceptions. In this respect, we are given few clues as to the actual mechanisms of co-production or the ways in which technologies, devices or graphic inscriptions for that matter can mediate and shape ideas. We thus find a need to supplement our analytical toolbox with concepts more attuned to considering the affordances and constraints of (particularly graphic) devices.

9.2. MATERIAL AGENCY: AFFORDANCE AND CONSTRAINT

Scholars have flagged the role of 'mediating instruments', 'market devices' and 'intellectual equipment' in facilitating processes of calculation within markets (Miller & O'Leary 2007, Callon et al. 2007, MacKenzie 2009). In contrast to those approaches that foreground individual actors in market decisions, it has been argued that actions and calculations are always collective achievements. Moreover, they are always propped up and aided by various kinds of material artefact. In this view, artefacts are seen to have 'agency', as they produce specific kinds of effects. In terms of who or what makes someone—or something—an agent, Latour argues that: 'anything that [can] modify a state of affairs by making a *difference* is an actor' (Latour 2005: 71, *emphasis in original*). Thus, Preda (2008) discussed how the 'price ticker' in the early years of the stock market was an agent in leading to different forms of decision making in the trading of stocks. Miller and O'Leary (2007), in their account of the history of integrated circuits, treat future-based graphs or technology roadmaps in a similar way. Instruments were, in their case, central in channelling discussions concerning the funding and development of integrated circuits across different scientific and industrial domains.

Both examples suggest that material devices play key roles in mediating or constituting behaviour (Akrich & Latour 1992). Miller and O'Leary's concern was with how roadmaps worked to mediate between the interests and strategies of multiple organizations involved in the development of the new market of post-optical lithography (Miller & O'Leary 2007: 720). In Preda's case, the price ticker produced a constant flow of prices that could be visualized in new ways. The ticker constituted the stockbrokers' practices in that they found themselves having to adapt to the continuous flow of price data such that they switched from being 'observers of the market' to 'observers of the tape' (Preda 2008: 232).

Another way of describing this agency—which sidesteps the controversy over ANT's invocation of non-human actors—is to suggest that artefacts have affordances and constraints. Although the original idea of affordance stems from the work of Psychology (Gibson 1979), it has been taken up within recent discussions within STS and especially the Sociology of Technology (Hutchby 2001, David & Pinch 2008). Gibson defined affordance as the 'perceived and actual properties of the thing, primarily those fundamental properties that determine just how the thing could possibly be used' (ibid: 9). Hutchby (2001), seeking to avoid technology deterministic overtones, proposed a softer definition in terms of those material aspects which frame but do not necessarily determine the actions of people. In this latter relational view, affordances exist in tandem only with how people take them up and the particular conditions of the local context. Writers like David and Pinch (2008) have recently built on this in their discussion of online book reviews where they describe how there can be 'material' and 'social' affordances shaping reviews. Physical affordances mean that reviewers can write as much as they want (limited only by their patience and the capacity of the computer's hard disk) but social practices (such as publishing conventions) dictate that reviews are normally limited to a handful of pages. Scholars such as Orlikowski (2007) have noted that since these two things are inseparable it is necessary to theorize the 'social' and 'material' as elements that mutually constitute one another: 'the social and the material are considered to be inextricably related—there is no social that is not also material, and no material that is not also social' (ibid: 1437). Underpinning this discussion is a core intellectual project in the social analysis of technology never to simply 'black box' objects but to study the intricate entanglement of social and material elements. Since there are no clear boundaries between what is social and what is material, scholars refer to these more precisely as 'sociomaterial'. Whilst adopting this particular terminology in the book we will also at times refer to the 'social' and 'technical' as there are analytical benefits from treating these empirically entwined features separately.

9.3. RANKING DEVICES

We are now in a position to set out more clearly what we mean by a 'ranking device'. Whilst our term builds on the idea of 'market device', defined as '...the material and discursive assemblages that intervene in the construction of markets' (Callon et al. 2007: 2), we attempt to operationalize this idea specifically for the way visual devices mutually constitute calculative practices. We do so by drawing on and making use of insights provided by more established ways of thinking (the 'programmes and technologies' framework, 'sociomateriality', 'affordance' and 'graphic inscription', and so on). Specifically, we propose that these are the 'format and furniture' implicated in the materiality of a ranking. The analytical value of the term is that it foregrounds how a ranking (the 'calculation', the 'commensuration') can be shaped through its incorporation in particular sociomaterial objects. Those constructing a ranking are required to take into account the device's various affordances and constraints—for example when they plot a dot on a graph. To lay the foundations for our empirical study we discuss some of the furniture commonly found within rankings. This is followed by a discussion of some of the sociomaterial affordances and constraints surrounding the production of graphs.

9.3.1. Format and furniture

Rankings are shot through with various kinds of devices in and through which they are embedded and become material. Some may come in the form of lists or tables. Others are more graphical in nature. One finds many examples of ranked lists (our informal research on Google, for instance, suggests at least several hundreds). Stark (2011) argues that this format became popular in the 1950s and cites the 'jukebox' as a possible source. Since jukeboxes held 40 single records this apparently led to the development of 'top 40' record programmes on radio stations (see also Anand & Peterson 2000). Today the list has become the format of choice for many ranking organizations. One of its affordances appears to be that it is relatively unconstrained by the number of subjects of evaluation. The 'top 10 MBA programmes' can (and often are) extended to include the 'top 50', 'top 100' degrees, for instance. Kwon and Easton (2010), in their discussion of the Financial Times' list of MBA programmes, suggest that, the longer the list, the more comprehensive or 'global' it may appear in certain peoples' eyes: '...individual consumers can find comfort in the perception that they can choose the "best" among hundreds or thousands of alternatives, rather than the "best" among several "good enough" alternatives arising through the search process. The FT MBA 100 allows buyers to maximize their choice of a highly ranked school, given personal constraints such as budget, geographical preferences and entry requirements' (ibid: 133). We flag this feature because it is not a capacity found in all rankings (see the following empirical discussion).

Rankings are also supported by specific furniture. In their discussion of consultancy reports, for instance, Qu and Cooper (2011: 358) highlight the role of the furniture of 'bullet points' and 'checklists' as providing a 'topographical image of how various employee groups within an organization are relevant to achieving strategic objectives'. In the case of rankings, there are stars, lines, waves, tics, dots and so on. Kwon and Easton (2010: 132) argue that the use of such furniture constitutes a particularly novel feature or form of contribution. Whilst rankers have not been particularly innovative with regard to methodology, or to how assessments are put together, they have been at the forefront in terms of developments in 'format and presentation'. Kwon and Easton (2010) describe how the Michelin Red Guide, for instance, was amongst the first of the major rankers to supplement complicated forms of quantitative data with 'qualitative descriptors'. It rated restaurant quality by producing the 'now famous three-star scale to denote relative excellence' (ibid: 132). These descriptors are now very much part of the machinery for ranking restaurants around the world (see Karpik 2010).

However, we still know very little about how and why such furniture has become popular or what, if anything, it has meant for these particular settings. We would argue that they are important because, they render the calculation visible through some kind of large-scale ranking apparatus of which these descriptors form a part. They are thus an aspect of the calculative practices for turning 'qualities into quantities' (Miller 2001) (see Kornberger & Carter [2010] and Jeacle & Carter [2011] for a discussion of calculative practices involved in ranking). While the importance of this furniture has been acknowledged, their effects have not been demonstrated. The latter become clear, we suggest, when one considers the production of graphical rankings where rankers are forced to entertain and take account of quite specific affordances and constraints. To understand what these are we turn to a discussion of the construction of graphs.

9.4. GRAPHIC VISUALIZATION: FROM LOOKING *AT* GRAPHS TO LOOKING *IN* GRAPHS

Latour famously argued that 'he who visualises badly loses the encounter' (1986: 13). The 'scientific graph' was originally said to be one factor that gave science its influence over other forms of knowledge production. For Latour, the graph was an 'inscription device'; the key idea behind this concept was that of 'mobility' (this was a method by which the product of a laboratory could circulate widely without taking with it the apparatus that led to its production). Accounting research has focused on the inscriptions that construct performance measures more generally (see Robson 1992, Dambrin & Robson 2011), with particular attention being given to 'graphs'. Qu and Cooper (2011: 358), for instance, highlight how 'graphical inscriptions are generally persuasive in communicating information. They solidify ambiguous concepts into concrete forms . . .'.

Scholars have mobilized the notion of inscription to capture how material substances are translated into figurations that can travel. However, it would be fair to say that they have looked *at* the graph but not necessarily *in* the graph. Some partial exceptions include Miller and O'Leary (2007) and Quattrone (2009). In his discussion of the history of the book, for instance, Quattrone (2008: 109) suggests that it is because graphs are 'partial' and 'simplified' that they have an effect:

> Graphical representations . . . are always so partial and simplified that they essentially contain very little; they have little truth in them; for, if it ever existed, it has been lost in the process of diagrammatic representation which has sacrificed details and context for the sake of clarity. This is the only way in which they can effectively communicate and engage the user in a performative exercise.

From sources further afield, Espeland and Stevens (2009: 423), in their review of the Communication Studies literature, argue that graphs are successful because they are produced according to 'aesthetic ideals' (ibid: 423, see also Bloomfield & Vurdubakis 1997). This includes how they should have clarity and be parsimonious: ' . . . people who make pictures with numbers typically prize representations whose primary information is easily legible (clarity), and which contains only those elements necessary and sufficient for the communication of this primary information (parsimony)' (Espeland & Stevens 2009: 423; see also Tufte [2001] on whom Espeland and Stevens draw). This is because those who construct graphs as part of their professional activities want them to be 'not only errorless but also compelling, elegant, and even beautiful' (Espeland & Stevens 2009: 422).

The contributions above suggest that graphs place 'limits' on designers. We supplement this with work from STS where Lynch (1988: 202) argues that graphs (in science) do more than constrain; they also add features and affordances not found in original understandings.

> The [graph] does not necessarily *simplify* the diverse representations, labels, indexes, etc., that it aggregates. It adds theoretical information which cannot be found in any single micrographic representation, and provides a document of phenomena which cannot be represented by photographic means (*emphasis in original*).

Even the simplest graphs, in Lynch's view, add rather than reduce information. They contribute:

> . . . visual features which clarify, complete, extend, and identify conformations latent in the incomplete state of the original specimen. Instead of reducing what is visibly available in the original, a sequence of reproductions progressively modifies the object's visibility in the direction of generic pedagogy and abstract theorizing (ibid: 229).

An example of those things added can be found in an earlier paper where Lynch discusses a common but little discussed graphic resource: the 'device of the dot'. Analyzing a field manual describing the anatomy of a lizard he makes the following point:

> Note that each observation of a marked individual is rendered equivalent to all others through the use of the device of the 'dot'. The only material difference between one dot and another on the chart is its locale. Locales are reckoned in terms of the grid of stakes, and all other circumstantial features of observation 'drop out' (1985: 43).

Dots are 'additive' rather than 'reductive' (we take this terminology from Ingold's discussion of another type of notation, 'the line' [Ingold 2007]). Lynch (1985) flags how graphs provide for commonplace resources of graphic representation. It is therefore important to understand the interplay between graphic resources and the thing they purport to describe. Lynch (1988) suggests one can witness how the properties of graphs go on to merge with and come to incorporate the thing represented. He writes: '. . . one theme which applies to many, if not all, graphs is that of how the commonplace resources of graphic representation come to embody the substantive features of the specimen or relationship under analysis' (Lynch 1988: 226). In turn: '. . . efforts are made to shape specimen materials so that their visible characteristics become congruent with graphic lines, spaces, and dimensions' (ibid: 227).

To summarize, we have found it necessary to bring together a number of complementary disciplinary schools to discuss this seemingly simple phenomenon. Specialization in this respect has traditionally posed a major barrier to analysis and understanding (Hopwood 2007). Linkages across different scholarly fields provide important new insights into how we understand, represent and theorize the tools and practices of performance measurement. In this respect, the 'programmes and technologies' framework (Miller & O'Leary 2007) tells us how areas are conceptualized in certain ways so that they can become 'calculable', often through interventions made possible through devices. The literature from STS directs attention onto how devices do not simply support but can act within calculations (in the sense they actively shape calculations). The idea of a 'ranking device' drills down further still to show how a ranking (and 'calculation') can be shaped by its incorporation in a specific format and furniture, and, in turn, with how sociomaterial features can shape aspects of the IT market.

We organize our empirical material around a discussion of three aspects of how specific furniture—'the dot'—is moved around a graph. The first section focuses on how the ranking helps create a 'competitive space' in relation to the shaping of the visible market of players. We define a 'competitive space' as the space of confrontation and struggle that is created between various economic players in a specific technological field, often through the use of various social and material strategies linked to a ranking. We discuss how new expertise, practices and routines are created and emerge as vendors attempt to improve their placing in the competitive space (what actors call 'moving the *dot*' activities). The second section investigates how the competitive space is shaped not only by '*people* moving dots' but also by sociomaterial constraints, in particular the affordances and limitations found within the ranking device (here the focus is on how '*dots* move people'). Specifically these are material affordances (for instance how players in a market can be brought together and compared in one space) and social constraints (not all players can be included on one graph). The final section discusses how these constraints encourage rankers to make interventions in the competitive space (that is how 'dots move *markets*').

9.5. A MONOPOLY?

The ranking discussed here is the Magic Quadrant. Whilst we have already introduced this graph in Chapter 7, we note some further characteristics of relevance here. As noted previously, whilst Gartner is just one of a number of such industry analyst firms within this area, it is widely recognized as the largest and most influential. Despite not having a monopoly over the production of IT analysis, commentators suggest it has something close (Hopkins 2007). This point about 'monopoly' is important for what is described below. It is clear that rankers are stronger when there is only one dominant evaluator in an area. Sauder and Espeland (2006), for instance, provide evidence to show that because US Law Schools are subject to a single dominant ranker and Business Schools to many, the influence of rankings on the former is much more direct and obvious than on the latter. Kwon and Easton (2010: 124) note how an individual ranker ' . . . can become powerful to the point where they are able to monopolize the information required for the efficient functioning of markets and thereby influence the behaviour of other market actors'. In the case of multiple rankings, by contrast, Sauder and Espeland (2006) point to the fact that because people see how rankings can come to quite different conclusions about the same topic, they can become sceptical of their value and of the robustness of rankings overall.

Gartner are prolific in the production of Magic Quadrants: they author nearly 240 for different IT markets (Drobik 2010) and this number changes all the time as Gartner continually create new Magic Quadrants to reflect the development of new types of technology markets and occasionally 'retire' older ones to represent the fact certain markets have matured. Authorship of Magic Quadrants is not a one-off process. They are updated and released each year. As a result, how vendors are placed within the matrix will change over time. There may also be the introduction or exit of players onto the Magic Quadrant.

As we saw in Chapter 7, decision makers draw on these rankings to help make choices when procuring IT equipment and software. It is common for those looking to buy solutions to invite tenders only from those in the top right quadrant. It is perhaps no surprise then that vendors seek to influence the ranking. Some are even said to construct aspects of their business (marketing and product development strategies) in line with the ranking's underlying assumptions (Hopkins 2007).

Box 4. Research note

We have been studying the Magic Quadrant for several years now. Our attention was alerted to its significance whilst carrying out an ethnographic study of IT procurement in a large municipal council at the turn of the century (Pollock & Williams 2007) and then a couple of years later during a study of how users bring influence to bear on ERP vendors (Pollock & Williams 2009). These initial dealings prompted us to plan and develop a research project that would enquire into the production of this ranking and the nature of the expertise surrounding it. The fact our project was funded filled us with both excitement and (it must be said) a certain amount of trepidation! There is a perception that it is difficult to gain access to Gartner (a point said to be true of rankers more generally [Kwon and Easton 2010]). Nevertheless, we set out to conduct fieldwork in the hope that we would get lucky (and 'fortune' does seem to feature in a lot of research). In our initial attempts to gain access, we wrote to one particular analyst whom we had come across in previous fieldwork. He agreed straightaway to an interview, which meant we were able to visit Gartner's European headquarters in London and begin what turned out to be a highly productive period of fieldwork.

Since this particular analyst worked in the area of 'Customer Relationship Management' (CRM) technologies and was able to provide specific details on how the CRM Magic Quadrants were constructed, we devoted most of our time to following events and people in this area.

We circulated a research paper within Gartner (an early version of Chapter 7), which not only served to build our confidence that we had produced a reasonable interpretation of events but also led to further episodes of fieldwork. One analyst with whom we had interacted previously had been forwarded the article via a

---

(continued)

Box 4. Continued

---

colleague and contacted us to tell us that he thought that we had produced a 'critical but fair' analysis of Gartner's work. He also reflected on how we had missed some of the more 'internal' aspects by which Magic Quadrants were constructed. Later, in a hastily arranged interview, he would tell us about these aspects. These form part of the material presented here.

Our study is further informed and contextualised by interviews and discussions we conducted with other actors involved in and around the ranking. i) We conducted formal interviews with some of the vendors subject to Gartner's assessment ii) we held informal discussions, especially during our attendance at Gartner conferences, with the IT managers and practitioners who consume this kind of knowledge iii) we interviewed analysts from rival firms to ascertain their view on Gartner's ranking process and its wider effects on the market iv) and we also interviewed and observed the activities of a new breed of (analyst relations) professional that has emerged to offer advice to vendors on how to interact with ranking organisations like Gartner.

Within the larger IT vendors there are now commonly 'analyst relations' departments which contain experts whose role is to liaise with and represent the vendors to industry analysts, consultants and other commentators. These experts attempt to understand the details of how industry analyst firms work and what kinds of influence they can wield. They will be particularly keen to identify how the analyst organisation currently views their particular firm and what they might do to influence that opinion. Moreover, there are now hundreds of independent 'analyst relations consultants' operating in and around the IT marketplace. During our research, we were able to interview a large number of these consultants.

9.6. DOT-OLOGY

What could be more banal than a 'dot'? However, if we want to understand the constitutive nature of a visual ranking then we have no choice but to focus attention on this particular graphic furniture. Dots form the basis of every conversation and consideration with regard to the Magic Quadrant. Everything that happens typically occurs around the dot. Dot-ology, which is a development of an actor's category, attempts to capture how this mundane furniture can offer new possibilities, place limitations on actors, and encourage processes of co-production between graphs and settings.

9.6.1. How rankings shape the practices of those ranked (*people* moving dots)

Rankings wield significant influence over a field of activity (Sauder & Espeland 2006). However, the organizations subject to these measures have not stood still. Certain groups have begun to set up independent 'agencies' and

Figure 9.1. Responding to the rankers
Source: Author photo (NP)

'consultancies' and to make available their experience on a more commodified basis, leading to the creation of a market for advice and supplementary knowledge-based products related to the management of rankings. Initially this involved simply collating information about rankings but today it includes the codification of specialist knowledge and its communication, through the production of guides and practitioner handbooks, seminars and workshops. A market has been created that sells information on the details of how major rankings are constructed, together with strategies for the improvement of placings (see Figure 9.1). Below we report on our interactions with a number of analyst relations consultants who produce and trade this kind of knowledge. We show how one effect of their work has been to establish the ranking as a space of confrontation and struggle between competing vendors (Kornberger & Carter 2010).

9.6.1.1. Moving the dot activities: A social affair

In the material we quote below, Carter Lusher from SageCircle has prepared a presentation to other analyst relations professionals. Having previously worked as a Gartner analyst, this expert now offers advice to others on how to interact with industry analysts. His presentation is organized around various 'moving the dot activities'. He is careful to tell the audience that, if they are to be successful in shaping the Magic Quadrant and other rankings, they will have a significant amount of work to do:

> Now, these activities that we're going to talk about, although we're going to call them out and highlight them as specific 'Moving the Dot activities', they should be part of your overall AR [analyst relations] Strategic and Tactical Plan . . . . I'm going to remind you, tremendous effort is required to influence the Magic Quadrant. The data that we've gathered indicates that our clients spend anywhere from 60 to 200 hours on a single Magic Quadrant . . . understand that this is not an insignificant amount of work (webinar, Carter Lusher, SageCircle).

In terms of the type of work necessary, firstly, this includes gathering insights about the makeup of the Magic Quadrant and, then secondly, feeding information back to Gartner about a vendor's products, strategy and specifically 'thought leadership'. Vendors are encouraged to do the latter through building personal relationships with individual rankers, often through engineering periods of 'social time' between them and particular analysts (conducting discussions 'over a meal' being one of the favoured methods) (webinar, Carter Lusher, SageCircle). Thus, there appear to be rich and direct interactions between rankers and those they rank (albeit increasingly mediated by these new kinds of intermediaries).

Another analyst relations consultant, Jonny Bentwood from the public relations firm, Edelman, described how he had engaged in a similar process when one of his own clients had received a negative placing:

> We used enquires with specific analysts in the channel to understand who they should be approaching to help go to market with specific vertical analysts at Gartner to understand the best approach to solve the business problems in that particular industry. And we focused on specific analysts to help us make sure our message and our persistent focus directly for that individual, that individual market (interview, Bentwood).

Bentwood went onto explain that the key reason for these 'briefings', 'enquiries', 'touches', or 'deep dives' was to bridge the 'gap' in knowledge between the ranker and the vendor. In evidencing this, Bentwood gave an example of a successful set of interactions:

> [O]ne of our clients was getting involved in a Magic Quadrant and . . . we tried to understand what the analyst thought about our company, and we realized that there were several areas where there was a gap. So we made sure we filled those gaps . . . we did enquires to understand whether what we believed the message should have got across, whether the analyst got that across, and if it wasn't we tried to fill that gap. So when the Magic Quadrant finally came out we positioned, we knew the analyst had sufficient information, we knew where we had weak

points and we addressed those, so it wasn't a shock. In fact, we were positioned in the top right hand corner. It was fantastic! (interview, Bentwood).

Both consultants describe how the rationale for these briefings and meetings is that the vendor should understand the 'evaluative criteria' the ranking organization applies when assessing vendors/products. These are the specific ways in which individual rankers conceive of the nature and characteristics of the various technologies covered by their particular Magic Quadrant. Carter Lusher tells his audience:

> I need to understand the criteria and current opinion and the publishing schedule, and I need to see what I can do to influence that criteria and that opinion. Now we're going to use the analysts by doing inquiry to find out this information, like what is changing in the criteria . . . consulting with them, perhaps even use some of their information and criteria to influence the way in which my product roadmap is going to go (webinar, Carter Lusher, SageCircle).

The suggestion given is that once a vendor understands the ranker's evaluative criteria they should then use this information to influence their own product development strategies. In other words, they should develop products and strategies in a way that more closely resembles the ranker's description of the technology/market (this is reported to be a common strategy amongst many IT vendors [Hopkins 2007]). If it is not possible (or desirable) to realign product development around the ranking then another solution is to attempt to modify the criteria of the ranking:

> . . . we might even give consideration to trying to change the character of the Magic Quadrant [through] influencing the definition of exactly what this Magic Quadrant is. That's part of changing the criteria. If I can sort of say 'Look, this is not the same Magic Quadrant as it used to be, now it has a new set of objectives and a new set of criteria because the market has changed', that has an interesting possibility of radically changing the position of all the dots (webinar, Carter Lusher, SageCircle).

What is being recommended is that vendors should attempt to move the ranker's conception of the technology assessed. In so doing, there will be obvious advantages for the vendor that is able to help shape the criteria by which products in a particular market are judged. The analyst relations consultant Carter Lusher then closes this particular segment by giving some practical examples of what kinds of benefits might be gained from (re)setting criteria.

9.6.1.2. *Bringing vendors into the same competitive space*

The issue of competition—and shaping of the competitive landscape—is a key theme surrounding the Magic Quadrant. The analyst relations consultant suggests that if a vendor has a product that is significantly different from those of competitors then it may be possible to suggest to Gartner that it needs to create a new Magic Quadrant. This they can do through feeding analysts their thoughts on how particular technologies and technology markets are developing. Alternatively, through similar kinds of interactions and briefings, there may also be the possibility of 'killing' a Magic Quadrant in which a vendor is not doing so well. Carter Lusher describes it thus:

> Alternatively, there's the chance of creating a completely new Magic Quadrant. Gartner does retire old ones and create new ones. Working with an analyst that doesn't have a Magic Quadrant, you might be able to create a new one. Working with the analyst that has two Magic Quadrants, you might be able to alter the characteristics. Working with an analyst that has lots of Magic Quadrants, you might be able to kill a Magic Quadrant (webinar, Carter Lusher, SageCircle).

The suggestion is that a vendor may be able to create a Magic Quadrant for an area where it is the 'leader'. It may even be able to help retire a Magic Quadrant where its competitors are doing particularly well by comparison. Carter Lusher suggests that, whilst a firm may not always be able to move its dot up, it should nonetheless give consideration as to how it might be able to move its competitor's dot down:

> An alternate objective is to move your competitor dot down, to the left . . . So that might be an interesting approach . . . if I had the ability to push my competitor down then by inference I've pushed myself up. I might look at an objective as increasing the distance between you and the competitors, or preventing a competitor from leapfrogging over you (webinar, Carter Lusher, SageCircle).

What is being described here is how it is the ranking itself that mediates and constitutes competition. Even though a vendor may not necessarily have thought of itself as directly competing with specific others, through placement on the Magic Quadrant the competitive space has been mapped out. Vendors are seen (and increasingly treated) as direct rivals (Kornberger & Carter 2010). In the consultant's view, the Magic Quadrant clearly indicates a vendor's standing in relation to those immediately surrounding it. And whilst vendors could not previously rank their performance against others, they can now measure the dots on a graph (and the use of a ruler by executives to capture even slight movements between successive versions of a Magic Quadrant appears to be common). Interestingly, whilst vendors have been brought together in the same competitive space, the consultant is advocating that a vendor should not simply accept but potentially attempt to reconfigure this space. Vendors are given advice on how to shape the boundaries surrounding the competitive space; they are encouraged to develop tactics and strategies to push themselves up and to the right, which, by default, will push their competitors down and to the left.

To summarize, we see how dots have come to mediate a vendor's interaction not only with the ranking organization but also with other vendors. Some have gone as far as to develop strategies and plan for modes of interaction with the rankers to help move places and shape spaces around the ranking device. Thus at a basic level dot-ology captures the practices and routines that develop as actors focus attention around the details of a ranking in order to influence, firstly, their own position in relation to competitors and, secondly, the boundaries of the competitive space. However, we want the notion of dot-ology to capture more than these 'social' strategies at play. It is not simply about how people contrive to move dots but how the competitive space is being (re) shaped in other ways too. In particular, we want to introduce the idea of sociomaterial agency, by which we mean that the field is influenced by the various affordances and constraints contained within the ranking. It is not simply people moving dots but also 'dots moving people'. To demonstrate this, we begin by discussing how dots are placed on the matrix in the first instance.

9.6.2. Individual rankers and ranking organization (*dots* moving people)

9.6.2.1. Production of ranking is not static

The calculation of the Magic Quadrant has generated much discussion within IT practitioner circles. During fieldwork, we had the opportunity to interview a number of Gartner employees about how Magic Quadrants were developed. 'The accusation we were always given', responded one to our question, 'was that we threw darts at the chart' (interview, Thomas). Here the analyst is responding to a widely held belief that the calculation of places lacks any form of process or systemization (see for instance Violino and Levin 1997). One issue that apparently vexed practitioners was the thought that placings were plotted by hand. Presumably, this was problematic because it lent the ranking a discretionary quality (ibid). Another was the fact that Gartner described the Magic Quadrant as resulting from predominately 'qualitative research' (Soejarto and Karamouzis 2005). As we saw in Chapter 7, Gartner would informally solicit opinions from customers of those vendors being assessed. But this was seen as 'flawed' since it gave a paramount role to analysts who could choose which customers to listen to (and this raised the issue of 'bias' and 'partiality').

In our interviews with Gartner analysts, however, they went to great lengths to dispel the idea that rankings were judgmental or approximate. They pointed to how the production of rankings, whilst relying on a range of sources including informal discussions with customers, are also circumscribed by standardized measures and technology: 'The actual dot

Table 9.1. Evaluation criteria for Magic Quadrant

Completeness of Vision	Ability to Execute
Market understanding	Product or Service
Marketing strategy	Overall viability
Sales strategy	Sales Execution, Pricing
Product strategy	Market responsiveness
Business Model	Marketing execution
Industry strategy	Customer experience
Innovation	Operations
Geographic strategy	

Source: https://www.gartner.com/doc/2804921/markets-vendors-evaluated-gartner-magic

scoring, there is a standardized spreadsheet we have to use [and] standardized scoring mechanism' (interview, Thomas). Dots are plotted within a 'spreadsheet' and populated with numbers from a 'standardized scoring mechanism' (interview, De Sousa). Scorings derive from a number of 'evaluation criteria' that have been divided along the two axis of the Magic Quadrant. These break down to reveal a number of further standard criteria (see Table 9.1).

Set criteria are then given a weighting ('high', 'standard', 'low', or 'no rating'). If 'no rating' is applied this means that this particular factor will not be counted in the calculation. However, whilst individual rankers have the flexibility to choose whether to apply a criterion or not, it was reported that the bulk of analysts would use most of them:

> So for example, of the standard, I think it is eight criteria on the two dimensions, eight criteria on each [sic], you could theoretically get rid of four or five of them, and just weight it on three—so you could weight something zero if you want to—but most analysts are using most, if not all of those criteria, and weighting them to different degrees, on every single Magic Quadrant (interview, Thomas).

The primary reason for these changes in calculating places was the increasing pressure exerted by analyst relations consultants and practitioners who were probing Gartner—through 'briefings', 'enquiries', 'touches', etc.,—to understand the detailed practice of ranking construction. Another reason was the fear of 'litigation'. As a result, the production of the Magic Quadrants is more regulated so as to create an 'audit trail' (see Free et al. 2009 for a discussion of the auditing of rankings):

> ...individual analysts have to follow the same procedure, and we have to document that, and you have to have an audit trail of how it was created, and usually you have to have scoring sheets to demonstrate how you got to that point but on the actual spreadsheet that creates the quadrant there is a scoring, a whole scoring system which is standardized across the whole company (interview, Thomas).

Gartner had even gone as far as setting up a 'Methodology Team' to ensure that the standards for plotting the graph were maintained across the entire organization (interview, Erskine). A former Director of the Methodology Team describes how this did introduce a certain amount of systemization into the work of individual analysts: '... there is some leeway in the methodology but [the Methodology] team is responsible for making sure that their methodology is sound and that it is followed, and that it is updated as technology changes and as we see things unfold in the marketplace' (interview, Erskine).

An analyst notes that this is a more regulated and standardized process than that from just a couple of years ago (interview, De Sousa). Apparently, individuals had more freedom in the past to plot graphs in different ways. An ex Gartner analyst describes this freedom:

> When I first wrote Magic Quadrants you sat there and said, 'wait a minute, I think these guys are here and these guys are over there'. 'Can I justify why I'm saying that?' 'Yes I can. Here are the reasons why'. It wasn't a bottoms-up, it was entirely a top-down kind of view but over time that's, somebody's coming after you over that. That's much more difficult to defend so they became much more robust in the methodology in enforcing that there must be something that you can go back to that you can show, here's a bottom-up set of numbers, even if at some point they got tampered with, top-down to get them to where I want them, they're still there and I can put them out to you and I can argue my case whatever the number is anyway, you can't argue against it, it's entirely a qualitative, it's my judgement, they're very rarely something that's purely quantitative, it's normally my view on what that means (interview, Levin).

Another analyst describes how the old way of calculating Magic Quadrants had both advantages and drawbacks:

> ... they were more comprehensive in those days but they weren't consistent. So the way I would have my criteria would be nothing like my colleague sitting next to me. We weight in a very different way and the dots are arrived at very differently. And the vendors didn't like that. The vendors didn't like being top right in one and bottom left in another and not knowing why. Often that was because they were trying to negotiate about how they were treated (interview, Thomas).

Magic Quadrants were more comprehensive because vendors could be scored according to criteria the individual ranker felt was important at the time, or relevant to the specific circumstances. However, this meant the process of plotting the dots differed widely across the analyst firm. This seemingly caused problems for Gartner's relationship with vendors who wanted greater clarity and uniformity around scoring mechanisms (interview, De Sousa). One analyst notes that because the process of placing dots was now similar across Gartner certain aspects of the ranking construction process had 'improved'. However, he was also of the view that that not all these changes in production were leading to improvements in the overall 'quality' of the Magic Quadrant:

> ... the purpose of the Methodology Team, and the purpose of all these extra steps, and more rigorous procedures, is to improve quality. The question really is about what quality means? And I would argue that the definition of quality being used there is about consistency, repeatability and audit trail. It is that level of quality. In other words, we have a process, we're following it, no one is getting out of the process (interview, Thomas).

Improvements, in his view, were related to control over the process and the repeatability of the same evaluative measures. He then goes on to describe why he thought Magic Quadrants were better in previous years:

> So I would argue that the value of the Magic Quadrants ten years [ago] was actually better, even though they were less accurate in some ways ... there were bigger movements on Magic Quadrants from year to year. But the point being made was that analysts' were changing the weightings much more dramatically to reflect what the customers were telling them. Now we reflect the customers ... less well, because we have to go through a lot more steps to reflect what the customers are asking. So it is an interesting trade-off really. Who is the value for? (interview, Thomas).

His point is that there used to be more 'movement' between rankings at each new release. Since individual rankers had the freedom to set criteria and plot dots this reflected what the client references were actually telling them about vendors. By contrast, today, even though an analyst might hear critical comments about a vendor, these may not be so easily reflected within the Magic Quadrant (they may fall outside the available criteria). The clear impression we gained from our interviewees with Gartner analysts was that in recounting these moves towards transparency and standardization they were also describing a decrease in their own discretion. As a result of corporate efforts to remove the idea of bias and partiality from the ranking, individual analysts were now increasingly circumscribed by a new material and organizational reality (increasingly explicit assessment criteria, a methodology team scrutinizing their work, the need to provide explicit evidence for choices, a spreadsheet that plotted dots, etc.). We now turn to look in more detail at these constraints.

9.6.2.2. Actors are constrained in producing rankings

We want to show how dot-ology relies on an extensive organizational apparatus that patterns the activities of individual analysts in placing dots. Below we focus on two particular aspects: technology and bureaucracy.

9.6.2.2.1. Technology

The 'spreadsheet' has become a central feature of the production of Magic Quadrants. Law (2001) argues that spreadsheets are among those technologies that help create powerful actors (by allowing them to manipulate data so as to see and project things and positions that others cannot see). However, at Gartner, the spreadsheet appeared not to be a malleable tool but one that placed limitations on individual analysts. Let us first consider how the spreadsheet could be manipulated. An ex-Gartner analyst describes how the process of building the graph was very much based on personal 'judgement':

> ... actually if you look at what really goes on inside the business and the way you do it, of course what they do is, they do all this scoring at this micro-level, you see all the dots appear on the quadrant then you say, wait a minute, knowing those two companies that doesn't look quite right, in my view that should be more over there. So then they start adjusting it, see what that means you have to do to the score to adjust it back again. So it's not quite as simple and logical a process as you imagine, there's a bit of judgement that goes on at the end (interview, Levin).

However, when scores had been entered into the spreadsheet and the graph plotted it was then more difficult to move a vendor: '... you just can't put the dots where you want. The dots are all related to each other. So if you move one score up it impacts all the dots on the chart' (interview, Thomas). A vendor might be moved if the analyst thought the calculative apparatus had failed to position a dot in the way they considered 'fair'. Fair meant a placing that reflected the individual ranker's own knowledge as opposed to that which results from the organizational machinery. However, moving a vendor once a graph had been generated would create further movement across the ranking. One small change could affect the position of all vendors and this would almost always certainly attract the attention of colleagues elsewhere in the organization.

For one particular analyst, this was further evidence that dots were not arbitrarily placed but that individuals were constrained by the scoring mechanism and technology. This analyst then goes on to describes how one of the few changes they could actually make to the graph was to:

> ... move the box around a bit. So, in other words, if all the dots are clustered in the centre you can reset the axes to get the box more spread out so they look more attractive. Otherwise, you would have a scale where all the dots are clustered around the centre or clustered around one spot. The idea there is just to make them spread out so you can actually read who compares to whom. So, there is a little bit of flexibility on the edges, but frankly, you can't really rig it anymore (interview, Thomas).

Analysts had the freedom to adjust the scale within the spreadsheet but not specific dots. If vendors were all clustered together, it was possible to adjust the box to create distance between them, that is, to enhance or develop a greater distinction between the entities ranked than was initially revealed in the spreadsheet. This was apparently an attempt to make the rankings more 'attractive'. Another issue, which leads to our discussion below, was that the space within the graph was limited, which could lead to unusual incidents. Carter Lusher from SageCircle describes how:

> . . . a particular analyst had put in the Magic Quadrant into editorial and editorial of course goes through and deals with all the little formats and graphics and all that kind of stuff and makes certain that all the pieces are done before they actually publish. It came back from editorial and one of the dots had moved on the graph, and the analyst got irate and went to editorial and said 'Why did this move, what happened?' and fortunately they actually saw that it had happened. And the editorial person responded with 'I couldn't fit the name in next to the dot so I had to move the dot over'. And that actually, as funny and ridiculous as it sounds, is one of the problems with the Magic Quadrant. Because the definition of exactly where the dot falls is so grey and the criteria can be so flexible, that sometimes you do think that the way they establish the dots was with a dart board or based on the space available on the graphic. So don't laugh about it, it does have the potential for happening (webinar, Carter Lusher, SageCircle).

9.6.2.2.2. Bureaucracy: Review process

The analysts reported increased scrutiny of their work. The Methodology Team dictated that Magic Quadrants and other forms of assessment should pass through various kinds of review. This includes, firstly, the discussions analysts would have amongst themselves. Most Magic Quadrants were produced by more than one individual, meaning that the ranking emerged from a consensus amongst a group of authors. There was also a 'peer review committee' where analysts from the same technology area would scrutinize the calculation. According to one analyst, it was now practically impossible to 'rig' Magic Quadrants because they were subject to so much scrutiny:

> If you have sat down and set the criteria out—I suppose mentally you could if you sat down—but there is a lot of heart felt discussion that goes on between usually a couple of the authors and, there is usually two authors, one author, sometimes two on each, and then there is a team of maybe three or four who are very closely involved (interview, Thomas).

Moreover, in recent years, a further check was also introduced where the placement of the larger vendors was also given a further round of review. It was inspected by what was called a 'lead analyst' within Gartner (interview, Old). This was someone who had overall responsibility for research produced on specific vendors:

> But now there is something else that happens as well. Say there is fifteen vendors on the Magic Quadrant, you might have lead analysts on some of the biggest

vendors out there. So for the biggest vendors we tend to have a lead analyst on them to keep a consistent viewpoint of the whole vendor. So they might be in ten different areas of technology and one analyst will have an overview across the whole lot. So if there is any form of escalation or, you want to go to one person and say 'give me an overview of that whole vendor'. And they are a sixty billion dollar company or something, you've got somebody with a view across the whole company. Those people have to review where the dot is and what the wording of the text is (interview, Thomas).

One final part of the review process was that graphs were also sent out to vendors themselves prior to publication who, in turn, were free to comment. A consequence of this, according to an analyst with responsibilities for the Gartner Ombudsman office, was that this often led to 'thorny' interactions between Gartner and the vendors:

> . . . a thorny one would be a vendor is dissatisfied or believe that they haven't been treated objectively in a . . . Magic Quadrant . . . So a typical issue might be well I am too far down and to the left and I deserve for my dot to be higher and more to the right. So they'll come to us and say I haven't been treated fairly (interview, Erskine).

Interestingly, it was not only in the management of existing Magic Quadrants that various new kinds of bureaucratic measures could be found. They were also visible in other aspects of the ranking. In particular, this was in the creation of new Magic Quadrants. Developing a new Magic Quadrant turned out to be more difficult than in the past because a 'committee' had now been put in place to approve them:

> Before you could just do it. 10 years ago you could just create one if you wanted to. You just had to negotiate with the boss. But now you have to go to a committee. There is a senior research committee that has to approve all new proposals for Magic Quadrants. So you have to justify there is a market, it's big enough, it's growing at this rate, there's lot of market clients, here's the enquiry volume coming from the customers, 'OK then, you've got a Magic Quadrant' (interview, Thomas).

Asked whether this particular analyst had been involved in or seen such a committee, he replied that he had closely observed the workings of a number. In particular, in recent months, he had seen the workings of a committee for a type of development called 'Social Software' (discussed in more detail below): 'I didn't go through the committee but I saw the forms you have to fill in, and you have to go to a meeting, and you have to, in effect, propose it and negotiate why it has a right to exist' (interview, Thomas). Added to this, and this is where we get to the substance of our argument, there was a further reason as to why setting up a new Magic Quadrant had become difficult. It appeared that the affordances and constraints of the device itself was a mediating feature.

9.6.3. Affordances and constraints

Creating a Magic Quadrant was reported by those we interviewed to be ineffective at certain key times in a technological lifecycle. It was said to be difficult to set a ranking up at the outset and then during the more mature stages of the career of a technology (interview, Lebber). There could be difficulties in the initial stages in the emergence of a new technological field because there might simply be too many vendors. An analyst describes how:

> When there is a 100 [vendors], that's not very good for us . . . because then [the market] is not mature enough for us to actually say, so what we are doing is watching that very carefully, and going, I will give you an example, Social Media Monitoring devices. There is tonnes of them at the moment (interview, Thomas).

When asked to explain why the presence of too many vendors was problematic our respondent replies: ' . . . graphically, you can't, [. . .] we've done it, you can have a 100 dots on the chart but it is unreadable. It is just garbage. It is just a bunch of dots' (interview, Thomas). In other words, if all players producing (or claiming to produce a) new technology were to be included then this would mean graphs would be too cluttered. There would just be too many dots and vendor names on the device. This would presumably create confusion for those attempting to consume and make sense of the ranking (see Figure 9.2).

Another analyst notes that, at the outset therefore, Magic Quadrants may not be very useful for those seeking insights into developing trends: 'Possibly if you have 200 vendors in the space that is probably not the right time to do a Magic Quadrant' (interview, Winter). Gartner analyst Thomas goes onto

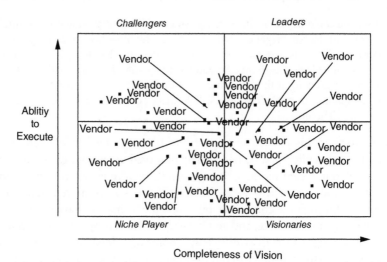

Figure 9.2. The Magic Quadrant is too *cluttered*

Source: Author depiction

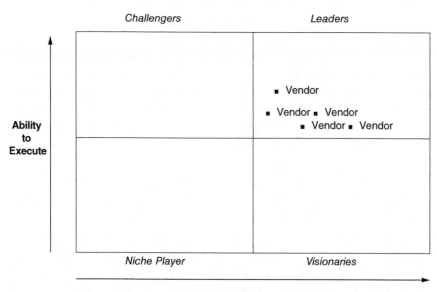

Too Empty

Figure 9.3. The Magic Quadrant is too *empty*
Source: Author depiction

describe how, equally, too few vendors is also a problem: 'And likewise when there is 3 dots on it, it is meaningless. What's the point of having a Magic Quadrant with 3 dots?' (interview, Thomas). Too few dots meant that little is being described in terms of how the market is developing (see Figure 9.3). The analyst gives a recent example:

> . . . we used to do things like operating systems . . . But when Microsoft started dominating operating systems on desktop or desktop applications it was pointless having 4 dots on a chart . . . But the ones that I have seen that have gone, have basically just dwindled to a point where through mergers and acquisitions they are down to less than 8 vendors, and the colleagues all turn around and go 'what was the point in that?'. The clients don't read them anymore, they are not so interesting. The only people who read them then are clients who want to justify what they are already doing—it is an insurance policy kind of thing. But their value is very, very low. The dots hardly move. And nobody is very interested (interview, Thomas).

Those analysts that we had interviewed had come to realize that there was an ideal number of dots that could be pictured at any one time:

> So, I would argue that Magic Quadrants are almost like, if you imagine a market always going theoretically going a 100 down to 10, to 5 vendors or something as it

consolidates and the barriers to entry get put up by the incumbent. Gartner's Magic Quadrant is the beautiful picture when you have gone down to about 20, 25 to 15, or 10, and then once you go below that it ceases to be useful. And before that it is not particularly useful (interview, Thomas).

The desired number is somewhere between 10 and 25 dots. This is what this individual ranker identifies as the 'beautiful picture'. Another analyst makes the same point: 'Typically, we would cream off all the vendors by inclusion criteria, and we work that in a way so that there is 20, 25 dots' (interview, Winter). It is seemingly a beautiful picture because the graph is neither too crowded nor too empty. It is also a beautiful picture because it apparently keeps Gartner *in the game* so to speak:

> So, while it is in that sort of state between about 25 down to maybe 10 vendors, there is a choice, there's a multiple different dimensions to it, and different ways of evaluating, how you write each vendor up. There is complexity in it, and therefore there is a game for us to play (interview, Thomas).

We do not think this is a feature that is unique to this industry analyst firm. For instance, an analyst from Gartner's competitor Forrester, who produce the 'Forrester Wave', describe how 'in general we try to be clutter cutting and we don't want more than 10 to 12 vendors cluttering up a Wave, right. We've seen quadrants where you have 40 and they are all blasted on there and your eyes start to glaze over. Our job is to prioritize' (meeting between Forrester analyst Tom Pohlmann and the IIAR).[1]

To summarize, dot-ology attempts to capture some of the interaction between the social and material aspects of producing a ranking. For instance, whilst (technically) it might have been possible to move individual placings on the spreadsheet, the analysts were constrained by the (social) review process where a moving dot would have to be explained and justified. Alongside this, the affordances of the Magic Quadrant meant that creating the figuration was difficult both at the initial and later stages of a technological field. At the outset, there were simply too many players and at the end, because the market has consolidated, there were too few. The individuals we interviewed appeared to agree that their experience had shown them that there was an optimal number of vendors that could be represented. In other words, the Magic Quadrant set limits on the kind of competitive space that could be created— and this was what one individual called the 'beautiful picture'. In terms of teasing out what the analysts were attempting to achieve we find Miller and O'Leary's (2007) 'programmes' and 'technologies' framework useful. Programmes refer to the conceptualization and envisioning of a domain so that it might become open to calculation/commensuration (the 'beautiful picture'), whereas technology refers to the various interventions that are made through a range of devices so as to bring about such ordering. We now turn to look as such interventions.

9.6.4. How the ranking encourages actors to intervene in the wider economy (dots moving *markets*)

9.6.4.1. Capturing *the beautiful picture*

The constraints dictated by the matrix appeared not only to have a spatial but also a time-related dimension. Although Gartner had identified the picture that furthered their interests and those of the market, this particular competitive space appeared temporally bound. At times, the number of players in an emerging field was changing so fast that Gartner could not capture the picture. Sometimes Gartner were simply to slow to react to an emerging field and by the time they had reacted, the beautiful picture had long gone. To illustrate this point we include the comments of an analyst talking about the case of 'Web Analytics':

> Sometimes they move through so fast that . . . Gartner's Magic Quadrant never quite . . . hits it. And a good example of that would be Web Analytics where . . . it was 68 vendors about 4 years ago and now there is about 20 or so. But there is only 3 big ones who control a vast majority of the market, followed by Google which is free and then there's a couple of specialists. So really to have a Magic Quadrant with about 5 or 6 on, there is not much point anymore. So it went from 68 to 6 in about 3 years and so there was little window there where Gartner could have managed to get a snapshot of the market when there was 20 in, but then it was gone (interview, Thomas).

In this case there were initially too many vendors and then later too few for them to 'get a snapshot' of the market (the technology field of Web Analytics had just passed them by). Gartner was unable to capture the beautiful picture. This was because the particular technology field was too fast moving for Gartner to mobilize its large organizational machinery in a timely fashion (particularly with the standardized processes, committees, review cycles described above that it currently deploys). If this was the case for Web Analytics, it seems also to be true for a new kind of technology called 'Social Software':

> So a classic example is Social Software at the moment where there is a team of 7 or 8 analysts in Gartner now on that area . . . But Social has been around for—you know Facebook and all that stuff—has been around for quite a few years now . . . What happened was they went: 'Wait a minute people are making money in that area' . . . . I don't mean Linked-in and that, they are not making money, but the stuff companies are buying to manage social networks or to deal with social networks. They are starting to invest and there is companies piling into that area and Gartner is going, at some point Gartner—I think it was 18 months ago—Gartner went 'Oh my god. We're late. Go. Boom!' (interview, Thomas).

Here the analyst finishes the conversation by noting how, in contrast to other smaller industry analysts and market commentators, Gartner were typically 'late' with their ranking:

> An analyst will take it upon themselves and say 'that's mine', and they will go leap
> after it. Then a couple will follow them and they will go after it. So we are, that's
> why I say that . . . we are not setting the pace. The only time we do set the pace is
> when we are quick followers I think is the best way I would describe it and we are
> useful in that we bless things (interview, Thomas).

Capturing the beautiful picture could also prove difficult because the grouping
might simply no longer exist. That is, there was once a vibrant competitive
space but now, because of mergers and takeovers, failures and collapses, and so
on, there remained only a few competing players within a market. When this
happened, the only solution apparently was to withdraw a Magic Quadrant:

> I haven't seen many [retired] recently because analysts don't like giving up turf
> but, it tends to be where you have got down to just a handful like 5 vendors in a
> market . . . So, there is no formal process that says we review them and anyone
> with less than 'x' dots gets shot. It is more that the analyst knows that and goes
> and finds a new market to go cover and research, if they are bright, which they
> usually are. So often you find an analyst has 2 Magic Quadrants: one old one that
> is dying; and then they got another one with a slightly different definition which
> has a newer and more buoyant market. And then eventually they stop doing that
> one, but there is no formal process as far as I understand it (interview, Thomas).

If a Magic Quadrant is 'old and dying', an analyst may then decide to 'retire' it.
What all of this suggests is that the ranking organization was not completely
passive in searching for the beautiful picture. If the beautiful picture was not
there then the Magic Quadrant prompted them to set about trying to
create one.

9.6.4.2. Creating *the beautiful picture*

The affordances and constraints of the Magic Quadrant were such that it could
encourage Gartner to attempt to make interventions in/to markets. During
our research, for instance, we noted how Gartner appeared to have at least two
strategies for creating beautiful pictures. The first of these relates to the
standardized evaluation criteria described above. When there are too many
vendors to be included, for instance, an individual ranker will continually set
and reset these criteria in order to reduce the competitive space. One analyst
describes this by talking through the example of Social Software:

> There is a lot of discussion [internally within Gartner] about . . . what stage do
> Magic Quadrants have in a lifecycle of a market? And they are not good at the
> start of a market; they are hopeless! When a market is in its first couple of years
> and there is, Social Software and I'm looking at Social CRM at the moment and
> we've identified 92 vendors in the last three days. Can't put 92 dots on a chart! So,
> it is pretty clear that we will set some high criteria to cut people out. And that is
> what the big debate will be about is how you set those criteria. But two years ago

there was probably more than that. It all depends on how you define that market (interview, Thomas).

To paraphrase the words from above, these criteria are usually set around 'quantitative' aspects as well as more 'qualitative' elements. These will then be set and reset to 'cut people out'. The second strategy is to divide spaces up to get the required picture. An analyst describes how this is done: 'Clearly there is a kind of optimal number of dots on a chart which Gartner kind of ends up almost dividing markets up in order to get that number of dots on a chart, which is readable, which is about 15 to 25' (interview, Thomas). The analyst acknowledges not only that Gartner reduce the market down, but that they reduce it down to a particular size: 'So in effect you'll find almost every analyst is setting the criteria, the bounds—not consciously really but we are doing it—to get 15 to 25 dots. Because if it drops to 5 dots, there's 5 vendors in this market, it's highly consolidated, so why would they ring us?' (interview, Thomas).

Let us unpack more carefully the implications of what is being described here. Gartner set the bounds of the competitive space so as to arrive at what it thinks is an optimal number of vendors. Because there are too many vendors in an area—and since the emerging field cannot be captured in its entirety on a single Magic Quadrant—analysts will literally divide markets up. This means Gartner will attempt to create new competitive spaces and distinctions between technologies. The easiest way to do this appears to be through the introduction of alternative nomenclatures (as described in Chapter 6). During the period of our research, for instance, we observed how Gartner introduced three new terminologies within the category of 'Social Software'.

9.6.4.2.1. Social Software

Social Software is a relatively new area in which there is currently a great deal of activity and interest as well as considerable uncertainty. Gartner describe Social Software as the area where they are fielding most questions from clients and prospective purchasers. One key issue is that Social Software is something of an 'umbrella term' (also described as 'Social CRM' or 'Social Media'). The problem is that large numbers of vendors are rebranding their products as 'Social' in some way. We attended a Gartner CRM conference in London, for instance, where an analyst makes this point to the audience:

> Social CRM is a huge topic. There has been tonnes of calls about it. I am tracking currently about 90 vendors who have some area of Social CRM. Some vendors are calling themselves that and they are not. Some people are that. Some people don't know that they have it when they have it. So there is a lot of movement going on as people try to make sense of just Social Media in the first place, and that is a hard nut to crack: 'What is Social Media?' (Sarner, conference floor).

The analyst notes how, in the last couple of days alone, Gartner had identified nearly a hundred new players claiming to offer some kind of Social Software.

There appears within the market a need for some form of clarity. Gartner's response has been to break this technological field down into further sub-segments. They have defined Social Software as containing 'Social CRM', 'Social Software in the Workplace', and 'Externally Facing Social Software' (EFSS). Another Gartner analyst presents the rationale for these splits during a conference presentation:

> ... we initially had one Magic Quadrant for Social Software and it really covered quite a few different technologies. Increasingly ... we have been looking to split that up because, as the market matures, we start to see some of the kind of submarkets or other kinds of segmentation .... these Magic Quadrants that are being issued in 2010, we're building on the Social Software in the Workplace which is looking at how these kinds of ideas can be used behind the firewall ... [t]he newest one that was released was EFSS or Externally Facing Social Software. What that is essentially doing is going beyond the firewall ... Now we also see the public social media, and I will also be talking about in a moment the Social CRM Magic Quadrant, that is the third one which we are releasing (Mann, conference floor).

Out of one category, and because of the difficulty of representing all the possible vendors in the Social Software Magic Quadrant, they had crafted three new (sub)spaces. Creating these new kinds of technological categories turned out not to be a straightforward process as we show in the final empirical section.

9.6.4.3. Pragmatics of making meaningful distinctions

One way to bring a new competitive space to life seems to be to create Magic Quadrants for them. However, during a presentation, a Gartner analyst notes some of the difficulties surrounding the pragmatics of doing this, particularly in separating out the Social Software category and making clear distinctions between the vendors operating within in it. The three new categories are presented on a slide as circles that overlap with each other:

> Across these different segments you can see some examples of the kinds of vendors that we see. You can also see that these circles do kind of overlap. We do see that there are some vendors that are active in several different markets and that is reflected also when we start looking at the Magic Quadrant. There are vendors that are present on several of the Magic Quadrants and a couple who really are active on all three. Now ... when we first started doing this analysis and we first started looking at the criteria we actually were ... a little afraid that [we] would see a great deal of overlap (webinar, Mann).

The analyst notes how there were vendors producing software that could be counted as belonging to all three technology categories. Their fear was that there would be a great deal of overlap. However, he goes on to say that, there turned out to be fewer than anticipated: '... the overlap we had in the final publication is really quite small. There is only a couple really that appear on several different ones' (webinar, Mann). The reason for this was that Gartner was able to impose differences on vendors through redefining the evaluation criteria: 'And parts of that is down to how we defined the criteria and what were the criteria and qualifications for being included in each Magic Quadrant' (webinar, Mann). Setting and resetting the criteria meant that the rankings plotted exactly as they should do!

This pragmatics of making meaningful distinctions can be seen more specifically in the creation of the Social CRM Magic Quadrant. Here an analyst describes the difficulty Gartner have had in producing this particular ranking: 'We're in the process of creating a Magic Quadrant for this. There isn't one yet . . . It is a very onerous task because so many of these vendors are very new and hard to define' (Sarner, conference floor). Some months before the release of the Social CRM Magic Quadrant, an analyst speculated about how many vendors would be included. He shows the audience not the Magic Quadrant but a 'list' of some representative vendors:

> Again this is a representative list—we are checking out 80 or 90. I think we are probably going to come out to 25 to 30 based on the criteria. One thing that we are looking over is vend over five million and putting in things like 'Are we being asked about you?' So, there is a lot of things in here . . . (Sarner, conference floor).

He makes clear the quantitative and qualitative evaluative criteria to be used. He also notes the use of 'the list', which he views as a standin for the real ranking, which has yet to be devised. Yet a few months later, the Magic Quadrant is published. The same analyst describes the final number:

> Gartner just got finished with a Social CRM Magic Quadrant. We started with about a 120 vendors that we looked at. Many vendors had some sort of social aspect included in their CRM—Social CRM aspects to it. We, finally, we were left with around '19' for various reasons that I will discuss (webinar, Sarner).

To summarize, evidence shows that when faced with a large number of vendors claiming to work in a new technological field, and in order to create a competitive space, Gartner sets the evaluation criteria to reduce the numbers of vendors included within each space. This is done by dividing up the field into new competitive groupings. If the beautiful picture that Gartner desires is not there, then it sets about trying to create it. Dot-ology, therefore, also captures the strategies deployed to influence the setting that the ranking describes. This pragmatic work is complex. Garner struggles to differentiate between vendors within classifications. This is because it is imposing boundaries onto the market. This can create difficulties. Many vendors, for instance, could be included in more than one specific ranking. Deciding where a particular instance sits across a number of technology classifications therefore requires taking an explicit decision, which often proves to be an ambiguous process.

9.7. DISCUSSION: FORMAT AND FURNITURE
OF A RANKING

According to Espeland and Sauder (2007: 36–7) the 'proliferation of public measures of performance' is one of the most 'important and challenging trends of our time'. The starting point for this chapter was the suggestion that these measures wield forms of influence that have yet to be adequately characterized in existing scholarly debates. Whilst there is a growing number of studies that analyse the power of rankings (Shrum 1996, Wedlin 2006, Blank 2007, Espeland and Sauder 2007, Free et al. 2009, Kornberger and Carter 2010, Karpik 2010, Kwon and Easton 2010, Jeacle and Carter 2011, Scott and Orlikowski 2012), very few have provided insights into their makeup and minutiae (but see Schultz et al. [2001] who point to some aspects of their construction). However if our analysis of such a crucial market mechanism is black-boxed, we only ever develop a partial understanding of its constitutive capacity. There is perhaps a tendency (or certainly a dangerous temptation) for researchers, when faced with an incomplete vantage point, to elevate the importance of those aspects of the phenomena that can be studied. Specifically, rankings are seen to influence domains through changing the way actors make sense of and interpret the world (Wedlin 2006, Espeland and Sauder 2007, Kornberger and Carter 2010).

We have worked up the idea of a 'ranking device' to capture how, alongside the way rankings cause people to adapt behaviour, graphic format and furniture can also be significant. Taking the example of the Magic Quadrant, we have shown how, in ways that are both social and material, this ranking has shaped the market for various technologies. Through describing how the ranking brought together and counterposed players in a 'competitive space', the chapter has considered three related aspects of the sociomaterial shaping of that space. Firstly, we focused on attempts by those technology vendors ranked by the assessment to affect the shape of the competitive terrain. Our evidence suggested that, because the ranking created the space by which various players could compete with each other (Kornberger & Carter 2010), vendors were advised to adapt and orient themselves to the nuances and measures of the ranking. These included employing strategies to help improve their position and weaken that of competitors. The players were in this process brought together into one space, and, importantly, with the help of new forms of expertise, this space appeared tractable.

Secondly, whilst our initial discussion emphasized the social strategies at play ('people moving dots'), we later introduced the theme of material agency. We demonstrated the sociomaterial constraints surrounding the shaping of the competitive space ('dots were moving people'). We saw this in relations between individuals and Gartner and then between the ranking organization and the market. Until recently within Gartner, individual analysts could wield notable amounts of discretion in placing vendors. More recently however, because of moves towards transparency and standardization, there had been changes in ranking practices (the discretion of individual analysts had become entangled in and increasingly stifled by layers of technology and methodology at Gartner). Added to this, the graph itself (its affordances and constraints) also placed limitations on how the competitive space could be captured and represented. The rankers could not capture and represent all the players in a market on one Magic Quadrant. This meant they were forced to adopt alternative strategies.

Thirdly, we showed in particular how the industry analysts, as a result, were required to intervene directly in the market to attempt to shape the competitive space to account for the limitations of this two-by-two matrix. This meant they did not use the graph to represent a competitive space conceived prior to its inclusion in the ranking. Rather, they conceived of new competitive spaces—or more particularly they were forced to conceive of these spaces—through taking the capacities of the ranking into consideration. We could say that the Magic Quadrant prompted such an intervention and that this was a prompt that individual analysts appeared willing to accept. Analysts would thus attempt to modify the competitive space to fit the ranking (rather than the other way around). It is specifically this aspect, a situation we conceive of as 'dots moving markets', that identifies one of the main contributions of this chapter (and perhaps the book).

9.7.1. New visual and temporal dynamics

We propose that graphical performance measures (and figurations more generally) contribute a powerful instance of the process by which markets and material things mutually constitute one another (Miller & O'Leary 2007, Callon et al. 2007, Pinch & Swedberg 2008, MacKenzie 2009). We attempted to get at this through analyzing the interactions between 'programmes' and 'technologies'. These refer to the imaginings and conceptualizations of an arena and the various devices and inscriptions that mediate and shape these envisionings, such that a domain may be acted upon and calculated (Miller & O'Leary 2007, Miller 2008). We have studied the production of the ranking not as 'knowledge' but as a 'practice'. This is to consider the idea of a ranking not in an abstract representational idiom (Espeland & Sauder 2007, Kornberger & Carter 2010), but one which captures the nuanced interplay involved between the conceptualization of a market domain and its incorporation within various format and furniture. What our analysis sought to show was how these devices both shaped and were shaped by the market. In particular, the format and furniture helped create a new visual dynamic and a new temporal dynamic within the IT domain. We explore these in turn.

9.7.2. Visual dynamic

We use the term 'visual dynamic' because Gartner analysts are attempting to specify what a market should look like. They sought a conceptualization that made the information technology domain amenable to calculation and commensuration (Miller & O'Leary 2007, Miller 2008). This meant they strove to produce a ranking that would allow everyone to see and compare how one technology vendor was performing in relation to another, in the most straightforward manner, where there were neither too many nor too few players in the competitive space. They apparently found the optimal number that could be included—and this represented the 'beautiful picture'.

What is the beautiful picture? The beautiful picture is part of what we might think of as an 'aesthetic economy' operating within Gartner and other industry analysts organizations. This is not to say that it is the picture of an ideal or perfect market (cf. Garcia-Parpet 2007). Rather, it is the result of a *negotiated, devised* and *contrived* intervention. The beautiful picture was a set of compromises (i) *negotiated* between the imaginings and conceptualizations of Gartner and the sociomaterial possibilities of the ranking. Material affordances potentially allowed for the placing of many vendors on a graph but (conventional) constraints meant that the rankers could not overburden the picture (Quattrone et al. 2012). The latter would not only produce a figuration that would be difficult for clients to understand, but also give the impression of an overly complex market (and this would have adversely affected the aesthetic economy deemed crucial by Gartner). Thus, the ranking was also conventionally (ii) *devised* (Espeland & Stevens 2009. There were not only material aspects limiting the construction of the competitive space but also 'social' ones (David & Pinch 2008).

The ranking was also (iii) *contrived* for bringing about certain kinds of (potentially contradictory) results. It was necessary to reduce the level of 'confusion' for decision makers and practitioners (there should not be too many dots). However, there should never be too few players on a graph because then there would appear insufficient complexity in the market. It was still important to maintain sufficient complexity that further advice was needed. If everything appeared straightforward, why would technology adopters continue to seek Gartner's expertise? The beautiful picture was one that kept this firm *in the game* so to speak.

Attempts to engineer the beautiful picture were consequential for the shaping of the actual market. It meant the Magic Quadrant was not neutral with regard to what constituted a competitive space. It appeared ill-suited to new, fast moving areas, for instance, where there were many new entrants in a technological area. Whilst individual rankers could spot multiple vendors entering an emerging category, in practice they could not capture or represent them within the ranking (the figuration lacked the affordances of a *list* in this respect). This issue resembles what Lynch (1985: 43), talking about scientific graphs, has called the 'problem of visibility'. Scientists determine what is 'natural' based on what their graphs are able to depict. Translated to our concerns, this means that the industry analyst firm decided what a market 'is'—the competitive space: which players make up the market, the boundaries of the field, etc.—partially based on what the Magic Quadrant was able to capture and communicate. This suggests that information technology markets today are a product of format and furniture as much as any other calculative aspect of this particular ranking.

What was also salient in our study was the finding that, if the beautiful picture could not be captured, then the ranking organization would try to create it. Because the graph was seen to embody key features of the markets under analysis, efforts were made to intervene in competitive spaces, so that the characteristics of these spaces were made congruent with the affordances of the ranking. Our fieldwork revealed how analysts performed this in one of two ways: through limiting the number of vendors operating in a particular competitive space or by creating entirely new spaces. They achieved the former through setting 'inclusion criteria' and the latter by attempting to divide technological fields into new designated areas of activity (with their own unique nomenclatures, definitions, inclusion criteria, Magic Quadrants, etc.). The designation of a new technological field of activity, or 'competitive space' as we have called it here, is not trivial. It can draw boundaries around a set of artefacts and their suppliers and create a space in which sorting and ranking becomes possible. If taken up it can go on to provide crucial resources and constraints within which vendors and management and technology consultants articulate future offerings. It could, in other words, go on to become a fully-fledged market in its own right (see below).

One problem Gartner now faces in competitive-spaces-constructed-according-to-the-affordances-of-a-ranking is the pragmatics of making meaningful distinctions. Since new boundaries were imposed onto the space, individual analysts have struggled to differentiate between vendors in these new groupings. This was evidenced by the fact that certain vendors appeared in *all three* of the new Magic Quadrants. This outcome was thought less than ideal because it suggested a lack of distinction within the ranking. Similar issues were apparent when the ranker was forced to intervene because vendors clustered together (which might occur because the market was converging or, over time, vendors were conforming to the evaluative criteria [Espeland & Sauder 2007], or, as in the case above, because there was no meaningful distinction to be made). Clustering was thought problematic because it suggested that all those on the graph had the same or similar qualities. This was troublesome because there would be little value found in the ranking. Decision-makers required the vendors to be graded in a way that signalled a distinction. Without this, why would people contact Gartner, to paraphrase one respondent? A further feature of this pragmatics therefore was the process whereby rankers were forced to devise distinctions by means of manipulating organizational machinery (for example through resetting the axes of the spreadsheet to increase the distance between dots).

9.7.3. Temporal dynamics

We use the term 'temporal dynamics' because during fieldwork we were alerted to the fact that the affordances of the ranking were not static but evolving over time. Espeland and Sauder (2007: 36) discuss how rankings are a 'moving target'. That is, as people learn to 'game' them, their authors are forced to update evaluative criteria more or less on a continuous basis. Whilst this was also a factor in our case, we note how the ranking was similarly surrounded by a 'moving organizational apparatus' (see Chapter 5). The Magic Quadrant had begun its career as a relatively informal, subjective ranking but there had subsequently been (quite vigorous) demands placed on Gartner to recreate it as a formal assessment, subject to auditing (see Free et al. 2009 for a discussion of these processes whereby rankings are audited). This meant individual rankers could no longer grade vendors exactly as they wished. It also limited their capacity to respond (rapidly) to innovation.

Today, the provision and administration of the Gartner Magic Quadrant is circumscribed by new technology and bureaucracy. This has affected Gartner's ability to produce 'snapshots'. The industry analyst firm is not always able to react in time to capture specific innovations. Some beautiful pictures may disappear before these experts can mobilize their committees, spreadsheets etc. The pictures are there for a moment and then they are gone, to paraphrase one respondent. This meant that certain technological innovations completely pass the industry analyst firm by. Pockets of the market can remain unranked in what is typically a highly graded arena. We suggest that instances where ranking devices and organizational apparatus create situations of 'unrankability' deserve further attention. It is a situation where the market escapes dots. This begs the questions: were the markets for these products adversely or positively affected? Were the vendors who remained outside the competitive space punished or rewarded in some way?

Our evidence also showed how the affordances of the ranking created cyclical pressures on Gartner to intervene at certain key moments. The beautiful pictures they sought were time limited. They were not there at the outset of an innovation (there were too many dots to be represented), and nor were they there as the technology matured (either there were too few dots to allow anything meaningful to be said, or all the players had clustered in the same segment of the quadrant). This prompted the industry analyst firm to engineer interventions not arbitrarily but at certain key points in the lifespan of a technology. This included, for instance, the moment when a distinctive new technological field first took form and then later as it matured.

9.7.4. What does a focus on graphic format and furniture show?

This chapter has developed some of the analytical tools used to consider the sociomaterial influence of a ranking. This begs the question as to whether a focus on format and furniture draws attention to aspects not visible under more 'social' approaches. Existing modes of analysis give particular emphasis to how rankings influence peoples' behaviour. The 'mechanisms of reactivity' concept (Espeland & Sauder 2007), for instance, explicitly captures this through showing how rankings evoke self-fulfilling prophecies that encourage people to adapt their behaviour towards the calculation. Extending this, we have emphasized how ranking devices can also play a role through offering specific affordances and constraints and encouraging others to modify the settings within which action takes place. For example, we have shown how the graphical ranking came to suggest a particular order for a market, prioritizing one market view over another (a beautiful rather than a cluttered or sparse picture), which the rankers then set about creating. The corollary is that a ranking can influence a setting in more diverse (and perhaps more fundamental) ways than previously thought.

The point above is about the shape of the landscape within which actions take place, but there is also a temporal issue. In this respect, our approach raises the question as to whether a sociomaterial influence, as opposed to simply a social one, is a more enduring form of influence. It could be argued that a ranking located 'in the back of everybody's head', as Espeland and Sauder describe (ibid: 11), may only have a fleeting influence whereas one residing in a specific format and furniture can endure if not indefinitely, for a prolonged period. As long as Gartner retains this particular format and furniture, the order described in the device above may continue to produce a particular shape to the market regardless of the actions of individual players at specific times.

What we are foregrounding is how the processes of market making are inscribed in and flow from the sociomaterial negotiations surrounding a ranking. Clearly the episodes of market (re)construction described here are very different from those formal accounts beloved of economists, where supply and demand comes together to form a price (Callon & Muniesa 2005). We thus offer an example of how new markets are constituted by the seemingly mundane constraints of a graph. This also contrasts with those scholars who view market creation as the results of primarily 'social interactions'. Kornberger and Carter (2010: 330) write that 'competition is something that is created out of interaction between market players'. Our work, by contrast, has shown how devices are also party to these interactions (see also Miller & O'Leary [2007], Robson [1992] and Quattrone et al. [2012] who similarly highlight the link between devices and processes of market making). Future inquiry would be to see whether the arguments set out in this chapter hold true for other areas. Do format and furniture hold similar implications for other kinds of performance measures?

9.8. CONCLUSIONS: IT IS BEAUTIFUL PICTURES THAT SHAPE ECONOMIC LIFE

The capture of business by the two-by-two matrix (Lowy & Hood 2004) in particular suggests that figurations are no longer a supplement but intrinsic and constitutive part of market settings. Whereas calculative practices have predominately been conceived of as 'numerical operations' (Miller 2001), Quattrone et al. (2012: 9) argue that there is a need to devote more attention to the 'visual nature of numbers' (see also Justesen & Mouritsen 2008). We believe this chapter meets elements of this call. Calculative practices turn 'qualities into quantities' (Miller 2001). In our case, this would be the translation of a subjective opinion about a vendor—rendered through a large-scale ranking apparatus—into a quantity, such as placing a dot on a graph. We suggest that the form of dot-ology described here represents a unique instance of these kinds of calculative practices. On the one hand, this is how a calculation can come to be shaped by mundane graphic resources (and vice versa), and, on the other, how there is an aesthetic element to the construction of visual numbers. In terms of the former, those producing visual numbers may come to determine what is 'calculable' based on what graphs are able to depict. It is not just a matter of how corporate and market performance are revealed and ordered by dots (or stars, lines, waves, tics, etc); it is rather how the format and furniture of graphs interact and merge with the calculations. Visual resources constitute calculative practices, such that any numbers that result bear the imprint of graphic sociomateriality.

This latter element is also important because, as Quattrone et al. (ibid: 9) notes, little attention has been given to the 'imaginative power' of an inscription. This is their ability to envision what business and markets could and should look like. In this respect, we speculate that the two-by-two matrix is different from other formats, such as lists (Cardinaels 2008), because it creates a particular way of representing and intervening in situations. As one of the premier modes of representing business activities—one only has to think of the 'cost benefit matrix', the 'product and market matrix', the 'BCG Product Portfolio Matrix', etc.,—this creates a particular kind of aesthetic economy

(Espeland & Stevens 2009). Through visualizing the elements of a competitive situation, one alters the way in which that situation is thought about and acted upon or practiced. Their allure is such that the situation appears amenable to intervention. They encourage various forms of co-production such that settings are modified to become congruent with graphic affordances and vice versa. Ultimately, the predominance of figurations across industries means that their sociomateriality should become a feature of academic study. We call for serious and detailed study of the format and furniture of the major business and accounting visualizations, for it is not simply engines but beautiful pictures that shape economic life.

NOTE

1. This is a widely recognized problem in these circles. For instance, an analyst relations consultant from SageCircle writes how 'Another problem is that there is only so much room on a MQ and therefore only a subset of vendors can be included. This is also an issue with the Forrester Wave. Often the criteria for excluding vendors can be arbitrary and inflexible. Some analysts will include a sidebar or footnote mentioning interesting vendors who did not make the cut, but this is not a universal practice'. http://sagecircle.wordpress.com/2008/12/29/vendor-complains-in-a-very-public-blog-post-about-gartners-data-integration-magic-quadrant/. Accessed 9 December 2014.

10

The Expertise Ecosystem

In this chapter, in an effort to integrate the previous empirical material and address the bigger picture, we reflect on the industry analysts 'ecosystem' that appears to be emerging, which raises questions about how we conceptualize markets for expertise in terms of the role of individuals and organizations.

We examined in Chapter 2 how the IT industry analyst emerged in response to the particular difficulties experienced by organizational adopters in assessing supplier offerings. Their properties and suitability for a specific organization cannot readily be determined (e.g., by inspection as might be used for simple physical products). This creates an opportunity for the emergence of a new kind of market intermediary (Sharma 1997, Carruthers & Stinchcombe 1999) who makes available commodified knowledge about a range of vendor offerings. However, as we noted in Chapter 4, this resort to external expertise in turn throws up new problems of identifying 'the best' expertise and ensuring the quality and independence of the knowledge being offered. This paradox of expertise threatens an apparently unending regression about who can advise about the choice of external consultancy and advisory services. In the case of industry analysts, we have suggested that the 'Gartner brand' provides some assurance about the quality and independence of advice offered. As happened in the case of Gartner and the other larger IT advisory firms, brand succeeds as a proxy for quality of expertise where a single organization (or a small number of reputed organizations) has established cognitive authority.

Gartner emerged in a context of marked asymmetry of access to information about the burgeoning supply of complex organizational IT solutions. This was a market that at the time was dominated by IBM. Gideon Gartner's IBM background gave him exceptional access to understanding that world, as did his work on analyzing IBM's competitors and his membership of two IBM user groups. The industry analyst firm he set up was able to trade on the asymmetry of access to information about vendor offerings. However, this knowledge asymmetry has contradictory effects and mobilizes other developments. In particular, we find a continued space for the emergence of individual experts and small analyst organizations. There are returns to scale in this sector and a major source of growth for Gartner and other leading industry analysts has been through the absorption of smaller industry research and analysis firms. At the same time, there are also opportunities and incentives for individuals to spin-out from larger firms and set up by themselves. There are, however, significant differences between small and large players in the sector. Our respondents from Gartner and other larger analyst firms distinguished themselves from the smaller players. Different kinds of research and analysis firms seemed to be playing different kinds of role. At this point in our research, we began to encounter another class of expert actor, an emerging community specializing in what they described as *analyst relations,* who sought to differentiate between different kinds of analysts. These groups were salient in suggesting that there was an *ecosystem* of analyst expertise.

In this chapter, we first analyse the structure of this intricate ecosystem of expertise. We examine the continued importance of the individual expert in Gartner (and more generally in contexts where clients are making strategic decisions). As we saw previously, individual analysts are subject to internal examination within Gartner (Chapter 3). Their performance is also subject to external scrutiny insofar as Gartner monitors client satisfaction with their advisory services (both directly through client feedback and indirectly through subscription renewals) and their performance at public events (Chapter 8). Moreover, as we will see shortly, third party organizations have also emerged which rate the perceived performance and influence of analysts. In this way, we see how the reputation of individual analysts depends on more than the Gartner brand.

Finally, we examine how this ecosystem of expertise is changing over time as a result of what we have described as the evolving knowledge infrastructures of the IT market. We note the increasing availability of information through the internet, which potentially erodes the asymmetries in knowledge distribution that underpinned the status and trading of industry expertise (but which perhaps generates further problems, including navigating this abundance of information). Here we note the emergence of new models for provision of analyst expertise—the 'open analyst' model—drawing analogies with developments in open source software. Although the big industry analyst organizations such as Gartner continue to grow, we also see the continuation of large numbers of small and medium-sized analyst firms together with many individual and boutique players. To help technology vendors navigate this bi-modal, 'long-tail' market for research and analysis, new forms of expertise are beginning to emerge, and seeking to professionalize their role as 'analyst relations' specialists.

10.1. INDUSTRY ANALYSTS EMERGE IN A CONTEXT OF INFORMATION ASYMMETRY

A key historical element of the formation of Gartner was the dominance of IBM in the growing market for IT applications software. Gideon Gartner had initially been working for IBM. As well as holding insider knowledge of IBM products, he explained that his job gave him insights into how these products related to those of IBM's competitors: 'I knew the layout of the computer industry because I was working in the competitive analysis department of IBM, which was studying the competition' (interview, Gideon Gartner). At that time, IBM was the major supplier of industry applications software. In this context, IBM did not need to provide extensive information about its products to potential customers. As David Mitchell, Research Director, Ovum Research, explained, this generated a deep information asymmetry:

> It started because of information asymmetry. Particularly IBM at the time, because IBM was the big player in the industry, didn't publish thing like brochures on its products, didn't explain what they were all were, didn't explain what each product line was for, didn't explain how they were all priced, didn't explain anything about them. So there was a huge favouritism for IBM against the purchaser. The purchaser didn't know how to navigate through it and had to trust IBM. Gideon studied it and wrote it down and sold it to people (interview, Mitchell).

We saw in Chapter 2 how Gartner succeeded in establishing itself as the hub for exchanging and trading knowledge about vendors and their offerings, in particular by collating the diffuse experience of multiple user organizations—knowledge which had otherwise spread only slowly and imperfectly through informal networks. We also observed how Gartner analysts sustained this by establishing extensive networks of contacts with vendors and with large numbers of users. These networks opened up a channel for information and influence to be exchanged and traded. Gartner (in conjunction with a number of other large analyst firms such as Forrester and Yankee Group) established themselves as *obligatory passage points* (Callon 1986) for access to this information. They were able to do this because of the character and distribution of the knowledge involved. Knowledge about technology products and their organizational use is changing rapidly (as a result inter-alia of frequent vendor product launches and revisions). The dynamism surrounding such knowledge makes it too expensive for knowledge users to collect (Sharma 1997). It also resists attempts to codify and share in a way that might become appropriated by a professional body.[1] Instead, Gartner succeeded in establishing and sustaining itself as the repository for collecting and organizing this information, and making it available in a dependable way (i.e. produced subject to particular methodologies and governance structures). Gartner's services gave user organizations (and vendors) access to knowledge but in a way that sustained their own central position. These developments addressed but did not eliminate the knowledge asymmetry between players. *Au contraire*, Gartner (and other research and analysis organizations) traded upon this knowledge asymmetry. It enabled them to develop and sustain a very successful business selling its knowledge products through very profitable subscription services. Following Turner (2001) we argued that, for this group of experts, this position of cognitive authority cannot be taken for granted but is an achievement that has to be constantly fought for in a context in which an array of organizations are competing to provide knowledge services.

10.1.1. Structure of industry analysis sector: Differentiated by firm size and client base

This brings us to examine the structure of the industry analysis sector. Bernard and Gallupe (2013) have highlighted the diversity within what they call the 'IT Industry Analyst sector'. A similar account is offered by Dennington and Leforestier (2013). This currently comprises a handful of very large organizations notably 'the Big Three' Gartner, Forrester, IDC; a modest number of smaller firms such as Aberdeen, GigaOM, Ovum, Yankee Group, including various industry specialist organizations; and 'hundreds of boutique firms'— very small organizations and individuals (Dennington & Leforestier 2013: 6).

The industry has grown substantially over three decades. The larger firms have absorbed many smaller players. However, this has been offset by the formation of new firms and by spin-offs where individuals and groups leave the big analyst organizations to set up on their own. The field has a complex history and structure, which has not yet been fully characterized (Bernard & Gallupe 2013). We already noted in Chapter 2 the heterogeneity of firms within the industry analyst sector and how this is only partly because of the diverse origins of these firms (in technical publication, marketing, investment analysis). Analyst firms continue to be differentiated. David Mitchell, Research Director, Ovum Research noted how '[t]here are lots of different shades within analysts . . . [with] different business models in different analysts firms' (interview, Mitchell). Here we note critical differences in where firms get their money from especially in terms of whether their main customer base is IT adopters versus software vendors. Firm size is also a key factor. It seems that larger and smaller firms may be doing different things. Moreover, these two dimensions appear linked together.

Many of our respondents drew attention to the influence of firm size over the role that industry analysts played. Size of analyst organization was important both directly and indirectly. Most directly, it was an indicator of breadth and depth of expertise. The larger analyst organizations were better placed to keep abreast of a more comprehensive sample of developments across a wide range of application domains. This was particularly important, as already noted, for technology adopters, keen to be aware of the full-range of relevant technologies. Moreover, the largest firms, such as Gartner and Forrester, had many subscriptions from technology user organizations, which gave them extensive access to community knowledge about adoption experience. Size and breadth of client base was also an important indirect indicator of the ability of an analyst to be independent of powerful vendors.

Technology adopters do not want to be tied to a part of the market but want to have information about the full range of potential solutions available. They are therefore looking for breadth of knowledge from their advisors. As Toby Old, Gartner's Senior SAP Analyst, told us 'from an end customer perspective you want to have a broad grasp of vendors' (interview, Old). They therefore tend to look to the larger companies (such as Gartner). Thus Neil Ward Dutton, co-founder of a small advisory firm and active blogger in the contemporary industry analyst field, observes that:

> the buy side tends to favour the larger companies to an extent because you get a larger coverage from the larger companies . . . Small companies are challenged because they tend not to be able to cover that breadth of things . . . So, typically speaking, a lot of the vendors like the small analysts. A lot of the buyers like the large analysts. So, you tend to find the small analysts are skewed in where they get their money from; they tend to get it more from the vendors. The larger analysts tend to get it more, either more of a 50–50 kind of mix, or in fact very, very explicitly primarily from the buyer community (interview, Ward Dutton).

Thus the larger firms emphasize that their large client base gives them a certain level of independence from powerful vendor organizations. They distinguish themselves from the smaller firms, which were described by David Mitchell, as operating more like consultants:

> A lot of the smaller firms live off the side of IBM, or IBM and a couple of other firms. They don't have an end-user client base they only have a vendor client base. Some of the smaller firms work on almost a consulting model, so they produce some IP, but their business model is essentially: I'll do a speaking engagement there or a small project there, so economically they will look like consultancies (interview, Mitchell).

So whilst adopter organizations prefer large firms and firms whose independence from vendors is underpinned by significant buy-side income,[2] vendors may find it advantageous under some circumstances to engage with smaller analyst firms, which may be more responsive to their needs and concerns. They may also find advantage in sustaining diversity in the analyst market. It gives them greater room to manoeuvre. For example, it allows vendors to reduce the risks of being excluded from a market by a negative assessment by a major analyst committed to a different view of how that technology field will develop:

It is very easy for . . . vendors to feel excluded [by established analysts like Gartner and Forrester]. That is why they like the idea of lots of these small players. People will dress it up in all kinds of altruistic language but basically . . . it allows them to have a channel into that whole market even when the big guys aren't . . . amplifying the right kind of messages if you like . . . So lots of choice in the analysts ecosystem is a good thing for some of the vendors (interview, Ward Dutton).

This problem might arise, for example, where a vendor offering did not fit with the established product market categorizations used by the large industry analysts (Chapter 6). As Jonny Bentwood, Head of Analyst Relations at the public relations firm Edelman observed 'Gartner and all the technology houses see the world according to their own taxonomy. What do we do when we don't fit into that taxonomy?' (interview, Bentwood). These taxonomies may be undermined by changes in technology and evolving technologies: 'And that is where Gartner fails and some of the more niche, boutique analyst houses succeed because they don't rely on that traditional method of looking at things' (interview, Bentwood). To overcome this obstacle he was in a position, as we will see shortly, to identify other smaller and more specialized analyst firms whose advice would be trusted and influential in that product market. In turn, the larger industry analysts firms question whether these smaller sell-side players should really be considered industry analysts when what they are doing amounts to 'marketing consultancy' for large vendors:

> Who takes their money from vendors? Who takes their money from enterprise buyers? I could cheekily argue that at least one of those wasn't an analyst firm [pointing to a list of analyst firms on one of the author's office wall]; it is a marketing consultancy for one of the large vendors, which isn't necessarily a bad thing; it is a good living to be had (interview, Mitchell).

Analyst firms that were seen as 'guns for hire', i.e. willing to write favourable reports for vendors fees, would lose credibility (interview, Bentwood). Independence is 'a frequently debated term' in the field of industry analysis (Dennington & Leforestier 2013: 5). It must be noted that all our industry analyst respondents, whether from large firms, small firms or solo operations, all tended to emphasize and reiterate their independence of view. Indeed (and this represents another somewhat paradoxical verbal convention in the field), the smaller firms which typically secure a large proportion of their income from vendors are often described as 'independent analysts' to distinguish them from the big players in the field (Dennington & Leforestier 2013: 5).[3] Industry analysts do not reveal all their sources of income. As we noted in Chapter 2, many have a 'hybrid' business model, selling their information and services to vendors and investors as well as the technology adopter organizations, which by convention are the players they describe as their 'clients'. However, a distinction is often made between analyst firms that generate most of their revenues from vendors ('sell-side') and IT adopters ('buy-side') (Bernard & Gallupe 2013).

10.1.2. Industry analyst sector as an ecology

These considerations highlight the complexity of the field of industry analysis, made up of firms of different sizes and performing somewhat different roles broadly (albeit not exclusively) geared to the differing customer needs of vendors and adopters.

The industry analyst sector appears to exhibit features for which Abbott's (2005: 248) concept of 'ecology' seems apposite. He identifies the particular contexts for which the concept of ecology, rather than for example market or organization, is appropriate:

> When we call a set of social relations an ecology, we mean that it is best understood in terms of interactions between multiple elements that are neither fully constrained nor fully independent. We thus contrast ecology with mechanism and organism on the one hand and with atomism and reductionism on the other (Abbott 2005: 248).

Revisiting his earlier (1988) work on the Sociology of Professions that we extensively covered in Chapter 3, Abbott (2005) suggests that the analysis of 'internal' jurisdictional competition between professional groups needed to be supplemented by investigating how this expertise gains legitimacy with players outside the profession.[4] In language that seems remarkably congruent with Turner (2001), Abbott argues 'The several professions' claims for legitimate control are judged by various "audiences": the state, the public, co-workers in the workplace' (Abbott 2005: 246). He focuses attention on how professions are shaped by their insertion into a wider setting. Abbott thus offers a more general framework for understanding these developments. Rather than take any ecology as central he proposes a more symmetrical analysis of these as a system of 'linked ecologies': 'Instead of envisioning a particular ecology as having a set of fixed surrounds, I reconceptualize the social world in terms of linked ecologies, each of which acts as a (flexible) surround for others' (Abbott, 2005: 246). Abbott's framework also explores how linkages ('hinges') are established between knowledge ecologies and their audiences.

However, if the industry analysis sector is an ecosystem, it would appear to be a markedly asymmetrical and a rather complex ecosystem. As we have just noted, big and small players—and analysts oriented towards the buy and sell side—seem to be fulfilling different roles! The consultancy firm Knowledge Capital Group takes further the asymmetry of this field distinguishing what they call the 'Buyer Advice Ecosystem' from the 'Vendor Mindshare Ecosystem' (Hopkins & England 2012). The former group involves technology vendors, analysts and buyers; the latter includes, in addition, 'Tech Media' that may play a key role in raising awareness of a new product. Moreover, the sell side analysts merge into marketing and what is termed media relations [Hopkins & England 2012]). This suggests that the buy-side and the sell-side articulate contrasting viewpoints on this analyst ecosystem, drawing different boundaries around overlapping but not identical memberships, depending upon their purposes and relationships.

As we began to explore this question, we encountered a group of actors that were specifically arguing that analysts needed to be understood as an 'ecosystem'.[5] Indeed these players were seeking to make rather fine distinctions about the structure of this ecosystem. These were part of a community that was beginning to come together under the banner of 'analyst relations'. Many of these were linked to the Institute for Industry Analyst Relations (IIAR), a UK body established to support this emergent community. It appears that a new form of expertise is emerging of 'analyst relations' specialists. The marketing and communications departments of larger vendors have appointed specialized staff and departments to coordinate their relationships with the industry analysts. The category of analyst relations comprises these staff and others (often experienced industry analysts) who advise technology vendors on which analysts to engage with and how to achieve visibility and influence in the technology market. We will come back below to explore how this new form of expertise emerges and how the industry analysis sector is changing with the emergence of new technologies and organizational forms for knowledge exchange.

But first, we will explore how they have been particularly active in making distinctions about different kinds of industry analyst. In the Introduction, we discussed an Institute of Industry Analyst Relations (IIAR) best practice paper '*Who are industry analysts and what do they do?*', which defines industry analysts as individuals or organizations 'whose business model incorporates creating and publishing research about, and advising on how, why and where ICT-related products and services can be procured, deployed and used' (Dennington & Leforestier 2013: 4). This distinguishes them, for example, from financial analysts and market researchers. Though the latter research may be used by analysts, these groups 'do not rate vendors, and rarely offer advisory services' (idem.). Dennington and Leforestier (2013) draw attention to firm size, which is closely correlated with the kind of service that is offered. Apart from the 'Number crunchers' (i.e. those selling market research) they distinguish 'buy-side' (analysts such as Gartner, Celent, Forrester, who they also describe as '*Prescribers*') who advise end-users from 'sell side' analysts whose customers are vendors and service providers. The latter are often small and medium sized players but constitute by far the largest number of firms.

An even more detailed breakdown is provided by The Knowledge Capital Group (KCG) who produce *The Technology Vendor Executive's Guide to the Industry Analyst* (Hopkins & England 2012). They distinguish analysts in terms of their 'influence' over enterprise technology buyers and 'exposure' in the IT product market. The positioning of analyst firms is thus charted on a two-by-two matrix that closely resembles Gartner's Magic Quadrant. They

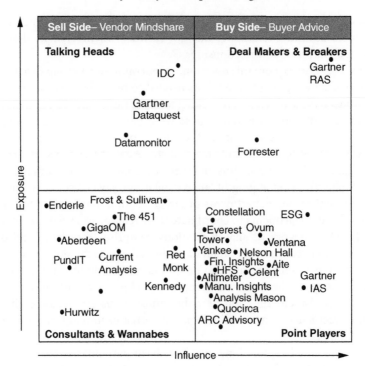

Figure 10.1. KCG (Knowledge Capital Group) Mystical Box Chart

Source: © The Knowledge Capital Group (2013) (www.knowledgecap.com)[6]

name this (with delicious irony) the KCG *Mystical Box Chart*. Like the Magic Quadrant, this sorts industry analysis into four quadrants and then positions them within it along two dimensions: influence and exposure (see Figure 10.1).

At the top right with high influence and exposure are the large firms like Gartner and Forrester whose links with end-user technology buyers give them such influence over procurement choices that they are characterized as 'Deal Makers or Breakers' (Hopkins & England 2012). A further group of firms whose buy-side links provide 'ability to generate influence in areas where they have high levels of core competency' are categorized as Point Players. Though analysts working primarily with the Sell Side may have less direct influence with buyers, some, who Hopkins and England (2012: 6) describe as 'Talking Heads', are able to be 'heavy hitters' on the basis of their 'exposure in the media'. The remaining group making up 90 per cent of the firms that KCG track are described as Wannabees and Consultants 'who work almost exclusively with vendors to help with market positioning' (Hopkins & England 2012: 6). In other words these players have only limited direct influence on the market but can help a vendor develop a strategy to engage with more influential players.

These analyst relations experts thus seek to differentiate industry analysts primarily in terms of the influence they are able to exert over adopter awareness and choice of supplier offerings. They articulate a vendor perspective on the field. (It is intriguing to see analyst relations experts applying analogous tools and presentation formats to differentiate and rate industry analysts to those that industry analysts had developed to rate vendors and their products.) We will return below to the emergence of analyst relations experts. But first, we will examine the structure of the sector.

10.2. INDUSTRIAL STRUCTURE OF THE ANALYST EXPERTISE MARKET

Many industrial research and advisory activities would appear to offer significant economies of scale and also economies of scope. This seems to underpin the increasing centralization of business consultancy organizations—and especially the case of the (now) Big Four international accounting firms (favouring both organic growth by large firms and mergers and acquisitions) (Greenwood & Suddaby 2006). This also pertains to IT research and industry analyst firms. As noted in Chapter 2, the upfront costs of generating this knowledge of the IT market are very high. This is compounded in the case of advice for technology adopters who wish to have access to information about the broadest range of issues and products and require breadth of expertise.

Knowledge has peculiar features as a commodity. It is expensive to acquire. However, information is a resource not destroyed by its consumption; once generated, it can be sold repeatedly (Shapiro & Varian 2013). To ensure a return on the huge investments sunk into knowledge acquisition, research and analysis organizations employ large sales teams to sell their publications or subscription services widely to ensure a good return on their investment. Marketing costs are in consequence high for research and analysis firms: marketing staff numbers, if not salaries, exceed the number of analysts (Snapp 2013; and as noted in Chapter 7).

Given these economies of scale it can be difficult to set up new firms and difficult for smaller firms to sustain their business. As David Mitchell from Ovum observed:

> lots of 'one man, one dog' firms are setting up and their influence is very different, because very few of them can rely on a syndicated business. Once you have got a syndicated business, you have got predictable cash flow. Great! But until you have built one, you need to live, which means you need to start doing consulting type things to get cash now, which means you don't have the time to spend on building a syndicated or subscription offering (interview, Mitchell).

Arguably no less important than the costs of creating knowledge and marketing it are the *costs of establishing reputation*—and reputation, as we have seen, serves as a proxy for the quality of research and advice provided (Gross & Kieser 2006). Smaller firms face particular problems in establishing and maintaining their brand. Given the non-fungibility of their services, buyers are forced to resort to reputational indicators of past performance in projects. Here small firms are confronted by 'reputation stickiness'. Reputation stickiness refers to the difficulty of transferring reputation from one product or service to another (Greenwood et al. 2005: 664). How can quality of performance be communicated? In particular, how can the success of one project be established in relation to other clients, in different settings and perhaps facing different challenges? Larger organizations in contrast are able to deploy breadth of expertise—demonstrated by a wider portfolio of clients.

The success of the largest (now Big Three) IT industry analyst firms demonstrates the importance of economies of scale. Bigger firms can employ many analysts bringing a broad scope of knowledge which both rests upon and underpins their large client base with technology adopters. This also helps explain the dominance that the largest of these players, Gartner Inc. has achieved. As Figure 2.1 shows, the 2013 revenue of $1.2m per analyst for Gartner was about twice the figure for the nearest rival Forrester. Two related questions follow on from this.

The first question is why, given these economies of scale, the small and medium-sized players continue to exist. Here our analysis has highlighted the intricacy of the market for industry research and analysis. As Noble (2014a) notes, the 'analyst business is a classic "long tail" industry'—there are hundreds of companies which fit the broad definition of 'analyst firm' and there are 'few barriers to entry' (see Anderson 2006). There are now hundreds of so-called new 'upstarts'. This in turn reflects the extended and poorly bounded structure of the IT application and service markets. Analysts must engage with a huge array of technologies and operate over many territories. The Big Three may seek to cover the full range of generic technologies. However, there is still scope for smaller firms to cater for specialized products, technical fields and industrial settings. The market is also segmented in terms of role and by size. As discussed above, (though many players are 'hybrids') small and medium-sized firms play different roles than the larger players. The pronounced economies of scope and scale for the biggest firms are rooted in the substantial costs involved in acquiring a broad knowledge base and developing reputation amongst the whole sector including adopter organizations. Smaller players find advantage in focussing their activities around specific industries/technologies and/or targeting vendors who place less emphasis than technology buyers do on analysts possessing complete knowledge of the market.

Arguably, this is reinforced by the different exigencies surrounding the development of reputational indicators amongst a smaller and more focused community. Informal reputational indicators may be more rapidly circulated and more effective amongst relatively closed circles of industrial vendors, consultants and media players than amongst the large adopter community. For example, trust is less sticky amongst close communities; it can be built up locally from one project and one client to the next. So in contrast to the universalizing discourses of economic analysis (Williamson 1975), we do not find 'a market' for industry research and analysis. Instead, we see diverse 'markets' for industry analyst expertise, conditioned by the exigencies of knowledge creation and its validation.

The pressures towards economies of scale and scope in the industry analyst sector may thus be countered by the scope for *specialization* in a context in which accelerating technological dynamism means that knowledge about IT products and services is becoming ever-more extensive and subject to rapid change. The product of these divergent vectors, coupled with differences between vendor and buy-side needs is an (at least) bi-modal market for analyst expertise. We return to discuss specialization in the next chapter through the notion of 'involution'.

The second question that arises very acutely when we examine Figure 2.1 is why experienced analysts continue to serve as employees, and thus only receive salary and bonuses, which, though high, constitute but a small share of the fees paid by their clients. Why do they not instead opt to trade their expertise as individuals and receive the full benefit? This is a dilemma that besets many kinds of service work, for example architecture (Cohen et al. 2005) in which individual practitioners possess both the requisite expertise and links to previous clients. Such a move might be risky. As industry analyst Phil Fersht observed:

> Many of the analysts in the traditional firms would love to join the boutiques (the CVs flying around are quite numerous), but if they do not have the self-confidence, or the risk-appetite to take a cut in their $175K base pay for a leveraged commission model with equity, then they will stay where they are . . . (posted at Gartner 2010d).[7,8]

Internal specialization within some kinds of research and advisory organization may involve the creation of specialized resources such as databases, facilities for conducting and analyzing surveys, which may mean that the work can only be conducted within an organization (what Transaction Cost Economics describes as asset specificity—one of the key features favouring resort to hierarchy rather than market [Williamson 1975] and by extension, larger firms over boutique players). The division of labour may also fragment the expertise of carrying out, analyzing and interpreting (and marketing) research in ways that might prevent individuals from setting up on their own. This specialization was, for example, a feature of Ovum's traditional methods for producing technical reports, described in Chapter 2, and of conventional market surveys.

However, other factors may push in the opposite direction. In particular, the specific organizational form adopted by Gideon Gartner, as discussed in Chapter 2, departed from the traditional market research model (Berghoff et al. 2012) in various ways, of which two in particular stand out. This was first the decision to employ highly experienced staff and second, the decision to integrate research and analysis into a single process, conducted through the analyst's informal networks of contacts (Chapter 7). As Elias Thomas, Gartner's Senior VP for Research, told us, discussing how he helps Gartner sell its services to clients, 'I am a walking talking product that has got value' (interview, Thomas). Further to this, in Chapter 6, we discussed how Gartner analysts do not work with centralized kinds of information but maintain their own individual 'pods of knowledge'.

Here we note that Gartner trades not just upon generic brand but also on the specific reputations of its expert staff. Individual analysts have their names and brief biographies on public Gartner web pages.[9] This is in contrast to many corporate websites—of the large management consultancies for instance—that seek to conceal the identities and role of individual specialist staff within the organization (Kipping & Clark 2012). Gartner's 'craft' model of expertise, with very little specialization of role, would appear to present few obstacles to staff trading their expertise externally rather than exclusively through the internal labour market.

These features of industry analyst work are reflected in the high level of occupational mobility within the sector. Though we had previously drawn attention to the high costs of developing reputation within the sector, we also saw how Gartner analysts, in advancing their careers within a competitive environment, needed to establish their expert reputation within the firm and the sector. Though our analysis in Chapter 4 emphasized the importance of corporate brand, these observations point to a situation in which individual expertise and reputation 'punches through' the status signifiers conferred by the company brand. We have already examined the ways in which the performance of Gartner analysts is subject to formal ranking and assessment, both within the firm and through the efforts of third party evaluators. Whilst a system of internal controls may operate to improve the authority of the corporate brand, publicly available assessments of individual expertise and influence would seem to reduce the barriers for these reputed analysts to leave big firms like Gartner in order to trade their expertise independently.

There has been discussion within the sector of the scope for experienced industry analysts to leave analyst firms in order to trade their expertise as individuals or in small partnerships. This is exemplified by our respondent Neil Ward Dutton who, having got to a point where his career was unlikely to progress within Ovum, decided to set up with some colleagues as an independent analyst organization. He and his associates brought some client relationships with them but were uncertain whether their personal recognition was enough to establish a sustainable business:

> Well we had a number of relationships absolutely. We had to be pretty careful obviously, it is quite tricky to steal clients . . . but, you know, at the end of the day . . . you build up strong relationships with people, so those carried forward. And the big unknown was, I suppose it boils down to one question, which is, in this game what is more important the brand or the person? Is it more important that we work for Ovum or did we have our own brands as individuals that would carry us forward, not to be millionaires overnight but to sustain us to build up a brand And, we didn't really know, but we tried it anyway. And it turned out that we had enough personal recognition—so that was the big unknown (interview, Ward Dutton)!

The importance of recognition/reputation drives the idea of setting up what some in the sector have described as a 'star analyst' group (Chapter 8). One analyst reflects that to do this you need to: 'hit hard with high quality and name recognition off the back. You need to set the bar high . . . The goal—bring in the top 10% of the analysts in the world together. This is how you command the billing rates. You'll need to retain stars' (Wang 2010).

What is at stake here? Why do analyst firms feel the need to bring together and retain so called 'star analysts'? The emphasis on star analysts underlines the importance of individual reputation (which may be growing with the availability of published reputational indicators). It also brings us back to observations in Chapter 8 about the changing character of analyst expertise. Why does the conception of the expert individual industry analyst appear to be shifting from the more research oriented 'backroom' figures to those who can perform well in front of large audiences? Preda (2009) draws our attention to the 'charismatic' features of expertise as well as commodified knowledge. In such settings, it is not just the experience of the analyst that seems to count but also their character and personality. Amongst the Chartists that Preda discussed, '[p]ersonal authority is combined now with the authority of technical systems' (Preda 2009: 245). This echoes Abbott's observation (1988: 191–2) that 'character retains a surprising foothold in the legitimating structures of many professions'. Here we also found helpful Shapin (2008) who, in invoking Weber's account of charismatic authority, argues that personal 'virtues' are as central as they ever were. He writes (2008: 3–5):

> insofar as late modernity's technoscientific experts are almost wholly professionalized, organized . . . we are tempted to talk straightforwardly about the 'waning of charisma'. There are, however, reasons to reject, or severely to qualify much of this academic common sense about late modern realities. First, while the irrelevance of the personal in scientific knowledge making has been vigorously asserted

at least since the seventeenth century, familiar people and their virtues have always been pertinent to the making, maintenance, transmission, and authority of knowledge.

Shapin describes the world (not so distant from the one set out in this book) of the venture capitalists who have to routinely deal with enormous levels of uncertainty when choosing between (the hundreds of) promising ventures to fund. Shapin (ibid: 270) writes that what these decision makers want just as much as detailed knowledge of the proposed projects is direct knowledge of the entrepreneurs' 'virtues'. In a language highly pertinent to our own case, he writes that where there are 'radical uncertainties' in the spawning of high tech futures, it is in the 'quotidian management of these uncertainties that the personal, the familiar and the charismatic flourish' (Shapin ibid: 270).

10.3. THE CHANGING ECOLOGY OF ANALYST EXPERTISE

10.3.1. Emergence of new models of analysis

This brings us finally to consider how we understand the overarching field of industry analyst expertise and how this may be evolving as a result of changes in the ways in which knowledge is collected, circulated and assessed, underpinned *inter-alia* by new information technologies and organizational forms in the sector.

Gartner continues to grow in terms of income and headcount. In 2013 with an annual revenue of $1.784bn, Gartner was 6 times larger than its nearest rival Forrester (up from 5 times larger in 2010) (Noble 2014). Gartner's public pronouncements suggest that for them it is 'business as usual', emphasizing the scale and scope of Gartner's expertise:

> There are few limits to our information resources and research coverage. Through our powerful client network and global research organization, we are able to see patterns and trends that others don't see. Our size and scale allow us to commit vast resources towards broader and deeper analyst coverage and proven methodologies, and to deliver insight to our clients based on what they need and where they are (post on Gartner website by Daryl Plummer Chief Gartner Fellow).[10]

At the same time, a growing number of voices can be heard suggesting that Gartner's industry analysis model is today facing growing challenges. In particular, though Gartner emerged in a context of information asymmetry, its position may be being eroded in a post-internet world characterized by an overflow of information linked to the growth of social media.

Though analysts lagged behind everyday Facebook users in their uptake of social media, once some early adopters started using them there were strong incentives for analysts to adopt blogs, Twitter, Linked-in and other social media. As a SageCircle webinar observed, 'If there is a conversation happening online, can you afford not to be part of it?' (SageCircle 2009). James Governor drew our attention to the extraordinary rapidity with which analysts have embraced Twitter, with how by 2009 there was already 'about 250 analysts on Twitter' (interview, Governor).

Analyst firms have been experimenting with how best to use these media in a context of few established models. Their uneven success is reflected in a pattern that has been characterized as 'expanding, but lumpy, adoption'.[11] Some analysts have invested particular attention in developing strategies to exploit social media. The fluidity of communication afforded by social media has enabled faster two-way communication between individuals and firms within the ecosystem. James Governor suggests this has allowed a new informal, collective spirit: 'And it is interesting because . . . there has been conversational, collaborative dynamics across different individuals and firms [and] that normally doesn't happen' (interview, Governor).

These developments seem to have been the starting point for a growing discussion within the industry analyst world of the challenges that it may face and of alternative models for the provision of industry analyst expertise. As a post on Gideon Gartner's blog by Jonathan Yarmis, former vice president of Gartner, warns, Gartner may become less relevant as just one voice in a cacophony: 'We used to have too little information. Then, Gartner could be king, as the one place you could go to reliably find an answer. Now we have too much information and Gartner is just another voice in that cacophony. Even worse, it's a voice that can't be found by Google' (Yarmis 2011).

We see suggestions emerging within Gartner of how new technologies could be applied within the firm's existing *modus operandii*, for example that Gartner might exploit the potential of internet-based communications to improve the operation of its knowledge networking. Thus Gartner analyst Di Maio (2009) proposes that Gartner might, in this way, use its client-base as a 'peer community'.

Other industry analysts outside the big firms such as Gartner have also been exploring the implications of the internet for their activities. Members of a small industry analyst operation came to realize the potential value of social media in not only disseminating their work but also subjecting it to wider scrutiny. James Governor, CEO Red Monk, discovered, after they started blogging, that 'the internet is a really aggressive peer reviewer' (interview, Governor). This formed the basis for what became Red Monk's *open source analysis model*: 'We decided, wait, let's externalize this, and let the outside world decide what's a good idea, and where the bugs are, and what we have got wrong, and check our facts' (interview, Governor).

Others reported similar experiences. Neil Ward Dutton, Co-founder and Research Director of the small firm MWD Analysis described how he had put up a blog opposing a Gartner naming intervention (the neologism: 'Software Oriented Architecture 2.0' that had a few months earlier been proposed by Gartner together with Oracle) that he considered unhelpful. He was encouraged by initial responses to post it as a petition. He told us 'within very short order we got something like 500 signatures, including people from Oracle, interestingly, including people from all across the industry'. This had important lessons for him: 'I suppose it tells us a couple of things: small companies can be influential; I think the nature of the debate is changing, the way the web kind of changes the nature of the debate as well, I think is quite interesting' (interview, Ward Dutton).

The 2002 formation of Red Monk and the subsequent success of this and other blog-based providers was seen as 'shaking up' industry research and analysis (Greenemeier 2006). Red Monk, which has as its strapline (a reworking of Abraham Lincoln's famous phrase), 'analysis for the people, by the people', describes itself as open source on the basis that it shares its reports for free. However, it and other blog-based analysts use the linkages and reputation established by circulating these reports as a basis for selling more traditional advisory services—typically to vendors but also potentially to technology buyers. Thus, Neil Ward Dutton observed:

> all the research we published was free . . . we have got a community now of about two and a half thousand people who read the stuff regularly. What we have started to do is to build a platform where we can make a much more significant part of our money from the buyer side, from the demand side (interview, Ward Dutton).

The use of blogging and social media—'a medium that facilitates interaction and commentary' (O'Grady 2006)—is seen as at the heart of this model. Stephen O'Grady, another of the founders of the open source analyst firm Red Monk, discusses the advantages of this new model. He presents this openness to external comment (and the resort to the 'wisdom of the crowd') as a way to combat the risk that analysts will be unduly influenced by their supply side customers. The open analyst model is presented as having benefits over conventional industry analysis in terms of both the quality of the advice and the reliance that can be placed on the advisor. O'Grady (2006) notes: 'ask yourself whether you'd like to work with analysts whose research has been disseminated and dissected in a very public fashion, or that which is conducted and published behind closed doors'.

O'Grady further draws attention to the influence exercised by blogs—influence which has been achieved through, and can be demonstrated by, their high ranking in Google searches (O'Grady 2006). However, elsewhere he also acknowledges the difficulties small players like Red Monk face in achieving credibility when much of their income comes from vendors. 'Frankly, we haven't achieved a high level of credibility among end users' (O'Grady, cited in Greenemeier 2006). Nevertheless, technology bloggers have been highly successful. For example former Forrester industry analyst Ray Wang can claim that his insights are widely drawn upon, as evidenced not only by multiple consultancy roles and speaking invitations but also by '10s of millions of page views a year'.[12]

In these pronouncements, an alternative model of expertise is being mapped out that (more or less explicitly) challenges the established position of the large industry analysts such as Gartner, whose authority is rooted in their ability to collect information from their wide array of contacts (especially amongst adopter organizations) and the methods by which their conclusions are generated and tested (subjected to internal review or review at their conferences). The new model differs sharply both in terms of how knowledge will be accumulated and outputs will be assessed. Some commentators suggest that this 'new breed' of blog-based IT analysts will present a challenge to traditional IT research and advisory firms (Greenemeier 2006). Rather than seek to find one firm that can meet all their needs, vendors and other industry research users may seek to identify various individual analysts and smaller outfits best suited to provide particular kinds of support (Gartner 2010c, d, Chapple 2014).

Gideon Gartner having retired from the firm he founded and now maintaining critical distance, has contributed to discussion of the future of the industry analyst sector,[13] suggesting for example that Gartner Inc. might wish to constitute peer panels with external experts to advise its work. He also highlighted weaknesses with the reward model used by large industry analyst firms who charge clients standard annual subscriptions, whatever the quantity and quality of research actually delivered. He flagged the possibility of moving to a more complex reward mechanism, based on the complex market for investment analyst expertise that would allow multiple sources of advice to be exploited with rewards being based on the calculated value analysts are seen to have delivered (Gartner 2010c, 2010d).

The large firms do *not* appear to be panicking, however—partly because their influence in the market does not immediately seem to be threatened. Gartner Inc. continues to point to its breadth of expertise that exceeds smaller advisories by 50 to 1 (Gartner 2010d). The growth of social media, as far as we are aware, has not displaced the client telephone calls through which Gartner analysts continue to conduct their research in the course of providing personalized advice. Moreover, the rapid collation of community information through blogs and tweets produces knowledge that is relatively 'unfiltered'. This knowledge has different affordances to, and does not displace, the carefully produced, authoritative formal outputs of the major analyst organizations (Greenemeier 2006, SageCircle 2009). A 2008 study of

'All The Analysts' shows the Big Three (Gartner, Forrester and IDC) as still accounting for two thirds of total web page views (ATA 2008). The established players still exercise influence. As David Mitchell, Research Director, Ovum Research, observed:

> . . . in the current economic climate . . . a few of the vendors are becoming less keen on some of the smaller firms. For example, I was talking to one of the larger vendors who said, we used to worry about what the little guys were writing on the blog sites and the MD would come down and scream when one of the small firms had written something nasty about us. We have really stopped caring because it does not affect any of the deals. It might affect thought patterns for the future but we can tackle that with marketing siege guns in the future. It doesn't affect the dollar of the deal now. Then we are not as interested as we were. So I think some of that social media gloss is fracturing a bit (interview, Mitchell).

The plethora of voices may seem to redress the asymmetry of information but still leaves unanswered questions about which knowledge can be relied on. This situation was described by Steve Pozgaj, former technology vendor Chief Information Officer (cited in Greenemeier 2006), 'Today, there's an abundance of data, but there's a dearth of information'.

The established players in the industry analysis market have considerable resources. They are adapting to take on board some elements of these new models. For example Forrester launched an online 'leadership board peer network' in 2003 as well as various blog pages (Greenemeier 2006). Competitor analyst organizations have followed suit. However, they have tended to develop what others have described critically as 'walled gardens' or 'gated communities', only available to clients of those firms.[14] At this point in time, the outcomes of this contestation over the future of industry analysis are by no means clear. Another development that may influence the further evolution of the research and advisory sector is the emergence and increasing influence of 'analyst relations' specialists.

10.3.2. Analyst relations: An emergent body of expertise on expertise

We have already touched upon the competing exigencies that give an (at least) bimodal structure to the market for industry analysts. Technology adopters will tend to rely on the larger research and advisory firms that are able to deploy the breadth of expertise needed to keep abreast of the full range of potentially relevant solutions; vendors, however, may find advantage in the existence of a more diverse expertise ecosystem with space for a wider range of voices. In addition the emergence of new technologies and organizational models, based upon the use of the internet and especially blogging and micro-blogs tweets linking peer communities, provided an alternative infrastructure to the large analyst firm for collecting, organizing and validating community opinion. As a result, as one active analyst relations blogger suggests: '[two distinct analyst firm business models are arising: one which only works with scale, and the other which is immune to competition from the large firms' (Chapple 2014a). The latter involves a wider array of smaller boutique and 'upstart' analyst operations.

If the industry analysis sector is not just big firms such as Gartner but includes many smaller players, how are their customers able to make choices about where to obtain research and advice? Vendors, in particular, may need to exercise 'choice in the analysts' ecosystem' (interview, Ward Dutton). This raises questions about where to source this knowledge—that is, which analysts to turn to. We saw in Chapter 4 how the reputation and brand of the major analyst firms provided a means to resolve questions about the quality of expert advice. How might reputational indicators like this work where there are large numbers of smaller analyst outfits catering for particular vendor needs (competing based on price or specialist services). This seems to have reopened the question about how to choose between analysts firms, particularly in a highly competitive context, which has perhaps forced technology vendors to look more carefully at where best to invest their limited budgets for research and marketing.

The abundance of information and opinion does not resolve the expertise problem. Paradoxically it creates new scarcities for the knowledge user in terms of the time and expertise needed to sift and sort between these myriad competing sources of advice (Anderson 2006). It is in this context that we see the coming together of various specialists offering advice, in particular to vendor organizations, on how to navigate the industry analysis space. This perhaps involves advising on which industry analysts they should work with in terms of how they may project their offerings into the market and what might be the most successful strategy for engaging with and influencing industry analysts and other commercially important players.

Members of this heterogeneous group have begun to present themselves as a distinct community of 'analyst relations' specialists and have embarked on a strategy of professionalization. Analyst relations involves a rather heterogeneous array. It encompasses staff employed by vendors (perhaps in their marketing functions) and public relations firms to advise on how to interact with industry analysts as well as a number of independent analyst relations consultants and small 'boutique' firms. Some of the analyst relations firms active today, including their geographical reach, are shown in Table 10.1.

Analyst relations specialists have begun to claim to have the expertise and techniques needed to understand the structure, dynamics and methods of the industry analyst sector and to help vendors make such choices. Thus, in the IIAR paper *Who Are the Analysts*, Dennington and Leforestier (2013: 1) observe, analyst relations professionals 'understand where the value is to be

Table 10.1. Some of the main analyst relations consultants in 2014[15]

US	European
Analyst Strategy Group	AnalystClix
AR Insights	Magnolia
Knowledge Capital Group	SmartCircle
Spotlight AR	
Kea Company	
The Skills Connection	

had from which analysts, to be selective about which analysts to use where, and to ensure that all parties involved get maximum value from analyst interactions'. The main activities undertaken by analyst relations specialists are of two sorts. First, they provide briefings and advice to vendors on how best to present their offerings most effectively to analyst firms. Second they develop tools to advise research users (especially vendors) upon which analysts to focus their attention on.

10.3.3. How to present offerings to analyst firms

Vendors often face difficulties in presenting the qualities of their new offerings to industry analysts and other opinion shapers. These difficulties may be particularly acute where a product differs significantly from existing applications in terms perhaps of its technical features or of the business challenges that it addresses. Analyst relations specialists observe that those involved in technology development tend to highlight technical features and have more difficulty conveying the business case for a new product. Analyst relations specialists thus coach and mentor marketing and technology development staff on how to conduct product briefings or 'pitches' to industry analysts. This is partly a question of ensuring that the information the analyst requests is provided—that the forms are filled in correctly, that the briefing runs on time etc.. Ex-Gartner analyst and Managing Director of The Skills Connection, Simon Levin explains:

> Gartner have created an industry of jobs for people just to respond to assessments, just to do all of that logistics. But that's only the logistics, because at the end of the day what you put in [the Gartner forms] could be complete crap, and in many cases it is complete crap. But what I've managed to do is get it together and get it to Gartner on time, that's what most analyst relations do. Now that's not what we do because we think it's pointless getting it all together on time and then sending in something that isn't actually the right information in the right format that's going to help tell your story. All you've done otherwise is spend lots of people's time with no likelihood of getting any different result (interview, Levin).

As he points out, it is not just a matter of providing data to these firms it is also a question of understanding the analyst's perspective:

> So we concentrate on content, we act like the analysts, like a pre-filter. We say [to the vendor], give us the information, we'll tell you what information to give us, don't give us any of that stuff, don't waste time on any of that because it's a complete waste of time, we don't care about it, just give me these things, give me facts, don't give me lots of marketing. And then we put that into the response for [the vendor] so that what they're giving the analyst is something that the analyst can actually use and is more likely to get a decent result (interview, Levin).

Here analyst relations specialists draw on their understanding and often direct experience of the culture and practices of industry analyst firms to achieve 'recipient design' i.e., to craft their messages in a way that will increase the likelihood they are understood and acted upon. Jonny Bentwood described a notable example where they were trying to encourage Gartner to create a Magic Quadrant in a new technological area. Bentwood understood Gartner's internal processes for creating a Magic Quadrant. As we saw in Chapter 9, this includes establishing that there is a market with enough players for Gartner's work of assessment to be pertinent to clients. Bentwood therefore liaised with other vendors to ensure that they would be able to meet the requisite criteria in terms of number of vendors and revenue volumes:

> We knew that for it to become a Magic Quadrant in its own right I had to have a certain amount of revenue within it, I had to have a certain number of vendors competing within it, lots of different scenarios. So we made sure that we actually had all these facts to hand and say look, this is not a Market Scope, it is a [Magic] Quadrant, it is this part of the technology cycle. And it worked. They actually developed a new way of looking at things (interview, Bentwood).

It does not seem to be the case that analyst relations players can influence analysts directly. However, they can change the dynamics of influence. As Bentwood modestly observes, when he did manage to change Gartner's assessments, 'I must admit that I had help from some hefty vendors behind me who were trying to push it, so it wasn't all thanks to me, but there was part of the process of trying say no this is what we need to do to make sure that Gartner recognize this as an area' (interview, Bentwood).

10.3.4. Identifying which analysts to target

Vendors are concerned to identify the individuals and organizations that can best influence technology adoption decisions. This may be directly through their links to technology buyers, or indirectly through their reach through direct engagement or media coverage to players in the field and their perceived

Figure 10.2. Industry analysts and analyst relations experts network at an event
Source: Thom Erbé from KeaCompany[16]

cognitive authority. Although the larger analyst firms may operate across many industries and application areas, others may only be reputed for their expertise over particular segments. Personal familiarity and networking appear a dominant resource in this community (Simakova 2013). The work of analyst relations experts appears primarily concerned with mining and exploiting professional contacts and the informal channels within the analyst bodies to create the space and occasion for interaction (see Figure 10.2). They explained to us how, in their work, they seek to foster a more pro-active approach. Thus preparation for a vendor briefing may start 6 months ahead of the meeting. These actors frequently meet with industry analysts for a briefing or informally over lunch or at an event where they can quiz rankers on the characteristics of their evaluations. These meetings provide valuable information that helps in the compilation of 'tiering strategies': lists that sort and prioritize rankers according to perceived importance and influence, and which are then used to direct resources (i.e. the experts pay more attention to those at the top as compared to those at the bottom).

Here analyst relations specialists have begun to monitor analyst firms and individuals. For example, the 'Analyst Value Survey' has been conducted since 2000. It examines the opinions of various players (analyst relations specialists, industry analysts, vendor staff and others) and addresses various factors but focuses in particular on the *influence* exerted by industry analysts. This is particularly their influence over technology buyers (Hopkins & England

2012, Dennington & Leforestier 2013) but also on IT investors and on trade journalists, etc.[17] One of the authors of the Analyst Value Survey, Duncan Chapple at KeaCompany, told us why they conduct the survey:

> I think one of the key reasons is, I believe most analysts relations effort is wasted and I think most of it is wasted because people are under-allocating efforts on influential analysts [and] much of that is because of a lack of understanding... So what I like about diagrams [from the Analyst Value Survey] is that they are used really widely. I was talking to a client recently to a $8bn IT services firm, their CEO did a presentation to their 100 top managers and they used pie-charts on the diagram in the presentation in order to help them to develop a common picture of which analysts were reporting them and how they were seen by analysts. That's really potent because there isn't wide understanding of the analysts, not wide accurate understanding (interview, Chapple).

It is common practice amongst analyst relations professionals to collect, present and increasingly 'sell' such data. Indeed a market for this new kind of knowledge is being established. Certain analyst relations groups have begun to set up independent 'agencies' and 'consultancies' and to make available their experience on a more commodified basis, leading to the creation of a market for supplementary knowledge-based products related to the management of industry analysts. Initially this involved simply collating information about rankings like the Magic Quadrant but today includes the codification of specialist knowledge and its communication, through to the production of guides and practitioner handbooks, seminars and workshops. It also includes such assessments as 'rankings of the rankers' (see Figure 10.3).

10.3.5. Constitution of analyst relations as a new form of expertise

The idea of constituting analyst relations as a new form of expertise emerged early in the new millennium (though there had been awareness since the late 1990s that this was a role that needed to be fulfilled). Jonny Bentwood, Head of Analyst Relations for the public relations firm Edelman describes how, around 2005, 'a group of analyst relations pros got together to form the Institute of Industry Analyst Relations—IIAR'.

> people on the vendor side of things... and people on the agency side got together and had a chat.... And that is when people started taking it as a group, a small clique of people who like getting together to have a chat to actually trying to be an industry body and trying to create a profession out of it (interview, Bentwood).

The proliferation of small firms and individual consultants in the analyst relations field undermines the scope to resort to brand and other reputational indicators of quality of expertise. Many of the analyst relations specialists are,

Figure 10.3. The Analyst Value Survey
Source: Author photograph (NP)

moreover, employees (of vendors and public relations/marketing firms) so are not able to trade their expertise in external knowledge markets. They need to find other ways to valorize their knowledge and skills. As Jonny Bentwood explained:

> One of the problems that [analyst relations] has is that the only people who really understand it are the people doing the job all the time. So we come across a problem which is how do you persuade your own bosses that your job is important and how do you persuade people who aren't on the agency side but are in the vendor side that they need their budget to carry on doing the work. And so a lot of it came about because we needed to show that our job was important (interview, Bentwood).

Bentwood, Levin and Chapple (whose comments we discussed above) went on to become founders and Directors of the IIAR. This community would appear to be pursuing a more traditional professionalization strategy based for example on upon skill development, training and certification (see Figure 10.4).

Figure 10.4. An analyst relations workshop where the topic of 'certification' is being discussed

Source: Author photograph (NP)

A particular role seems to have been played by blogging over the last decade. Indeed a key factor in pulling together the diverse players who today are described as the analyst relations community has been online exchanges around an interlinked set of blog postings. Thus the IIAR website[18] lists a number of blogs that its members operate: Analyst Equity (now called Influencer Relations), Analyst Insight, ARcade, KCG (Knowledge Capital Group), SageCircle and Technobabble 2.0. Several of these specialists are also experimenting with technology to rank influential industry analysts. Another development that has become particularly important in the context of multiple industry analyst firms is 'search' (Stark 2011). This is the process to find the industry analysts who actually count or make a difference in a particular product or service area which entails efforts to estimate the influence of an industry analyst either in absolute terms or relative to others. This includes making use of new, widely available online influence measurement tools (Klout, PeerIndex, Kred etc.) and in a few cases some of these people are going as far as to develop their own versions of these technologies. Jonny Bentwood from Edelman, for instance, has developed 'TweetLevel' and 'BlogLevel' which produce an automatic score based on a variety of criteria related to the popularity of various industry analysts. TweetLevel, for instance, on the day when we tried it, awarded the Magic Quadrant a score of '300' in terms of its influence and its main rival, the Forrester Wave, a '40'. These influence measurement tools are becoming increasingly popular (Gerlitz 2012), but it is far from clear how they will become integrated into practice.

10.4. CONCLUSION: ECOLOGIES OF KNOWLEDGE

How may we understand the distinctive structure of the industry analysis sector? Much writing from Economics and Business Studies has (unhelpfully, we suggest) taken as a starting point the 'firm' as an economic actor and theorized its operation within an impersonal market in terms of price/efficiency factors. However the economic 'theory of the firm' (Coase 1937) explains the formation and size of firms as a function of efficiency and the relative costs of resorting to the market or to the organization (hierarchy). In general the market is seen as a more efficient coordination mechanism—the resort to organizations arises because 'there is a cost of using the price mechanism' (Coase 1937: 390). This includes for example the costs associated with price discovery, marketing, contract negotiation and enforcement (as has been explored in more detail by Transaction Cost Economics [TCE] [Williamson 1975, 1991]). Firms can exploit economies of scale in production and in marketing; however, these may be offset as the size of the organization increases by growing inefficiencies in resource deployment and costs of avoiding and repairing error (Coase 1937). This framework would seem to provide an effective explanation for the emergence and increasing market dominance of the large industry analyst firms such as Gartner. Nevertheless, it leaves under-explained some of the current developments including the continued presence of smaller players in the field. These are not effectively explained by these 'economic functionalist' arguments in terms of the respective economic efficiencies and inefficiencies of smaller and larger firms. TCE does go on to address the emergence, in highly uncertain markets, of inter-firm relationships and other phenomena that go beyond the market-hierarchy dichotomy but does this by constructing a residual category of 'hybrid' economic governance structures (Husman 2003, Ménard 2011). These are particularly a feature of markets for informational products such as software or advisory services (Fincham et al. 1994, Miller et al. 2006). Our analysis has highlighted how expertise may be embodied (simultaneously) in individuals, organizations and networks. Fleck (1998) introduced the concept of the 'tradeability of expertise' to examine the social distribution and utilization of expertise. This, as we have seen, may take place within organizations (i.e. through internal labour markets) or externally through wider labour markets or product/service markets. Expertise cannot thus be understood simply in relation to firms or to markets.

Here we turn to the rich conceptual model that Abbott (2005) has produced for analyzing professional work based around the concept of 'ecology'. The metaphor of ecology has also been applied with much the same analytic purposes by writers from our own field of Science and Technology Studies as a means to understand how science as a form of social practice can be achieved successfully amongst heterogeneous distributed communities. Thus Star and Griesemer (1989) characterize science as an *institutional ecology* involving coordination amongst heterogeneous actors, differing in their institutional insertion and knowledges. The purpose of 'the ecological analysis is anti-reductionist in that the unit of analysis is the whole enterprise' (p. 389) rather than foregrounding any particular stakeholder. Star's (1995: 2) later concept of 'ecology of knowledge' similarly emphasizes the 'complex interdependencies' between scientific practice, knowledge and social organization.

Fujimura (1995: 304) applies the concept of ecologies to emphasize the complexity and contingency of knowledge production across multiple sites. This is offered as an alternative to the 'warlike' accounts offered by Actor-Network Theory (ANT) that revolve around goal oriented individuals able to colonize other worlds, discipline other actors and stabilize linkages.[19] Drawing upon this, Akera (2007) builds a complex model to represent what he describes as 'ecologies of knowledge' in order to study the dynamic relationships between knowledge, its material infrastructure and social institutions. In place of the 'flat' ontologies of ANT, which focus on the constitution of networks by a narrow range of entities and overlook historical antecedents, Akera proposes a layered schema that emphasizes the relations of connection but partial disassociation between diverse constituents. Thus he argues 'there can be no profession of bookkeepers without the knowledge, skills, and instruments with which they ply their trade ... Nor could the profession exist apart from the financial institutions and the historical development of mercantile and industrial capitalism' (Akera 2007: 418).

10.4.1. The field of industry analysts as a knowledge ecology

Abbott's concept of linked ecologies would seem to apply readily to the industry analyst sector as an analytical framework. This sector cannot effectively be understood simply as an array of firms operating independently within an impersonal market. Instead we have shown that it is constituted by an intricate web of relations linking individuals, formal groups within (technology vendor, adopter and analyst) organizations and informal networks. The role of particular individual and organizational actors has to be understood in the context of these multiple relations. And as we saw in Chapters 7/8, the production of key industry analysis knowledge outputs such as Gartner's Magic Quadrant is conditioned by a complex set of inter-locking interests and relationships between vendor, analyst and user organiza-tions, each of whom (as the actors themselves recognize) may be playing sharply different games. These features in turn underpin the paradoxical features of analyst knowledge identified in Chapter 7 (for example that it is both widely contested and exerts considerable influence).

Industry analysis expertise thus arises within an ecology. Here Abbott (2005: 249) reminds us that 'no social world ever exists without a pre-existing topology of some sort'. And the industry analysis ecology is by no means an undifferentiated 'flat' space. Instead, it has its own very distinctive topology, characterized by multiple asymmetrical relations between the various classes of player (different groups of analyst organization, technology buyers, tech-nology vendors, and most recently analyst relations experts).

In Chapter 4, we discussed the paradox that the emergence of a market for complex (enterprise systems) technologies in turn creates the basis for the emergence of a new body of specialized technical expertise—that became known as industry analysts. But this in turns provokes a further regression, opening up questions about who are the right experts that particular firms should employ. Juvenal's ancient dictum *Quis custodiet ipsos custodies?* be-comes *who assesses the assessors?* or in this case, *who analyses the analysts?* We saw how in the case of business knowledge, questions about the quality of expert advice were resolved not through a traditional professionalization model but through reputation and the brand of the analyst firm. This worked well enough when Gartner and a handful of other players dominated the world. Still the asymmetrical distribution of knowledge that Gartner traded upon continues to attract new entrants and encompasses players differing both in size and position within the field. New organizational models have emerged for collecting and validating evidence. This seems to have reopened the question of which analyst firms should one turn to, particularly in relation to technology vendors where in a context of financial crisis they are perhaps under pressure to look more carefully at where limited marketing funds are invested.

A group of actors—analyst relations specialists—arising within the industry analyst ecology have constituted themselves as experts in exercising choice between analysts. By circulating measures of the performance (especially market influence) of analyst organizations and individuals, they are helping transform the setting in which industry analysts operate, helping to change the way their knowledge is leveraged. Analyst relations experts suggest their knowledge can help research users to 'refine' how they use industry analysts' expertise, targeting particular firms and individuals (Chapple 2014).

This analysis points to continued knowledge asymmetries in a burgeoning IT market, which are only partially allayed by the development of this new expert group. We see the emergence of new distinctions. A salient feature is the classification and ranking by analyst relations experts of industry analyst organizations in terms of their (direct) adopter and (indirect) media influence. Thus, as we saw, KCG's *Mystical Box Chart* positions analysts into four classes: Deal Makers and Breakers, Point Players, Talking Heads, Consultants and Wannabees (Hopkins & England 2012) (see Figure 10.1). In the same way that the Magic Quadrant helped define the properties of technologies and their suppliers (see Chapter 7), these rankings help users of industry research and advisory firms—and especially vendors—make new distinctions. The rankings give form to properties (exposure and influence) and relative positions that had not hitherto been defined. The proliferation of smaller analyst firms creates an opportunity for ecosystem players with requisite experience, knowledge and tools to make distinctions within the field of analysts; it also creates an incentive make these distinctions. Individuals and groups with experience seek to enhance this expertise by elaborating specialist information resources and methodologies. This allows them to trade upon their expertise—to enhance their status and perceived value with their organization or to trade this on the market.

We conclude this reflection by observing that business knowledge is not knowledge from nowhere but is conditioned by the point of insertion of knowledge producer and knowledge consumer into the ecosystem and the incentives and penalties that they consequently face. However, these players, in developing and trading their expert knowledge, are also involved in the creation and reworking of this system of linked ecologies. In this way, our analysis charts the emergence and continued elaboration of an increasingly intricate knowledge infrastructure of the IT applications market.

NOTES

1. We also examined, in Chapter 4, why a market model of expertise was selected rather than other possible mechanisms for assessing and disciplining expertise. For example the Sociology of Professions (Abbott 1988) had highlighted how medics and similar technical specialists had developed professional bodies to provide a mechanism to ensure professional performance and avoid opportunistic behaviour by experts which protect the expert from undue influence by powerful clients.

2. And some analysts, like Gartner, place limits on the level of income from vendors and associated constraints (e.g. confidentiality clauses) on their operations.

3. Here we see a somewhat different notion of 'independence', in this context 'based primarily on the fact that they have an external view and so are not hampered by the internal perspectives, structures and politics of a given vendor or end-user business' (Dennington & Leforestier 2013: 5).

4. Abbott (2005) explains how he reaches this conclusion from his efforts to analyse the expertise of university academics. 'The university ecology thus requires that we

generalize the image of ecology implicit in the "system of profession". It forces us to see that professional jurisdiction is only one type of location and that the topologies of other ecologies may be more overlapping and cross-cutting' (Abbott 2005: 251). In this Abbott argues the need to 'replace the "audience" concept (from the analysis of professions given at the outset) with the notion of "linked ecologies", it is important to say something about the audiences for the university ecology. In the professional ecology, it is fairly clear who are the actors and who are the audiences for actors' claims: the professions on the one hand; the workplace, public, and state on the other. But in the university ecology, it is not clear exactly where the ecology ends and the audiences of the various claims within it begin' (Abbott 2005: 250).

5. Thus the SageCircle Blog which was established as a forum for 'Analyst Relations News and Views Category Archives' has a category of Industry Analyst Ecosystem News. See '2009 the year that was in the analyst ecosystem'. Available online at: http://sagecircle.wordpress.com/2009/12/10/2009-the-year-that-was-in-the-analyst-ecosystem Posted 10 December 2009 by SageCircle. Accessed 19 March 2014. Another analyst relations blog network, bramweerts.com also has posts under this category (http://bramweerts.com/category/industry-analyst-ecosystem-news/. Accessed 29 November 2014.

6. Thanks to The Knowledge Capital Group for permission to reproduce this diagram.

7. Comment by Phil Fersht, posted 1 July 2010 on Gideon Gartner's blog (Gartner 2010d). Accessed 22 January 2015.

8. The professionals involved may be required to sign agreements not to exploit these links and set up in competition to their employers. Such agreements, however, may be hard to enforce. Indeed their very existence highlights the difficulty in preventing such moves. In the case of Gartner, the sensitivity of information that analysts elicit from vendors and clients mean that particular emphasis is paid when an analyst leaves to enforcing the Confidentiality Agreement that all employees are required to sign (Erskine 2014). As Gartner VP Christian Byrnes observes (cited in Chapple 2014b), 'every employee of Gartner is subject to our Confidentiality Agreement. And, in the case of analysts, we are very aware of the trust given to us by vendor clients during inquiries, SAS and briefings. As such, analysts are trained in the proper handling of such information. When an analyst leaves Gartner, they are reminded of that fact and they must acknowledge that they understand that their responsibility concerning confidentiality goes with them. This even includes when analysts retire. I realize that this is a very sensitive issue for any client who has entrusted Gartner with its strategic plans. You should know that this is something that we take very seriously at the highest levels of the company'.

9. Analyst profiles for Gartner Analysts include a brief description of 'Roles and Responsibilities', the areas they cover, a note of how many years' experience they have at Gartner and the IT industry and even a photograph. http://www.gartner.com/analysts/name. Accessed 1 December 2014.

10. http://www.gartner.com/technology/research/methodologies/reach_resources.jsp. Accessed 19 March 2014.

11. '2009 the year that was in the analyst ecosystem' http://sagecircle.wordpress. com/2009/12/10/2009-the-year-that-was-in-the-analyst-ecosystem Posted 10th December 2009 by SageCircle. Accessed 19 March 2014.

12. http://blog.softwareinsider.org/r-ray-wang/. Accessed 2 December 2014.

13. http://analystinsight.blogspot.co.uk/2009/12/gideon-gartner-on-future-of-industry.html Video: Gideon Gartner on the Future of the industry analyst. Posted 4 December 2009. Accessed 19 March 2015.

14. SageCircle blog: Looking ahead to 2010: Forrester or Gartner launch a client-only social network. https://sagecircle.wordpress.com/2009/12/28/forrester-or-gartner-launch-a-client-only-social-network/ /Posted on 28 December 2009 by SageCircle. Accessed 21 July 2015.

15. Source: Personal communication from Duncan Chapple, Influencer Relations 3 December 2014.

16. Thanks to Thom Erbé for giving us permission to use this photo here.

17. The Analyst Value Survey was conducted by The Kea Company till 2014 when it was taken over by Influence Relations. http://www.keacompany. com/capabilities/analyst-relations-measurement/analyst-value-survey/. Accessed 3 December 2014.

18. http://analystrelations.org/about/. Accessed 4 December 2014.

19. Thus Fujimura (1995: 334–5) offers an alternative to Latour's (1987) idea that scientists make their laboratory a 'centre of authority' (e.g. an 'obligatory passage point') by emphasizing distributed centres of authority, that allows for 'contingent articulations of . . . research at different sites'.

11

From IT Markets to the Sociology of Business Knowledge

The intellectual challenge identified in this book has been to deepen our understanding of the shaping of the digital future. Economists (Fransman 2010) have pioneered the study of information technology (IT) markets. More recently, institutionalist organizational theorists have studied the 'organizing visions' (Swanson & Ramiller 1997, Ramiller & Swanson 2003, Currie 2004) or 'managerial fads and fashions' (Abrahamson 1991, 1996, Newell et al. 2001, Baskerville & Myers 2009, Hirschheim et al. 2012) that herald in wider technological and market change. However, these broad-brush approaches do not adequately engage with the detailed processes involved. We have attempted to bring the rather 'abstract' (Callon & Muniesa 2005) study of information technology markets down to earth, by grounding it in the knowledge, practices and artefacts of particular groups of market intermediaries known as 'industry analysts'. Industry analysts have arisen in response to uncertainty in the marketplace, uncertainties brought about by rapid changes in technology, but also latterly by their own role in this increasingly complex knowledge ecology.

Industry analysts have made their mark on the digital economy in ways that few outside the immediate domain have thus far recognized or acknowledged. Indeed their work and influence seems to have gone largely un-noticed by academics and others. The remarkable aspect about the rise of this body of expertise is not only the degree of authority these people now wield over technological selection and innovation but how quickly they have established this authority and on what it seems to rest. We have developed a number of insights into their growth and influence. This chapter reviews and brings together the three themes that run though the book.

The first concerns the *influence* of industry analysts addressed through detailed empirical examination of how they go about shaping IT markets. We have sought to understand how industry analysts pattern the selection and procurement of technology solutions and, consequently, how they influence the offerings of technology vendors. Whilst industry analysts are by no means the only source of influence on technology adopters, their knowledge outputs do appear able to push technology adoption decisions towards certain vendor products and away from others. As a result, responding to the proliferation of industry analysts is amongst the most pressing challenges facing technology vendors today. Few aspects of the work of technology vendors today remain untouched by potent analyst reputational and performance indices of one form or another. Industry analysts create new problems for technology vendors as being positioned below a rival, or where they fail to appear on a significant measure, can directly affect their standing. They thus have no choice but to take industry analysts seriously.

The second theme has been the emergence of industry analysts as a new form of *expertise*. We have painted a picture of the life of the industry analyst, and described the specialists who hold and exercise this technical knowledge, and the organizations in which they work and from which their knowledge products develop. The analyst's ability to publish a vendor ranking, to make a technology prediction, to classify a new emerging trend etc., depends upon gathering and interpreting large amounts of data. These experts have developed the capacity to make sense of and present that information. That industry analysts exercise considerable autonomy in the way they go about their activities, does not mean that their work is not also shaped by the contexts in which they are located. We have been interested in the various constraints and restrictions industry analysts encounter. Here we have sought to capture the rise of this new and quite distinctive 'knowledge infrastructure', or what Knorr Cetina (1999) calls 'machineries of knowing', that can pattern and shape the work of these experts.

We have investigated primarily, but not solely, the leadership role of the research organization Gartner Inc. Gartner is the acknowledged frontrunner in this young industry, having shaped it over several decades through a number of consequential innovations. Chapter 2 described the 'ten innovations' instigated by Gartner's founder in the early 1990s. We have sought to track these innovations historically and contemporarily to understand how they have shaped Gartner's distinctive machinery of knowing. What is striking about these innovations is that they played a central role in the initial constitution of this expertise and, although modified and translated substantially over the subsequent years, continue to have importance today. These innovations provide the fulcrum for many of our chapters and in this final discussion we take the opportunity to say something about the ideas that sit behind them.

The final theme we explore in this concluding chapter is what our discussion of these experts might tell us about how the *performativity programme* (Callon 1998, 2007) might be extended to new contexts such as IT markets. With the increasing market-based provision of business knowledge, this exercise has also thrown light on how we might understand the difficulties of trading and verifying industry analyst knowledge. We make some tentative suggestions with regard to both these aspects through pointing towards a possible *Sociology of Business Knowledge*.

11.1. DO INDUSTRY ANALYSTS DIRECT MARKETS?

What does our empirical examination of industrial analysts contribute to a sociological understanding of the shaping of IT markets? One danger of ignoring the knowledge practices of these experts is that we tend to assume their outputs and actions are 'monolithic' or that they construct their research in 'isolation' from others. The book has attempted to describe how Gartner shapes the market in a variety of ways—not just directly and not always with full forethought but also indirectly as a consequence of their many interactions with market players. We note how industry analysts are not external, but part of and connected to market practices. We draw attention to a series of looping effects between industry analyst knowledge of the market and the market itself. However, whilst we have used well-worn metaphors like 'holding the ropes' and 'setting the rules of the game' to describe their influence, we have also been careful to pay attention to the limitations of this expertise and how it is constantly being reworked in the effort to retain cognitive authority.

11.1.1. From disinterested research to active intervention

It is widely thought that Gartner's role is to help consumers make decisions through 'describing' the market, as their research material puts it (Gartner Inc. 2015). Industry analyst outputs tend not to be purely descriptive, however. Our observations suggest that Gartner regularly moves from the descriptive to the imperative. Gideon Gartner's decision to extend his firm's offerings from 'market research' into 'advisory services' set in train a shift towards prescribing and recommending action. This has a key consequence for how Gartner acts in the world today. In our discussion of the emergence of Customer Relationship Management (CRM) systems in Chapter 6, for instance, we saw how Gartner sought to formulate distinct presuppositions about what *should* be included within this new paradigm. We also show how they then went on to actively 'police' the boundaries of this development based on these presumptions.

We find it instructive that these experts, when asked, distinguished between the notions of 'describing' and 'directing', and reflected on the difference between them. On the one hand, they pointed towards the similarities between their research and disinterested academic enquiry. That is, they were concerned with 'a truth thing', and had a disciplined approach to knowledge production such that they describe their work as 'pseudo academic'. On the other hand, they were also cognisant of the conflicts of interest and pressures they faced in working so closely to actual market processes, and understood that the distinction between how things 'are' and how they 'could' or 'should' be was not a firm but a porous boundary. It was not that individual industry analysts were uninterested in such distinctions it was that there was a flow of directives, ideas and devices coming from within the firm that nudged them from one point to another on a spectrum between disinterested research and active intervention.

11.1.2. Shaping markets in different ways

We have drawn attention to the plurality of Gartner's work through setting out a typology of future-oriented knowledge, differentiating between at least three distinct types of knowledge product. These are differences in terms of how these products are produced, legitimated, distributed, consumed (Suddaby & Greenwood 2001) and achieve influence. Firstly, we illustrate the example of what we describe as *infrastructural knowledge* through discussing technology classifications. Behind Gartner's highly public naming interventions, for instance, sitting in the background, lies a range of equipment that is crucial for the framing of markets and to help analysts discriminate between products within a particular frame. Chapter 6 discussed the seemingly mundane example of the 'list'. We develop this notion of infrastructure to move away from a view of market and product classifications as mere mental constructs (as Economic Sociologists have conceived of them, where 'critics' flexibly interpret whether a vendor belongs to a particular category [Zuckerman 1999, Rosa et al. 1999, 2003]). Presumptions about technologies that exist in the heads of analysts are clearly important. However, when a technology field is materialized in a list of vendors the process by which an individual industry analyst discriminates between one vendor and another is from then on highly prescribed.

Secondly, there is a more transitory form of intervention that we describe as a *vision let loose*. Visions let loose are a technique that Gartner has developed to test whether there are shifts in sentiment across technology markets. Gartner faces a battle to stay ahead of the game. It needs to identify areas where things are moving or changing. Gartner thus continually sends out various provocations or probes across its networks and conferences to provoke a response. Where these visions achieve some purchase in the community, they may point to the emergence of what Rip et al. (2000) have described as 'fashions', promising areas of innovation that can be exploited (Abrahamson 1991, 1996). But visions let loose may have a rather short-lived level of influence. This is because they fail to command the internal apparatus of infrastructural knowledge forms like classifications and lists. Where successful, they can become the basis for naming interventions and Magic Quadrants. Eventually, however, the area of technology opportunity becomes exhausted.

Thirdly, we discussed *statements and their world* which are episodes where industry analysts make strenuous effort to bring into being new ways of thinking about market activity. Gartner will look to exercise leadership around certain knowledge claims. Chapters 7 and 9 discussed the example of the Magic Quadrant. Here Gartner is attempting to set out a distinctive evaluative world or culture that differs from how others view vendor performance. Given that Gartner is offering differential assessments of particular offerings, it must attempt to construct defensible kinds of knowledge (unlike the areas above). This did not come about spontaneously or easily. It is an achievement. There is a struggle for the renewal of substantive knowledge, the management of its human resources, and a continued reworking of methodologies and formats for knowledge elicitation and presentation.

In offering this typology, we repeat a number of caveats for fear of being misunderstood. In distinguishing between the different forms of Gartner's work, we are not suggesting a 'fixed' typology because these different forms of influence, as part of an 'epistemic system' (Knorr Cetina 1999), are in constant movement. The prediction (vision let loose) that survives the conference and builds up internal support, where other Gartner analysts 'line up behind it' (interview, Thomas), could wield a more enduring form of influence (i.e. become infrastructural). Just as we found instances where industry analysts could direct areas of activity, we also found examples where their knowledge was incomplete and fragile. The 'Technology Enabled Relationship Management' terminology, for instance, appeared infrastructural but ended up wielding only temporary/limited influence. This latter observation reinforces our argument for attention to be paid to the ways in which knowledge is not only produced but consumed (Knorr Cetina 2010), including the ways that analysts actively manage the reception of their knowledge outputs.

11.2. MACHINERIES OF KNOWING

Scholars like Preda (2009) in the new field of the Sociology of Markets have pointed to how we cannot understand the formation and operation of markets without also looking at the material apparatus that sustains the economy. A key argument of the book is that the influence of industry analysts is affected by the various machineries of knowing in play. Let us mention a seemingly mundane example from the early days. When he first started out at the investment firm Oppenheimer, Gartner was worried about how he would 'make a mark' in competing against what he describes as the 'awesome concentration of MBA brainpower across Wall Street' (Gartner 2010e). His solution—highly routine but beautifully indicative of how much attention he gave to the material detail that could set his firm apart from competitors—was to bring 'props' to meetings with prospective clients:

> When visiting with clients, other analysts would invariably simply chat across the clients' desk, hardly ever using props. I chose to almost always present my pitch via a presentation 3-ring binder, propped on the desk while I leafed through my hand-drawn arguments. This style, which seems trivial, definitely helped differentiate me (Gartner 2010e).

In some respects, this focus on simple material props has characterized the firm ever since. We have looked into the minutiae of a variety of such artefacts. Gartner's figurations in particular have become an important influence on how technology adopters and others view and act in markets. We have described how Gartner Inc. has elaborated a range of tools for engaging with technology fields in their *emergent* phases (Hype-Cycles), further *evolution* (MarketScopes and Cool Vendor Lists), *maturation* (Magic Quadrants) and *closure* (IT Market Clocks). These devices are about giving adopters particular 'market pictures'. For instance, an anticipatory tool like the Hype-Cycle provides technology adopters with a frame to consider their medium to longer-term courses of action (e.g., to help generate an acquisition strategy) and the Magic Quadrant would be used later in the process, where a field is stabilizing, as a tool for discrimination (e.g., to support procurement).

As well as enhancing what actors can do, however, we have shown how these devices can severely limit action and have unintended consequecnes for the shaping of markets. For instance, Gartner analysts talked of how, at a certain point in the maturation of a field, the Magic Quadrant could deliver the 'beautiful picture' (where there was somewhere between 10 to 25 vendors depicted). However, we should be careful not to mistake these beautiful pictures for 'realist paintings' (Latour 1999: 78). In constructing its figurations, Gartner is not attempting to make 'an exact copy of the world', to recall Latour's discussion of representation practices in science (ibid: 78). Rather, the Magic Quadrant can depict only a *small* number of potential players. To portray just a fraction of the market can generate pressures and anger from within the vendor community. Vendors become angry because even though Magic Quadrants are described as market 'snapshots' (Snapp 2013), they know that adopters treat them as if they were the entire marketplace of possibilities (see Chapter 7).

Chapter 9 discussed how Gartner issued a Magic Quadrant to capture a new and dramatically evolving technological field. However, quickly afterwards, it was forced to issue further Magic Quadrants to capture the many other entrants outraged at not being included in the original picture. These further

Magic Quadrants, however, demand their own nomenclatures and definitions to mark them out from existing pictures. Because the launch of a new terminology can generate processes of 'reactivity' (Espeland & Sauder 2007), where vendors begin to realign their activities around a new name, Gartner had (unwittingly?) sparked the important processes that lead to market segmentation. It seems that the release of a Magic Quadrant that does not possess or is unable to sustain an organic (i.e. lived) relationship between vendor and adopter communities can finish with the creation of new distinct technology/market categories.

Even though these figurations have severe limits, it is not the case that Gartner can easily replace them. We found it 'locked in' to producing particular pictures. Seasoned analysts, harking back to the early days of the 'think-tank' mentality, observed that analyst firms developed ways of doing things that continue to be replicated regardless of changing circumstance (interview, Thomas). Even though the Magic Quadrant was 'disliked' by those who compiled it as well as those negatively affected by its assessments, it is extremely difficult for Gartner to get rid of it (interview, Lebber). They remain the most popular of Gartner's outputs, where an entire 'community' has been built around it. And because it is the device that differentiates Gartner from all others, they find it difficult to move beyond it.

11.2.1. Hodgepodge of ideas

In studying the devices undergirding markets/business, Miller (2008) further reminds us that we require a simultaneous investigation into the 'ideas' behind these objects. Not only do we need to understand the performative role of market devices but we also need to appreciate how these objects take on an importance that extends well beyond the direct tasks to which they are put. Building on Miller (ibid), we might argue that there is a 'hodgepodge of ideas' behind even the most mundane business device. Through the notion of a 'hodgepodge' Gideon Gartner provided insights into how Gartner's outputs are entangled with broader visions of consumer decision making, the role of research in shaping those decisions, how such research should be organized and presented, and so on.[1] In order to throw further light on the thinking behind tools such as the Magic Quadrant, and taking partial inspiration from Gartner's ten innovations, we discuss the following themes: 'capturing the client', 'staying in the game', 'relevance and actionability' and 'audience'.

Capturing the client: Let us note a crucial difference in how contemporary industry analyst research is produced today as compared to the models for industry and market research that existed before Gideon Gartner developed his idea of selling advisory services to support decisions. The focus then was upon selling databases and long technical reports that the user would purchase and have to make sense of (Sherden 1998). What appeared important was generating data through comprehensive surveys of the 'whole' market. Research revolved around the enormity of data, making reports 'lengthy' and 'academic' (Berghoff et al. 2012). Today the goal is not to gather together data simply to create general taxonomies; Gartner's research is designed to serve a different purpose. The firm's strapline is that it 'wants to be involved in every IT decision' (interview, Thomas). Thus it formulates its outputs in a way that attracts and makes things easier for the consumer; it attempts to produce research that *captures its clients* (see Cochoy & Venn [2007] who discuss devices for the 'captation' of publics).

For instance, the Magic Quadrant and similar graphs are widely dismissed as 'simplifications'. But scholars who only see the visual simplicity of these outputs underestimate these figurations. This is because they are purposely simplified. Gartner attempts to create a view of the market that the consumer can make sense of. Chapter 9 shows that even the most apparently basic figurations are surrounded by a specific rationalization process. They are 'commercial' and 'consumer oriented' (Karpik 2010: 52) and deliberately designed to capture and retain the user/client. Those who produce these rankings deploy dedicated and methodical practices to create a particular viewpoint. There is a delicate balance between too much and too little information. There should be no need to 'sit down and discuss in detail these charts', to repeat the words of one informant (interview, Vale). How do buyers draw up shortlists when there are so many vendors? From the many possible options available, the Magic Quadrant offers the buyer a ready solution—choose not between infinite numbers but between these selected few! Its authors hope to identify a clear point that allows people to comprehend the situation straight away. That is, there should be enough information for the reader to understand 'the battlefield' (interview, Muller) or 'the landscape' (interview, Doorly), what we have described elsewhere as the 'subitizing range' (Pollock & Campagnolo 2015).

Staying in the game: Easy to read formats such as the Magic Quadrant are not entirely evaluative. They are also created as a 'hook' to enable further conversations. They are devoted, on the one hand, to the conquest of the client, and, on the other, to keeping industry analysts *in the game*. Gartner's outputs are deliberately 'incomplete' in contrast to traditional comprehensive market surveys (Berghoff et al. 2012). They provide an effective tool for potential adopters to conduct triage and focus efforts on the most promising offerings. They act as a prelude, rather than a substitute, for more detailed direct discussions between analysts and the adopters who subscribe to their advisory services, reflecting the importance of 'staying in the game', which permeates all Gartner outputs. We were struck in Chapter 9 by how precisely industry analysts could identify the 'amount' of information needed to be included in their research outputs. For the Magic Quadrant it is somewhere between '10 and 25' vendors whilst for the Forrester Wave it is '10 and 12'. These numbers are clearly not arbitrary. Just as the graphs should not be (overly) complex, nor could they be (too) simple. There should be enough information and complexity that clients will still have questions for the industry analyst. Though there is a process of 'simplification' (Quattrone 2009: 109), our research shows that this process is not crude; these figurations were artfully contrived with sophisticated intent. Those producing Magic Quadrants can 'increase' as well as decrease information portrayed. Gideon Gartner wanted these shorter kinds of reports not to substitute but to serve as a starting point for consultations.

Relevance and actionability: Our argument is not only that specific forms of action and processes of decision-making have resulted from the work of industry analysts, but that these experts have created or shifted the practices of knowledge production and warranting of knowledge. One highly unusual feature of the various provocative predictions, described above under the heading 'vision let loose', is that, at first glance, it does not seem to matter if Gartner gets these forecasts 'wrong'. How might we explain this? The argument developed in Chapter 8 was that Gideon Gartner got around this by making it a problem of 'geography'. He shifted this particular form of knowledge making from the circulation of paper to direct engagement at the venue. Furthermore, the events where predictions were communicated became part of a 'circuit' (Thrift 2005) with the same or similar conferences repeated at different locations and times throughout the year. This meant that the predictions could be constantly tested and updated at each event.

What was being improved over the series of conference events, and what was ultimately being evaluated by the audience, was not the verisimilitude of the prediction but its potential to stimulate 'activities'. In setting up his firm, Gartner adopted and applied ideas from decision theory (Montgomery & Weinberg 1979). He purposely reconfigured his outputs from research as a process of *reflection* to research as a process of *action*. Thus when a prediction is developed before the conference, thought is given to how it must challenge conventional thinking: it must be 'provocative' (a 'Stalking Horse' to use Gideon Gartner's suggestive term). More importantly, it must also be *relevant* and *actionable* (Nilsson & Helgesson 2015. And just as we seem unlikely to evaluate the activity of swimming or running as 'right' or 'wrong' (du Gay 2010), the audience appears not to want to decide about predictions in the same way.

We found interesting in this respect Knorr Cetina's (2007: 368) discussion of how, in her study of investment analysts, fundamentals like 'truth' or 'facts' became less important as they were replaced with 'news' and 'surface events'. 'Surface events', as we understand it, is not a pejorative term. Knorr Cetina develops it to signal how particular epistemic systems can come to be governed by alternate priorities (where 'alternate' means those not directly inspired by the scientific model [Porter 1992]). This idea, that surface rather than fundamental issues also dominate the contexts studied in this book, would seem to be confirmed by the form of validation regime that has emerged amongst industry analyst events in recent years. One only has to look at the example of the conference and how the assessment includes whether the speaker 'performed well', whether the content was 'useful', was the event 'well organized', did it allow the audience to 'make changes and decisions' once back in their office, etc. We return to discuss the notion of 'validation regime' below.

Audience: Industry analyst outputs are not constructed in one single place or by one set of actors but are co-created in a multi-audience arena. The understanding of the role of the audience in helping to form this knowledge evolved throughout our study. Initial characterizations depicted the audience outside the shaping of the outputs and with limited interactions with the firms supplying it (Burks 2006). Our research has shown them to play a central role in how these outputs are put together: audiences are 'informants' and 'sources' of seemingly objective opinion about vendor capacities and performance; and they are 'co-producers' who play a part in elaborating and determining the shape of powerful indicators. The development of the conference as a focal means of interaction has further stretched the notion and role of the audience. Indeed, today, in these venues, it is far from clear who are the creators of predictions and who are the audiences for this promissory work.

11.3. DOES THE PERFORMATIVITY THESIS TRANSPORT WELL?

The last couple of years have seen a growing body of empirical analysis (Doganova & Eyquem-Renault 2009, Czarniawska 2011, D'Adderio & Pollock 2014) and related conceptual discussions (Muniesa 2014, Mason et al. 2015) that point to the gradual extension of the performativity programme. A simple Google Scholar trace provides evidence of the growing influence of these arguments. There is now a fairly clear web of connections emerging between performative analyses across STS (Callon 1998, Callon et al. 2007, MacKenzie 2006, Preda 2008), Economic Sociology (Pinch & Swedberg 2008, Stark 2009, Beckert & Aspers 2011), Accounting (Milller & O'Leary 2007, Miller 2008, Vollmer et al. 2009), and more recently critical perspectives in Business Studies (Thrift 2005, Czarniawska 2011), Marketing (Cochoy 1998, Kjellberg & Helgesson 2006, Araujo 2007, Mason et al. 2015), Organization Studies (Cabantous & Gond 2011, Muniesa 2014, D'Adderio & Pollock 2014) and Information Systems (Pollock & Williams 2007) etc. This dialogue points to the potential for an exciting programme of work around the constitutive nature of business knowledge or what some have begun to identify as 'Market Studies' (Mason et al. 2015). However, it also raises questions about the pertinence of the performativity thesis when applied beyond the areas in which it was first developed. Though our review has shown that industry analysts share some of the characteristics of financial analysts say, we find that their effective study is not well served if we simply extend to them wholesale concepts honed on the study of financial/economic markets. In trying to make sense of industry analysts we need different analytical templates. Here we are arguing for a necessary extension of the performativity programme to look at the knowledge production practices in industry analyst firms. This in turn informs our conception of a specific programme of work that gives central attention to how knowledge is produced, warranted and consumed within business contexts—a *Sociology of Business Knowledge* perhaps.

11.3.1. Dichotomy between implausibly 'weak' and 'strong' readings of knowledge

One reason for this latter suggestion is that we find existing templates offer either an implausibly *weak* or implausibly *strong* reading of the effects of knowledge. In terms of the former, the critical instincts of scholars seem to favour a sceptical reading of the outputs described in this book, portraying them (when they are portrayed) as *content-less* or *arbitrary*. We have already discussed, from the Sociology of Expectations, Rip's description of the Gartner Hype-Cycle as mere 'ritual' or 'folk theory'. This is a form of expectations, as he sees it, ' . . . based in some experience, but not necessarily systematically checked' (2006: 352–3). Its 'robustness derives from [it] being generally accepted, and thus part of a repertoire current in a group or in our culture more generally' (ibid). He concludes by pointing to how these kinds of business tools are 'lacking research' and, in some cases, 'plainly wrong' (ibid). Whilst understanding the scepticism towards this form of knowledge, we argue for a more symmetrical and balanced account (Porter 1992). This is because our fieldwork tells us something different. If these tools were mere 'folk theories' and their robustness derived *only* from their acceptance (by *dupes?*) then Gartner would not have been obliged to construct the intricate research apparatus described in these pages—it could literally throw darts at a chart when constructing its Magic Quadrant ranking.

Indeed one explanation for Gartner's success that we have implicitly explored in various parts of the book is the (continued) development and extension of standard techniques and tools. This process of 'standardization' was visible at the beginning (the internal 'discipline' imposed by Gideon Gartner in setting out and ensuring that recruits adhered to 'Theory G') and it is still apparent today (with the standard methods that exist around tools such as the Magic Quadrants). We are not claiming that Gartner is forced to operate these standardized research processes as some kind of objective mechanical calculation—as we saw, there is considerable scope for discretion and judgement but rather that, it can be held to account if it is seen to depart from standardized methods (interview, Erskine).

In this respect, several of the large analyst organizations have been more forthcoming about (and in some cases made public) their methodologies and research processes, pointing to the collective and, in some cases, 'collegiate' nature of their research process whereby analysts 'peer review' and critically scrutinize each other's work prior to publication. Their research (and the process of constructing that research) is subject to increasing levels of external scrutiny. Furthermore in the recent period, actors have emerged who have taken upon themselves the specific task of throwing light on this research apparatus (e.g., the 'analyst relations' groups described in Chapter 10). Visible divergences can be seized upon. This compels Gartner to give increased attention to issues like standardization and conformance. It also explains why we have seen organizational innovations such as the 'methodology team' and the 'Ombudsman's office' etc.

We find it something of a paradox that social scientists, especially those from our home discipline of STS, have criticized the privileging of scientific knowledge, and argued for the study of 'alternate', 'lay' or 'marginal' knowledge, but largely shied away from addressing the proliferation and construction of new forms of business expertise. The paradox is that these scholars largely overlook the explosion of business knowledge and other emerging forms of expertise in our so-called Knowledge Society and instead follow the contours of the long-discredited 'hierarchy of science' (Porter 1992). Arguably, industry analyst assessments may be seen as constituting a new kind of privately provided public good (Brante 1988, Fournier 2000), which is not subject to the strict controls of independent 'scientific' knowledge (Shapin 1994), but which does have its own particular forms of accountability.

This brings us to the 'strong' readings found in recent work on the Sociology of Economic (Callon 1998, 2007) and Financial (MacKenzie et al. 2007) markets. Influenced by the Sociology of Science (Barnes et al. 1996), the power of the performativity programme is that it gives central attention to the 'content' of knowledge. However, there is a very real danger that this analytical template could unintentionally convey the impression of a theory or model that is able to drive change. Despite Callon's (1998) foregrounding of the study of 'overflows' and MacKenzie's (2009) deployment of the notion of 'innofusion', one can still find a portrayal of theory doing things to people. Actor Network Theory-based discussions in particular (Holm & Nielsen 2007), deploying the 'follow the actors' (Latour 1987) methodology, tend to track from theory out and deploy a template of colonization, involving warlike language (Fujimura 1995). In researching material for this book, we found few accounts that draw attention to the *interplay* between theory and actors in a wider ecology (D'Adderio & Pollock 2014). There is also a difference between the 'espoused' view and the 'practice' of doing performativity studies (Kjellberg & Helgesson 2006). In adopting performativity as model of study, it is common for scholars to reject the suggestion of a 'linear' description or to call for more complex templates of study; in practice, however, this is not what we end up with (Mason et al. 2015). These failings are closely linked to epistemic issues of finding adequate analytical templates, research designs and methods to engage with the kind of complexity described in this book. We need new templates to address the rich fabric of business settings.

11.3.2. New templates to address business settings

Let us recap our point of departure from existing approaches to the analysis of financial and economic markets and at the same time discuss how we went about our study. Early contributors to the self-styled 'Anthropology of Markets' (Callon 1998, 2007) make little distinction between market actors that produce theories and models *on* markets and those that design various tools and devices *in* markets. To repeat Callon's words from before, an economist may be both an 'academic researcher whose job is to produce theories on the market ... [o]r he or she may be a market professional who designs market devices, algorithms for comparing supply and demand' (2007: 336). This symmetrical view, whilst consonant with ANT, underplays the very different texture of the fabric of social and material relations that can exist between these settings. These shortcomings are particularly problematic when we use frameworks honed on well-established institutional settings to analyse the development of industry analysts and other instances of business knowledge.

In his recent critique of the upsurge in interest of how economics performs the economy, Miller (2008) flagged the danger of assuming that all modes of ordering are a direct derivative of Economics. Different disciplines, such as Accounting and Finance, will constitute markets in different ways. This begs the question as to whether there are further forms of performativity, perhaps those that stem from the kinds of business setting described in this book, which we might need to consider. Indeed scholars have noted the distinctive, hybrid characteristics of the business domain and how it is influenced and constituted by lots of disciplines—not just Economics, Finance or Accounting but also, going back a century, Engineering, Psychology and Sociology etc. (Khurana 2010). Miller argues that it is exactly this 'hybridisation of practices' (2008: 59) that shapes business life (though he does not spell out what form this hybridization might take or how business contexts might differ).

One important difference, we would argue, is that the world of business knowledge has not developed the kind of highly elaborate (e.g. disciplinary) formal institutional apparatus one finds in modern academia or science (Knorr Cetina 2010). Business school theories and models, for instance, are assessed primarily in terms of their relevance and utility in domains of business practice (Suddaby & Greenwood 2001), reflected for example in the resort to case-based teaching (though Fourcade & Khurana [2011] note the influence of economic agency theory in changing corporate governance and reward systems). Instead our study points to the less-formalized, flatter, market-based knowledge infrastructures that have emerged through processes that we describe as 'involution'.

This notion of involution attempts to capture the way in which industry analysts (and other new forms of business expert) emerge through the concentration of expertise and experience within the agora of technology supply and use. Specialization goes hand-in-hand with the market-based provision of this knowledge. The shift to market supply opens up an organizational, indeed industrial, division of expert labour that facilitates specialization (echoing elements of what Rosenberg [1976] described a few decades earlier as 'convergence'). The market-based forms of the supply and coordination of business knowledge impart complex dynamics that shape further developments. This includes the commodification of offerings in the form of knowledge products.

We have foregrounded this ongoing process of specialization through indicating first how the industry analyst resulted from the difficulties adopters had in assessing complex computer solutions, and second how the presence of industry analysts and their growing influence over the IT domain (especially powerful rankings like the Magic Quadrant) directly led to the constitution of a further distinctive form of expertise—expertise about expertise (e.g. analyst relations). Thirdly, as seen in Chapter 10, the analyst relations groups within IT vendors have sought further forms of knowledge that they were seen to lack, which has led to the birth of a market for commodified advice and consultancy related to analyst relations.[2]

We intend the term involution to capture this constant elaboration of business knowledge that leads to the formation of specialist divisions within the firm. The involution of business knowledge constitutes rather different circumstances for exploring the performativity thesis than, for example, the case of building new markets around particular financial and economic theories. The latter also refers to a context with a more pronounced social and institutional gulf between knowledge producers and knowledge consumers with correspondingly increased risk of misalignments in mutual understanding and trust (MacKenzie & Millo 2003). In the world described in this book there is nowhere near the same divide between industry analysts and those who consume their knowledge that one seemingly finds between the various economists described by MacKenzie and Millo (2003) and the Chicago financial derivatives markets. Industry analysts are in no way part of a separate evaluative realm but might more usefully seen to be embedded in an 'interactional arena' or 'community of reputation' (Sauder & Fine 2008). Because these experts find it necessary to operate in close proximity to practice, this provides the possibility for more than just immediate contact between players; there is sustained interaction. This provides an unusual quality to the form of knowledge production and verification, which we have attempted to capture in this book. These features, we would argue, can be found across other forms of knowledge/sectors.[3]

11.3.3. A new model for understanding the interrelation knowledge production and shaping of industries: A focus on 'interstices'

Studying industry analysts and related knowledge groups arguably requires a new model for understanding the interrelations between tools, knowledge production and the shaping of industries. We maintain that this also calls for careful attention to *research design*. The research frameworks we adopt in an enquiry are important for they too can be performative, in that they shape the kinds of understanding we are likely to reach (Law 2004). The dominant viewpoint emerging in the Sociology of Markets is to start from economic theory and work outwards. In choosing this point of entry over others, it implicitly prioritizes particular assumptions about the world and about how we may investigate it. The focus is upon how (economic) theory does things to people (Holm & Nielsen 2007), notwithstanding an interest in what happens when this breaks down (e.g., 'overflowing' [Callon 1998]). To avoid this presumption we need concepts and methods that attend to the distribution of authority (Fujimura 1995) and shift our focus to how outputs like theories or models *interact* with the affordances of the wider knowledge system. Rather than focus our lens solely on the theoretical models of these specialists we have taken as our focus 'interaction' (Barry 2001). It is the series of interactions between those writing, described in, and using industry analyst research that together make up the complex and distinctive epistemic cultures that we have attempted to describe here.

We share Suddaby and Greenwood's (2001: 934) surprise that, despite the unprecedented growth in new forms of business knowledge provider, relatively little attention has been given to the study of the producer/user 'nexus' and the complex web of relations that exist between those who supply and those who consume business knowledge. Our interest in addressing these kinds of interactions was also linked to our concern to shift away from a research model based on simple 'snapshots'—for example of the role of industry analyst expertise or of (economic) theory. In this study, rather than extrapolating the effects of organizations/markets from the production of theory, we engage with the production and consumption of knowledge outputs *in tandem*.

Our methodology started with following the circuit of Gartner's knowledge production and consumption. We pursued a longer-term view that engaged across multiple sites and over extended temporalities with the evolution and co-production of industry analyst tools and markets. Searching for the various interfaces between the suppliers and the users of this knowledge, which constitute key nexuses in which competing requirements are presented and worked out, allowed us to construct different viewpoints and points of entry to this circuit. For example, we addressed the Magic Quadrant by studying its production and consumption, and explored in particular detail how various actors interacted with its authors to shape it. This allowed us to follow the intricate relations at play here, the complex web of players, and the multi-faceted games played between vendors, research users and the analysts. We would argue that rather than projecting forwards from particular discourses or promises, a more 'biographical' (Pollock & Williams 2009) research template was needed where scholars follow artefacts and theory through space and time (Williams & Pollock 2012, D'Adderio & Pollock 2014). This includes understanding the longer-term dynamics of markets. The ground-breaking studies in the Sociology of Markets have focussed on the formation of new markets, leading to the tacit presumption that a market once set up remains stable. We argue that we need tools to understand the maintenance and longer-term evolution of the knowledge infrastructures of the IT markets, as these epistemic systems are in constant transformation (Knorr Cetina 1999).

We find ourselves diverging from the performativity programme because we seek to give attention to how the form and content of outputs relate to the particular exigencies of knowledge production and its validation, patterned as they are by various forms of accountability, incentives and penalties arising through the validation regime. In developing this analysis of the knowledge infrastructures of the IT markets, we have obtained considerable insight from a group of scholars who have been exploring and developing understandings of epistemic systems. This includes the work of Knorr Cetina (1999, 2010, 2012), Star (Star & Griesemer 1989, Star 1995) and Fujimura (1995), who suggest that knowledge is related to the knowledge ecology in which it is produced, evaluated and consumed. It also includes Abbott (2005: 246) who has moved from the idea of an ecology as having a 'set of fixed surrounds' to explore the idea of 'linked ecologies' and connections (or what he calls 'hinges') between knowledge ecologies and their audiences. We think these approaches can be taken further, however, to look at the specificities of the knowledge infrastructure of business acumen.

We use the term 'validation regime' to highlight the argument that the processes and content of industry analyst knowledge are closely related to the features of the epistemic system in which it is generated, circulated and consumed, and in the process legitimated with particular internal and external audiences and subject to various forms of verification and test. In other words, what we are arguing is that industry analyst knowledge is produced and achieves influence as part of a complex ecology. In this respect, it might be better to say that *business knowledge is performed* rather than just knowledge is performative.

11.3.4. Business knowledge *is performed* and not just performative

We note a number of aspects that the analytical template we have constructed here has allowed us to uncover in the case of industry analysts. Firstly, we have shown how industry analyst research is not simply the product of individuals but shaped by the affordances of the knowledge infrastructure. In tracing these knowledge outputs it is not clear where the machinery ends and the input of the analyst begins. One only has to think of the kinds of insight that come out of the 'conference' as described in Chapter 6. To make it to conference, predictions are peer-reviewed internally, picked over by copy editors and others, before being submitted to an audience for external review and possible reshaping, depending on their reactions (a process that repeats itself several times, as predictions are recycled along with other conferences around the globe). We also threw light on how Magic Quadrants resulted from a dispersed production process and how this very 'distributedness' was built into Gartner's machinery. The Gartner analysts we interviewed told us that there was little choice but to accept that their work would be subject to review as the technology supporting the production and circulation of outputs like Magic Quadrants physically demanded it (interview, De Sousa).

Secondly, taking this perspective also allowed us to show how the production processes and content of industry analyst knowledge are legitimated with particular internal and external audiences and subject to various forms of 'test' (the 'so what?' assessment, the 'hands-up' interactions, the 'Google test' etc.). Moreover, these tests are far removed from visions of the verification of objective truths articulated under 'Mertonian' norms of scientific practice. They are closer to what Knorr Cetina (2007) describes as 'surface events'. Though we might distinguish the more stable epistemic world of industry analysts from the rather chaotic and fast moving world of investment analysts described by Knorr Cetina (see below), we find this idea of a shift from a fundamental to a surface attitude useful as it foregrounds how particular kinds of 'priorities' have developed in relation to the production and validation of business knowledge.

Thirdly, since industry analysts find it necessary to operate in close proximity to practice, this approach allowed us to throw light on how their outputs, like rankings, are shaped by those they are evaluating (e.g., the technology vendors). There have been a number of pioneering studies on the impact of powerful evaluations and rankings on processes of consumption and markets; however, there has as yet been little focus on the prior issue of their construction and, in particular, on how those constructing rankings increasingly depend on and interact with a wide range of others in what might be thought of as the broader 'ranking chain'. This includes, for example, the extended network of actors from which information is drawn and who, in turn, play a role in shaping or attempting to shape the placing of a vendor and its products/services. Fourthly, and related to this last point, our lens shows that, despite the various information asymmetries within the ecology, those responding to industry analysts have a complex understanding of proximal players in the arena. The actors we found were not the 'dupes' one sometimes finds implicitly described in accounts of business knowledge but critical, indeed hyper-reflexive, actors, with enhanced sensibilities and understandings of the role and work of industry analysts, constantly probing and game playing to improve a position etc., (see particularly Chapter 7).

11.4. TOWARDS A SOCIOLOGY OF BUSINESS KNOWLEDGE?

The commodification and spread of business knowledge is a theme that various disciplinary perspectives have turned to time and time again. It might be argued that scholars have *already* embarked upon a Sociology of Business Knowledge in that much attention has been given over to the *circulation* of business ideas and theories. In calling for such a programme we are anxious not to overlook extant debates but to extend and deepen them. One need only think of the extensive literature on the diffusion of management consultancy knowledge reviewed in Chapter 4; and the work on managerial 'fads and fashions' (Abrahamson 1996) and 'organizing visions' (Swanson & Ramiller 1997) discussed in Chapter 2. We identify how, with some notable exceptions, existing work has tended to focus on the rhetorical shaping accompanying the diffusion of particular knowledge artefacts. This is not to deny the importance of such discursive processes as we find useful this focus on how technology and knowledge suppliers promote their offerings.

We could also mention Czarniawska's discussion of how business ideas, objects and practices travel in a global economy (Czarniawska & Sevón 2005). Similarly, Thrift (2005: 11), drawing on Carrier and Miller's (1998) notion of 'virtualism', describes the 'cultural circuits of capitalism' where ideas and theories about business are circulated and enacted by management specialists.

We see our work adding to this latter debate through our insistence that a focus on the circulation of business knowledge analysis should look to capture not only the processes whereby knowledge is constructed but also how that knowledge is legitimated by those who consume it.

Some of the exceptions, and a platform on which to build our understanding of industry analysts, is Abbott (1988) and Suddaby and Greenwood's (2001) discussions of 'knowledge commodification'. In early studies of organizational expertise, the problem of the management of expertise was primarily an issue of managing intra-organizational communication and politics (Burns & Stalker 1959). With the increasing market-based provision of business knowledge the difficulties of trading and verifying knowledge have come to the fore. Fleck (1998) draws attention to two dimensions in the validation of expertise: the *credibility cycle* (Latour & Woolgar 1979) through which the efficacy of expertise could be demonstrated and the *tradeability* of expertise either informally (e.g. in competitions for status and influence within organizations and networks) or formally through the market. Let us look at the tradeability of knowledge and then at how it can be demonstrated and verified in practice.

11.4.1. Tradeability of business knowledge

There have been discussions about the commodification of business knowledge, for example within the Sociology of Professions (Abbott 1988) and the Sociology of Professional Service Firms (Suddaby & Greenwood 2001). These writers focus on how management experiences may be extracted from specific contexts. In Suddaby & Greenwood's (2001) terminology knowledge could be *codified* and then converted into a form that meant it could be moved elsewhere, what they describe as *abstracted* knowledge, before eventually being *translated*, i.e. reapplied in particular organizational contexts. These accounts, however, have arguably not given adequate attention to the challenges of trading knowledge and other informational products (Fleck 1998). The circumstances of trading informational products impart a number of paradoxical features to the market provision of business knowledge (e.g., how do people know the value of knowledge before they have consumed it? If they did know its value then they probably would not need the knowledge in the first place). Abbott (1988) and Suddaby and Greenwood (2001) argue that commodification, by promoting the development of routines and templates (i.e. codification/abstraction/translation), makes knowledge more accessible and thus increases imitability, opening up scope for competition. We would argue, by contrast, that the commodification of business knowledge instead sets in train somewhat contradictory impulses. For example:

i) specialists collectively need to sell the *generic effectiveness* of a set of ideas as reflecting the state of art in improving business performance; and,

ii) experts individually seek to demonstrate the *particular benefits* of their knowledge and its relevance. This may be cast in terms of representing generic best business practice or its specific benefits to the particular organization.

As the quality and benefits of this expertise cannot be directly observed—except through slowly and expensively obtained hindsight—potential adopters are forced to resort to proxy measures (e.g. community reputation [Glückler, & Armbrüster 2003] or more formalized rating systems, as we saw in Chapter 10).

11.4.2. Demonstrating relevance of knowledge in practice

Suddaby and Greenwood (2001) have analysed the process by which business knowledge is produced: innovations in management practice need to be 'disembedded' from local contexts, 'objectified' and made 'portable'. However, particular prescriptions must also be tested and validated. On the one hand, their analysis highlights the role of Business Schools[4] as well as consultants, gurus and adopters in disseminating these ideas and also in their legitimation. On the other, prescriptions must ultimately be verified and validated at the level of practice.[5] This is one reason, they argue, why 'case studies' of successful implementation of an innovation become a currency to validate particular forms of business knowledge (and an indicator of the expertise of a management consultant involved) (Graham & Williams 2005, Heusinkveld & Benders 2005, Gross & Kieser 2006, Muniesa 2014). 'New' programmes for business improvement may emerge, supported by a community of academics, consultants and successful adopters, providing testimony of the generic effectiveness of the set of ideas as reflecting the state of the art in improving business performance (as we saw for example a few decades ago in the area of Business Process Redesign [BPR, see Fincham 1995]). There is, however, often little incentive to retain these as distinct, standardized formal practices and techniques. Instead, we see the local appropriation/reworking of these generic prescriptions. This occurs at two levels:

i) concepts are reworked to meet local relevancies—to implement them and demonstrate their utility within adopter organizations

ii) to meet exigencies of trading knowledge in the market, generic concepts (such as BPR) become appropriated by private consultancies as distinctive proprietary solutions—alongside claims about advantages these methodologies have over generic prescriptions. This is couched in terms of both their general effectiveness and their specific appropriateness for particular adopter organizations.

These dual exigencies of validating and trading knowledge can be seen to have also shaped the evolution of industry analyst expertise. Gideon Gartner started with a view that industry analyst research was about the generation of a new form of knowledge and that this knowledge could be shown to have value for users and traded profitably. He thus simultaneously promoted 'research methods' and 'sales goals' (Gartner 2011c) in equal measure. Though our analysis has given much attention to analyst knowledge, we have been careful not to background Gartner's distinctive sales emphasis (see Chapter 7). Gartner describes how, in developing his early model, he codified research methods into a staff handbook described as 'Theory G', which emphasized an orientation to clients and the value that their services would bring. His guidance to sales staff even included modelling specific ways in which clients would obtain value from advisory services to support the propositions of a 5:1 ratio between client benefits and subscription fees (Gartner 2011c). He would circulate sales staff with daily 'Gideon says' bulletins to provide occasions for them to contact potential customers. He recounts how these took on a fabled status amongst the sales staff: 'one salesperson coined these messages "Sunflowers", because "parrots ate sunflowers" and the sales people were there to 'parrot' my research' (Gartner 2010e).

Right from the beginning, then, Gideon Gartner realized that his research outputs would not travel under their own steam. What we have attempted to show is how industry analysts found it necessary not only to create a following but also to continuously prove themselves to their audience(s) (Turner 2001, Preda 2008). Thus the development of industry analysis methodology and knowledge was simultaneously about attracting attention, validating knowledge and developing cognitive authority amongst potential customers. However, there are important nuances related to the specific temporalities of this form of knowledge in terms of how it is validated that need to be considered. There are also different levels of the generality of this knowledge between different industry analysts firms. In order to unpack this, we find it instructive to compare industry analysts to an apparently similar group—financial analysts as described by Knorr Cetina (2010, 2012). Contrasting our study with Knorr Cetina's account also further underscores our argument as to why existing templates from the Sociology of Finance offer rather 'disembodied' accounts of the performativity of knowledge.

11.4.3. Comparing industry analysts with financial analysts

Knorr Cetina (2010) draws our attention to differences between natural scientific knowledge and the 'information knowledge' deployed by the financial analysts she studied trading in foreign exchange and security markets. Scientists deploy relatively stable forms of knowledge whose significance, once established, decays only slowly. In contrast, she argues that it is *immediate* news that drives investment decisions. Moreover, there is no need to assess whether statements about possible investments are correct: '[E]ven if the time were available for collecting or verifying relevant information this need not be done,' (idem: 188). This is because, as she describes it, the market is only interested in the next piece of news rather than raking back over already consumed knowledge. However, Knorr Cetina's findings have to be seen against other features of the world of finance (the wider ecology) that her study does not foreground. In these settings, what ultimately matters can be reduced to a single metric (of price and thus profit and loss).

i) *Foreign exchange traders* are more likely to be interested in the trade or, to be more specific, their aggregate financial outcomes rather than the correctness of specific decisions. The settlement and reconciliation of trades requires rapid and accurate machinery for recording and aggregating these financial outcomes (Preda 2008).

ii) *Buy-side analysts* within institutional investors may be working over longer timeframes. However, the outcomes of their decisions are expressed directly in profit and loss terms: quantitative measures of trading outcomes provide a self-evidently valid, direct proxy of the thing that matters. So we see in financial analysis a situation where buy-side players are rewarded and build reputations in more or less direct proportion to the net outcomes of their investment choices. They need to be 'right' and in particular avoid expensive mistakes[6]— but, importantly, their performance is immediately visible within the organization.

iii) *Sell-side securities analysts* (who have been the focus of most research in this field [Wansleben 2012]) tend to develop deep knowledge in relation to particular groups of firms in order to generate forecasts of earnings and advice on whether to buy sell or hold stock (Zuckerman 1999). Knorr Cetina (2010: 34–7) highlights the contribution of direct contacts with firms, and in particular, company visits which she describes as 'proxy ethnographies', to fill the gaps left by publicly available information. This expertise is highly individuated on both the buy- and sell-side (the focus is on the performance of individuals rather than the firms they work for) (Gartner 2010y), and rewards are closely tied to performance measures. Whilst buy-side analysts are directly rewarded on the basis of their investment decisions, the sell-side analysts, who provide information on a daily basis to support the huge numbers of investment decisions on Wall Street are rewarded based on perceptions of the aggregate contribution of their advice to financial outcomes—allocated through a 'poll' of buy-side analysts and money managers at the end of the trading year (Hong & Kubik 2003).

Industry analysts in contrast are subject to very different temporalities and mechanisms of validation and offer different levels of generality of knowledge. Contrast the short-term cycle and immediately visible outcomes of currency or stock trades with the long timeframes for an organization's strategic IT procurements. The consequences of particular procurement decisions extend long into the future (and the long-term associations they herald between vendor and adopter may extend over decades) (Pollock & Williams 2009). Particular choices thus have long-term and strategic implications for enterprise system adopters. This means that great diligence is needed in coming to decisions. However, it is extremely hard to achieve due diligence: there is a long time lag between claims about the suitability of vendor offerings and their potential validation through the implementation and use of technology within organizations (Pollock & Williams 2007). Moreover, outcomes are influenced by many intervening factors (notably the adopter's implementation strategy), so implementation outcomes in one organization may not be applicable in another (Pollock & Hyysalo 2014). There is therefore little scope to pursue direct forms of empirical 'verification' of the accuracy of vendor claims in practice. Instead, there is a need for expert judgements about vendor capacity and implementation experience with these or similar artefacts in other, more or less similar organizations (ibid). Industry analysts develop the expertise needed to support these judgements and throughout the book we have shown how they deploy extensive networks within specific application domains that give them access to exceptional arrays of vendors and adopters as well as the tools and experience needed to sift and sort their views.

One key difference between financial analysts and industry analysts therefore is that the significance of industry analyst knowledge has to be *established with clients*. Gartner analysts were induced through staff monitoring and remuneration systems to ensure that clients perceived their advice as *valuable*, and this value was measured directly through surveys of customers and conference participants and indirectly through subscription renewal rates. And at some level, the willingness to pay for advice provides a powerful testament to the significance of knowledge. Indeed, there is an growing body of work on the economics of consultancy work which suggests that in order for such forms of knowledge to be seen as valuable then high prices must be asked for (see Armbruster [2006] for a review). However, both the generation and warranting of the quality and independence of Gartner analyst expertise goes beyond individual trades and client/analyst relationships.

- As we have described throughout this book it is also the result of a corporate achievement vested in the Gartner brand (Chapter 2)
- It stems from 'signature' tools such as the Magic Quadrant and the wider array of outputs that are able to mark(et) Gartner out from all others (Chapter 7)

- It is the charismatic 'star analyst' who combines technical knowledge with personal attributes that allows them to test knowledge with audiences whilst on stage (Chapter 8)

- It comes from the creation of the Office of the Gartner Ombudsman ('a brand differentiator') (Chapter 3)

- It is the cognitive authority Gartner can establish through 'naming' and going on to 'police' new technological fields (Chapter 6)

- It results from the creation of 'beautiful pictures' that clients understand at a glance but which also become the starting point for more detailed discussions with analysts (Chapter 9), and so on.

Whilst industry analyst expertise is less individuated than financial analyst advice, this varies within the analyst ecosystem for several reasons.

Clients look for breadth of knowledge: Technology adopters (more specifically, adopter organizations considering procurement) turn to large industry analyst firms such as Gartner to identify (i) the most promising areas of application and (ii) the most appropriate providers within these fields. They are looking for the breadth of knowledge and the independence that the larger analyst organizations can potentially offer.

Industry analysts therefore need to establish authority over broad fields: Establishing and maintaining the perceived right to speak with authority over broad fields of technology development requires a constant struggle for cognitive authority over a relentlessly changing landscape of technology offerings and business prescriptions. This involves first identifying promising areas of technology as they emerge and then going on to discriminate between competing offerings before interest in the field as a source of competitive advantage becomes exhausted.

So we see the proliferation of a variety of Gartner knowledge outputs that extend their scope for intervention throughout the lifecycle of a promising technology. Timing was therefore a major factor in Gartner's 'core' project of identifying and exercising discrimination within emerging 'hot' fields. Their success depends on a very fine line between calling something prematurely (e.g., advancing field definitions like TERM that did not take hold) and being proved wrong by events (e.g. flagging emerging fields that subsequently fragment) and missing things or arriving too late (hence Gartner describes itself as a 'fast follower'). We also observed the creation of new arenas such as the 'conference event' in which industry analysts could calibrate its timing through simultaneously acquiring and validating community knowledge.

We also saw how there was a complex ecosystem of industry analyst expertise with smaller analyst organizations (often lacking a large technology adopter client base) providing advice on a boutique basis to technology vendors about the presentation of their products. These analysts found themselves rated by analyst relations specialists in terms of their influence, which might reflect their media profile as well as their reputation with peers and practitioners. These smaller analyst organizations tended to specialize in particular technologies or sectors. In this respect, they were closer to Knorr Cetina's (2010) sell-side equity analysts who developed individual reputations/ rewards by demonstrating success in predicting the relative performance of particular firms and sectors rather than cognitive authority over entire fields. So, in other words, different kinds of industry analyst are subject to different kinds of validation regime.

This book has explored how the exigencies of producing, validating and trading knowledge conditions the way in which Gartner's knowledge activities are organized. We have shown that the industry analyst ecosystem is internally differentiated and that other (e.g. smaller, vendor-facing) analyst organizations, confront different constraints and have accordingly developed alternative strategies for creating, validating and selling their knowledge. This brief comparison between industry analysts and various types of financial analysts (as revealed through the growing body of Social Studies of Finance) shows a pattern of similarities and differences. We have highlighted differences in the temporal durability and methods of validation and rewarding of different kinds of expertise. We linked these to the material consequences of particular decisions, the temporalities through which they unfolded, and the extent to which they could be subject to pragmatic measures versus indirect proxies of the quality of expertise. In the case of financial trading markets, the pragmatic outcome of trades represents a good indicator of the commercial goals of players. The extended timeframes and multiplicity of factors surrounding the effects of IT procurement choices, by contrast, resist direct measurement and call for complex forms of expertise able to exercise experience-based judgement.

11.5. BEYOND IT MARKETS

We have examined the rise of a new form of knowledge producer and knowledge production process set against a backdrop of the increasing market-based supply of business knowledge. Whilst there has been an extensive body of research into the emergence of various forms of managerial and technical specialist in the twentieth century, scholarship has not fully kept pace with changes that have become very visible in the twenty first concerning how knowledge is produced, validated, supplied and consumed through the market. A number of researchers, from a variety of approaches, have come to similar conclusions regarding the proliferation of experts similar to the ones described here. To paraphrase Knorr Cetina (2007: 361–2), a knowledge society is not simply a society of 'more knowledge' (Mokyr 2002) but also one permeated with new kinds of knowledge producer that attempt to redress the uncertainties surrounding the increased market provision of business knowledge. This expansive group might include those who participate in the production, evaluation and use of what Camic et al. (2012) describe as 'social knowledge'. By social knowledge they include those 'professional knowledge specialists located outside the academy' and whose knowledge is 'shaped directly at the point-of-practice' (ibid: 4). This definition—extremely broad, but useful—has much in common with Holmes and Marcus's (2006, 2008) investigations into the increasing numbers of experts performing 'research-like' roles in the economy. Knorr Cetina (2007: 367) similarly points to the 'macro-epistemic actors' that have arisen in recent years not just to supply but also to 'verify' the business knowledge produced and used by others.[7] Scholars have also begun to ask, as we have done here, whether the growth of a knowledge society is altering the composition and ecology of knowledge production and its validation (Camic et al. 2012).

There is a need for a specific Sociology of Business Knowledge to help understand the demands related to the increased market-based supply of knowledge. This begs the question as to what are the possible topics of investigation for such an enquiry. We take our cue from Knorr Cetina's early work on epistemic cultures (1999) which sought to understand both the production *and* warranting of knowledge. We have described in detail one highly particular (and potent) late modern form of knowledge producer. Their rise is interesting to study since their outputs were not (and in some circles are still not) judged as on a par with other expert knowledge making bodies. Yet their knowledge products are becoming extremely popular and influential in and beyond IT markets. We have described the rise of a technological expertise vested with increasing authority. We have examined how their authority seems to rest on the relationship between knowledge and the creation of an audience for that knowledge (Turner 2001).

The study of how specific forms of knowledge succeed or fail, including the circumstances that give rise to their acceptance or failure (Shapin 2001), came to prominence in the Sociology of Science in the 1990s (Bloor 1991). If the focus of initial studies were on what comes to count as knowledge in a specific time and place, according to particular groups or cultures, then the Sociology of Business Knowledge might usefully draw on a modified version of this template. Since, as we have shown here, the knowledge practices for building cognitive authority are co-extensive with the creation and maintenance of an audience, understanding the success of a body of knowledge must take certain necessary factors concerning audience construction into account. Here we have shown that what counts in the case of industry analysts is the production and circulation of *actionable* and *relevant* business knowledge, as well as with how that actionability and relevance is *verified* with potential audiences.[8] No matter its shape, scholars might usefully enquire into the reputed quality of business knowledge offered. How is business knowledge produced and verified in the twenty first century? What kinds of organizations are producing and proofing this knowledge? How does the authority of these knowledge producers relate to the followers of this knowledge? And most importantly, how do they go about verifying their knowledge products with their audiences?

We have reviewed cognate research into various forms of expertise including financial analysts, management consultants as well as industry analysts. We do not yet adequately understand how the suppliers of these new forms of business knowledge have achieved and continue to maintain such levels of authority. There is obviously much scope for developing a Sociology of Business Knowledge that attends to the content of knowledge and the process of its generation as well as variations across different epistemic systems in terms of the aforementioned exigencies of producing, validating and trading knowledge. This highlights the scope for developing, through more systematic comparison, a more general Sociology of Business Knowledge. There are likely to be key differences between these and other groups in how they establish and verify knowledge. These will be differences rooted in practices. There will also be different evidentiary grounds for what counts as effective knowledge and different ways for these different groups to create a following, and to prove the value of their outputs to an audience. We see a Sociology of Business Knowledge as able to maintain a focus on knowledge production whilst also offering insights into how knowledge outputs result from the particular demands of their production, which include verification by an audience. In a period when there are multiple new forms of business knowledge producer, we think that research on business knowledge, rather than simply lag behind practice, should be able to keep pace.

11.6. UNDERSTANDING THE ECOSYSTEM FOR INDUSTRY ANALYSIS: IMPLICATIONS FOR POLICY

We started this book by presenting an exchange between novice and seasoned industry analysts about the extent to which these experts direct markets. We hope we have presented evidence that throws light on this question. Although it was not our original goal to make policy prescriptions, we do in these final pages wish to make a couple of points about the implications of industry analyst influence for processes of technological innovation. This is because it was increasingly evident to us, during fieldwork, that industry analysts were not neutral with regard to wider processes of innovation within the IT sector. Yet there was a lack of clarity as to whether this influence was positive or negative. In the book we have sought to show how industry analysts are part of the knowledge infrastructures of the IT arena. We have also explored how the ecosystem for industry analysis has been changing in the face of new technologies for information exchange and the entrance of new players with different models for providing and trading expertise. The challenge today is that industry analysts, as they increase in number and compete for space, are both broadening and deepening their coverage.

This means that it is now common for IT vendors to be assessed many times over by different industry analysts firms. There are dozens of established players producing powerful rankings and assessments. It is important to understand not only the emerging heterogeneity of the evaluative ecosystem but also the kinds of friction that this creates for innovation. IT vendors are being assessed not by one or two but 'multiple' forms of ranking. They may also find themselves assessed quite differently by these rankings (i.e. according to different evaluative criteria) and with radically different results. In terms of the latter point, it is not unusual for a vendor to be assessed as the best on one industry analyst ranking, amongst the worst on another, and not listed whatsoever on a third (Sauder & Espeland 2006). Yet large and small IT vendors alike have little choice but to take industry analysts seriously, which creates new and pressing problems for them. Given the increasing numbers of industry analyst firms, which ones should they respond to? And how? Which may be the most receptive? And which have most influence over choices by adopters? And how should they be targeted?

We saw that organizational adopters and vendors might have rather different viewpoints on the industry analyst ecosystem. Thus, adopters sought the breadth and depth of knowledge over the whole IT market that the larger, established industry analyst firms could be trusted to deploy. Vendors might seek to engage a wider range of—smaller as well as larger—analyst organizations, and prioritize analysts according to their influence over the field (including influence with media as well as adopters). They may also find advantage in this plurality of analysts and their assessments, particularly if they feel disadvantaged by the framings offered by dominant players in the field, since diversity amongst analysts may provide other avenues for them to promote offerings.

As we have said, there is a lack of clarity about whether industry analysts are positive or negative with regard to processes of innovation. For instance, one set of studies suggest that being accountable to many, according to different criteria, is problematic. Technology vendors, in responding to multiple rankings, can be pulled in different directions (Sauder & Espeland 2006). Paraphrasing the words of the analyst relations consultant Jonny Bentwood (Chapter 10), when all the industry analysts see the world according to their own 'taxonomy', it is very easy to fall between different worldviews.

Others suggest that the proliferation of rankings and assessments could be positive because it could create new forms of 'entrepreneurship' (Stark 2011).

The friction created by multiple forms of assessment and ranking may not be a barrier but an essential requirement for innovation. It has been argued that economies face crises not because there are too many ranking bodies but because there are too few, they are too similar, or they are all located in one region. For instance, there is perceived to be a 'geographical' bias within industry analyst research. Many of the most important analyst firms are located in North America (see Appendix 1). As a result, vendors from outside the US or Canada are said to receive a more fragmented coverage. The analyst firms devote larger teams of analysts to assessing US/Canadian vendors as compared to other regions and this can be represented in the shape of research outputs. For instance, we heard numerous complaints of how some of the largest European vendors failed to even appear on Magic Quadrants or Forrester Waves. If this bias is correct then the non-appearance of technology vendors on some of the most important rankings could be a significant disadvantage. On the one hand, therefore, too much geographical alignment between industry analysts, or the presence of a dominant firm, reduces the scope for strategic manoeuvre by recipients. This can have a chilling effect that inhibits innovation and/or competition (ibid). On the other hand, if the arguments set out in this book are correct, that the 'heterogeneity' of the industry analyst ecosystem is increasing, this will be positive for innovation. Clearly, it is important for policy that scholars and others foster debate on this issue.

NOTES

1. The Oxford English Dictionary defines a hodgepodge as 'a clumsy mixture of ingredients'. This concept perhaps also has consequences for an emerging Sociology of Business Knowledge. Whilst the performativity thesis invites the reading that markets are a direct or partial consequence of theoretical economic models (Callon 1998, 2007, MacKenzie 2006), the hodgepodge notion suggests a much looser coupling between the various elements involved, and that these ideas might evolve out of, or at least be highly influenced by, practice.
2. Furthermore, it might be speculated that it is especially 'rankings' over other forms of business knowledge that create these specific dynamics. The introduction of a ranking radically changes the terrain in which non-fungible information-intensive products (technologies, expert services) are procured. As others have already noted, rankings create processes of 'reactivity' (Espeland & Sauder 2007) that means that actors and organizations will look to orient towards the evaluation (Chapter 9). This reorientation generates new forms of expertise (as well as markets for that expertise) (Sauder & Fine 2008).
3. See for instance, du Gay et al. (2012), who, like us, combine a performativity analysis with the work of Abbott (2005) to explicitly focus on the shift away from

single level accounts that operate within particular organizational boundaries to highlight 'assemblages'. They are interested in capturing the interstitial clusters where organizational events happen.

4. Scholars have looked at the role of external bodies in the circulation and certification of knowledge, especially most immediately the role played by the University Business School. These were, at least initially, practitioner dominated (Fourcade & Khurana 2011) but brought in more formal knowledge—initially from Engineering, and later on, the social sciences and latterly Economics and especially Financial Economics. However, Business Schools continue to be dominated by practical concerns, which conditions their struggle for authority (Fourcade & Khurana 2011). They are seen to mediate between academic (e.g. social science-based) knowledge and the world of business practice. Suddaby and Greenwood (2001: 936) argue that Business School research can be seen to follow rather than lead business practice, noting how 'much academic research . . . is devoted to testing the validity of managerial "concepts in use"'. They go on, 'Business Schools provide a forum for sober second thought, where managerial knowledge is evaluated and refined'. They thus serve as a locus for exercising 'a form of due diligence by ensuring that knowledge claims made by others are accurate' (Suddaby & Greenwood 2001: 943). Suddaby and Greenwood explore the interaction between Business Schools, consultant and business gurus who straddle these domains in legitimating particular kinds of knowledge output.

5. Fourcade and Khurana (2011: 6) highlight the ways in which Economics, and especially Financial Economics gains priority in Business Schools and in business practice (e.g., through mergers and acquisition). They talk of the 'hinged' evolution of the fields of Economics and Business.

6. Buy Side Vs. Sell Side Analysts http://www.investopedia.com/articles/ financialcareers/ 11/sell-side-buy-side-analysts.asp. Accessed 19 January 2015.

7. Knorr Cetina (2007) includes as examples of those supplying and verifying knowledge credit rating agencies (Sinclair 2014), patent offices, management consultancies, accounting firms and investment analysts. To her list we could also add accreditation bodies, press agencies (Czarniawska 2011), professional associations, international organizations (Harper 2000), standards bodies (Busch 2011), practitioner management journals (Thrift 2005) and of course industry analysts.

8. We are grateful to C. F. Helgesson for helping us think about our contribution in this way.

List of Industry Analyst and IT Market Research Firms[1]

6Sight, US
ABI Research, US
Acacia Research Group, US
Accenture, Ireland
Access Intelligence, LLC, US
AccuStream iMedia Research, US
ACG Research, US
ACSEITIS, France
Actionable Intelligence, Inc., US
Adaptive Path, LLC, US
Aging in Place Technology Watch
Aite Group LLC, US
AltaTerra Ltd., US
Altimeter Group, US
Ambient Insight Research, US
AMI Partners, Inc., US
AMR Research, US
Analysys Mason, UK
Analysys Research, UK
Anastasia, Italy
Andreas Weber Communciations, Germany
Apps Run the World, US
Arab Advisors Group Ltd, Jordan
Aragon Research, Inc., US
ARC Advisory Group, US
Arcati, UK
Arete Research, UK
Argus Research Company, US
Arlen Communications Inc., US
Ars Logica, US
Arthur D. Little, UK
Ashton, Metzler & Associates, US
A-Team Group, UK
ATLANTIC-ACM, US
Attributes Associates, UK
Avasant, US
Axendia, Inc., US
AxiCom, US
B2B Analysts, US
B2C Partners, US
Barometrix Software Corp., US

BASDA Ltd., UK
Basex, Inc., US
BDA China Ltd., China
Beagle Research Group, LLC, US
Benchmarking Partners, Inc., US
benchmark-it.co.uk, UK
Berg Insight AB, Sweden
Berkeley Design Technology, Inc., US
BERTL, Inc., US
Better Buys for Business, US
Beyond IT, US
BI Research, US
Big Picture Research, US
BigInsights, Australia
Bissett Communications Corp., US
Bloom & Wallace, US
Bloor Research, UK
Bluefin Research Partners, Inc., US
BMI-TechKnowledge, South Africa
Bock & Company, US
BPM Partners, Inc., US
BRAICONN, Germany
Brandon Hall Research, US
Branham Group, Canada
Breakaway Information Group, Inc., US
Brimstone Hill, US
Broadbandtrends LLC, US
Brockmann & Company, US
Bruce Silver Associates, US
BSRIA Ltd, UK
BuddeComm, Australia
Burton Group, US
Business & Information Tech. Group, France
Business Application Research Cen., Germany
Business Intelligence Group (BIG), US
Butler Analytics, UK
Butler Group, UK
Buyers Laboratory, US
Cambashi Limited, UK
Cambridge Computer Services, Inc., US
Camden Associates, US
Canalys, UK
Carmel Group, US
C-Core, Canada
CCS Insight, UK
CCW Research, China
CEB TowerGroup, US
Celent LLC, US
CERTPOINT Systems, Inc., US
ChainLink Research, US
Chapman Alliance LLC, US
CharisCo Ltd., UK
Chartis Research, UK

CIMdata, Inc., US
Clabby Analytics, US
Clear Thinking Research, Inc., US
Clipper Group, US
CLK Strategies, US
Cohasset Associates, Inc., US
Collaborative Product Dev. Assoc., US
COMMFusion, US
Common Sense Advisory, Inc., US
Communication Network Architects, US
Compass, UK
Compass Intelligence, US
Compete, Inc., US
Computer Economics, Inc., US
Constellation Research, LLC, US
ContactBabel, UK
CONTEXT, UK
Convergencia Latina, Argentina
Cornerstone Advisors, US
Corporate Integrity, LLC, US
Coughlin Associates, US
Counterpoint Tech. Market Research, China
CPA Computer Report, US
CRC-Pinnacle Consulting, China
Creative Strategies, US
CT Link, Inc., US
CTS (Computer Training Services), US
Current Analysis, Inc., US
Currid & Company, US
Cutter Consortium, US
CXP, France
CyberEdge Group, LLC, US
CyberMedia Research (CMR), India
Cyon Research, US
Cyveillance, Inc., US
DA Digital, LLC, US
Daratech, Inc., US
Data Mobility Group, US
DataGate, Inc., Japan
Datamonitor plc, UK
dBrn Associates, Inc., US
DCIG, US
DeepStorage.net, US
Dell'Oro Group, US
Delphi Group, US
DFC Intelligence, US
Diffraction Analysis, France
Digital Clarity Group (DCG), US
Digital World Research, LLC. (DWR), US
DigiTimes Research, Taiwan
Directions on Microsoft, US
Discerning Analytics, US
DisplaySearch, US

Disruptive Analysis Ltd., UK
Distributed Networking Associates, US
Dittberner Associates, Inc., US
DMG Consulting, US
Doculabs, Inc., US
Dow Brook Advisory Services, US
Dragon Slayer Consulting, US
Dresner Advisory Services, LLC, US
Duquesne Group, France
DW Channels Ltd, UK
ebizQ, US
EC Research Corp., Japan
Econsultancy, UK
Edison Group, Inc., US
eDJ Group, US
Eduventures, LLC, US
Eighty Twenty Insight, UK
Elemental Links, US
eMarketer Inc., US
Embedded Insights, US
Emerging Technologies Group, Inc., US
eMetaprise Research, Belgium
Encore Info, US
Enders Analysis, Ltd., UK
Endpoint Technologies Associates, Inc., US
Enterprise Application Consulting, US
Enterprise Computing Advisors, US
Enterprise Strategy Group (ESG), US
Ernst & Young, US
ERP Forum Japan, Japan
Essential Solutions Corp., US
Euroland, UK
Evaluator Group, Inc., US
Evans Data Corp., US
Everest Group, US
eVergance Partners, LLC, US
Everware-CBDi, Inc., US
Exact Ventures, US
Experton Group AG, Germany
Experture LLC, US
Explorasia, Philippines
FactPoint Group, US
Farpoint Group, US
Ferris Research, US
FiSite Research, US
Flanagan Consulting, US
Focus Consulting, US
Forrester Research, Inc., US
Forward Concepts Co., US
Fox Group Consulting, Canada
Freeform Dynamics Ltd., UK
FronTier Associates, France
Frost & Sullivan, US

Fuji Chimera Research Institute, Inc., Japan
Gabriel Consulting Group, Inc., US
gap intelligence, US
Gartner Inc., US
GCR Custom Research, LLC, US
GfK Boutique Research, US
GfK Marketing Services UK Ltd., UK
GfK Retail and Tech. GmbH, Germany
GigaOM, US
GlassHouse Technologies, Inc., US
Gleacher & Company, US
Global Smart Energy, US
GovWin, US
Grant Analysis & Consulting, UK
GRC 20/20, US
Green Research, US
GreenMonk, Spain
Greentech Media (GTM Research), US
Grey Consulting, US
Greyhound Knowledge Group, India
GroupM, US
Harvard Research Group, Inc., US
Harvey Spencer Associates, US
Heavy Reading, US
Hewson Group, UK
High Road Communications, Canada
Hoey Associates, Canada
Hong Kong Telecoms Users Group, China
Horses for Sources, US
HOT Telecom, Canada
HR.com, Canada
Hypatia Research, LLC, US
IANS Research, US
IBISWorld, US
IBM Global Technology Services, US
IDAnalyst, US
IDATE, France
IDC, US
IDC Energy Insights, US
IDC Financial Insights, US
IDC Government Insights, US
IDC Health Insights, US
IDC Manufacturing Insights, US
IDC Retail Insights, US
Ideas International Ltd, US
IDG, US
iGR, Inc., US
IHL Consulting Group, Inc., US
IHS Cambridge Energy Research Assoc., US
IHS, Inc., US
Ikam Systems, UK
Illuminata, Inc., US
iLocus, India

IMERGE Consulting
IMEX Research, US
Industry Analysts, Inc, US
iNet Interactive, US
Inflection Point Research, LLC., US
InfoCom GmbH, Germany
Infonetics Research, US
Informa Telecoms & Media, UK
Information Architected, US
Information Tech. Intelligence Corp., US
Information Tech. Research Corp., Japan
infoSource SA, Switzerland
InfoTech, US
Info-Tech Research Group, Canada
InfoTrends, Inc., US
InMedica, UK
Inmon Data Systems, US
Inside Digital Media, Inc., US
Insight 64
Insight Research Corp., US
Intellicom Analytics, LLC, US
Intelligent Business Strategies, UK
Interarbor Solutions, LLC, US
Intermedium, Australia
Int. Association of Outsourcing Profs, US
Internet Research Group, US
Interpret LLC, US
Interquest, US
Intersect360 Research, US
Intrepid Learning Solutions, US
ISG (Information Services Group), US
IT Data, Brazil
IT Strategies, US
IT-Harvest, US
J Arnold & Associates, Canada
J.Gold Associates, US
Jackdaw Research, US
Javelin Strategy & Research, US
Jeff Kagan, US
JEMM Research, France
JGunn Research, US
John Juliano Computer Services, US
John Morton Institute, US
Jon Peddie Research, US
Josh Krischer & Associates, Germany
JP Morgan, US
Judy Sweeney Research
Juniper Research Ltd, UK
K2 Enterprises, US
Kable Ltd., UK
Kelcor, Inc, US
Kennedy Information, Inc., US
KLAS Enterprises LLC, US

Knowledge Research Group, South Korea
KPMG, UK
Kuppinger Cole Ltd., Germany
Kusnetzky Group, US
Layland Consulting, US
Leichtman Research Group (LRG), US
LightCounting, LLC, US
Linley Group, Inc., US
Lippis Enterprises, Inc., US
LNS Research, US
Longhaus Pty Ltd., Australia
Lopez Research LLC, US
Lunendonk GmbH, Germany
Lux Research Inc., US
M:Metrics, Inc., US
M2 Research, Inc., US
MacArthur Stroud International, UK
Macehiter Ward-Dutton (MWD), UK
MachNation, US
Madison Advisors, US
Maravedis-Rethink, Canada
Mark H. Goldberg & Assoc. Inc., Canada
MARKESS International, France
Market Intell. & Consulting Inst., Taiwan
Marketing and Planning Systems, US
Marketing Research Consultants (MRC), US
Marsh, Inc., US
Masie Center, US
Mathison Group, US
Matterhorn Group, US
Maverick China Research, China
McGee-Smith Analytics, US
McLean & Company, Canada
Media Partners Asia Ltd (MPA), China
Megabuyte, UK
Mercator Advisory Group, Inc., US
Mercury Research, US
Mesabi Group LLC, US
MGI Research, US
MIC Research Institute Ltd., Japan
Mintel International Group Ltd., UK
MM Research Institute, Ltd., Japan
Mobile Ecosystem, US
Mobile Experts, US
Mobilocity, US
Moriana Group, UK
msmd advisors Ltd, UK
MultiMedia Intelligence, US
Multimedia Research Group, Inc., US
MZA Ltd., UK
Navigant Research, US
NBI/Michael Sone Associates Inc., Canada
NCW, Inc., US

NelsonHall, UK
Nemertes Research, US
Neo Advisory, US
NetConsulting, Italy
NetForecast, Inc., US
Neuralytix, US
New Hampshire Pub. Utilities Comm., US
New Paradigm Research Group, US
New River Marketing Research, US
Newton-Evans Research Company, US
Newzoo, Netherlands
Nomura Research Institute, Ltd., Japan
Northern Sky Research, LLC (NSR), US
Novarica, US
NPD Group, US
Nucleus Research, US
Occidental Comm. Pty Ltd., Australia
Offshore Insights, India
Om Advisory Pvt. Ltd., India
Opus Research, Inc., US
Orbys Consulting Ltd, UK
Orion Partners LLP, UK
OTR Global Ltd, US
Outsell, Inc., US
Ovum, UK
Ovum-RHK, US
PA Consulting Group, UK
Parks Associates, US
Partner Research Corp. (PRC), Canada
Patricia Seybold Group, US
Peerstone Research, US
PELORUS Group, US
Penteo, Spain
Performance Solutions International, US
Peter Carr Advisory, Australia
Petrosky.com, US
Pfeiffer Consulting, France
PhoCusWright, Inc., US
Photofinishing News, US
Pierre Audoin Consultants (PAC), France
Pike Research, US
Plant-Wide Research (PWR), US
Point Topic Ltd., UK
Points North Group, US
Precursor Group, US
PricewaterhouseCoopers (PwC), US
Prince & Cooke, Argentina
PrintCom Consulting Group, US
Probe Group LLC, US
ProCertify
Procullux Ventures, UK
Ptak Associates LLC, US
Pyramid Research, US

Quint Wellington Redwood, Netherlands
Quocirca Ltd., UK
RAAD Consult, Germany
Radcliffe Advisory Services Ltd., UK
Radicati Group, US
RampRate, Inc., US
Real World Technologies, US
Red Monk, US
Research In Action, Germany
Retail Systems Research (RSR), US
RetailNet Group, US
Reticle Research, US
RIT, US
Robert Frances Group, Inc. (RFG), US
RobertGrayDirect, US
S2 Intelligence, Australia
Saddletree Research, Inc., US
Sage Research, US
Salmon & Associates, Canada
Schwetz Consulting, Germany
SeaBoard Group, Canada
SecurityCurve, US
Select, Mexico
Sell More Now Inc., US
Semicast Research Ltd., UK
Semico Research Corp., US
Senza Fili Consulting LLC., US
Seraphim Group, US
Service & Support Professionals Assoc., US
Service Performance Insight Research, US
Seybold Seminars, Pubs. & Consulting, US
Shenandoah Analytics, LLC, US
Sherburne & Associates, US
Shosteck Group, US
Siemens, Germany
Signals Research Group LLC, US
Signals Telecom Consulting, Argentina
Silicon Insider, US
Silverton Consulting, Inc. (SCI), US
Simba Information, US
Sinn Consulting, Germany
SiriusDecisions, US
SIRMI SPA, Italy
SIS Market Research, US
SiteIQ, US
Sky Light Research (SLR), US
Smart Insights, France
SMB Group, Inc., US
SMB Research, US
Smith's Point Analytics, US
SNL Kagan, US
Software Strategies, UK
Solucom KLC, France

SOLUTIONS, US
SoundView Technology Group, US
Source+, UK
Spar Point Research LLC, US
SpencerLab Digital Color Laboratory, US
Standford Group Company, US
Standish Group, US
STKI, Israel
Storage Strategies NOW, US
Storage Switzerland, LLC, US
StorageIO Group, US
Strand Consult, Denmark
Strassmann, Inc., US
Stratecast Partners, US
Strategic Research Corp., US
Strategies UnLtd, US
Strategy Analytics, Inc., US
Strategy Meets Action, US
Strategy Partners, UK
Structure Research, Canada
Supply Chain Insights LLC
Synergy Research Group, Inc. (SRG), US
Synthexis, US
T3i Group LLC, US
Tabb Group, US
TAK Analytics Research, Inc., Japan
Taneja Group, US
Taxal Ltd, UK
Tebbo, UK
Tech Research Asia, Australia
Tech Research Services, US
Techaisle, US
TechCaliber Consulting, LLC, US
Tech-Clarity, Inc., US
TechConsult GmbH, Germany
TechIntelligence, LLC, US
TechKnowledge Strategies, Inc., US
TechMarketView LLP, UK
TechniCom, Inc., US
Techno Systems Research, Japan
Technology Business Research, Inc., US
Technology Evaluation Centers Inc., Canada
Technology Research Institute (TRI), US
Techtel Corp., US
TechVentive, US
TechVisor.JP, Ltd., Japan
TekPlus Ltd, UK
Telechoice, Inc., US
Telecom Pragmatics, Inc., US
TeleSpan Publishing Corp., US
Telsyte, Australia
Temkin Group, US
TEQConsult Group, US

The 451 Group, US
The Advisory Board Company, US
The Advisory Council, US
The AlignIT Group, LLC., US
The Bloor Group, UK
The Brian Madden Company, LLC, US
The CDI Institute, US
The Competitive Intelligence Unit, Mexico
The Data Warehousing Institute, US
The Diffusion Group (TDG), US
The Economist Intelligence Unit Ltd, UK
The Envisioneering Group, US
The Information Difference, UK
The Kelsey Group, US
The METISfiles, Netherlands
The Ogren Group, US
The Rayno Report, US
The Real Story Group, US
The Research Board, US
The Strategic Counsel, Canada
The Tolly Group, US
The Virtualization Practice, US
The W Group, US
ThinkBalm, US
ThinkJar LLC, US
THINKstrategies, US
Third Nature, Inc., US
Tholons, US
Tirias Research, US
TM Forum, US
TNS Global, UK
Toigo Partners International, LLC, US
Topology Research Institute (TRI)
TRAC Research, US
Treillage Network Strategies, Inc., US
Trends Consulting, Argentina
Triple Tree, LLC, US
tsm strategies, UK
Two Crows, US
UCStrategies, US
UniChina Consulting Corp., China
UniComm Consulting, LLC, US
Unified-View, US
Upside Research, Inc., US
Vanguard Communications Corp., US
VDC Research Group, Inc., US
Ventana Research, US
Verdantix Ltd, UK
Vertical Systems Group, Inc., UK
Viewpoint Research, US
Visiongain Ltd., UK
voke, inc., US
WebFeet Research, US

Webster Buchanan Research, UK
Welchman Consulting, LLC, US
Wellington Research & IT Policy Compliance
WhatTheyThink.com, US
Wikibon, US
WinterCorp, US
WinterGreen Research, Inc., US
Wireless Explorers, UK
Wireless Intelligence, UK
WiseAnalytics, US
WiseHarbor, US
Wohl Associates, US
Workgroup Strategic Services, US
Yankee Group, US
Yano Research Institute Ltd. (YRI), Japan
Yphise, France
Zona Research, US

NOTE

1. This list has been compiled from the Architect database maintained by ARInsights (http://www.arinsights.com). The database describes these firms as either market research or industry analyst firms. We have not included sole-traders in this list. Thanks to Duncan Chapple for making this data available to us.

Fieldwork Conducted

Interviews with industry analysts and other related actors

Name of interviewee directly referred to in book	Location of interview	Date of interview
Franco Arzuffi, Gartner client*	London	5 June 2013
Jonny Bentwood, Chief Innovation Officer, Edelman Public Relations	London	20 October 2009
Davide Bonamini, VTE CRM*	London	4 June 2013
Duncan Chapple, Director, KeaCompany	London and Edinburgh	7 March 2013, 18 October 2013
Jon Collins, Director, Freeform Dynamics	Tetbury	16 November 2009
Khalda De Sousa, ex-Gartner analyst and now Principal Analyst, HfS Research	London	17 September 2014
Jane Doorly, vice President European Research, IDC	Telephone	3 February 2014
Alex Drow (pseudonym), Managing VP, Gartner	London	15 March 2011
Nancy Erskine, Ombudsman, Gartner	Telephone	20 September 2011
Gideon Gartner, founder and previous CEO of Gartner	Telephone	5 May 2010
James Governor, Founder and Director Redmonk	London	3 March 2009
Jen Lebber (pseudonym), Global Vice President, Gartner	Telephone	6 January 2014
Ludovic Leforestier, Analyst Relations at BearingPoint Consultancy	London, and Telephone	14 February 2014, 13 December 2013, 24 May 2013
Simon Levin, ex-Gartner analyst. Now Director of The Skills Connection*	London	13 March 2013
Stefano Machera, Gartner client*	London	5 June 2013
Danile Matkovits, analyst relations, Deloitte*	London	17 September 2014
Efrem Mallach, analyst relations and Founder of Kenwood Group*	Edinburgh	18 September 2014
Paul Winter (pseudonym), Research VP, Gartner	Edinburgh	25 August 2011
David Mitchell Research Director Ovum Research	Edinburgh	19 March 2010
Alessandro Monza, Gartner client*	London	5 June 2013
Peter Muller, ex-Gartner analyst and now working for a technology vendor*	London	5 June 2013

(*continued*)

Continued

Name of interviewee directly referred to in book	Location of interview	Date of interview
Rick Nash, analyst relations, Director Spotlight Analyst Relations	Edinburgh	23 September 2014
Bill O'Hara (pseudonym), Research Director, Gartner*	London	5 June 2013
Toby Old (pseudonym), Research VP, Gartner	Skype	25 August 2011
Nick Patience, founder 451 Research*	London	17 September 2014
Robin Schaffer, analyst relations, NICE Systems*	London	16 September 2014
David Taylor, analyst relations at Vodafone*	London	16 September 2014
Elias Thomas (pseudonym), VP Distinguished Analyst, Gartner	London, Edinburgh	7 July 2009, 14 January 2010, 5 November 2015
Oliver Vale, Gartner client*	London	5 June 2013
Neil Ward Dutton, co-founder and Research Director at MWD Advisors	London	20 October 2009
Debleena Paul, analyst relations, SapientNitro*	London	16 September 2014
Samyr Jriri, Kea Company*	London	17 September 2014
Yash Khanna, Director, Analyst Relations, Tata*	London	16 September 2014
Roy (pseudonym), IT Director at 'Langdon'	Langdon	15 March 2006
Jono Smith, Marketing Director, Sungard	Altrincham	2 March 2006
Richard Forrest, Internationalisation Director, Sungard	Altrincham	2 March 2006
Buster Hale, IT Director at University	Orlando	20 October 2005
Udo Pieles, Pre-Sales Engineer, SAP	Edinburgh	16 August 2005

* Indicates interviewed either with or by Gian Marco Campagnolo

Observation of industry analysts

Name	Approx. hours observation	Location of observation	Date of observation
IIAR Webinar, Negotiating with Gartner	1 hour	Telephone	22 January 2015
Kea Company Analyst Relations Forum	2 days	London	16/17 September 2014
IIAR webinar, Tracking Analyst Influence: Is there an easier way?	1 hour	Telephone	6 July 2014
IIAR webinar, Is there Really Magic in the MQ?, Richard Stiennon	1 hour	Telephone	7 May 2014
IIAR webinar, How Big is the IT Research Market?, Outsell	1 hour	Telephone	26 March 2014
IIAR networking event	4 hours	London	4 December 2013
Gartner webinar, Jeffrey Mann, Build a Social Strategy to Encourage and Optimize Collaboration	1 hour	Telephone	24 July 2013
IIAR Webinar, Julie Thomas, Gartner Magic Quadrant Enhancements 2013	1 hour	Telephone	23 July 2013
IIAR webinar, Gartner's 'Ombudsman' Nancy Erskine	1 hour	Telephone	28 June 2013
Gartner Customer Relationship Management Summit*	2 days	London	4/5 June 2013
IIAR workshop at Tata	4 hours	London	13 March 2013
IIAR workshop at Edelman, including presentation by Forrester	4 hours	London	3 October 2012
IIAR Gartner exclusive: Your questions answered on great presentations	1 hour	Telephone	22 May 2012
Gartner webinar, Adam Sarner, Social CRM: The Next Generation of Customer Innovation	1 hour	Telephone	21 March 2012
IIAR Webinar, Jeff Golterman, Gartner Research and Analyst Relations Community	1 hour	Telephone	24 March 2011
Gartner Customer Relationship Management Summit	2 days	London	14–15 March 2011
Gartner Customer Relationship Management Summit	2 days	London	16–17 March 2010
SageCircle webinar, Carter Lusher, Moving the Dot	1 hour	Telephone	5 October 2009
EDUCAUSE conference	3 days	Orlando	18–21 October 2005

* Indicates observations carried out by Gian Marco Campagnolo

Further related fieldwork that informs the book

The book is further contextualized and informed by two different ethnographic studies of enterprise system procurement and implementation.

ERP implementation study discussed in Chapter 7 (1998–2005)	• We conducted approx. 40 semi-structured (and tape-recorded) interviews with members of the 'Langdon' IT team, users, and university managers.
	• We conducted 5 semi-structured (and tape recorded) interviews with SAP employees, which included the Pre-Sales Engineer, Solution Manager, and Sales team.
	• We conducted 1 semi-structured (and tape recorded) interview with the Langdon IT Director as well as a number of more informal conversations.
	• We conducted 2 focus groups with users of the ERP system. We conducted 1 focus group with the Langdon IT team and wider university managers (all focus groups were tape recorded).
	• Attended 5 vendor user group meetings where able to talk with other users making use of industry analyst research.
	• We had full access to the Langdon IT Director's email for more than a year (collected several hundred relevant emails). This contained exchanges between the IT Director, SAP and Gartner.
	• We observed Langdon IT project meetings (approx. 2 hours a month over a 2 year period).
CRM procurement study discussed in Chapters 5 and 6 (2000–2001)	• We carried out a year-long observation at a local government office that included one of the authors observing the CRM procurement team meetings (he attended meetings once every month over the period of a year).
	• We also conducted approx. 20 semi-structured (and tape recorded) interviews with members of the procurement team.
	• We had access to procurement team written communications, and exchanges between the procurement team and Gartner analysts.

Bibliography

Abbott, A. (1988). *The System Of Professions: An Essay On The Division Of Expert Labor*, Chicago & London: The University Of Chicago Press.

Abbott, A. (1995). Things Of Boundaries, *Social Research, Defining The Boundaries Of Social Inquiry*, 62(4): 857–82.

Abbott, A. (2005). Linked Ecologies: States And Universities As Environments For Professions, *Sociological Theory*, 23(3): 245–74.

Abernathy, W. J. & Utterback, J. M. (1978). Patterns Of Innovation In Technology, *Technology Review*, June/July: 40–7.

Abrahamson, E. (1991). Managerial Fads and Fashions: The Diffusion and Rejection of Innovations, *Academy of Management Review* 16(3): 586–612.

Abrahamson, E. (1996). Management Fashion. *Academy Of Management Review*, 21(1): 254–85.

Abrahamson, E., & Fairchild, E., (1999). Management Fashion: Lifecycles, Triggers, And Collective Learning Processes, *Administrative Science Quarterly*, 44: 708–40.

Abrahamson, E. & Fairchild, G. (2001). Knowledge Industries And Idea Entrepreneurs: New Dimensions Of Innovative Products, Services, And Organisations. In C. B. Schoonhoven & E. Romanelli (Eds.), *The Entrepreneurship Dynamic: Origins Of Entrepreneurship And The Evolution Of Industries*. Stanford, California: Stanford University Press: 147–77.

Adler, P. S. & Heckscher, C. (2006). Towards Collaborative Community. In C. Heckscher & P. S. Adler (Eds.), *The Firm As A Collaborative Community: Reconstructing Trust In The Knowledge Economy*. New York: Oxford University Press: 11–106.

Agarwal, R. & Tripsas, M. (2008). Technology And Industry Evolution. In S. Shane (Ed) *The Handbook Of Technology And Innovation Management*, New York: Wiley: Chap. 1, 3–55.

Akera, A. (2001). Voluntarism And The Fruits Of Collaboration: The IBM User Group Share. *Technology And Culture*, 42(4): 710–36.

Akera, A. (2007). Constructing A Representation For An Ecology Of Knowledge: Methodological Advances In The Integration Of Knowledge And Its Various Contexts. *Social Studies Of Science*, 37(3): 413–41.

Akrich, M. & Latour, B. (1992). A Summary Of A Convenient Vocabulary For The Semiotics Of Human And Nonhuman Assemblies. In W. Bijker & J. Law (Eds.), *Shaping Technology/Building Society*. Cambridge, Mass.: MIT Press. Chap. 9: 259–64.

Alexander, J. C. (2011). *Performance And Power*. Cambridge: Polity.

Aldridge, A. (1994). The Construction Of Rational Consumption In Which? Magazine: The More Blobs The Better?. *Sociology*, 28: 899–912.

Aldridge, M. & Evetts, J. (2003). Rethinking The Concept Of Professionalism: The Case Of Journalism, *British Journal Of Sociology*, 54(4): 547–64.

Alvesson, M. (2001). Knowledge Work: Ambiguity, Image And Identity, *Human Relations*, 54: 863–86.

Anand, N. & Peterson, R. (2000). When Market Information Constitutes Fields: Sensemaking Of Markets In The Commercial Music Industry. *Organisation Science*, 11(3): 270–84.

Anderson, C. (2006). *The Long Tail: Why The Future Of Business Is Selling Less Of More*, New York: Hyperion.

Anderson-Gough, F., Grey, C & Robson, K. (2006). Professionals, Networking And The Networked Professional. In Royston Greenwood & Roy Suddaby (Eds) *Professional Service Firms: Research In The Sociology Of Organisations* Bingley: Emerald Group/JAI Press, Vol. 24: 231–56.

Anleu, S. (1992). The Professionalisation Of Social Work? A Case Study Of Three Organisational Settings, *Sociology*, 26(1): 46–63.

Araujo, L. (2007). Markets, Market-Making And Marketing. *Marketing Theory*, 7(3): 211–26.

Argyris, C. (1954). *The Impact Of Budgets On People*. New York: Controllership Foundation.

Armbrüster, T. (2006). *The Economics And Sociology Of Management Consulting*. Cambridge University Press.

Aspers, P. (2007). Theory, Reality, And Performativity In Markets. *American Journal Of Economics And Sociology*, 66(2): 379–98.

ATA Research (2008). *Directory Of Industry Analyst Firms*, ATA Research. Available online at: http://ataresearch.alltheanalysts.com/industry_analyst_firm_directory.pdf. Accessed 20 May 2013.

Austin, J. (1962). *How To Do Things With Words*, Cambridge, Mass.: Harvard University Press.

Avgerou, C., Ciborra, C., & Land, F. (2004). *The Social Study Of ICT: Innovation, Actors And Contexts*. Oxford University Press.

Bakker, S., van Lente, H. & Meeus, M. (2011). Arenas Of Expectations For Hydrogen Technologies, *Technological Forecasting & Social Change* 78: 152–62.

Balnaves, M., O'Regan, T., & Goldsmith, B. (2011). *Rating The Audience: The Business Of Media*. London: A&C Black.

Barben, D., Fisher, E., Selin, C. & Guston, D. (2007). Anticipatory Governance Of Nanotechnology: Foresight, Engagement, And Integration. In E. Hackett, O. Amsterdamska, M. Lynch & J. Wajcman (Eds), *The Handbook Of Science And Technology Studies*, 3rd Edition. Cambridge, Mass.: MIT Press: 979–1000.

Barnes, B. (1983). Social Life As Bootstrapped Induction, *Sociology*, 17: 524–45.

Barnes, B., Bloor, D., & Henry, J. (1996). *Scientific Knowledge: A Sociological Analysis*, Chicago: University Of Chicago Press.

Barry, A. (2001). *Political Machines: Governing A Technological Society*. Bloomsbury Publishing.

Baskerville, R. & Myers. M. (2009). Fashion Waves In Information Systems Research And Practice, *MIS Quarterly*, 33(4): 647–62.

Becker, H. S. (1982). *Art Worlds*. Berkeley, California: University Of California Press.

Beckert, J. & Aspers, P. (2011). *The Worth Of Goods: Valuation And Pricing In The Economy*. New York: Oxford University Press.

Berg, M. & Timmermans, S. (2000). Orders And Their Others: On The Constitution Of Universalities In Medical Work. *Configurations*, 8(1): 31–61.

Berghoff, H., Scranton, P. & Spiekermann, U. (2012). *The Rise Of Marketing And Market Research.* New York: Palgrave Macmillan.

Bernard, J. G. & Gallupe, R. B. (2013). IT Industry Analysts: A Review And Two Research Agendas. *Communications Of The Association For Information Systems,* 33(1): 16.

Bessy, C. & Chauvin, P. M. (2013). The Power Of Market Intermediaries: From Information To Valuation Processes. *Valuation Studies,* 1(1): 83–117.

Beunza, D. & Stark, D. (2004). Tools Of The Trade: The Socio-Technology Of Arbitrage In A Wall Street Trading Room, *Industrial And Corporate Change,* 13(2): 369–400.

Beunza, D. & Garud, R. (2007). Calculators, Lemmings Or Frame-Makers? The Intermediary Role Of Securities Analysts, *The Sociological Review,* 55: 13–39.

Blank, G. (2007). *Critics, Ratings, And Society: The Sociology Of Reviews.* Lanham, Md.: Rowman & Littlefield.

Blau, P. M. (1994). *The Organisation Of Academic Work.* (2nd ed.) New Brunswick NJ: Transaction Publishers.

Bloomfield, B. & Vurdubakis, T. (1997). Visions Of Organisation And Organisations Of Vision: The Representational Practices Of Information Systems Development. *Accounting, Organisations And Society,* 22(7): 639–68.

Bloomfield, B. P. & Vurdubakis, T. (2002). The Vision Thing: Constructing Technology And The Future In Management Advice. In T. Clark & R. Fincham (Eds) *Critical Consulting: New Perspectives On The Management Advice Industry.* Oxford: Blackwell, 115–29.

Bloor, D. (1991). *Knowledge And Social Imagery.* Chicago: University Of Chicago Press.

Boot, A.W.W., Milbourn, T.T., & Schmeits, A. (2006). Credit Ratings As Coordination Mechanisms, *The Review of Financial Studies,* 18(1): 81–118.

Borup, M., Brown, N., Konrad, K. & van Lente, H. (2006). The Sociology Of Expectations In Science And Technology, *Technology Analysis & Strategic Management,* 18 (3–4): 285–98.

Bott, E. (2012). Why Does The IT Industry Continue To Listen To Gartner? *Zdnet.* Available online at: http://www.Zdnet.Com/Why-Does-The-It-Industry-Continue-To-Listen-To-Gartner-7000001394/. Accessed 5 August 2014.

Bourdieu, P. (2005). Principles Of An Economic Anthropology. In. Smelser & R. Swedberg (Eds) *The Handbook Of Economic Sociology,* Princeton NJ: Princeton University Press: 75–89.

Bowker, G. & Star, S. (1999). *Sorting Things Out: Classification And Its Consequences,* Cambridge, Massachusetts: MIT Press.

Brante, T. (1988). Sociological Approaches To The Professions, *Acta Sociologica,* 31(2): 119–42.

Bresciani, S. & Eppler, M.J. (2008). Gartner's Magic Quadrant And Hype Cycle, *Collaborative Knowledge Visualization Case Study Series,* Case Nr. 2, University Della Swizzera Italiana, Institute Of Marketing And Communication Management, Available online at: http://www.Knowledge-Communication.Org/Pdf/Gartner_Teaching_Case_Study_Updated.Pdf Accessed 22 October 2014.

Broniarczyk, S. M. & Alba, J. W. (1994). The Importance Of The Brand In Brand Extension. *Journal Of Marketing Research,* 31(2): 214–28.

Brown, N. (2003). Hope Against Hype: Accountability In Biopasts, Presents And Futures' *Science Studies* 2: 3–21.

Brown, N, Rappert, B. & Webster, A. (2000). Introducing Contested Futures: From Looking Into The Future To Looking At The Future. In N. Brown, B. Rappert & A. Webster (Eds), *Contested Futures: A Sociology Of Prospective Science And Technology*. Aldershot: Ashgate: 3–20.

Brown, N. & Michael, M. (2003). A Sociology Of Expectations: Retrospecting Prospects And Prospecting Retrospects, *Technology Analysis And Strategic Management* 15(1): 3–18.

Burks, T. D. (2006). Use Of Information Technology Research Organisations As Innovation Support And Decision Making Tools. In M. Murray & H. R. Weistroffer (Eds), *Proceedings Of The Ninth Annual Conference Of The Southern Association For Information Systems*. Jacksonville, Fla.: SAIS: 8–14.

Burns, T. & Stalker, G. M. (1959). *The Management Of Innovation*, London: Tavistock.

Burton, B. & Aston, T. (2004). How Gartner Evaluates Vendors In A Market, Document ID Number: G00123716.

Busch, L. (2011). *Standards: Recipes For Reality*. Cambridge MA: MIT Press.

Cabantous, L. & Gond, J. P. (2011). Rational Decision Making As Performative Praxis: Explaining Rationality's Eternel Retour. *Organisation Science*, 22(3): 573–86.

Callon, M. (1986). Elements Of A Sociology Of Translation: Domestication Of The Scallops And The Fishermen Of St Brieuc Bay. In John Law (Ed.), *Power, Action And Belief: A New Sociology Of Knowledge?* London, Routledge: 196–233.

Callon, M. (1998). An Essay On Framing And Overflowing. In M. Callon (Ed.), *The Laws Of The Markets*, Oxford: Blackwell: 244–69.

Callon, M. (1999). Actor-Network-Theory: The Market Test. In J. Law & J. Hassard (Eds) *Actor Network Theory And After*, Oxford: Blackwell: 181–95.

Callon, M. (2007). What Does It Mean To Say That Economics Is Performative? In D. MacKenzie, F. Muniesa & L. Siu (Eds), *On The Performativity Of Economics: Do Economists Make Markets*, Princeton: Princeton University Press: 311–57.

Callon, M., Meadel, C. & Rabeharisoa, V. (2002). The Economy Of Qualities, *Economy & Society*, 32: 194–217.

Callon, M. & Law, J. (2005). On Qualculation, Agency, And Otherness, *Environment And Planning D: Society And Space*, 23: 717–33.

Callon, M. & Muniesa, F. (2005). Economic Markets As Calculative Collective Devices. *Organisation Studies*, 26(8): 1229–50.

Callon, M., Millo, Y. & Muniesa, F. (2007). *Market Devices*, Sociological Review Monographs.

Camic, C., Gross, N. & Lamont, M. (Eds.). (2012). *Social Knowledge In The Making*. Chicago: University Of Chicago Press.

Cardinaels, E. (2008). The Interplay Between Cost Accounting Knowledge And Presentation Formats In Cost-Based Decision Making. *Accounting, Organisations And Society*, 33: 582–602.

Carr, D. (2014). Gartner Magic Quadrant: Netscout Says Secret Is Green, *Informationweek*. Available online at: http://www.Informationweek.Com/Strategic-Cio/Executive-Insights-And-Innovation/Gartner-Magic-Quadrant-Netscout-Says-Secret-Is-Green/A/D-Id/1297955. Accessed 17 March 2005.

Carrier, J. G. & Miller, D. (Eds) (1998). *Virtualism: A New Political Economy*. Oxford: Berg Publishers.

Carroll-Burke, P. (2001). Tools, Instruments And Engines: Getting A Handle On The Specificity Of Engine Science. *Social Studies Of Science*, 31(4): 593–625.

Carr-Saunders, A. M. & Wilson, P. A. (1933). *The Professions*, Oxford: Clarendon.

Carruthers, B. G. & Stinchcombe, A. L. (1999). The Social Structure Of Liquidity: Flexibility, Markets, And States. *Theory And Society*, 28(3): 353–82.

Chapple, D. (2002). *Industry Analysts Are All In The US, Aren't They?*, Lighthouse Analyst Relations, Updated Version Of Paper Available online at: http://www.Academia.Edu/405852/Industry_Analysts_Are_All_In_The_US_Arent_They. Accessed 20 May 2013.

Chapple, D. (2007). How Strongly Do Industry Analysts Influence Buyers Of High Technology? Lighthouse Analyst Relations, Available online at: http://www.Academia.Edu/405853/. Accessed 14 February 2013.

Chapple, D. (2014). Frustrated Customers Produce Opportunities For Upstart Analyst Firms, Available online at: http://www.Influencerrelations.Com/2833/Frustrated-Customers-Produce-Opportunities-For-Upstart-Analyst-Firms Posted 1st August 2014. Accessed 3 December 2014.

Chapple, D. (2014a). Parables: Sampsa Hyysalo On The Karakat, Available online at: http://www.Influencerrelations.Com/3239/Parables-Sampsa-Hyysalo-On-The-Karakat Posted 15 October 2014. Accessed 3 December 2014.

Chapple, D. (2014b). Don't Panic If A Competitor Hires Your Gartner Analyst, Available online at: http://www.Influencerrelations.Com/3275/Dont-Panic-If-A-Competitor-Hires-Your-Gartner-Analyst Posted 21st October 2014. Accessed 3 December 2014.

Chapple, D. (2015). Announcing The Top Ten Telecoms Analyst Firms, Available online at: http://www.Influencerrelations.Com/3584. Accessed 28 January 2015.

Chiasson, M. W. & Davidson, E. (2005). Taking Industry Seriously In Information Systems Research. *MIS Quarterly*, 29(4): 591–605.

Chua, W. F. (1995). Experts, Networks And Inscriptions In The Fabrication Of Accounting Images: A Story Of The Representation Of Three Public Hospitals. *Accounting, Organisations And Society*, 20(2/3): 111–45.

Coase R. H. (1937). The Nature Of The Firm, *Economica*, 4(16): 386–403.

Coburn, D. (1992). Freidson Then And Now: An Internalist Critique Of Freidson's Past And Present Views Of The Medical Profession, *International Journal Of Health Services*, 22(4): 497–512.

Cochoy, F. (1998). Another Discipline For The Market Economy: Marketing As A Performative Knowledge And Know-How For Capitalism. *The Sociological Review*, 46(S1): 194–221.

Cochoy, F. & Venn, C. (2007). A Brief Theory Of The 'Captation' Of Publics: Understanding The Market With Little Red Riding Hood. *Theory, Culture & Society*, 24 (7–8): 203–23.

Cochoy, F. (2014). The American Marketing Association: A Handrail For Marketers And Marketing History. *Journal Of Historical Research In Marketing*, 6(4): 538–47.

Cohen, L., Wilkinson, A., Arnold, J. & Finn, R. (2005). Remember I'm The Bloody Architect!' Architects, Organisations And Discourses Of Profession. *Work, Employment & Society*, 19(4): 775–96.

Collins H. M. & Evans, R. (2002). The Third Wave Of Science Studies: Studies Of Expertise And Experience', *Social Studies Of Science*, 32(2): 235–96.

Columbus, L. (2005). Gartner's Magic Quadrant May Need New Pixie Dust, *CRM Buyer*. Available online at: http://www.crmbuyer.com/story/42302.html Accessed 26 June 2006.

Cooper, D. & Hopper, T. (Eds). (1989). *Critical Accounts*. Basingstoke: Macmillan.

Coopmans, C. (2014). Visual Analytics As Artful Revelation. *Representation In Scientific Practice Revisited*. Chapter 3, In Coopmans, C., Vertesi, J., Lynch, M. E. & Woolgar, S. (Eds). Representation In Scientific Practice Revisited. Cambridge MA: MIT Press: 37–60.

Cornford, J. & Pollock, N. (2003). *Putting The University Online: Information, Technology & Organisational Change*, Milton Keynes: Open University Press.

Cowles, A. (1933). Can Stock Market Forecasters Forecast?, *Econometrica*, 1(3): 309–24.

Currie, W. (2004). The Organizing Vision Of Application Service Provision: A Process-Oriented Analysis, *Information And Organisation*, 14 (4): 237–67.

Czarniawska, B. (2011). *Cyberfactories: How News Agencies Produce News*. Cheltenham: Edward Elgar Publishing.

Czarniawska, B., & Sevón, G. (Eds). (2005). *Global Ideas: How Ideas, Objects And Practices Travel In A Global Economy*, Malmo: Liber and Copenhagen Business School Press.

D'Adderio, L. & Pollock, N. (2014). Performing Modularity: Competing Rules, Performative Struggles And The Effect Of Organizational Theories On The Organization. *Organization Studies*, 35(12): 1813–43.

Dambrin, C. & Robson, K. (2011). Tracing Performance In The Pharmaceutical Industry: Ambivalence, Opacity And The Performativity Of Flawed Measures. *Accounting, Organisations And Society*, 36: 428–55.

David, S. & Pinch, T. (2008). Six Degrees Of Reputation: The Use And Abuse Of Online Review And Recommendation. In T. Pinch & R. Swedberg (Eds). *Living In A Material World: Economic Sociology Meets Science And Technology Studies*, Cambridge MA: MIT Press.

Davidson, E. & Vaast E. (2009). Tech Talk: An Investigation Of Blogging In Technology Innovation And Discourse, *IEEE Transactions On Professional Communication*, (52), 1, March.

Deleuze, G. & Guattari, F. (1988). *A Thousand Plateaus: Capitalism And Schizophrenia*. New York: Bloomsbury Publishing.

Dennington, C. & Leforestier, L. (2013). Who Are Industry Analysts And What Do They Do? A Primer On Industry Analysts, *IIAR Best Practice Paper*, Institute Of Industry Analyst Relations, The IIAR Blog. Posted Tuesday 27 August 2013 By Caroline Dennington. Available online at: http://Analystrelations.Org/2013/08/27/New-Iiar-Best-Practice-Primer-Paper-Who-Are-Industry-Analysts-And-What-Do-They-Do/. Accessed 11 September 2014.

De Vaujany, F. X., Carton, S., Dominguez-Péry, C. & Vaast, E. (2013). Moving Closer To The Fabric Of Organizing Visions: The Case Of A Trade Show. *The Journal Of Strategic Information Systems*, 22(1): 1–25.

Di Maio, A. (2009). Vice President For Public Sector In Gartner Research, 'Taking My Own Medicine: Client-Sourcing Gartner Research'. Available online at: http://Blogs.Gartner.Com/Andrea_Dimaio/2009/11/30/Taking-My-Own-Medicine-Client-Sourcing-Gartner-Research/Posted November 30, 2009. Accessed 19 March 2014.

Dingwall, R. (2008). *Essays On Professions*, Ashgate, Aldershot.

Doganova, L. & Eyquem-Renault, M. (2009). What Do Business Models Do?: Innovation Devices In Technology Entrepreneurship. *Research Policy*, 38(10): 1559–70.

Drobik, A. (2010). Getting Gartner: How To Understand What We Are Talking About, Presentation Given To The Customer Relationship Management Summit, London, 16 March.

du Gay, P. (2010). Performativities: Butler, Callon and the moment of theory. *Journal of Cultural Economy*, 3(2), 171–9.

du Gay, P., Yuval M. & Tuck, P. (2012). Making Government Liquid: Shifts In Governance Using Financialisation As A Political Device. *Environment And Planning C: Government And Policy*, 30: 1083–99.

Edelman (2008). Edelman Trust Barometer 2008. Available online at: https://www.edelman.com/assets/uploads/2014/01/2008-Trust-Barometer-Global-Results.pdf. Accessed 20 July 2015.

Edwards, P. N. (2010). *A Vast Machine: Computer Models, Climate Data, And The Politics Of Global Warming*. Cambridge MA: MIT Press.

Eppler, M. J., (2006). *Managing Information Quality: Increasing The Value Of Information In Knowledge-Intensive Products And Processes*, Berlin/New York: Springer.

Erskine, N. (2014). "Forget Everything I Told You . . . ". Gartner Office of the Ombudsman http://blogs.gartner.com/ombudsman/ Posted 7 February 2014, sampled 21 July 2015.

Espeland W. & Sauder M. (2007). Rankings And Reactivity: How Public Measures Recreate Social Worlds. *American Journal Of Sociology*, 113(1): 1–40.

Espeland W. & Stevens M. (1998). Commensuration As A Social Process. *Annual Review Of Sociology*, 24: 313–43.

Espeland W. & Stevens M. (2009). A Sociology of Quantification. *European Journal of Sociology*, 49(3): 401–36.

Evans, R. (2002). *Macroeconomic Forecasting: A Sociological Appraisal*. New York: Routledge.

Evans, R. (2007). Social Networks And Private Spaces In Economic Forecasting. *Studies In History And Philosophy Of Science*, 38(4): 686–97.

Evetts, J. (2006). The Sociology Of Professional Groups: New Directions, *Current Sociology*, 54(1): 133–43.

Ezzamel, M., Lilley, S. and Wilmott, H. C. (2004). Accounting Representation And The Road To Commercial Salvation, *Accounting, Organisations and Society*, 29, 783–813.

Feen, J. (2007). *Understanding Gartner's Hype Cycles*, 2007, Gartner Research, ID Number: G00144727. Available online at: https://www.gartner.com/doc/509085/understanding-gartners-hype-cycles-. Accessed 13 October 2014.

Fenn, J. & Raskino, M. (2008). *Mastering The Hype Cycle: How To Choose The Right Innovation At The Right Time*. Boston MA: Harvard Business Press.

Fincham, R. (1995). Business Process Reengineering And The Commodification Of Managerial Knowledge. *Journal Of Marketing Management*, 11(7), 707–19.

Fincham, R. (2002). Charisma Versus Technique: Differentiating The Expertise Of Management Gurus And Management Consultants. In T. Clark, R. Fincham (Eds.). *Critical Consulting: New Perspectives On The Management Advice Industry*. Oxford: Blackwell: 191–205.

Fincham, R. (2006). Knowledge Work As Occupational Strategy: Comparing IT And Management Consulting, *New Technology, Work And Employment* 21(1): 16–28.

Fincham, R., Fleck, J., Procter, R., Scarbrough, H., Tierney, M. & Williams, R. (1994). *Expertise And Innovation: Information Technology And Strategy In The Financial Services Sector*, Oxford: Clarendon Press.

Fine, G. A. (2006). Ground Truth Verification Games In Operational Meteorology. *Journal Of Contemporary Ethnography*. 35(1): 3–23.

Fine, G. A. (2007). *Authors Of The Storm: Meteorologists And The Culture Of Prediction*. Chicago: University Of Chicago Press.

Firth, D. & Swanson, E. (2002). IT Research And Analysis Services: Surveying Their Use And Usefulness, Information System Working Paper, UCLA Anderson School, Los Angeles, California.

Firth, D. & Swanson, E. B. (2005). How Useful Are IT Research And Analysis Services?, *Business Horizons*, 48(2): 151–9.

Firth, D. & Lawrence, C. (2006). An Institutional Perspective On Customer Relationship Management, *Journal Of Information Technology Theory And Application*, (8)1: 21–31.

Fleck, J. (1988). Innofusion Or Diffusation?: The Nature Of Technological Development In Robotics', *Edinburgh PICT Working Paper* No.4, Research Centre For Social Sciences, University Of Edinburgh, Edinburgh.

Fleck, J. (1998). Expertise: Knowledge, Power And Tradeability. In R. Williams, W. Faulkner & J. Fleck (Eds), *Exploring Expertise: Issues And Perspectives*, Basingstoke: Macmillan: 143–72.

Fleck, J., Webster, J. & Williams, R. (1990). The Dynamics Of IT Implementation: A Reassessment Of Paradigms And Trajectories Of Development, *Futures*, 22: 618–40.

Flichy, P. (2007). *Understanding Technological Innovation: A Socio-Technical Approach*, Cheltenham, UK: Edward Elgar.

Fourcade, M. & Khurana, R. (2011). From Social Control To Financial Economics: The Linked Ecologies Of Economics And Business In Twentieth Century America, *Harvard Business School Working Paper*, No. 11–071.

Fournier, V. (2000). Boundary Work And The (Un)Making Of The Professions. In Nigel Malin (Ed.) *Professionalism, Boundaries And The Workplace*, London/New York: Routledge: 69–86.

Fransman, M. (2010). *The New ICT Ecosystem: Implications For Policy And Regulation*. Cambridge: Cambridge University Press.

Fredman, C. & Gartner, G. (2014). *About Gartner: The Making Of A Billion-Dollar IT Advisory Firm*, New York: Lemonade Heroes.

Free, C., Salterio, S. & Shearer, T. (2009). The Construction Of Auditability: MBA Rankings And Assurance In Practice. *Accounting, Organisations And Society*, 34: 119–40.

Freidson, E. (1970). *Professional Dominance*, New York: Atherton Press.

Freidson, E. (1994). *Professionalisation Reborn: Theory, Prophecy And Polity*, Cambridge: Polity Press.

Friedman, A. L. With Cornford, D. S. (1989). *Computer Systems Development: History Organisation And Implementation*, New. York.: John Wiley & Sons.

Fujimura, J. (1995). Ecologies Of Action: Recombining Genes, Molecularizing Cancer, And Transforming Biology. In S.L. Star, (Ed.), *Ecologies Of Knowledge: Work And Politics In Science And Technology*. Albany, New York: State University Of New York Press: 302–46.

Fuller, A. & Unwin, L. (2010). Knowledge Workers' As The New Apprentices: The Influence Of Organisational Autonomy, Goals And Values On The Nurturing Of Expertise, *Vocations And Learning* 3: 203–22.

Future Thinker (1988). Gartner Group: What A Gartner Group? *Future Thinker*, 1(2), 1 September, Available online at: http://Pcmine.Com/P/FT/Future%20Thinker%20v1%20n2.Pdf. Accessed 23 January 2015.

Garcia-Parpet, M. F. (2007). The Social Construction Of A Perfect Market: The Strawberry Auction At Fontaines-En-Sologne. In D. Mackenzie, F. Muniesa & L. Sui (Eds) *Do Economists Make Markets*, Princeton University Press.

Gartner Inc. (2000). Higher Education And The Magic Quadrant Process, Gartner Research, 3 January, ID Number: M-09-9829.

Gartner Inc. (2001). Top Ten Trends In CRM For 2001, Posted on 14 December 2000, Available online at: http://www.Gartner.Com/Webletter/Nortel/Article1.Html. Accessed 19 May 2010.

Gartner Inc. (2005). *Gartner Enhances Magic Quadrant And Marketscope Research Methodologies And Processes*, Gartner Newsroom; Press Release 8 November 2005. Available online at: http://www.gartner.com/newsroom/id/492217. Accessed 30 September 2014.

Gartner Inc. (2013). Gartner Highlights 2013 Cool Vendors That Are Transforming How Businesses Operate, Available online at: http://www.gartner.com/newsroom/id/2484715. Accessed 26 January 2015.

Gartner Inc. (2014). *Gartner 2013 Annual Report*, Stamford, Conn., Available online at: http://Investor.Gartner.Com/Phoenix.Zhtml?C=99568&P=Irol-Reportsannual. Accessed 1st September 2014.

Gartner Inc. (No Date). Vendor Briefings, Available online at: http://www.Gartner.Com/It/About/Vendor_Briefings.Jsp. Accessed 10 May 2010.

Gartner Inc. (2015). *Inside Gartner Research: How The Art, Science And Rigor Behind Our Research Process And Proprietary Methodologies Help You Make The Right Decisions, Every Day*. Available online at: http://www.gartner.com/imagesrv/research/methodologies/inside_gartner_research.pdf. Accessed 23 January 2015.

Gartner, G. (2007). 'Gideon Gartner On . . . The Genesis Of Gartner Group' *Q&A At The Computer History Museum*, May, 2007. Uploaded Onto Youtube 15 October 2007. Available online at: https://youtu.be/viRoBiMbvWE. Accessed 20 July 2015.

Gartner, G. (2010). Entrepreneurial Case Study From My Wall Street Days, Available online at: http://Gideongartner.Com/2010/03/A-Story-From-My-Wall-Street-Days/Posted 3 March 2010. Accessed 19 December 2014.

Gartner, G. (2010a). Gartner's Soundview: Its Rollercoaster Story (Part 1), Available online at: http://Gideongartner.Com/2010/03/Gartners-Stock-Brokerage-Arm-Its-Growth-And-Collapse/Posted 15 March 2010. Accessed 7 May 2013.

Gartner, G. (2010b). 'Gartner Innovation During Its Formative Years', Available online at: http://Gideongartner.Com/2010/04/Gartner-Innovation-During-Its-Formative-Years/Posted 10 April 2010. Accessed 4 April 2013.

Gartner, G. (2010c). 'Advisory Industry Future Redesign: The 'Payment' Model'. Available online at: http://Gideongartner.Com/2010/05/Advisory-Industry-A-Future-Redesign-The-'Payment'-Model/Posted 4 May 2010. Accessed 19 December 2014.

Gartner, G. (2010d). 'Advisory Industry Competition: Pushing Past "Business As Usual"' (Part 1). Available online at: http://Gideongartner.Com/2010/06/Advisory-Industry-Competition-Pushing-Past-Business-As-Usual/Posted 29 June 2010 In Non-Gartner Advisory. Accessed 19 December 2014.

Gartner, G. (2010e). 'Entrepreneurial Case Study From My Wall Street Days'. Available online at: http://Gideongartner.Com/2010/03/A-Story-From-My-Wall-Street-Days/Posted 3 March 2010. Accessed 27 January 2015.

Gartner, G. (2011). Early Research Process (RP), Part 1. Available online at: http://Gideongartner.Com/2011/01/Gartners-Original-Research-Processes-Part-1/Posted 31 January 2011. Accessed 5 May 2013.

Gartner, G. (2011a). Early Research Process (RP), Part 2 (Including Magic Quadrants). Available online at: http://gideongartner.com/2011/02/gartners-original-research-processes-part-2-including-mqs/ Posted 6 February 2011. Accessed 5 May 2013.

Gartner, G. (2011b). Early Research Process, Part 3 (80/20 Rule). Available online at: http://Gideongartner.Com/2011/02/Gartner-Early-Research-Process-Part3-Research-Meetings/Posted 8 February 2011. Accessed 5 May 2013.

Gartner, G. (2011c). 'Gartner's Original Research Process Part 4 Theory G – Sales'. Available online at: http://Gideongartner.Com/2011/03/Gartnerearly-Theory-G-Sales-Part-4/Posted 6 March 2011. Accessed 5 May 2013.

Gartner, G. (2011d). From Hutton, To Oppenheimer, To Gartner. Available online at: http://Gideongartner.Com/2011/04/The-Founding-Of-Gartner/Posted 14 Apr 2011. Accessed 7 May 2013.

Gartner, G. (2014). 35th Anniversary Of Gartner Inc.'s Founding. Available online at: http://Gideongartner.Com/2014/10/35th-Anniversary-Of-Gartner-Inc-S-Founding/Posted 9 October 2014. Accessed 19 March 2015.

Garud, R. (2008). Conferences As Venues For The Configuration Of Emerging Organisational Fields: The Case Of Cochlear Implants. *Journal Of Management Studies*, 45(6): 1061–88.

Geels, F. (2007). Feelings Of Discontent And The Promise Of Middle Range Theory For STS: Examples From Technology Dynamics, *Science, Technology & Human Values* 32: 627–51.

Geels, F. & Smit, W. (2000). Failed Technology Futures: Pitfalls And Lessons From A Historical Survey, *Futures* 32(9/10): 867–85.

Gerlitz, C. (2012). Acting On Data. Temporality And Self-Evaluation In Social Media. Goldsmiths Research Online. Available online at: http://Research.Gold.Ac.Uk/7076/. Accessed 30 March 2015.

Ghemawat, P. (2002). Competition And Business Strategy In Historical Perspective, *Business History Review*, 76: 37–74.

Gibson, J. J. (1979). *The Ecological Approach To Visual Perception*. Boston: Houghton Mifflin.

Gieryn, T. (1999). *Cultural Boundaries Of Science: Credibility On The Line*. Chicago: University Of Chicago Press.

Glückler, J. & Armbrüster, T. (2003). Bridging Uncertainty In Management Consulting: The Mechanisms Of Trust And Networked Reputation, *Organisation Studies*, 24(2): 269–97.

Goffman E. (1974). *Frame Analysis: An Essay On The Organisation Of The Experience*. New York: Harper Colophon.

Goody, J. (1977). *The Domestication Of The Savage Mind*, Cambridge: Cambridge University Press.

Grady, K. & Potter, J. (1985). Speaking And Clapping: A Comparison Of Foot And Thatcher's Oratory. *Language & Communication*, 5(3): 173–83.

Graham, I. & Williams, R. (2005). The Use Of Management Texts: Hammer's Reengineering, *Scandinavian Journal Of Management*, 21: 159–75.

Greenemeier, L. (2006). Blog-Based Analysts Shake Up IT Research, Information Week, Available online at: http://Reports.Informationweek.Com/Abstract/81/922/Business-Intelligence-And-Information-Management/Blog-Based-Analysts-Shake-Up-IT-Research.Html. 22 May 2006. Accessed 20 March 2014.

Greenemeier, L. & Mcdougall, P. (2006). Credibility Of Analysts, *Information Week*, 6 Feb. Available online: http://Informationweek.Com/Shared/Printablearticlesrc. Jhtm?Articleid=178601879. Accessed 31st August 2006.

Greenwood, R. & Suddaby, R. (2006). Institutional Entrepreneurship In Mature Fields: The Big Five Accounting Firms. *Academy Of Management Journal*, 49(1): 27–48.

Greenwood, R. Li, S. X., Prakash, R. & Deephouse, D. L. (2005). Reputation, Diversification, And Organisational Explanations Of Performance In Professional Service Firms. *Organisation Science* 16(6): 661–73.

Gregory, J. (2000). *Sorcerer's Apprentice: Creating The Electronic Health Record, Re-Inventing Medical Records And Patient Care*. Unpublished Doctoral Dissertation, Department Of Communication, University Of California San Diego, La Jolla, California.

Gross, C. & Kieser, A. (2006). Are Consultants Moving Towards Professionalization? In Royston Greenwood & Roy Suddaby (Eds) *Research In The Sociology Of Organisations* Special issues on *Professional Service Firms*: 24: 69–104.

Guice, J. (1999). Designing The Future: The Culture Of New Trends In Science And Technology, *Research Policy* 28: 81–98.

Gyurko, E. (2009). Managing The Gartner Magic Quadrant: A Tool For Analyst Relations Managers, IIAR White Paper Series, 25 March 2009.

Hacking, I. (1983). *Representing And Intervening: Introductory Topics In The Philosophy Of Natural Science*. Cambridge: Cambridge University Press.

Hacking, I. (1992). The Self-Vindication Of The Laboratory Sciences. In A. Pickering (Ed.), *Science As Practice And Culture*. Chicago: University Of Chicago Press.

Hardie, I. & MacKenzie, D. (2007). Assembling An Economic Actor: The Agencement Of A Hedge Fund, *The Sociological Review*, 55(1): 57–80.

Harper, R. (2000). *Analysing Work Practice And The Potential Role Of New Technology At The International Monetary Fund*. Cambridge: Cambridge University Press: 169–86.

Hennion, A. (1989). An Intermediary Between Production And Consumption: The Producer Of Popular Music. *Science, Technology & Human Values*, 14(4): 400–24.

Heusinkveld, S. & Benders, J. (2005). Contested Commodification: Consultancies And Their Struggle With New Concept Development, *Human Relations*, 58(3): 283–310.

Hill & Knowlton (2013). New Study From Hill+Knowlton Strategies Quantifies Impact Of Social Media And Industry Analysts On B2B Technology Sales In The US And UK, Available online at: http://www.hkstrategies.com/news/new-study-quantifies-impact-social-media-and-industry-analysts-b2b-technology-sales. Accessed 20 July 2015.

Hind, P. (2004). Self-Fulfilling Prophecies?, *CIO*, 12 July. Available online at: http://www.Cio.Au/Pp.Php?Id=885195886andfp=4&Fpid=1854618785. Accessed 29 March 2006.

Hirschheim, R., Murungi, D. M. & Peña, S. (2012). Witty Invention Or Dubious Fad? Using Argument Mapping To Examine The Contours Of Management Fashion. *Information And Organization*, 22(1): 60–84.

Holm, P., & Nielsen, K. N. (2007). Framing Fish, Making Markets: The Construction Of Individual Transferable Quotas (Itqs). *The Sociological Review*, 55(S2): 173–95.

Holmes, D. R. & Marcus, G. E. (2006). Para-Ethnography And The Rise Of The Symbolic Analyst. In M. Fisher & G. Downey (Eds) *Frontiers Of Capital: Ethnographic Reflections On The New Economy*, Durham, US: Duke University Press: 33–57.

Holmes, D. R., & Marcus, G. E. (2008). Collaboration Today And The Re-Imagination Of The Classic Scene Of Fieldwork Encounter. *Collaborative Anthropologies*, 1(1): 81–101.

Hong, H. & Kubik, J. D. (2003). Analyzing The Analysts: Career Concerns And Biased Earnings Forecasts, *Journal Of Finance*, (58)1: 313–51.

Hopkins, W. (2007). *Influencing The Influencers: Best Practice For Building Valuable Relationships With Technology Industry Analysts*, Austin, Tex.: Knowledge Capital Group.

Hopkins, W. S. & England, S. F. (2012). *The Technology Vendor Executive's Guide To The Industry Analyst*, KCG Executive Guide, The Knowledge Capital Group, Version 6.0.

Hopwood, A. (2007). Whither Accounting Research? *The Accounting Review*, 82(5): 1365–74.

Howard, P. (2004). Let's Play The Magic Quadrant Game, *The Register*, 24 December. Available online at: http://www.theregister.co.uk/2004/12/24/magic_quadrant/ Accessed 22 February 2006.

Howells, J. (2006). Intermediation And The Role Of Intermediaries In Innovation, *Research Policy* 35(5): 715–28.

Huczynski, A. (2006). *Management Gurus: Revised edition*. London and New York: Routledge.

Husman, T. B. (2003). Long Live The 'Hybrid': What Transaction Costs Economics Left Unseen DRUID Conference Paper Winter 2003. Available online at http://www.druid.dk/conferences/winter2003/Paper/Husman.pdf. Accessed 4 December 2014.

Hutchby, I. (2001). Technologies, Texts And Affordances. *Sociology*, 35(2): 441–56.

Hyysalo, S. (2006). Representations Of Use And Practice-Bound Imaginaries In Automating The Safety Of The Elderly, *Social Studies Of Science*, 36(4): 599–626.

Ikeler, A. (2007). The Under-Examined Public: Making Sense Of Industry Analysts And Analyst Relations, *Journal Of Promotion Management*, 13(3–4): 233–60.

Ingold, T. (2007). *Lines: A Brief History*. Abingdon, Oxon: Routledge.

Jeacle, I. & Carter, C. (2011). In Tripadvisor We Trust: Calculative Regimes And Abstract Systems. *Accounting, Organisations And Society*, 36: 293–309.

Jørgensen, U. & Sørensen, O. (1999). Arenas Of Development: A Space Populated By Actor-Worlds, Artefacts, And Surprises, *Technology Analysis And Strategic Management* 11(3): 409–29.

Justesen, L. & Mouritsen, J. (2008). The Triple Visual: Translations Between Photographs, 3-D Visualizations And Calculations. *Accounting, Auditing & Accountability Journal*, 22(6): 973–90.

Kaniadakis, A. (2012). ERP Implementation As A Broad Socio-Economic Phenomenon: The Agora Of Techno-Organisational Change, *Information Technology & People*, 25(3): 259–80.

Karpik, L. (2010). *Valuing The Unique: The Economics Of Singularities*. Princeton NJ: Princeton University Press.

Keil, M. & Carmel, E. (1995). Customer-Developer Links In Software Development. *Communications Of The ACM*, 38(5): 33–44.

Keiser, A. (2002). On Communication Barriers Between Management Science, Consultancies And Business Organisations. In T. Clark & R. Fincham (Eds), *Critical Consulting*, Blackwell, Oxford.

Kennedy, M. (2008). Getting Counted: Markets, Media, And Reality, *American Sociological Review*, 73: 270–95.

Khurana, R. (2010). *From Higher Aims To Hired Hands: The Social Transformation Of American Business Schools And The Unfulfilled Promise Of Management As A Profession*. Princeton NJ: Princeton University Press.

Kipping M. & Armbrüster T. (2000). *The Content Of Consultancy Work: Knowledge Generation, Codification And Dissemination*. CEMP-Report No. 13 October 2000. The Creation of European Management Practice (CEMP) A Research Programme Supported by the European Union. Available online at project website: http://www.fek.uu.se/cemp. Sampled 21 July 2015.

Kipping, M., & Clark, T. (Eds.). (2012). *The Oxford Handbook Of Management Consulting*. Oxford and New York: Oxford University Press.

Kjellberg, H. & Helgesson, C. F. (2006). Multiple Versions Of Markets: Multiplicity And Performativity In Market Practice. *Industrial Marketing Management*, 35(7): 839–55.

Kjellberg, H. & Helgesson, C. F. (2007). On The Nature Of Markets And Their Practices. *Marketing Theory*, 7(2): 137–62.

Kjellberg, H. & Helgesson, C. F. (2010). Political Marketing: Multiple Values, Performativities And Modes Of Engaging. *Journal Of Cultural Economy* 3(2): 279–97.

Knights, D. & Murray, F. (1994). *Managers Divided: Organisation Politics And Information Technology Management*. Chichester: John Wiley & Sons.

Knorr Cetina, K. (1999). *Epistemic Cultures: How The Sciences Make Knowledge*. Cambridge MA: Harvard University Press.

Knorr Cetina, K. (2007). Culture in global knowledge societies: knowledge cultures and epistemic cultures. *Interdisciplinary science review* 32(4): 361–75.

Knorr Cetina, K. (2010). The Epistemics Of Information: A Consumption Model. *Journal Of Consumer Culture*, 10(2): 171–201.

Knorr Cetina, K. (2012). Financial Analysis: Epistemic Profile Of An Evaluative Science. In Camic, C., Gross, N. & Lamont, M. (Eds), *Social Knowledge In The Making*. Chicago: University Of Chicago Press.

Kornberger, M. (2010). *Brand Society: How Brands Transform Management And Lifestyle*. Cambridge: Cambridge University Press.

Kornberger, M. & Carter, C. (2010). Manufacturing Competition: How Accounting Practices Shape Strategy Making In Cities. *Accounting, Auditing & Accountability Journal*, 23(3): 325–49.

Kwon, W. & Easton, G. (2010). Conceptualizing The Role Of Evaluation Systems In Markets: The Case Of Dominant Evaluators. *Marketing Theory*, 10(2): 123–43.

Lampel, J. & Meyer, A. D. (2008). Guest Editors' Introduction. *Journal Of Management Studies*, 45(6): 1025–35.

Lapsley, I. & Mitchell, F. (Eds). (1996). *Accounting And Performance Measurement: Issues In The Private And Public Sectors*. London: Paul Chapman Publishing.

Larson, M. (1977). *The Rise Of Professionalism*, California: California University Press.

Latour, B. (1986). Visualization And Cognition: Thinking With Eyes And Hands'. In H. Kucklick and E. Long (Eds.). *Knowledge And Society: Studies In The Sociology Of Culture, Past And Present*. Greenwich, Connecticut., JAI Press: 1–40.

Latour, B. (1987). *Science In Action, How To Follow Scientists And Engineers Through Society*, Cambridge, Mass.: Harvard University Press.

Latour, B. (1999). *Pandora's Hope: Essays On The Reality Of Science Studies*. Cambridge, Mass.: Harvard University Press.

Latour, B. (2005). *Reassembling The Social: An Introduction To Actor-Network Theory*. Oxford: Oxford University Press.

Latour, B., & Woolgar, S. (1979). *Laboratory Life: The Social Construction Of Scientific Facts*. Beverly Hills: Sage.

Law, J. (2001). Economics As Interference. In P. Du Gay & M. Pryke (Eds). *Cultural Economy: Cultural Analysis And Commercial Life*. London: Sage: 21–38.

Law, J. (2004). *After Method: Mess In Social Science Research*. London: Routledge.

Leonhard, W. (2013). Gartner And IDC Predictions: Oops, Forget What We Said Last Time. *Infoworld*. http://www.infoworld.com/article/2614009/microsoft-windows/gartner-and-idc-predictions–oops–forget-what-we-said-last-time.html. Accessed 21 July 2015.

Leyshon, A. & Thrift, N. (1999). Lists Come Alive: Electronic Systems Of Knowledge And The Rise Of Credit-Scoring In Retail Banking, *Economy And Society* 28: 434–66.

Lissack, M. & Richardson, K. (2003). Models Without Morals: Toward The Ethical Use Of Business Models, *Emergence*, 5(2): 72–102.

Lounsbury, M. & Rao, H. (2004). Sources Of Durability And Change In Market Classifications: A Study Of The Reconstitution Of Product Categories In The American Mutual Fund Industry, 1944–1985, *Social Forces*, 82(3): 969–99.

Lowy, A. & Hood, P. (2004). *The Power Of The 2x2 Matrix: Using 2x2 Thinking To Solve Business Problems And Make Better Decisions*. San Francisco: Jossey-Bass.

Lury, C. (2004). *Brands: The Logos Of The Global Economy*. London: Routledge.

Lynch, M. (1985). Discipline And The Material Form Of Images: An Analysis Of Scientific Visibility. *Social Studies Of Science*, 15: 37–66.

Lynch, M. (1988). The Externalized Retina: Selection And Mathematization In The Visual Documentation Of Objects In The Life Sciences. *Human Studies*, 11: 201–34.

Mabert, V., Soni, A. & Venkataramanan, M. (2001). Enterprise Resource Planning: Common Myths Versus Evolving Reality, *Business Horizons*, May-June: 69–76.

MacKenzie, D. (1996). *Knowing Machines: Essays On Technical Change*, Cambridge, Mass.: MIT Press.

MacKenzie, D. (2003). An Equation And Its Worlds: Bricolage, Exemplars, Disunity And Performativity In Financial Economics, *Social Studies Of Science*, 33(6): 831–68.

MacKenzie, D. (2005). Opening The Black Boxes Of Global Finance. *Review Of International Political Economy*, 12(4): 555–76.

MacKenzie, D. (2006). *An Engine, Not A Camera: How Financial Models Shape Markets*, Cambridge, Mass.: MIT Press.

MacKenzie, D. (2006b). 'Is Economics Performative? Option Theory And The Construction Of Derivatives Markets', *Journal Of The History Of Economic Thought*, 28(1): 29–55.

MacKenzie, D. (2009). *Material Markets: How Economic Agents Are Constructed*, Oxford: Oxford University Press.

MacKenzie, D. & Millo, Y. (2003). Constructing A Market, Performing Theory: The Historical Sociology Of A Financial Derivatives Exchange. *American Journal Of Sociology*, 109(1): 107–45.

MacKenzie, D. A., Muniesa, F. & Siu, L. (Eds). (2007). *Do Economists Make Markets?: On The Performativity Of Economics*. Princeton University Press.

Mallach, E. (1997). Vendor Support Of Industry Analysts, *Telematics And Informatics* 4(2): 185–95.

Mallard, G. & Lakoff, A. (2011). How Claims To Know The Future Are Used To Understand The Present. Techniques of Prospection in the Field of National Security', in C. Camic, N. Gross & L. Michele (Eds). *Social Knowledge In The Making*, Chicago: University of Chicago Press: 339–77.

Maoz, M. (2001). CRM: What's Right For Customers Is The Correct Approach, Gartner Research Document ID Number: AV-14-0605.

Marcus, G. E. (1995). Ethnography In/Of The World System: The Emergence Of Multi-sited Ethnography. Annual review of anthropology, 24: 95–117.

Marres, N. (2009). Testing Powers Of Engagement Green Living Experiments, The Ontological Turn And The Undoability Of Involvement. *European Journal Of Social Theory*, 12(1): 117–33.

Mason, K., Kjellberg, H. & Hagberg, J. (2015). Exploring The Performativity Of Marketing: Theories, Practices And Devices. *Journal Of Marketing Management*, 31(1–2): 1–15.

McDonald, D. (2014). *The Firm: The Inside Story Of Mckinsey, The World's Most Controversial Management Consultancy*. London: Oneworld Publications.

McDowall, W. (2012). Technology Roadmaps For Transition Management: The Case Of Hydrogen Energy. *Technological Forecasting And Social Change*, 79(3): 530–42.

McKenna, C. (2006). *The World's Newest Profession. Management Consulting In The Twentieth Century*. Cambridge: Cambridge University Press.

Mellet, K., Beauvisage, T., Beuscart, J. & Trespeuch, M. (2014). A 'Democratization' Of Markets? Online Consumer Reviews In The Restaurant Industry. *Valuation Studies*, 2(1): 5–41.

Ménard C. (2011). Hybrid Modes Of Organisation: Alliances, Joint Ventures, Networks, And Other 'Strange' Animals. In R. Gibbons & J. Roberts (Eds), *The Handbook Of Organisational Economics*, Princeton: Princeton University Press: 1066–108.

Mennicken, A. (2010). From Inspection To Auditing: Audit And Markets as Linked Ecologies. *Accounting, Organizations and Society*, 35(3): 334–59.

Merton, R. K. (1948). 'The Self-Fulfilling Prophecy', *The Antioch Review*, 8(2): 193–210.

Merton, R. K. (1982). *Social Research And The Practicing Professions* Cambridge: Abt Books.

Meyer, A. D., Gaba, V. & Colwell, K. (2005). Organizing Far From Equilibrium: Non-Linear Change In Organisational Fields. *Organisation Science*, 16: 456–73.

Meyer, M., & Kearnes, M. (2013). Introduction To Special Section: Intermediaries Between Science, Policy And The Market. *Science And Public Policy*, 40(4): 423–9.

Michael, M. (2000). Futures Of The Present: From Performativity To Prehension. In N. Brown, B. Rappert & A. Webster (Eds) *Contested Futures: A Sociology Of Prospective Science And Technology*, Aldershot, Ashgate: 21–42.

Miller, P. (2001). Governing By Numbers: Why Calculative Practices Matter, *Social Research*, 68(2): 379–96.

Miller, P. (2008). Calculating Economic Life. *Journal Of Cultural Economy*, 1(1): 51–64.

Miller, P., Kurunmä Ki, L. & O'Leary, T. (2006). Accounting, Hybrids And The Management Of Risk', LSE Centre For Analysis Of Risk And Regulation, *Discussion Paper* No: 40, November.

Miller, P. & O'Leary, T. (2007). Mediating Instruments And Making Markets: Capital Budgeting, Science And The Economy. *Accounting, Organisations And Society*, 32: 701–34.

Millo, Y. & Mackenzie, D. (2009). The Usefulness Of Inaccurate Models: Towards An Understanding Of The Emergence Of Financial Risk Management. *Accounting, Organisations And Society*, 34(5): 638–53.

Mirowski, P. (2011). *Science-Mart*. Cambridge MA: Harvard University Press.

Mok, A. L. (1971). Professional Innovation In Post-Industrial Society. In Eliot Freidson (Ed), *The Professions And Their Prospects*, Beverly Hills/London: Sage: 105–16.

Mokyr, J. (2002). *The Gifts Of Athena: Historical Origins Of The Knowledge Economy*. Princeton and Oxford: Princeton University Press.

Montgomery, D. B. & Weinberg, C. B. (1979). Toward Strategic Intelligence Systems. *The Journal Of Marketing*, 43: 41–52.

Morrison, A. & Wensley, R. (1991). Boxing Up Or Boxed In? A Short History Of The Boston Consulting Group Share/Growth Matrix. *Journal Of Marketing Management*, 7(2): 105–29.

Morrison, M. & Cornips, L. (2012). Exploring The Role Of Dedicated Online Biotechnology News Providers In The Innovation Economy. *Science, Technology & Human Values*, 37(3): 262–85.

Mulkay, M. J. (1976). Norms And Ideology In Science, *Social Science Information*, 15: 637–56.

Muniesa, F. (2014). *The Provoked Economy: Economic Reality And The Performative Turn*. London: Routledge.

Muzio, D., Kirkpatrick, I. & Kipping, M. (2011). Professions, Organisations And The State: Applying The Sociology Of The Professions To The Case Of Management Consultancy, *Current Sociology*, 59(6): 805–24.

Newell, S., Robertson, M. & Swan, J. (2001). Management Fads And Fashions. *Organization*, 8(1): 5–15.

Nilsson, J. & Helgesson, C. F. (2015). Epistemologies In The Wild: Local Knowledge And The Notion Of Performativity. *Journal Of Marketing Management*, 31(1–2): 16–36.

Noble, D. (2013). Crunching The Analyst Firm Numbers—What Do They Tell Us About Gartner, Forrester, IDC & Others?, Intelligenar Blog. Posted 1st May 2013. Available online at: http://Intelligenar.Wordpress.Com/2013/05/01/Crunching-The-Analyst-Firm-Numbers-What-Do-They-Tell-Us-About-Gartner-Forrester-Idc-Others/. Accessed 1st May 2103.

Noble, D. (2014). Gartner Just Bets Bigger & Draws Further From The Pack—Analysing Gartner's & Forrester's 2013 Financial Results, Intelligenar Blog Posted 13 February 2014. Available online at: http://Intelligenar.Wordpress.Com/2014/02/13/Gartner-Just-Bets-Bigger-Draws-Further-From-The-Pack-Analysing-Gartners-Forresters-2013-Financial-Results/. Accessed 1st December 2014.

Noble, D. (2014a). 'New Firms Sprout Roots In The Asia/Pacific IT Analyst Landscape', Intelligenar Blog Posted 28 May 2014, Available online at: https://intelligenar.wordpress.com/2014/05/28/new-firms-sprout-roots-in-the-asiapacific-it-analyst-landscape/. Accessed 3 December 2014.

Norton, D. (2000). The Latest Acronyms Will Keep You Up On CRM, *Tech Republic*, Available online at: http://Articles.Techrepublic.Com.Com/5100-10878_11-5030192.Html. Accessed 21st April 2009.

O'Grady, S. (2006). Open Source Industry Analysis: Not Such A Silly Idea Anymore. Available online at: http://Redmonk.Com/Sogrady/2006/06/20/Open-Source-Industry-Analysis-Not-Such-A-Silly-Idea-Anymore/. Posted 20 June 2006. Accessed 20 March 2014.

O'Shea, J. E. & Madigan, C. (1998). *Dangerous Company: Management Consultants And The Businesses They Save And Ruin*. New York: Penguin Putnam.

Orlikowski, W. J. (2007). Sociomaterial Practices: Exploring Technology At Work. *Organisation Studies*, 28(9): 1435–48.

Parsons, T. (1939). The Professions And Social Structure, *Social Forces*, 17(4): 457–67.

Parsons, T. (1954). *Essays In Sociological Theory*, Glencoe: Free Press.

Pels, D. (2003). *Unhastening Science: Autonomy And Reflexivity In The Social Theory Of Knowledge*, Liverpool: Liverpool University Press.

Perkmann, M. & Spicer, A. (2010). What Are Business Models? Developing A Theory Of Performative Representations. *Research In The Sociology Of Organisations*, 29: 269–79.

Pettigrew, A. M. (1973). *The Politics Of Organizational Decision-Making*. London: Tavistock.

Pinch, T. & Swedberg, R. (2008). (Eds). *Living In A Material World*, Cambridge, MA: MIT Press.

Pollner, M. (2002). Inside The Bubble: Communion, Cognition, And Deep Play At The Intersection Of Wall Street And Cyberspace'. In S Woolgar (Ed) *Virtual Society: Technology, Cyberbole, Reality*, Oxford University Press, Oxford: 230–46.

Pollock, N. & Williams, R. (2007). Technology Choice & Its Performance: Towards A Sociology Of Software Package Procurement, *Information & Organisation*, 17: 131–61.

Pollock, N. & Williams, R. (2009). *Software & Organisations: The Biography Of The Enterprise-Wide System Or How SAP Conquered The World*, London: Routledge.

Pollock, N. & Hyysalo, S. (2014). The Business Of Being A User: The Role Of The Reference Actor In Shaping Packaged Enterprise System Acquisition And Development. *MIS Quarterly*, 38(2): 473–96.

Pollock, N. & Campagnolo, G. M. (2015). Subitizing Practices And Market Decisions. The Role Of Simple Graphs In Business Settings. In M. Kornberger, L. Jusesen, J. Moursitsen & A. K. Madsen (Eds), *Making Things Valuable*, Oxford: Oxford University Press.

Pontikes, E. (2008). Fitting In Or Starting New? An Analysis Of Invention, Constraint, And The Emergence Of New Categories In The Software Industry, Working Paper.

Porter, T. M. (1992). Quantification And The Accounting Ideal In Science, *Social Studies Of Science*, 22(4): 633–51.

Porter, T. (1995). *Trust In Numbers: The Pursuit Of Objectivity In Science And Public Life, Princeton*, New Jersey: Princeton University Press.

Power, M. (2003). Auditing And The Production Of Legitimacy, *Accounting, Organisation And Society*, 28: 379–94.

Preda, A. (2007). Where Do Analysts Come From? The Case Of Financial Chartism. In M. Callon, Y. Millo & F. Muniesa (Eds) *Market Devices*, Oxford: Blackwell: 40–64.

Preda, A. (2008). Technology, Agency, And Financial Price Data. In T. Pinch & R. Swedberg (Eds). *Living In A Material World*. Cambridge, Mass: MIT Press: 217–32.

Preda, A. (2009). *Framing Finance: The Boundaries Of Markets And Modern Capitalism*, Chicago/London: University Of Chicago Press.

Qu, S., & Cooper, D. (2011). The Role Of Inscriptions In Producing A Balanced Scorecard. *Accounting, Organisations And Society*, 36: 344–62.

Quattrone, P. (2009). Books To Be Practiced. Memory, The Power Of The Visual And The Success Of Accounting. *Accounting, Organisations And Society*, 34: 85–118.

Quattrone, P., Puyou, F., Mclean, C. & Thrift, N. (2012). Imagining Organisations: An Introduction. In Puyou, F., Quattrone, P., Mclean, C. & Thrift. N. (Eds). *Imagining*

Organisations: Performative Imagery In Business And Beyond, London, Routledge: 1–15.

Raelin, J. A. (1989). An Anatomy Of Autonomy: Managing Professionals, *Academy Of Management Perspectives*, 3(3): 216–28.

Ramiller, N. C. & Swanson, E. B. (2003). Organizing Visions For Information Technology And The Information Systems Executive Response, *Journal Of Management Information Systems*, 20(1): 13–50.

Rao, H, Greve, H. R. & Davis, G. F. (2001). Fool's Gold: Social Proof In The Initiation And Abandonment Of Coverage By Wall Street Analysts, *Administrative Science Quarterly*, 46(3): 502–26.

Rao, H., Monin, P. & Durand. R. (2005). Border Crossings: Bricolage And The Erosion Of Category Boundaries In French Gastronomy, *American Sociological Review*, 70: 968–91.

Rip, A. (2006). Folk Theories Of Nanotechnologists, *Science As Culture*, 15(4): 349–65.

Rip, A., Jacob, M. & Hellstrom, T. (2000). Fashions, Lock-Ins And The Heterogeneity Of Knowledge Production. In M. Jacob & T. Hellstrom (Eds) *The Future Of Knowledge Production In The Academy*, Buckingham: Open University Press: 28–39.

Robson, K. (1992). Accounting Numbers As 'Inscriptions': Action At A Distance And The Development Of Accounting. *Accounting, Organisations And Society*, 17(7): 685–708.

Rosa, J., Porac, J., Runser-Spanjol, J. & Saxon M. (1999). Sociocognitive Dynamics In A Product Market, *The Journal Of Marketing*, 63: 64–77.

Rosa, J., Judson, K. & Porac, J. (2003). On The Sociocognitive Dynamics Between Categories And Product Models In Mature Markets, *Journal Of Business Research*, 58: 62–9.

Rosenberg, N. (1976). *Perspectives On Technology*. Cambridge: Cambridge University Press.

Rosental, C. (2013). *Toward A Sociology Of Public Demonstrations. Sociological Theory.* 31(4): 343–65.

Sage Circle (2008). Don't Obsess, Don't Ignore: the Magic Quadrant & Tech Vendors [part 1]. Available online at: http://sagecircle.wordpress.com/2008/05/26/dont-obsess-dont-ignore-the-magic-quadrant-and-tech-vendors-part-1/. Accessed 9 December 2014.

Sage Circle (2009). Launching a Social Media Strategy: A SageCircle Workshop. Available online at: https://sagecircle.wordpress.com/2009/04/08/announcing-launching-a-social-media-strategy-a-sagecircle-workshop/. Posted on April 8, 2009 by SageCircle. Accessed 9 December 2014.

Sauder, M. & Espeland, W. (2006). Strength In Numbers? The Advantages Of Multiple Rankings. *Indiana Law Journal*, 81: 205–17.

Sauder, M. & Fine, G. A. (2008). Arbiters, Entrepreneurs, And The Shaping of Business School Reputations. *Sociological Forum* 23(4): 699–723.

Sawyer, S. (2001). A Market-Based Perspective On Information Systems Development. *Communications Of The ACM*, 44(11): 97–102.

Schnaars, S. P. (1989). *Megamistakes: Forecasting And The Myth of Rapid Technological Change*. New York/London: Free Press/Collier Macmillan.

Schultz, E. (2003). Gartner's Prediction Concerning Intrusion Detection Systems: Sense Or Nonsense? *Computers & Security*, 22(6): 462–3.

Schultz, M., Mouritsen, J. & Grabielsen, G. (2001). Sticky Reputation: Analyzing A Ranking System. *Corporate Reputation Review*, 22: 24–41.

Scott, S. & Orlikowski, W. (2012). Reconfiguring Relations Of Accountability: Materialization Of The Social Media In The Travel Sector. *Accounting, Organisations And Society*. 37(1): 26–40.

Shapin, S. (1988). The House Of Experiment In Seventeenth-Century England. *Isis*, 79: 373–404.

Shapin, S. (1994). *A Social History Of Truth: Civility And Science In Seventeenth-Century England*, Chicago: University Of Chicago Press.

Shapin, S. (2001). Truth And Credibility: Science And The Social Study Of Science. In Smelser N. & Bates P. (Eds) *International Encyclopedia Of The Social And Behavioral Sciences*. Amsterdam: Elsevier: 15926–9.

Shapin, S. (2008). *The Scientific Life: A Moral History Of A Late Modern Vocation*. Chicago: University Of Chicago Press.

Shapin, S. & Schaffer, S. (1985). *Leviathan And The Air-Pump*. Princeton: Princeton University Press.

Shapiro, C. & Varian, H. R. (2013). *Information Rules: A Strategic Guide To The Network Economy*. Boston MA: Harvard Business Press.

Sharma, A. (1997). Professional As Agent: Knowledge Asymmetry In Agency Exchange, *The Academy Of Management Review*, 22(3): 758–98.

Sherden, W. A. (1998). *The Fortune Sellers: The Big Business Of Buying And Selling Predictions*. New York: John Wiley & Sons.

Shrum, W. M. (1996). *Fringe And Fortune: The Role Of Critics In High And Popular Art*. Princeton, N.J.: Princeton University Press.

Simakova, E. (2013). *Marketing Technologies: Corporate Cultures And Technological Change*, Abingdon Oxon and New York: Routledge.

Sinclair, T. J. (2014). *The New Masters Of Capital: American Bond Rating Agencies And The Politics Of Creditworthiness*. Ithaca NY: Cornell University Press.

Skov, L. & Meier, J. (2011). Configuring Sustainability At Fashion Week. In B. Moeran & J. Pedersen (Eds). (2011). *Negotiating Values In The Creative Industries: Fairs, Festivals And Competitive Events*. Cambridge: Cambridge University Press: 270–93.

Snapp, S. (2013). *Gartner And The Magic Quadrant: A Guide For Buyers, Vendors And Investors*, Scm Focus.

Soejarto, A. & Karamouzis, F. (2005). *Magic Quadrants For North American ERP Service Providers*, Gartner Document, ID Number: G00127206.

Star, S. L. (1995). Introduction. In S. L. Star (Ed.), *Ecologies Of Knowledge: Work And Politics In Science And Technology*, Albany, New York: State University Of New York Press: 1–35.

Star, S. L. & Griesemer, J. R. (1989). Institutional Ecology, Translations' And Boundary Objects: Amateurs And Professionals In Berkeley's Museum Of Vertebrate Zoology, 1907–39. *Social Studies Of Science*, 19(3): 387–420.

Star, S. L. & Bowker, G. C. (2007). Enacting Silence: Residual Categories As A Challenge For Ethics, Information Systems, And Communication. *Ethics and Information Technology*, 9(4): 273–80.

Stark, D. (2009). *The Sense Of Dissonance. Accounts Of Worth.* Princeton NJ: Princeton University Press.

Stark, D. (2011). What's Valuable? In P. Aspers & J. Beckert (Eds) *The Worth Of Goods: Valuation And Pricing In The Economy*, Oxford: Oxford University Press: 319–38.

Stewart, J. (1999). The Web Meets The TV: Users And The Innovation Of Interactive Television. In C. Toscan & J. Jensen (Eds) *Interactive Television: TV Of The Future Or The Future Of TV?*, Aalborg: Aalborg University Press: 25–66.

Stewart, J. & Hyysalo, S. (2008). Intermediaries, Users And Social Learning In Technological Innovation, *International Journal Of Innovation Management*, 12(3): 295–325.

Stiennon, R. (2012). 3 Things You Need To Know About Gartner Magic Quadrants *CIO*, 6 July 2012. Available online at: http://www.cio.com/article/2394373/ it-organization/3-things-you-need-to-know-about-gartner-magic-quadrants.html. Accessed 20 July 2015.

Suchman, L. A. (1987). *Plans And Situated Actions: The Problem Of Human-Machine Communication.* Cambridge and New York: Cambridge University Press.

Suddaby, R. & Greenwood, R. (2001). Colonizing Knowledge: Commodification As A Dynamic Of Jurisdictional Expansion In Professional Service Firms, *Human Relations*, 54(7): 933–53.

Swan, J. A. & Clark, P. (1992). Organizational Decision-Making In The Appropriation Of Technological Innovation: Cognitive And Political Dimensions. *The European Work And Organizational Psychologist*, 2(2): 103–27.

Swan, J., Scarbrough, H. & Robertson, H. (2003). Linking Knowledge, Networking And Innovation: A Process View In L. V. Shavinina (Ed.) *International Handbook Of Innovation*, London: Elsevier Science: 680–94.

Swanson, E. B. (2010). Consultancies And Capabilities In Innovating With IT, *Journal Of Strategic Information Systems*, 19: 17–27.

Swanson, E. B. (2012). 'The Managers Guide To IT Innovation Waves' *MIT Sloan Management Review*, 53(2): 75–86.

Swanson, E. B. & Ramiller, N. C. (1997). The Organizing Vision In Information Systems Innovation. *Organisation Science*, 8(5): 458–74.

Techra (No Date). *Analyst Firm Directory*, Techra. Available online at: http://www. techra.com/category/analyst-firm-directory/ Accessed 20 May 2013.

Teece, D. J., Pisano, G. & Shuen, A. (1997). Dynamic Capabilities And Strategic Management. *Strategic Management Journal*, 18(7): 509–33.

Thompson, B. (2004). The Reports Of CRM Failure Are Highly Exaggerated: An Interview With Gartner's Ed Thompson, *Customer Think*, 7 December, Available online at: http://www.Customerthink.Com/Interview/Reports_Crm_Failure_ Highly_Exaggerated. Accessed 18 August 2008.

Thrift, N. (2002). Think And Act Like Revolutionaries: Episodes From The Global Triumph Of Management Discourse. *Critical Quarterly*, 44(3): 19–26.

Thrift, N. (2005). *Knowing Capitalism*. London: Sage.

Timmermans, S. & Berg, M. (1997). Standardization In Action: Achieving Local Universality Through Medical Protocols. *Social studies of Science*, 27(2): 273–305.

Tingling, P. & Parent, M. (2004). An Exploration Of Enterprise Technology Selection And Evaluation, *Journal Of Strategic Information Systems*, 13: 329–54.

Tsoukas, H. (2010). Representation, Signification, Improvisation—A Three Dimensional View Of Organisational Knowledge, foreword to H. E. Canary & R. D Mcphee *Communication And Organisational Knowledge: Contemporary Issues For Theory And Practice*, Abingdon/New York: Routledge: i–xv.

Tsoukas, H. & Shepherd, J. (Eds). (2009). *Managing The Future: Foresight In The Knowledge Economy*. Oxford: Blackwell.

Tufte, E. R. (2001). *The Visual Display Of Quantitative Information*. Cheshire, Conn., Graphics Press.

Turner, S. (2001). What Is The Problem With Experts? *Social Studies Of Science*, 31(1): 123–49.

Tutton, R. (2011). Promising Pessimism: Reading The Futures To Be Avoided In Biotech. *Social Studies Of Science*, 41(3): 411–29.

Välikangas, L. & Sevón, G. (2010). Of Managers, Ideas And Jesters, And The Role Of Information Technology. *The Journal Of Strategic Information Systems*, 19(3): 145–53.

van Lente, H. (1993). *Promising Technology: The Dynamics Of Expectations In Technological Developments*, Amsterdam, Proefschrift.

van Lente, H. & Rip, A. (1998). Expectations in Technological Developments: An Example of Prospective Structures to be Filled in by Agency. In: Disco, C., van der Meulen, B. J. R. (Eds), *Getting New Technologies Together*. Walter de Gruyter, Berlin, New York, 195–220.

Violino, B. & Levin, R. (1997). Analyzing The Analysts. *Information Week*, 17 November, Available online at: http://Informationweek.Com/657/57iuana.Htm. Accessed 29 March 2006.

Vollmer, H., Mennicken, A. & Preda, A. (2009). Tracking The Numbers: Across Accounting And Finance, Organisations And Markets. *Accounting, Organisations And Society*, 34: 619–34.

Wang, P. (2009). Popular Concepts Beyond Organisations: Exploring New Dimensions Of Information Technology Innovations, *Journal Of The Association For Information Systems*, 10(1): 1–30.

Wang, P. & Swanson, E. B. (2007). Launching Professional Services Automation: Institutional Entrepreneurship For Information Technology Innovations, *Information And Organisation*, 17: 59–88.

Wang, P. & Swanson, E. B. (2008). Customer Relationship Management As Advertised: Exploiting And Sustaining Technological Momentum, *Information Technology & People*, 21(4): 323–49.

Wang, P. & Ramiller, N. (2009). Community Learning In Information Technology Innovation, *MIS Quarterly*, 33(4): 709–34.

Wang, R. (2010). The 7 Tenets Of Building A 'Star Analyst' Firm' Personal Log: Published 24 July 2010. Available online at: http://Blog.Softwareinsider.Org/2010/07/24/Personal-Log-The-7-Tenets-Of-Building-A-Star-Analyst-Firm/. Accessed 4 February 2014.

Wansleben, L. (2012). Financial Analysts. In Knorr Cetina, K. & Preda, A. (Eds), *The Oxford Handbook Of The Sociology Of Finance*, Oxford: Oxford University Press: 250–71.

Ward, J. M (1987). Strategic Information Systems. In Elizabeth K. Somogy & Robert D Galliers (Eds) *Towards Strategic Information Systems*, Abacus: Tunbridge Wells.

Webster, J (1993). Chicken Or Egg? The Interaction Between Manufacturing Technologies And Paradigms Of Work Organisation, *International Journal Of Human Factors In Manufacturing*, 3(1): 53–67.

Wedlin, L. (2006). *Ranking Business School: Forming Fields, Identities And Boundaries In International Management Education*. Chichester: Edward Elgar.

Werr, A. & Stjernberg, T. (2003). Exploring Management Consulting Firms As Knowledge Systems, *Organisation Studies*, 24(6): 881–908.

Whitehorn, M. (2007). Is Gartner's Magic Quadrant Really Magic?', *REG Developer*, 31st March. Available online at: http://www.theregister.co.uk/2007/03/31/myth_gartner_magic_quadrant/. Accessed 21 July 2015.

Williams, R. (1997). The Social Shaping Of A Failed Technology: Mismatch And Tension In The Supply And Use Of Computer-Aided Production Management. In C. Clausen & R. Williams (Eds), *The Social Shaping Of Computer-Aided Production Management And Computer Integrated Manufacture*, Vol. 5, ISBN 92 828 1569 2, COST A4, European Commission DGXIII, Luxembourg: 109–30.

Williams, R, Faulkner, W. & Fleck, J. (Eds) (1998). *Exploring Expertise*, Basingstoke: Macmillan.

Williams, R. & Procter, R. (1998). Trading Places: A Case Study Of The Formation And Deployment Of Computing Expertise. In Williams, R. Faulkner, W. & Fleck (Eds) *Exploring Expertise*. Basingstoke, Macmillan: 197–222.

Williams, R. & Pollock, N. (2012). Research Commentary-Moving Beyond The Single Site Implementation Study: How (And Why) We Should Study The Biography Of Packaged Enterprise Solutions. *Information Systems Research*, 23(1): 1–22.

Williamson, O. E. (1975). *Markets And Hierarchies: Analysis And Antitrust Implications*, New York: The Free Press.

Williamson, O. E. (1991). 'Comparative Economic Organisation: The Analysis Of Discrete Structural Alternatives.' *Administrative Science Quarterly*. 36(2): 269–96.

Wylie, L. (1990). A Vision Of The Next-Generation MRP II Computer Integrated Manufacturing, Scenario S-300-339, Gartner Group, 12 April.

Yarmis, J. (2011). Advisory Industry—Its Future Posted By Gideon Gartner on 4 July 2011, Available online at: http://Gideongartner.Com/2011/07/Advisory-Industry-Its-Future/#. Posted June 19 2011. Accessed 22 May 2013.

Zuckerman, E. (1999). The Categorical Imperative: Securities Analysts And The Illegitimacy Of Discount, *American Journal Of Sociology* 104: 1398–438.

Index

Note: f stands for figure and t for table